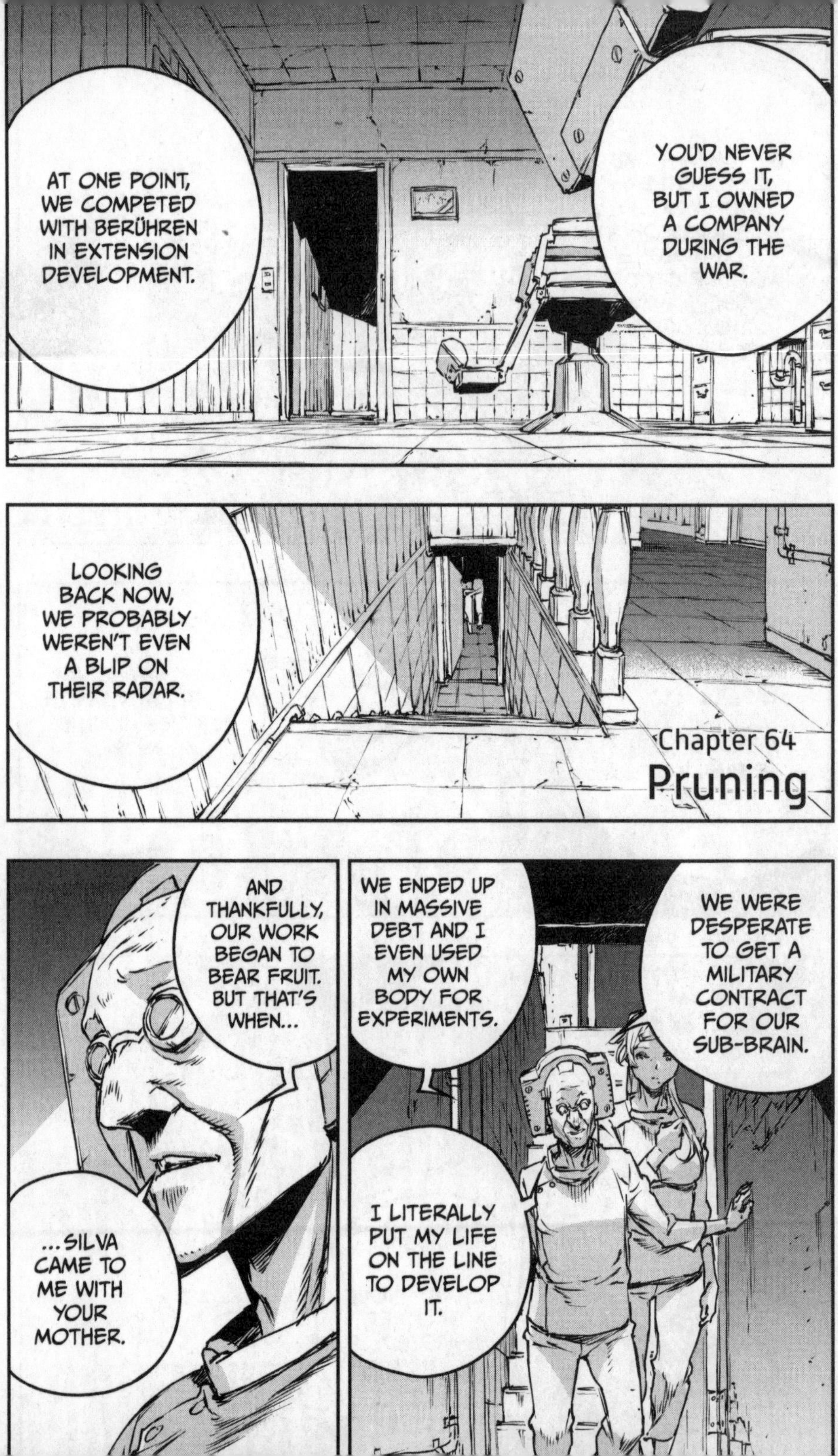
YOU'D NEVER GUESS IT, BUT I OWNED A COMPANY DURING THE WAR.
AT ONE POINT, WE COMPETED WITH BERÜHREN IN EXTENSION DEVELOPMENT.
LOOKING BACK NOW, WE PROBABLY WEREN'T EVEN A BLIP ON THEIR RADAR.
Chapter 64
Pruning
WE WERE DESPERATE TO GET A MILITARY CONTRACT FOR OUR SUB-BRAIN.
WE ENDED UP IN MASSIVE DEBT AND I EVEN USED MY OWN BODY FOR EXPERIMENTS.
I LITERALLY PUT MY LIFE ON THE LINE TO DEVELOP IT.
AND THANKFULLY, OUR WORK BEGAN TO BEAR FRUIT. BUT THAT'S WHEN...
...SILVA CAME TO ME WITH YOUR MOTHER.

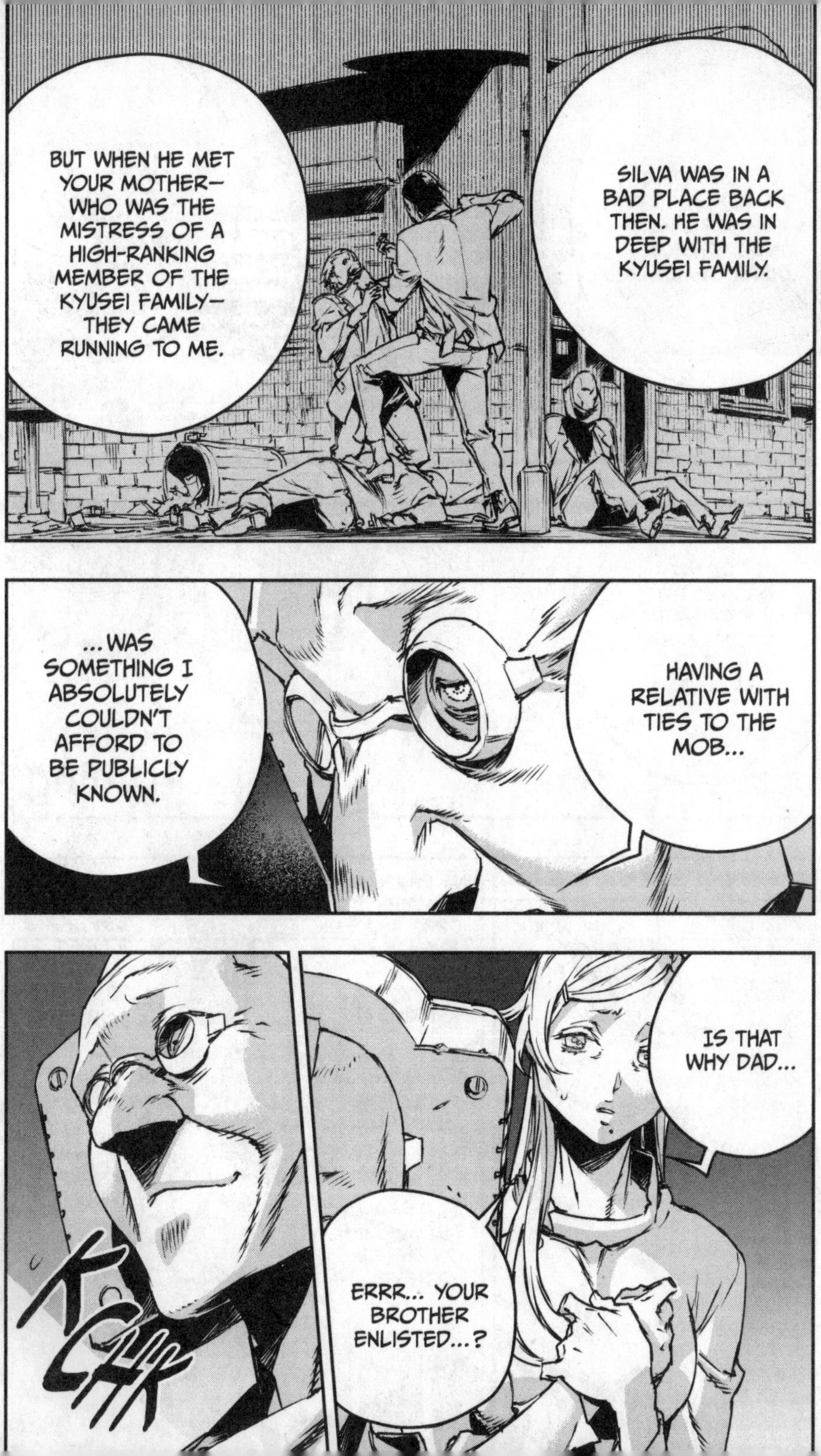
SILVA WAS IN A BAD PLACE BACK THEN. HE WAS IN DEEP WITH THE KYUSEI FAMILY.
BUT WHEN HE MET YOUR MOTHER—WHO WAS THE MISTRESS OF A HIGH-RANKING MEMBER OF THE KYUSEI FAMILY—THEY CAME RUNNING TO ME.
HAVING A RELATIVE WITH TIES TO THE MOB...
...WAS SOMETHING I ABSOLUTELY COULDN'T AFFORD TO BE PUBLICLY KNOWN.
IS THAT WHY DAD...
ERRR... YOUR BROTHER ENLISTED...?
KCHK

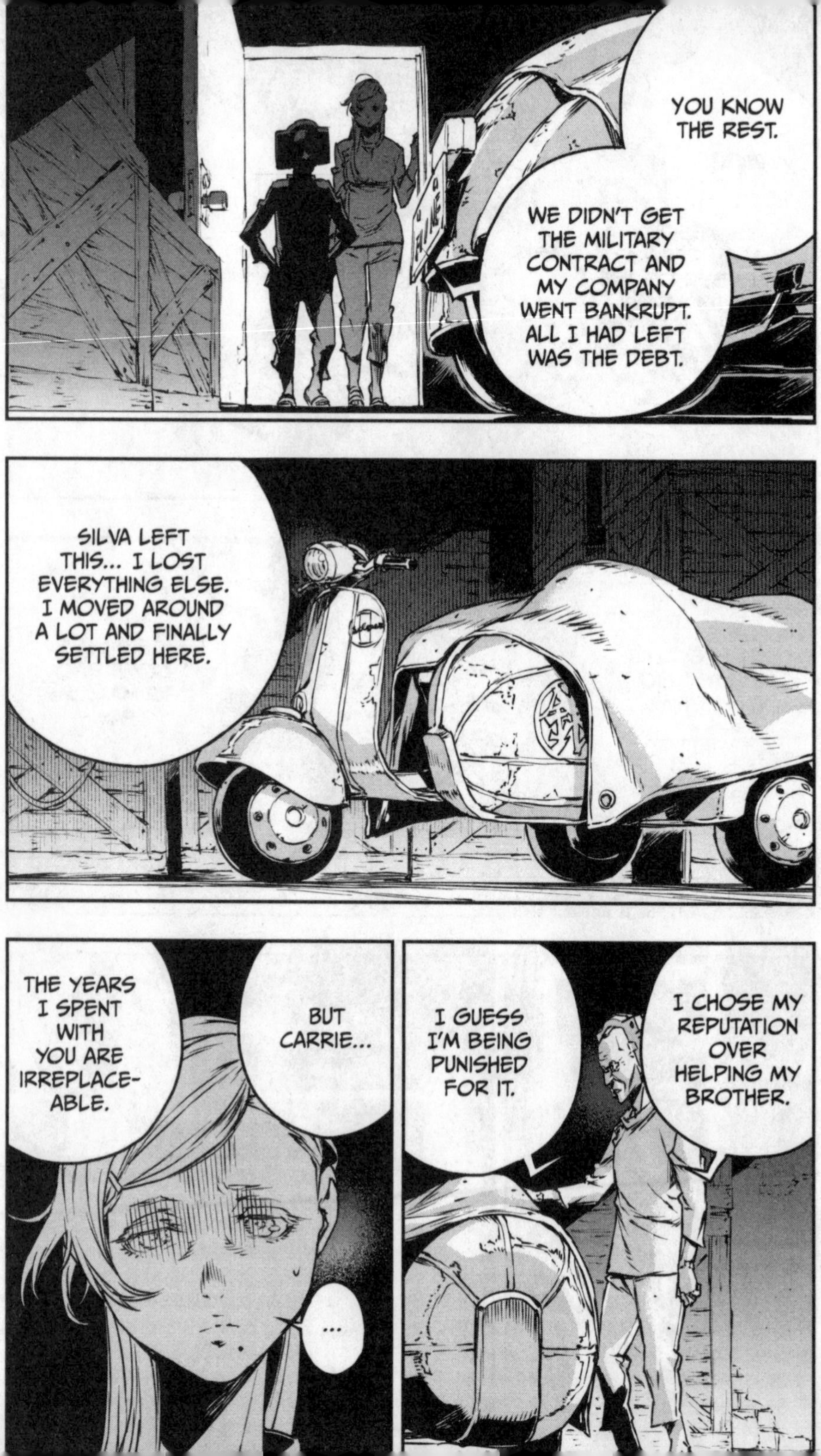
YOU KNOW THE REST.
WE DIDN'T GET THE MILITARY CONTRACT AND MY COMPANY WENT BANKRUPT. ALL I HAD LEFT WAS THE DEBT.
SILVA LEFT THIS... I LOST EVERYTHING ELSE. I MOVED AROUND A LOT AND FINALLY SETTLED HERE.
I CHOSE MY REPUTATION OVER HELPING MY BROTHER.
I GUESS I'M BEING PUNISHED FOR IT.
BUT CARRIE...
THE YEARS I SPENT WITH YOU ARE IRREPLACE-ABLE.
...

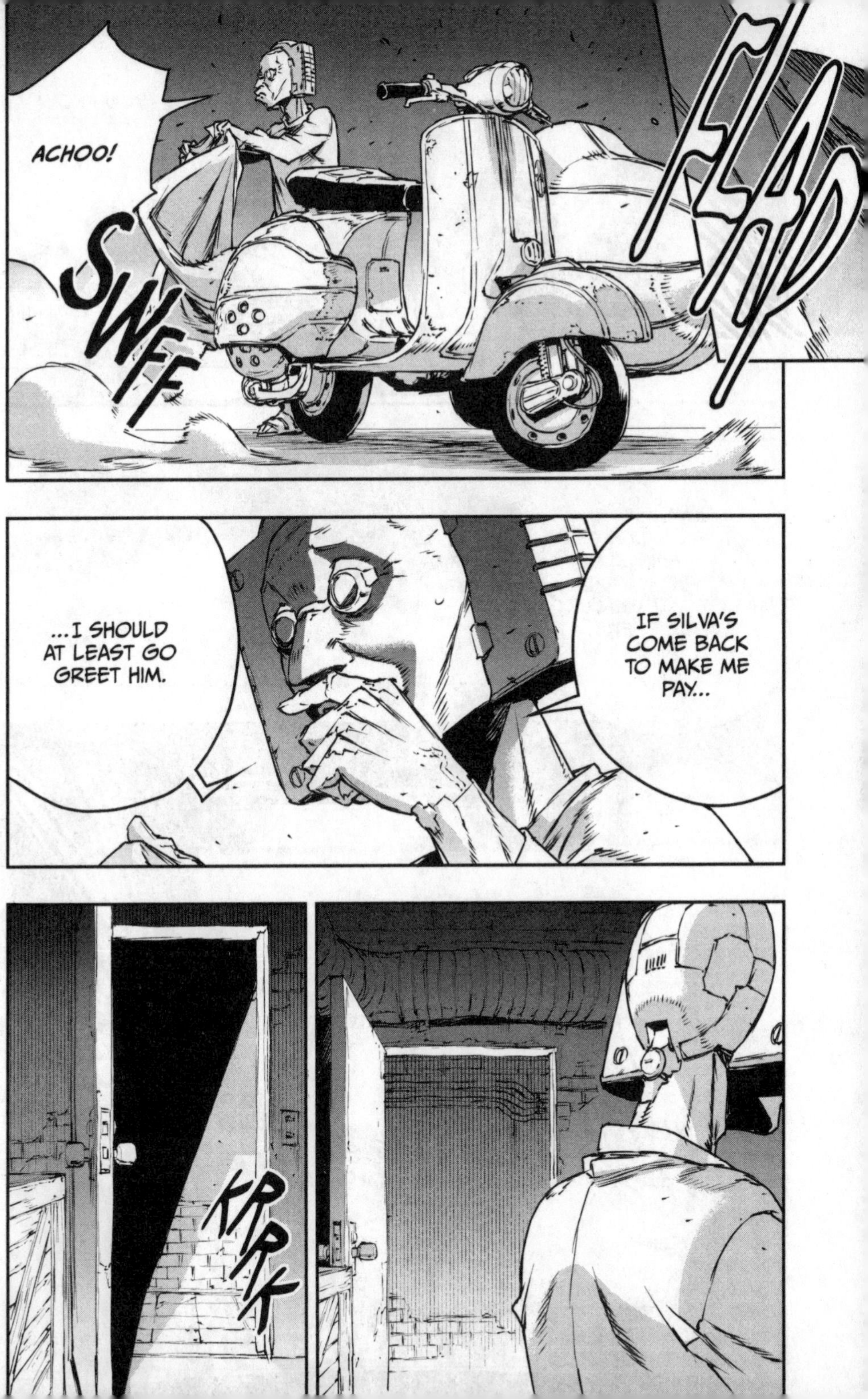
FLAP
ACHOO!
SWFF
IF SILVA'S COME BACK TO MAKE ME PAY...
...I SHOULD AT LEAST GO GREET HIM.
KRRK

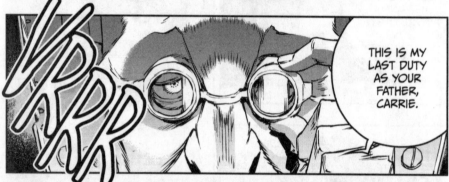

THIS IS MY LAST DUTY AS YOUR FATHER, CARRIE.

NO ONE ELSE NEEDS TO DIE... JUST ONE OLD MAN.

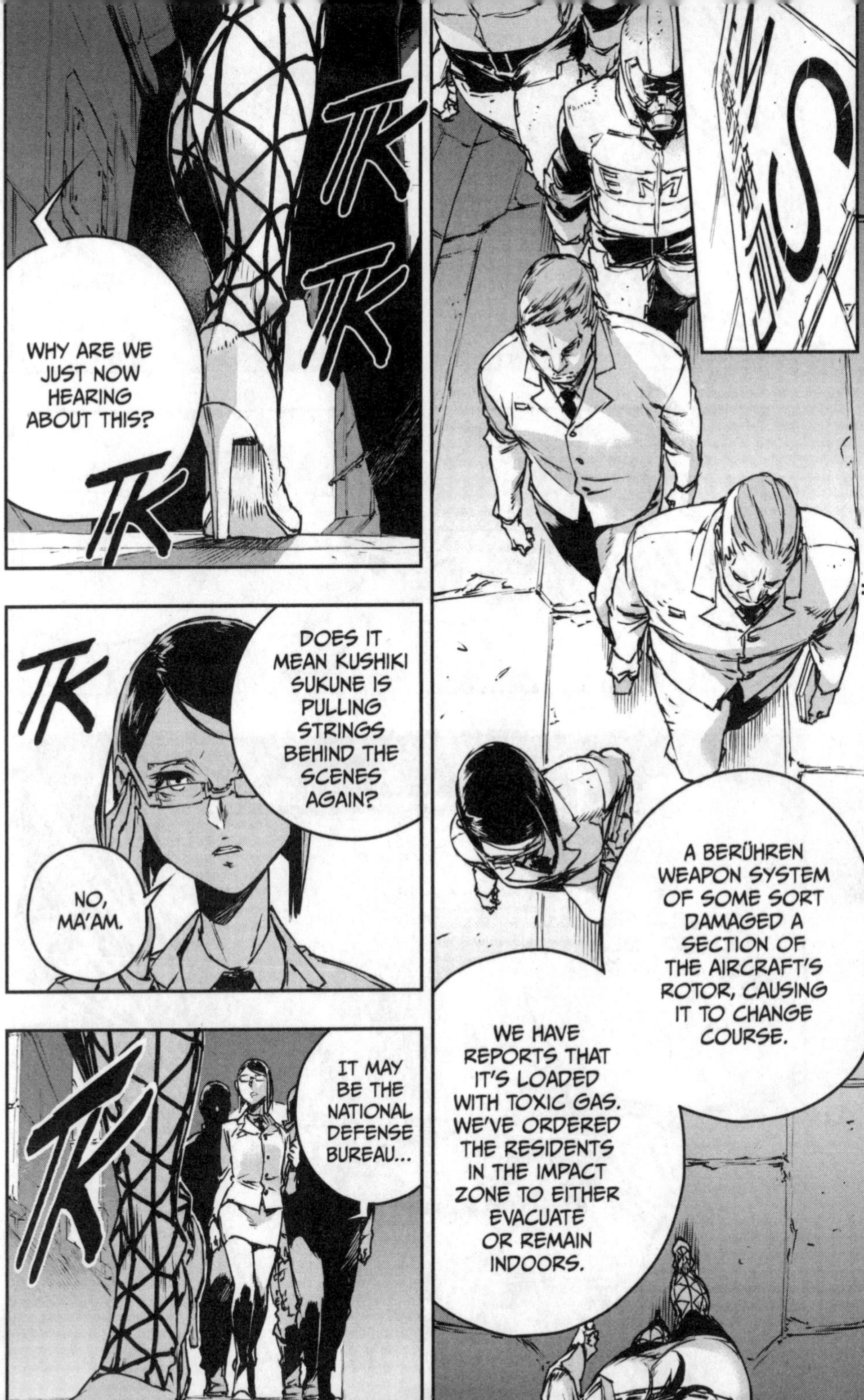
A BERÜHREN WEAPON SYSTEM OF SOME SORT DAMAGED A SECTION OF THE AIRCRAFT'S ROTOR, CAUSING IT TO CHANGE COURSE.
WE HAVE REPORTS THAT IT'S LOADED WITH TOXIC GAS. WE'VE ORDERED THE RESIDENTS IN THE IMPACT ZONE TO EITHER EVACUATE OR REMAIN INDOORS.
TK TK
WHY ARE WE JUST NOW HEARING ABOUT THIS?
TK
TK
DOES IT MEAN KUSHIKI SUKUNE IS PULLING STRINGS BEHIND THE SCENES AGAIN?
NO, MA'AM.
TK
IT MAY BE THE NATIONAL DEFENSE BUREAU...

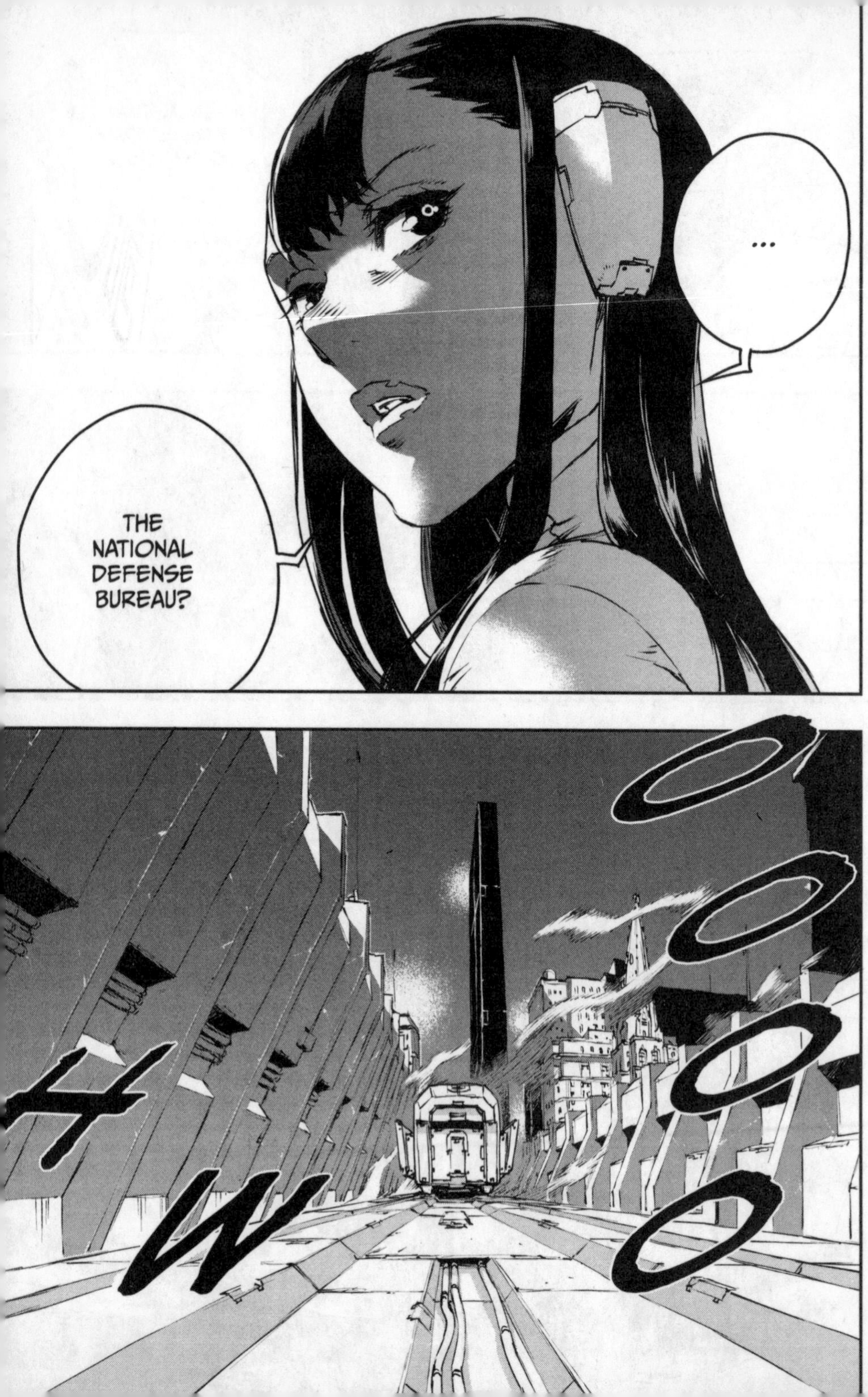
...
THE NATIONAL DEFENSE BUREAU?
WHOOOOOO

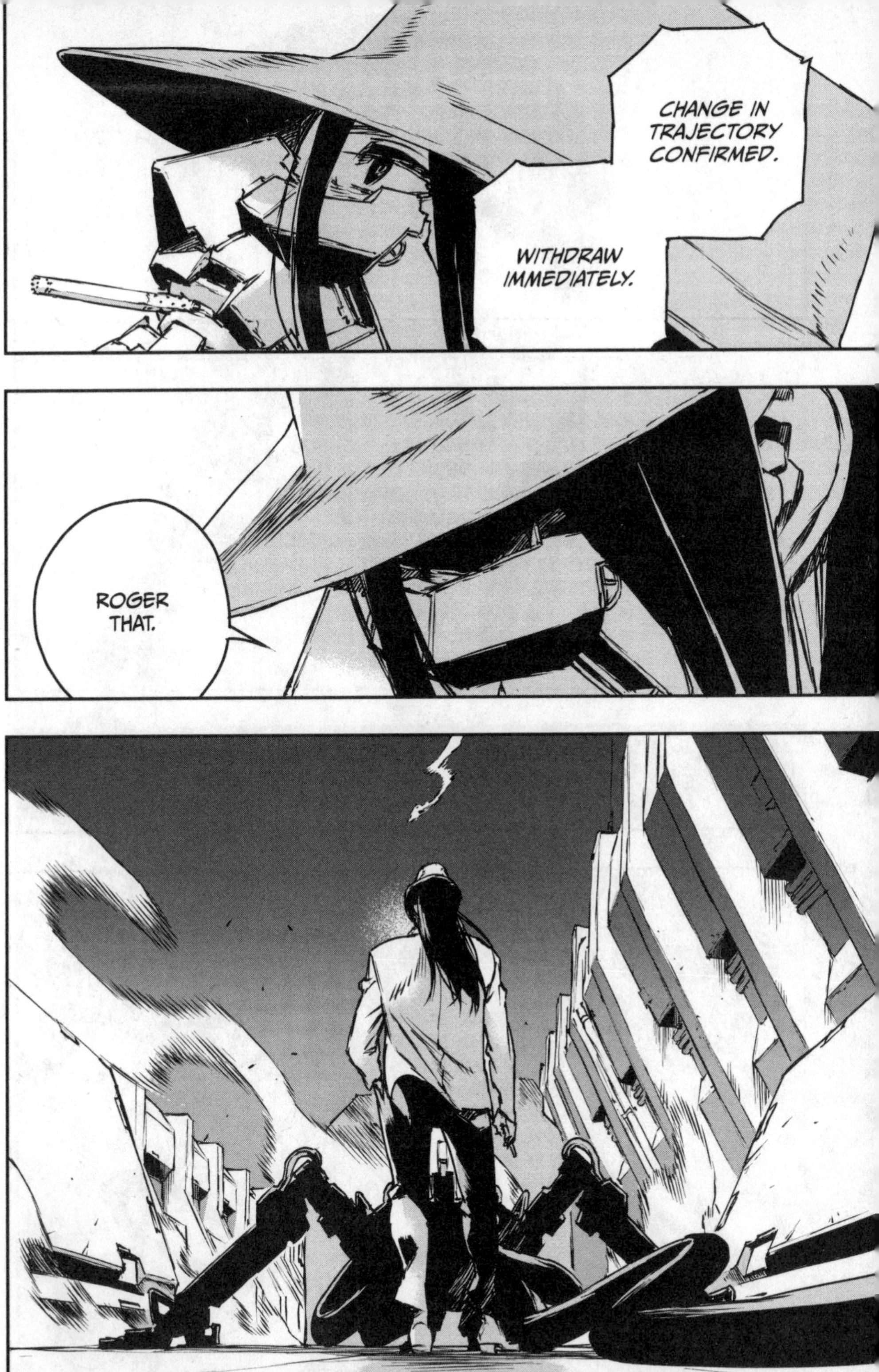
CHANGE IN TRAJECTORY CONFIRMED.
WITHDRAW IMMEDIATELY.
ROGER THAT.

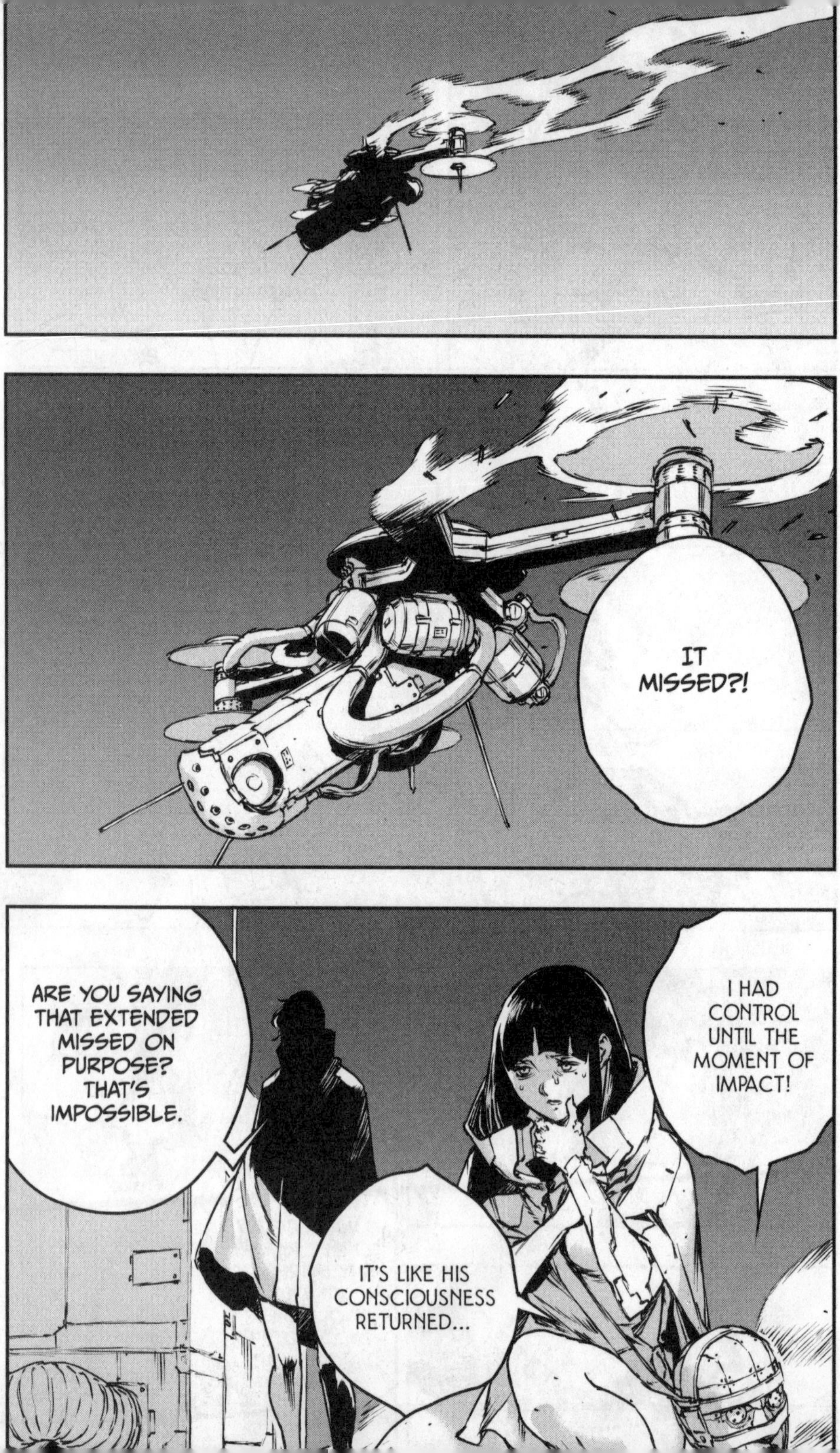
IT MISSED?!
I HAD CONTROL UNTIL THE MOMENT OF IMPACT!
ARE YOU SAYING THAT EXTENDED MISSED ON PURPOSE? THAT'S IMPOSSIBLE.
IT'S LIKE HIS CONSCIOUSNESS RETURNED...

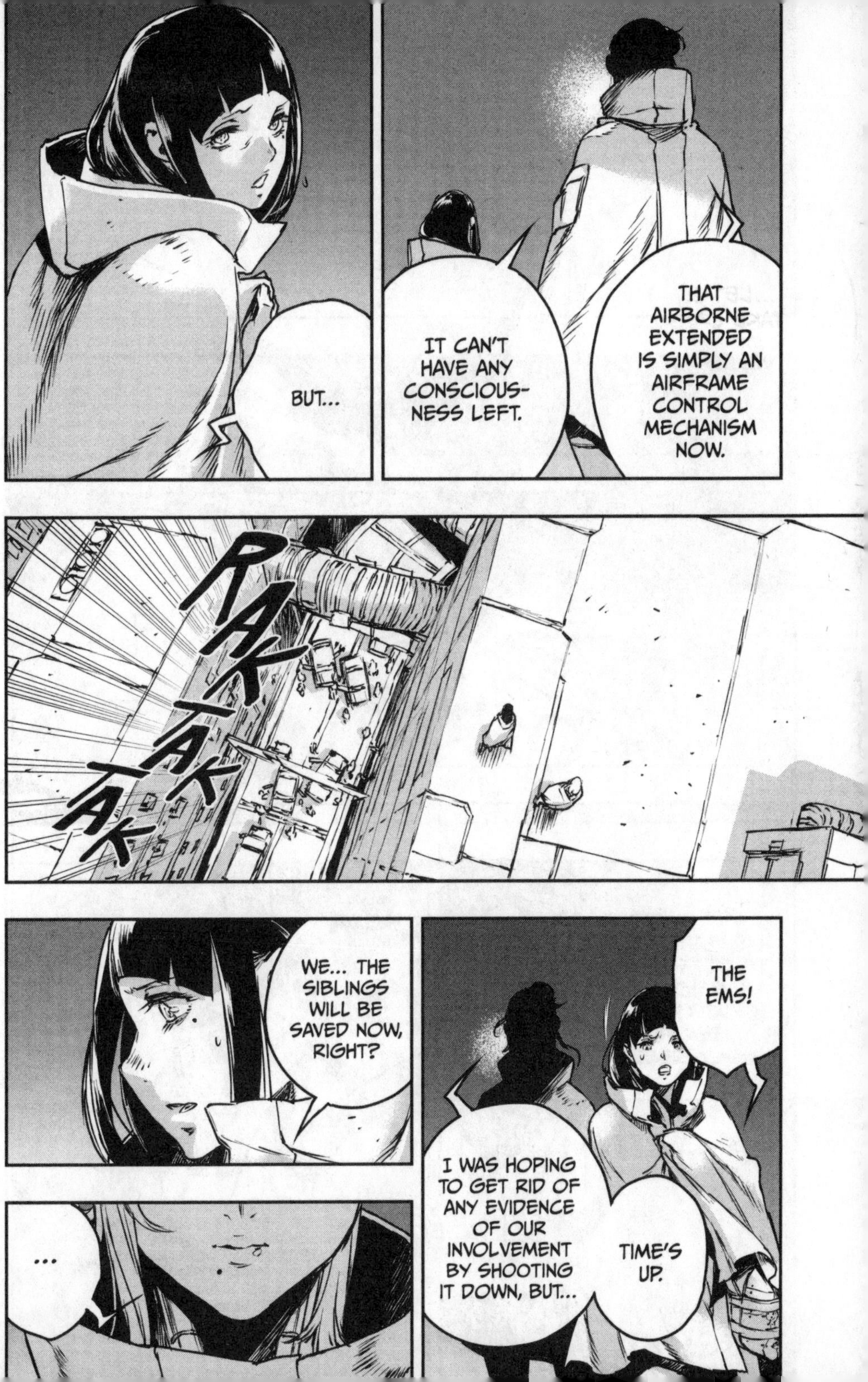
THAT AIRBORNE EXTENDED IS SIMPLY AN AIRFRAME CONTROL MECHANISM NOW.
IT CAN'T HAVE ANY CONSCIOUSNESS LEFT.
BUT...
RAK TAK TAK
THE EMS!
TIME'S UP.
I WAS HOPING TO GET RID OF ANY EVIDENCE OF OUR INVOLVEMENT BY SHOOTING IT DOWN, BUT...
WE... THE SIBLINGS WILL BE SAVED NOW, RIGHT?
...

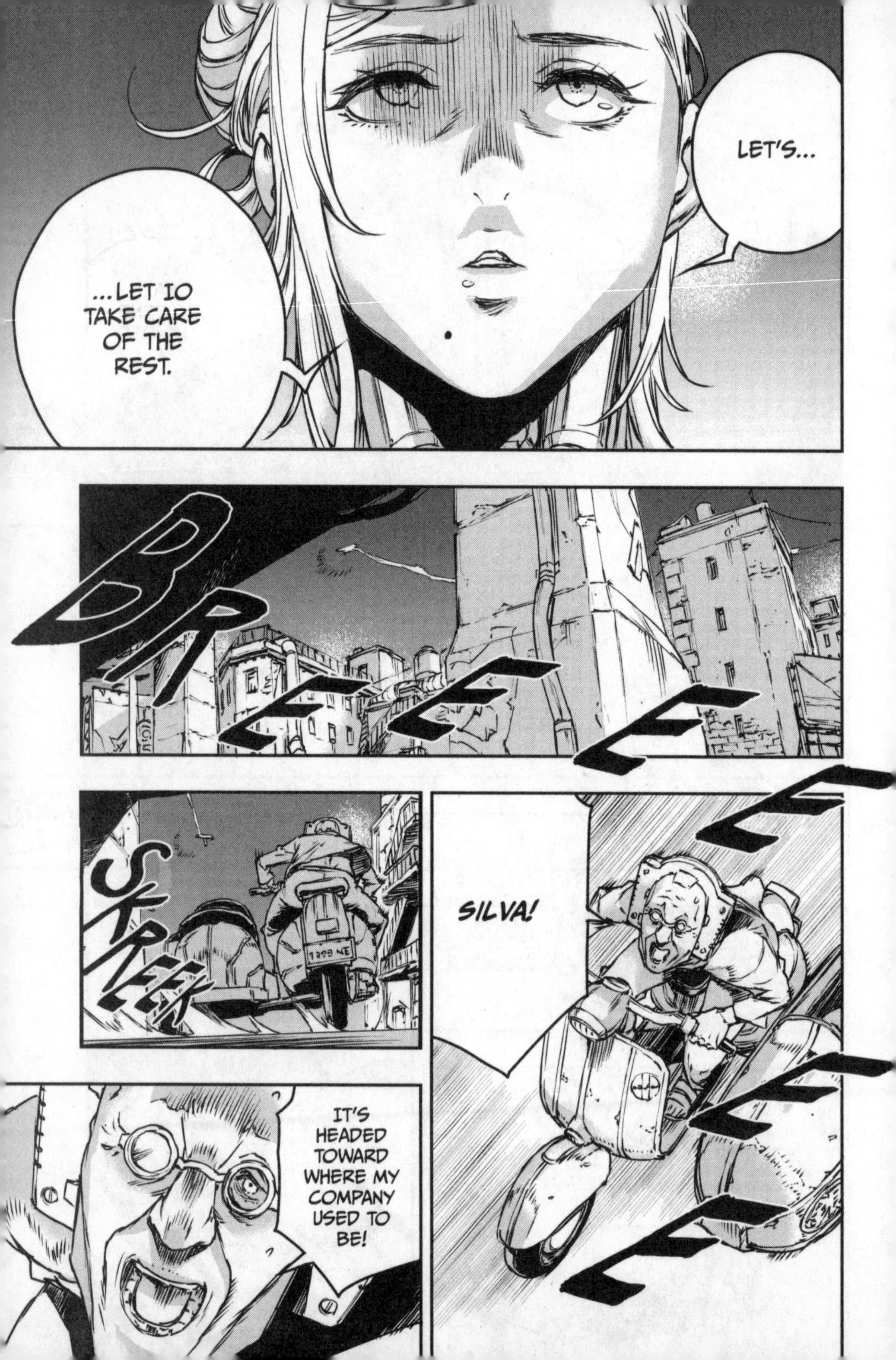
LET'S...
...LET IO TAKE CARE OF THE REST.
BREEEEEEEE
SILVA!
SKREEK
IT'S HEADED TOWARD WHERE MY COMPANY USED TO BE!

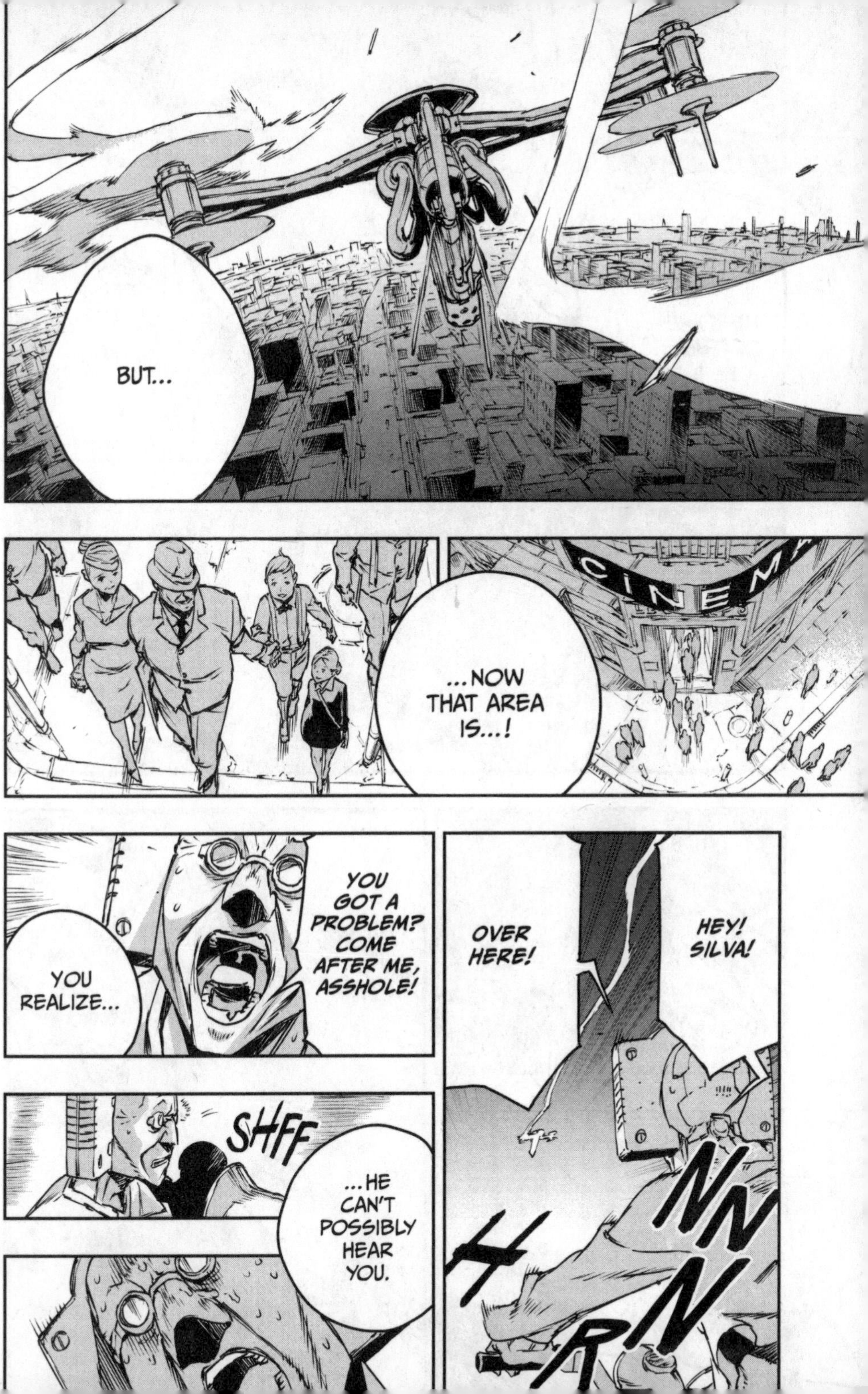
BUT...
CINEM
...NOW THAT AREA IS...!
HEY! SILVA!
OVER HERE!
YOU GOT A PROBLEM? COME AFTER ME, ASSHOLE!
YOU REALIZE...
SHFF
...HE CAN'T POSSIBLY HEAR YOU.

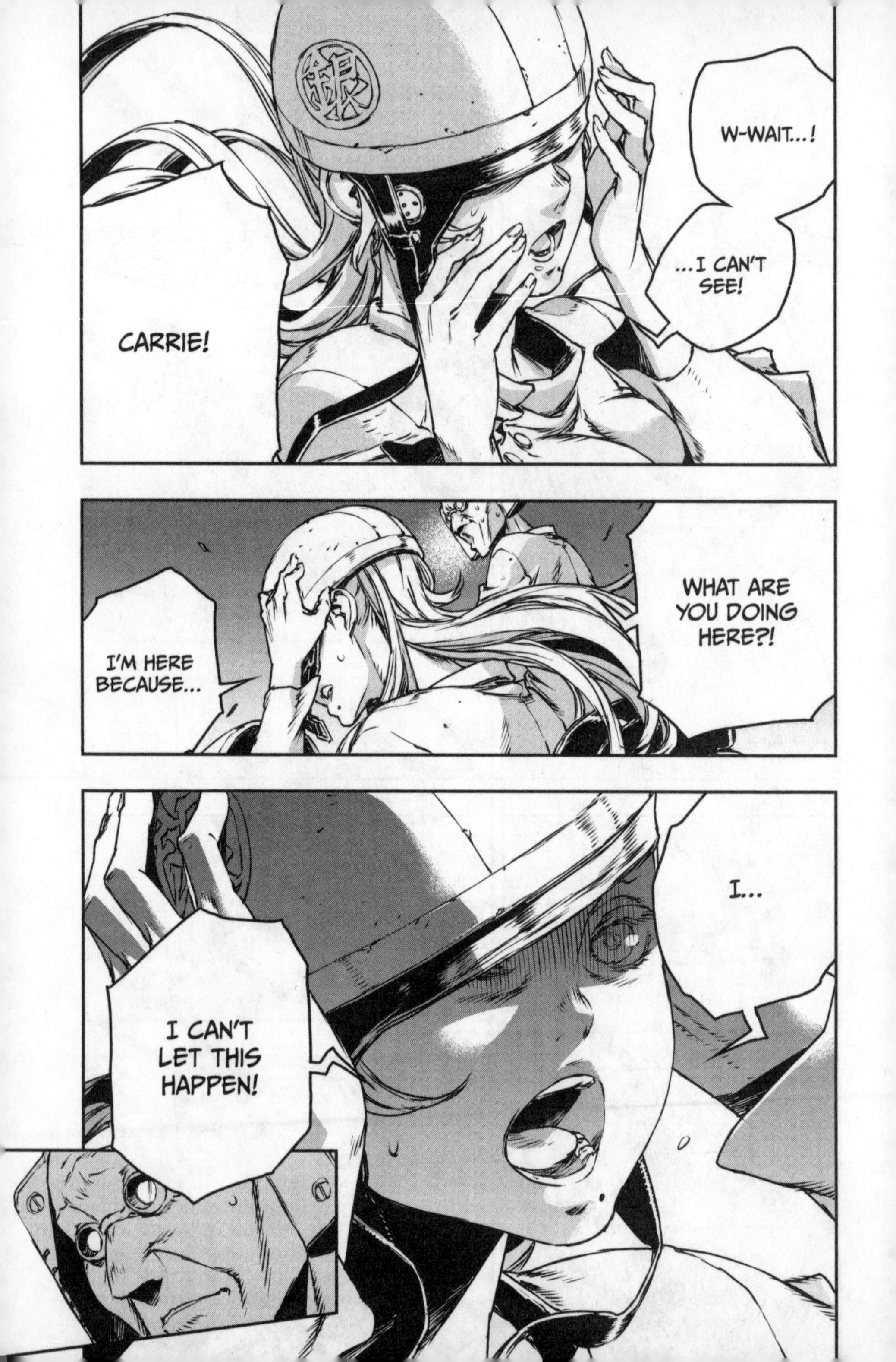
W-WAIT...!
...I CAN'T SEE!
CARRIE!
WHAT ARE YOU DOING HERE?!
I'M HERE BECAUSE...
I...
I CAN'T LET THIS HAPPEN!

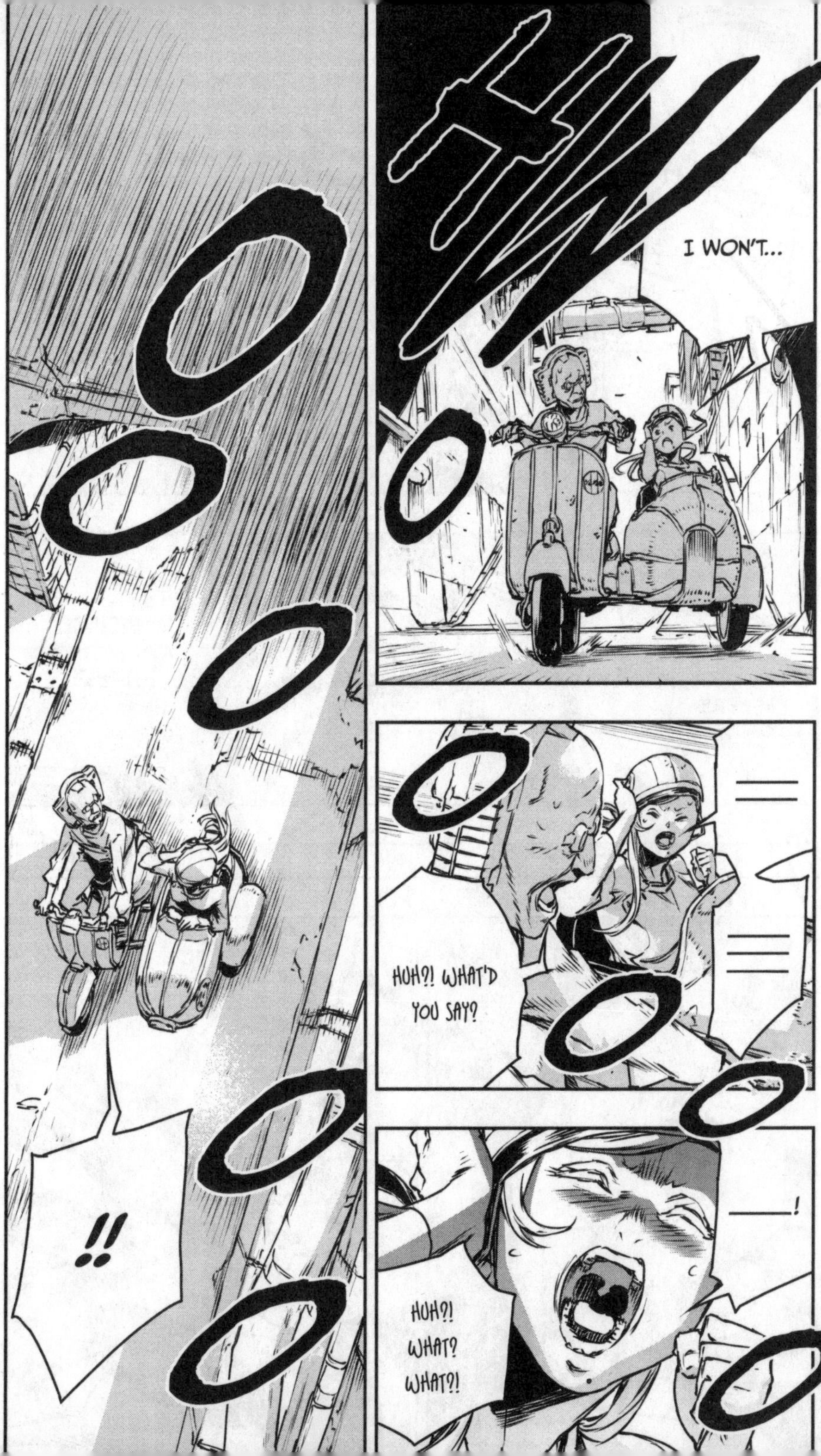
I WON'T...
HUH?! WHAT'D YOU SAY?
——!
HUH?! WHAT? WHAT?!
!!

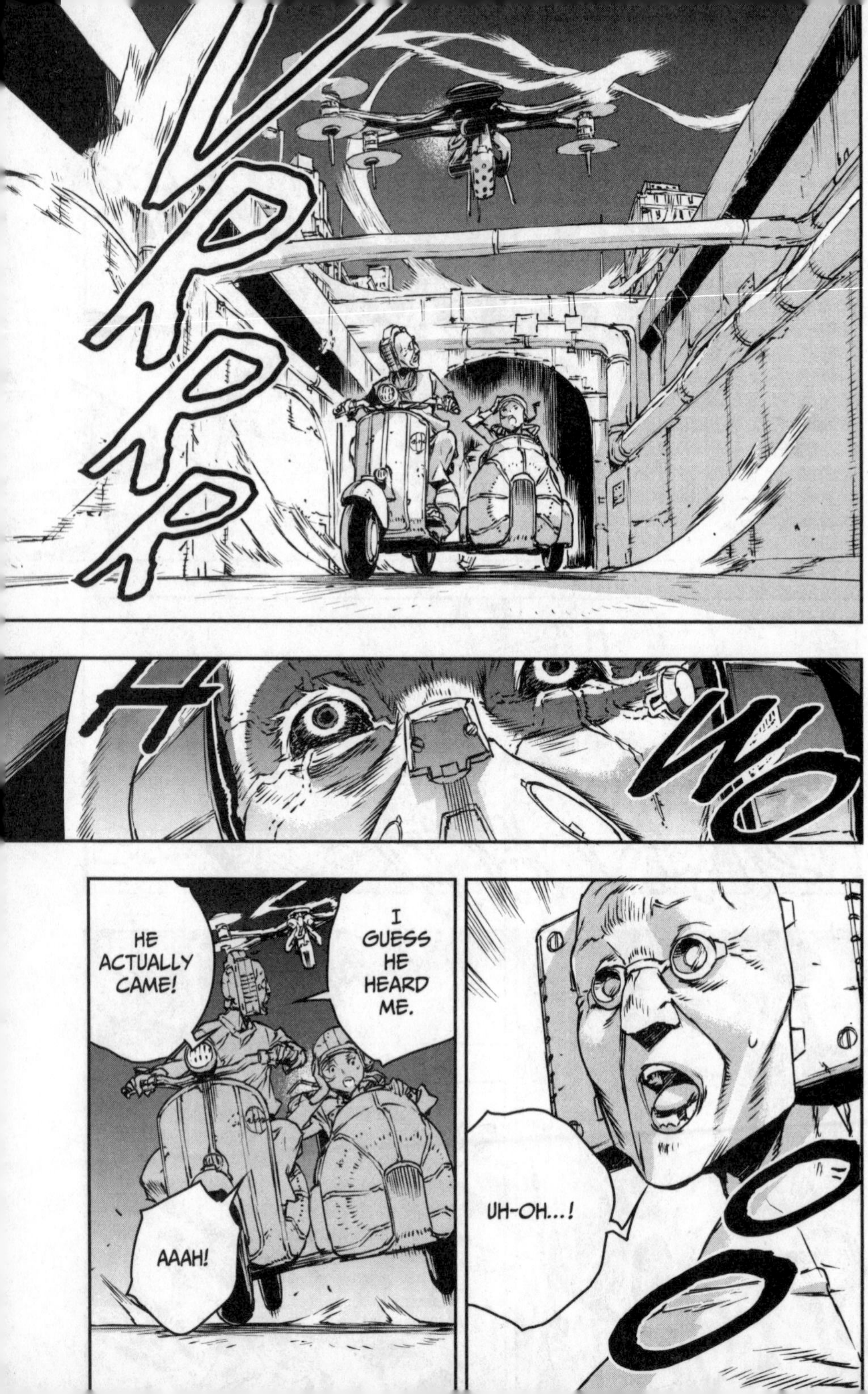
VRRRR
WO
H
UH-OH...!
OOO
I GUESS HE HEARD ME.
HE ACTUALLY CAME!
AAAH!

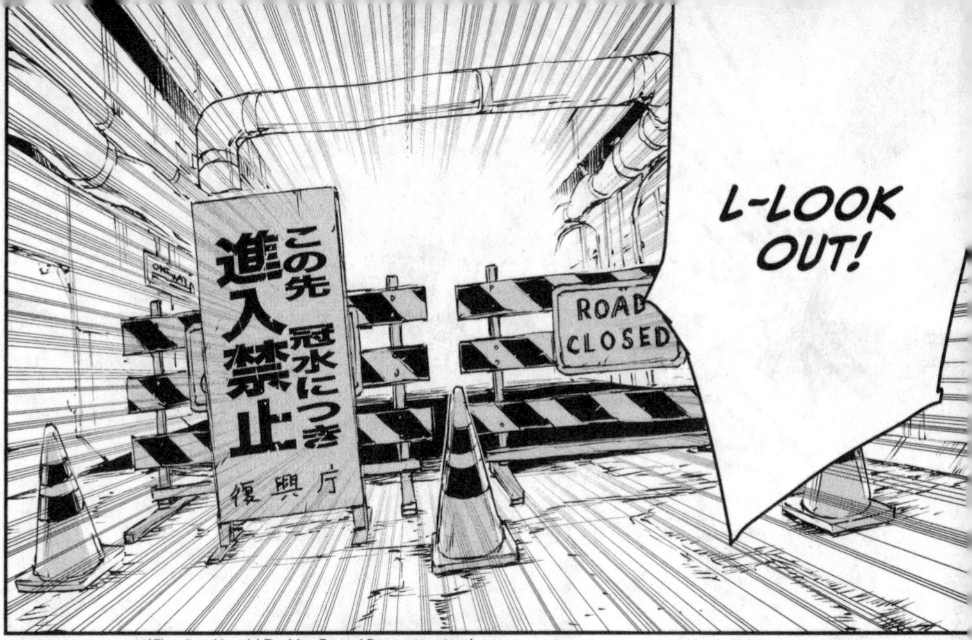
L-LOOK OUT!
ROAD CLOSED
この先冠水につき
進入禁止
復興庁
*Flooding Ahead / Do Not Enter / Reconstruction Agency

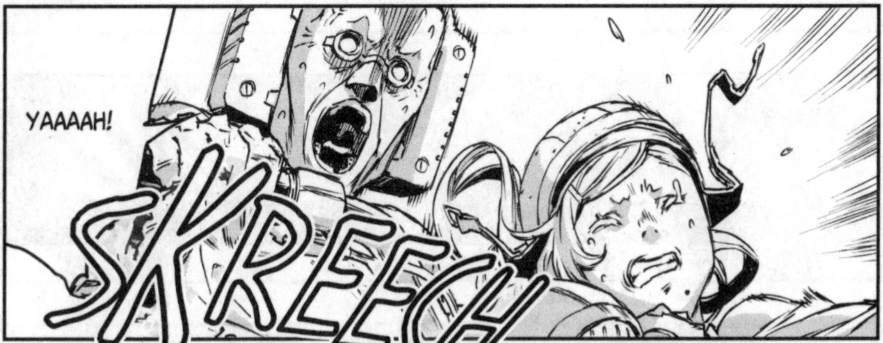
YAAAAH!
SKREECH

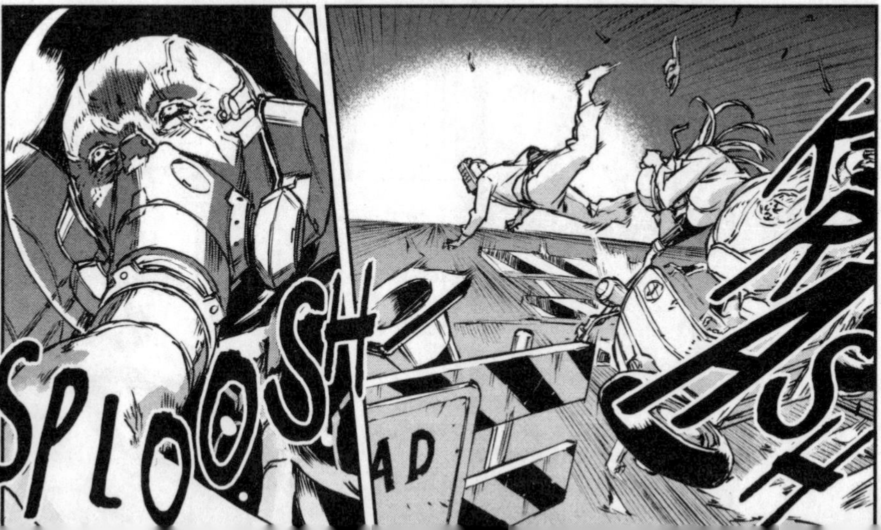
KRASH
SPLOOSH

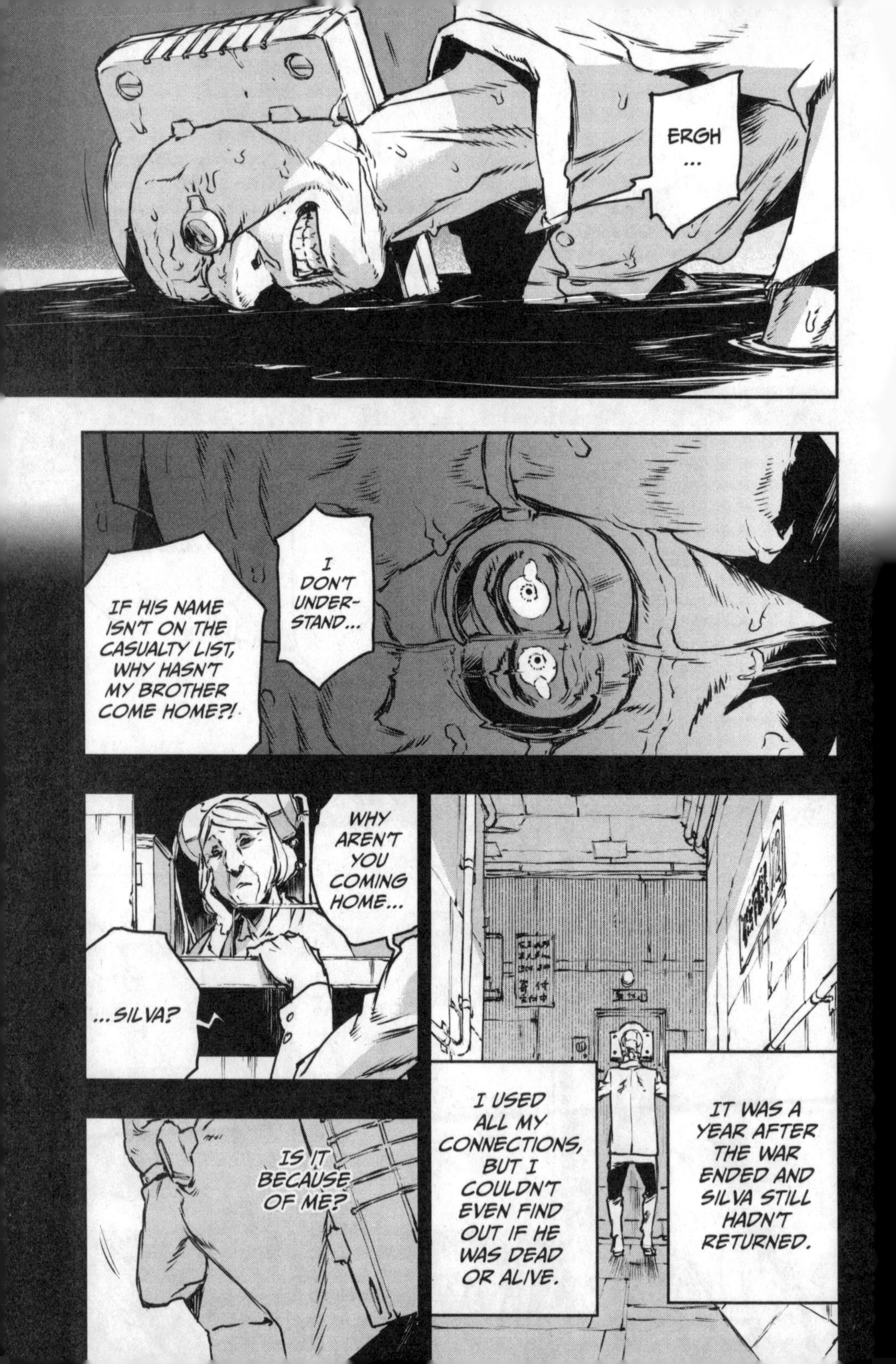
ERGH ...
I DON'T UNDER-STAND...
IF HIS NAME ISN'T ON THE CASUALTY LIST, WHY HASN'T MY BROTHER COME HOME?!
IT WAS A YEAR AFTER THE WAR ENDED AND SILVA STILL HADN'T RETURNED.
I USED ALL MY CONNECTIONS, BUT I COULDN'T EVEN FIND OUT IF HE WAS DEAD OR ALIVE.
WHY AREN'T YOU COMING HOME...
...SILVA?
IS IT BECAUSE OF ME?

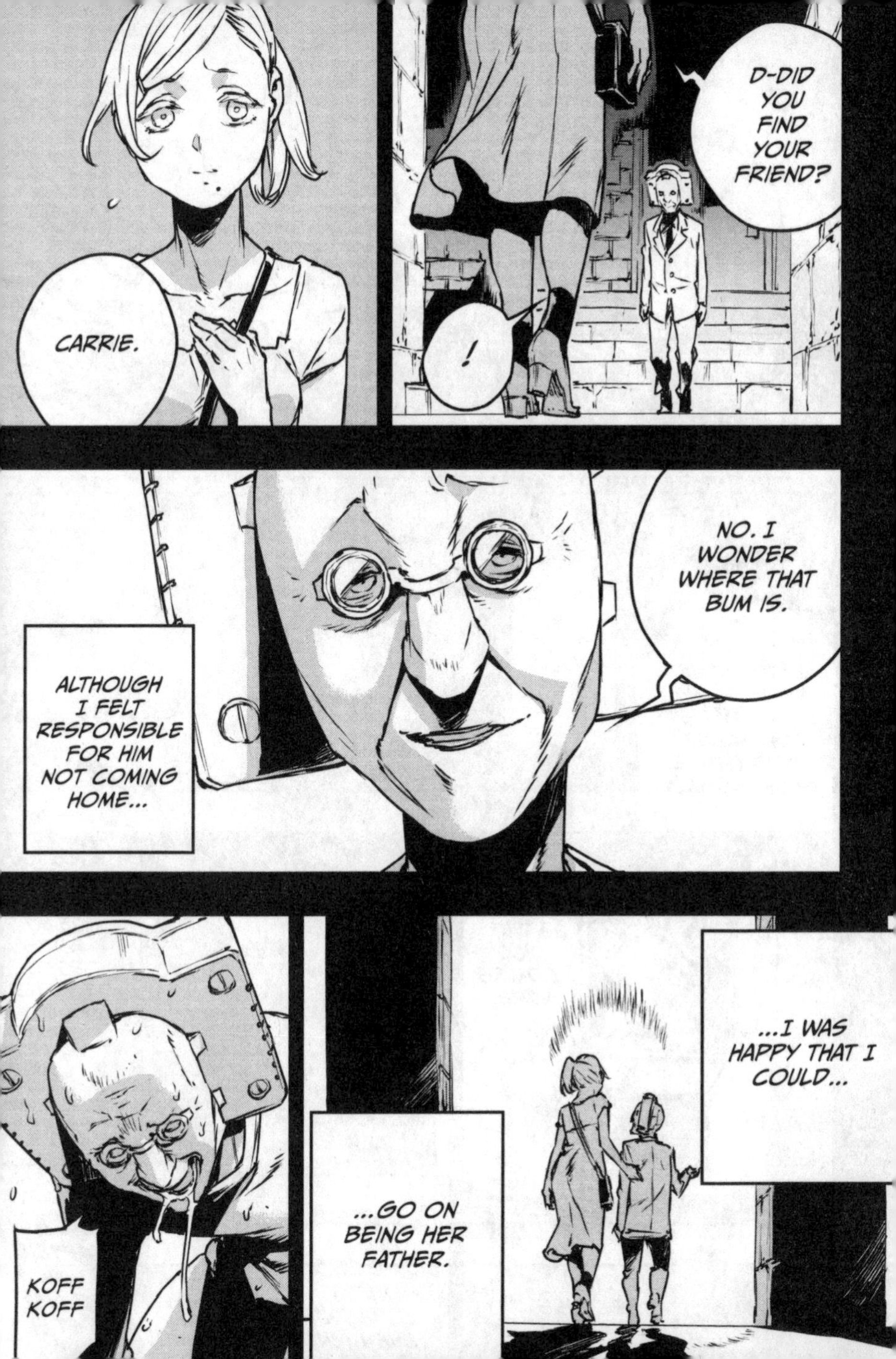
D-DID YOU FIND YOUR FRIEND?
!
CARRIE.
NO. I WONDER WHERE THAT BUM IS.
ALTHOUGH I FELT RESPONSIBLE FOR HIM NOT COMING HOME...
...I WAS HAPPY THAT I COULD...
...GO ON BEING HER FATHER.
KOFF KOFF

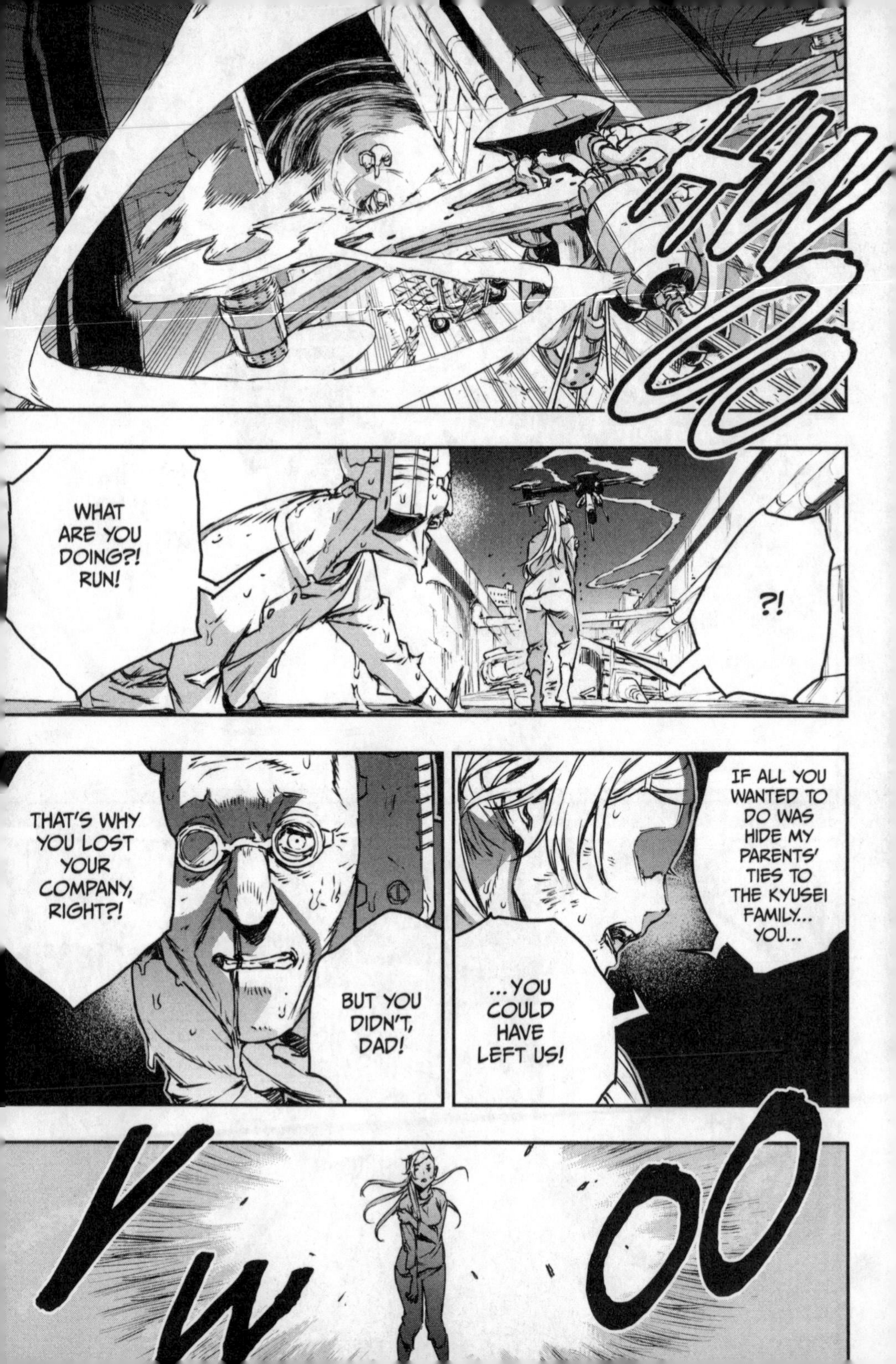
HWOO
?!
WHAT ARE YOU DOING?! RUN!
IF ALL YOU WANTED TO DO WAS HIDE MY PARENTS' TIES TO THE KYUSEI FAMILY... YOU...
...YOU COULD HAVE LEFT US!
THAT'S WHY YOU LOST YOUR COMPANY, RIGHT?!
BUT YOU DIDN'T, DAD!
YWOO

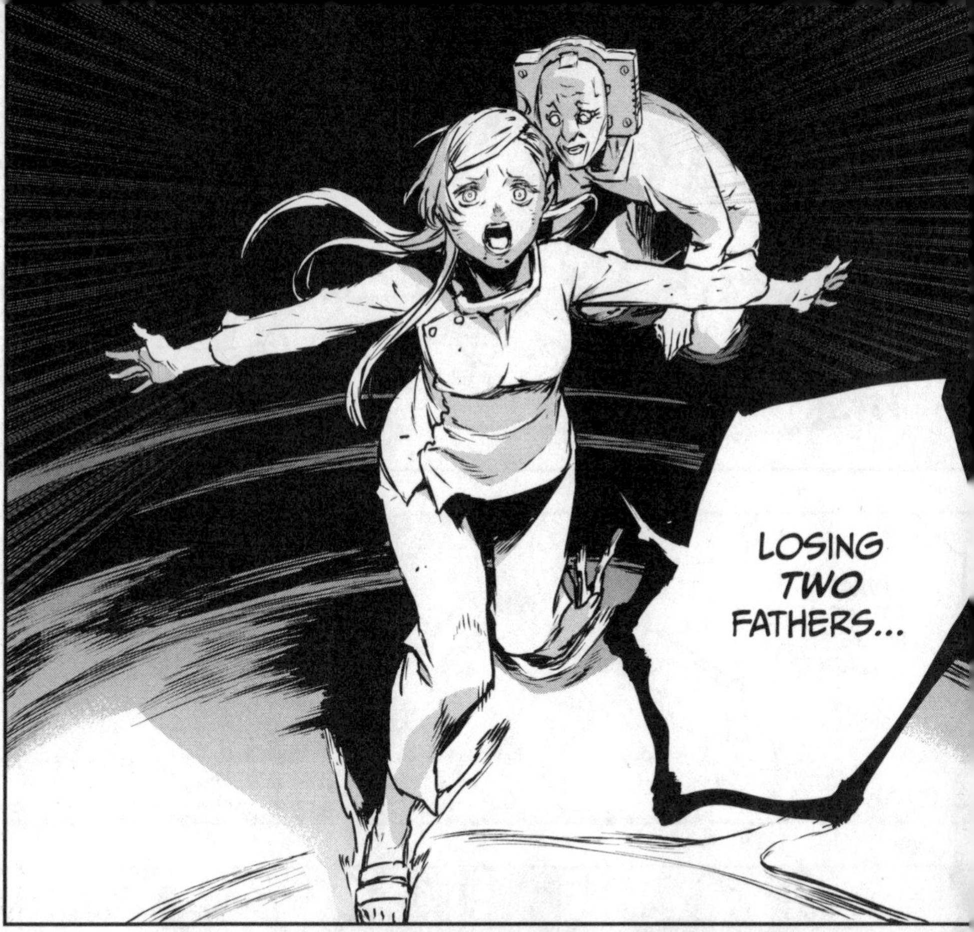
LOSING TWO FATHERS...
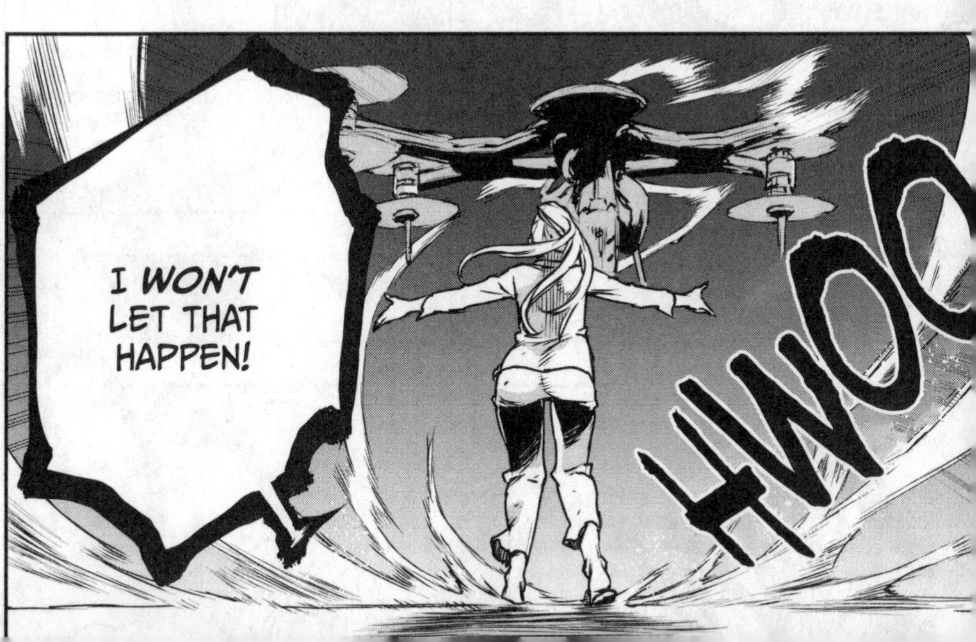
I WON'T LET THAT HAPPEN!
HWOO

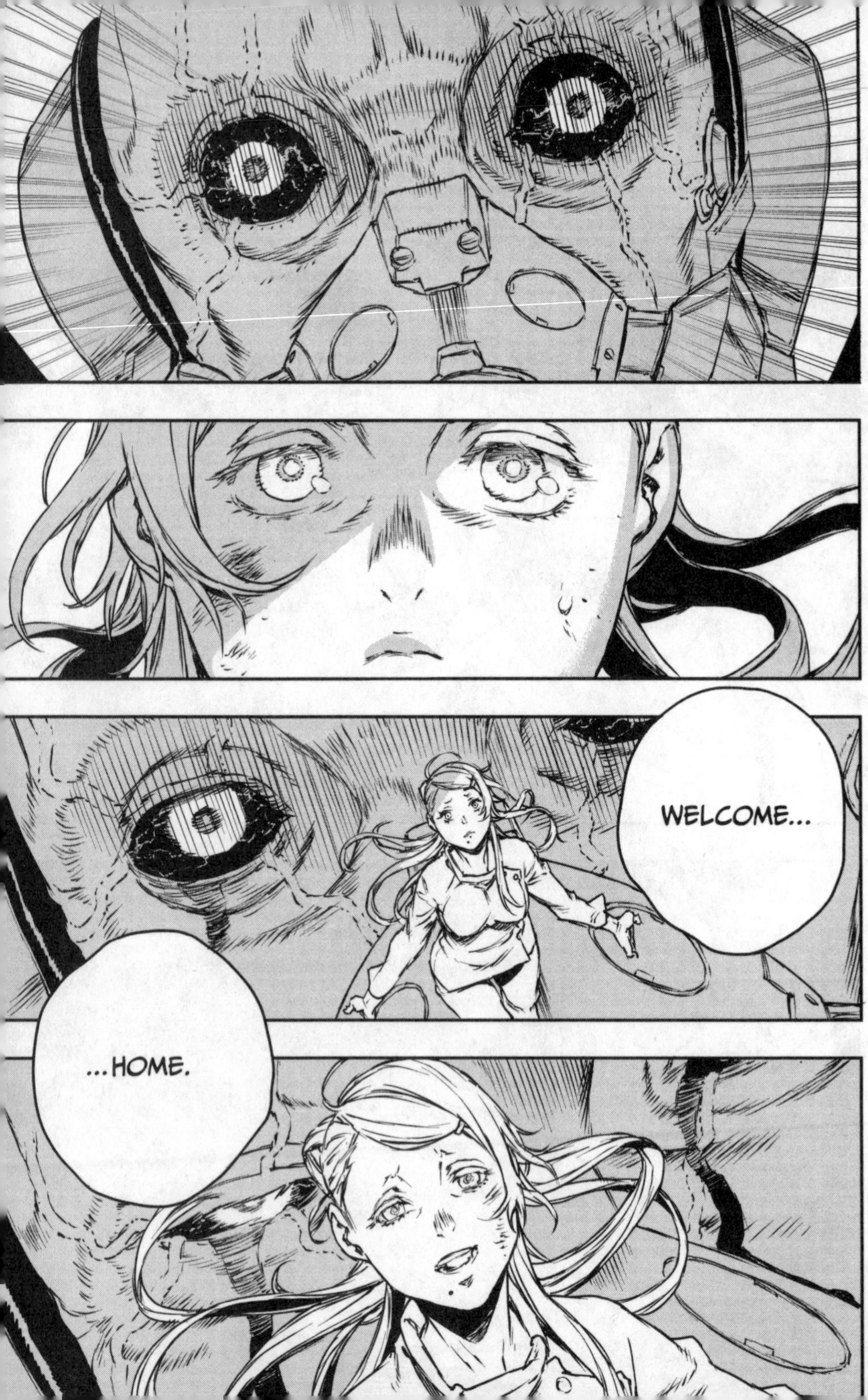
WELCOME...
...HOME.

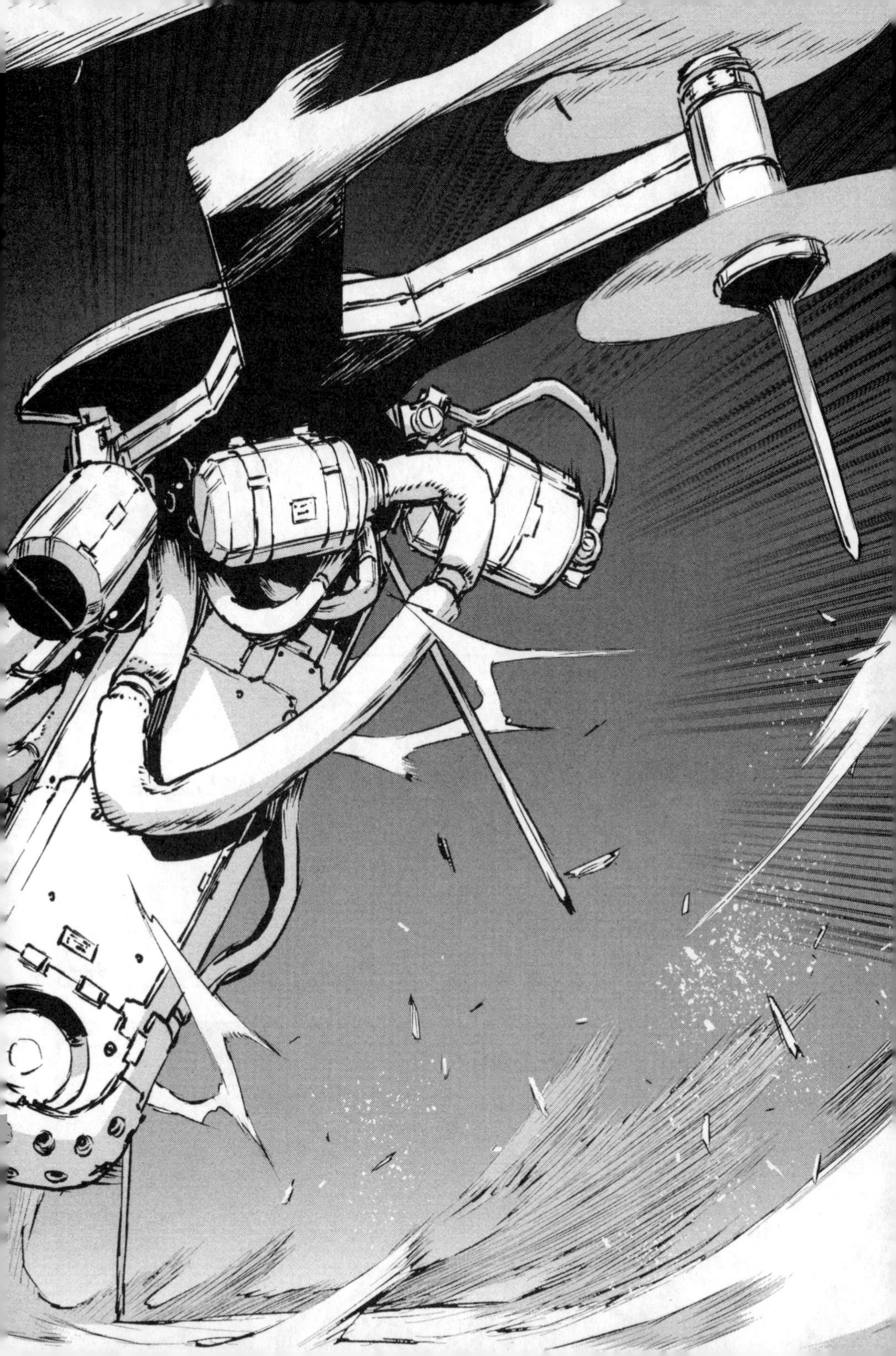

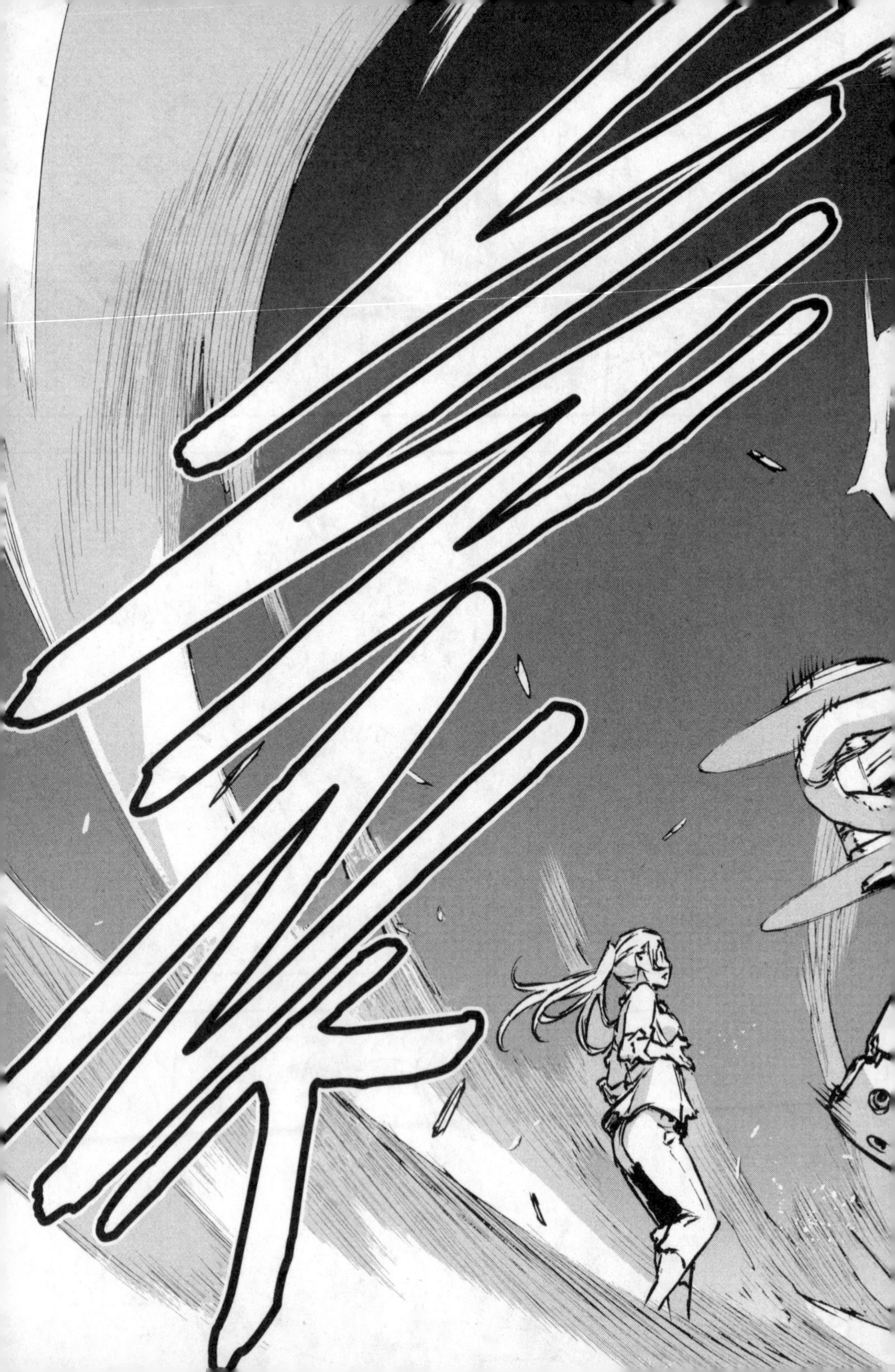

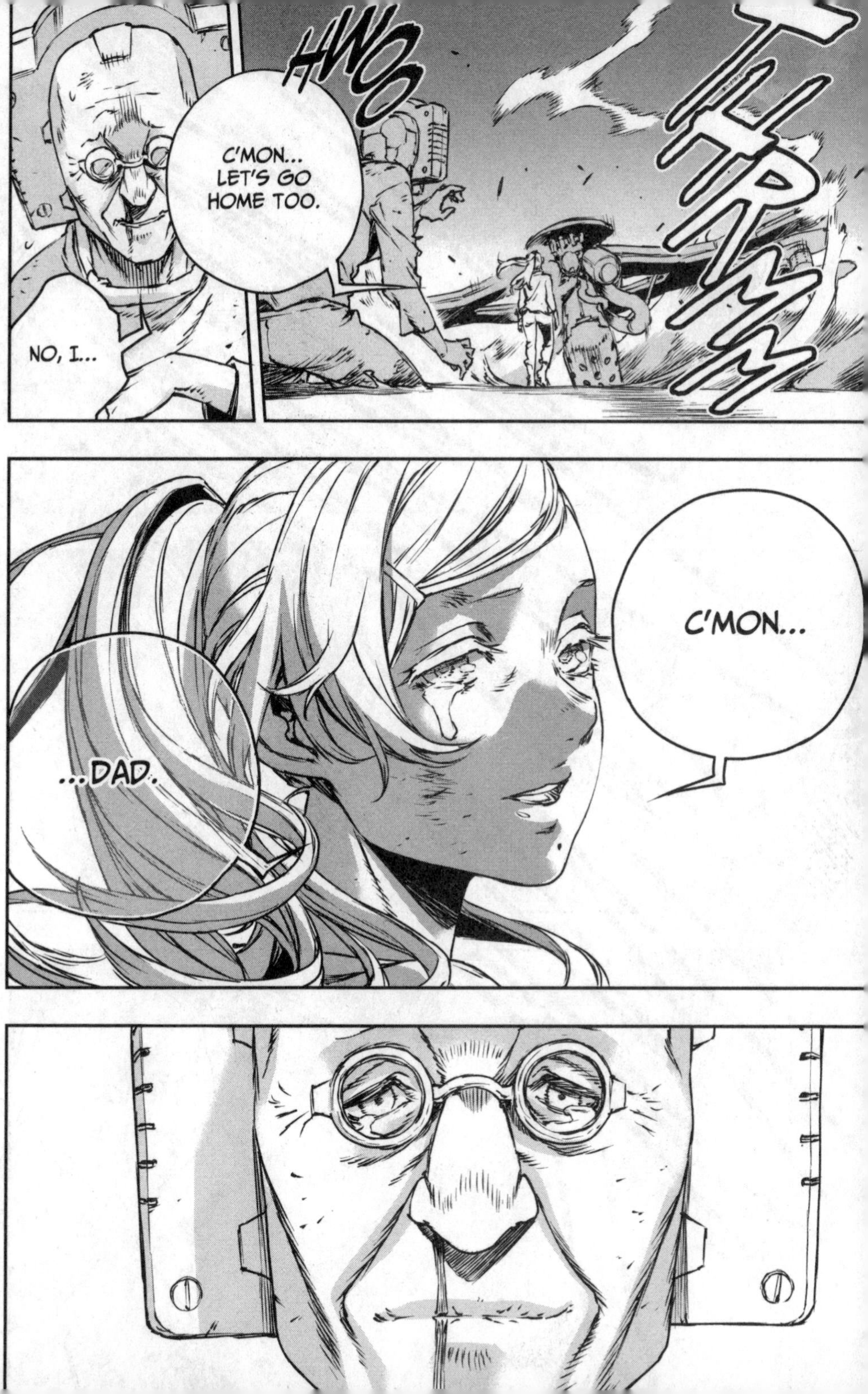
THRMMM
HWOO
C'MON... LET'S GO HOME TOO.
NO, I...
C'MON...
...DAD.

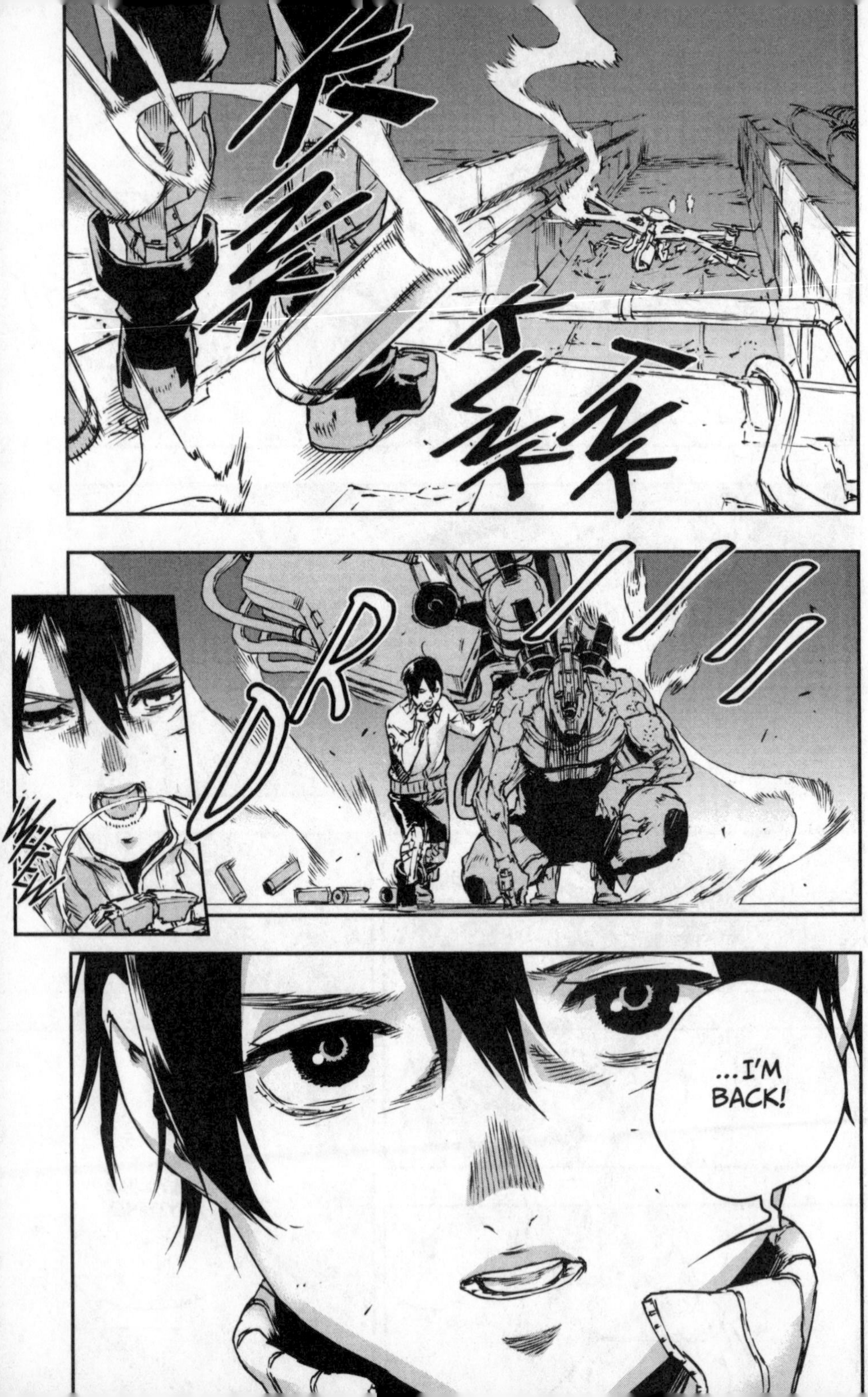
WHEW
...I'M BACK!

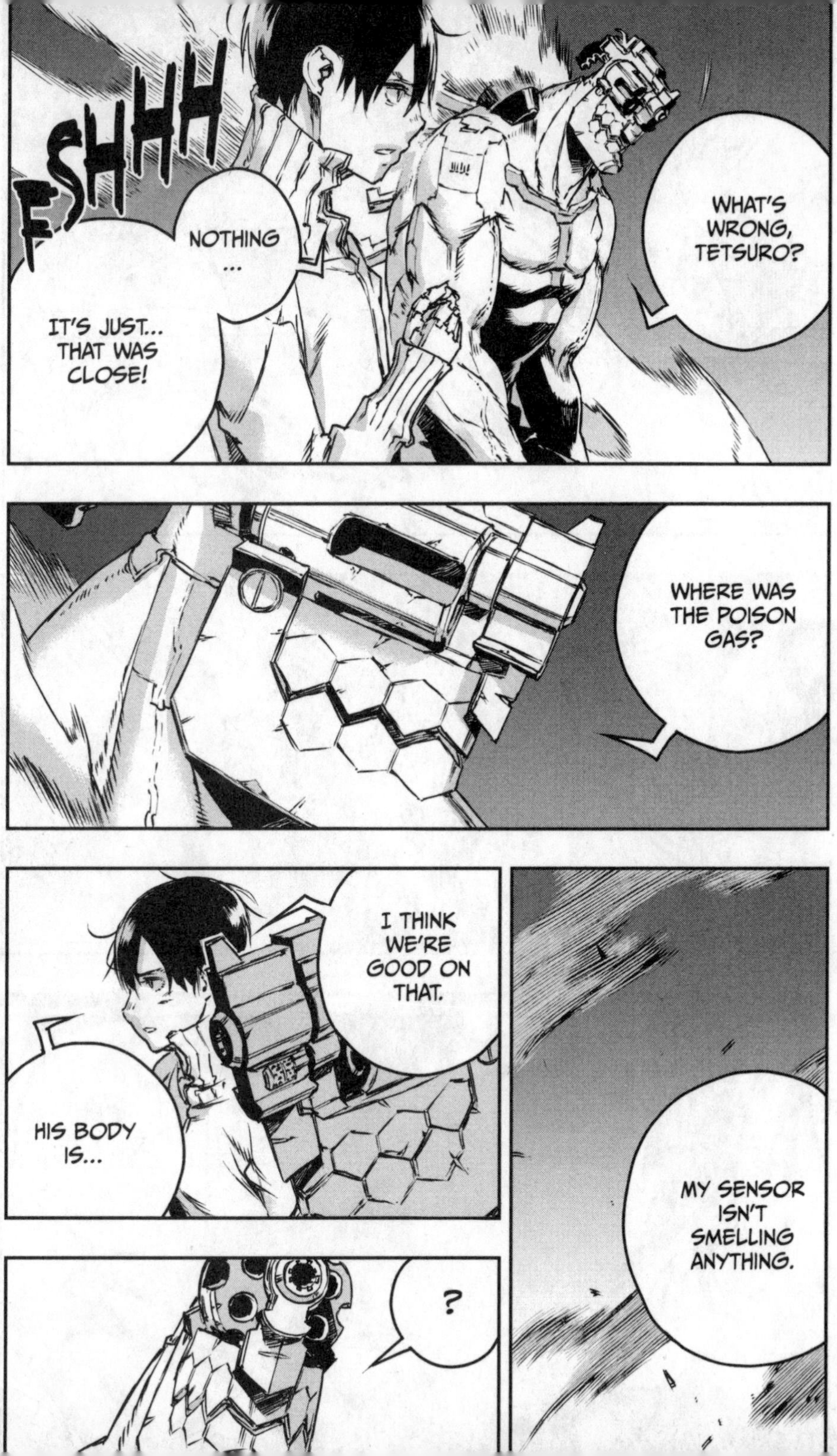
WHAT'S WRONG, TETSURO?
FSHHH
NOTHING ...
IT'S JUST... THAT WAS CLOSE!
WHERE WAS THE POISON GAS?
MY SENSOR ISN'T SMELLING ANYTHING.
I THINK WE'RE GOOD ON THAT.
HIS BODY IS...
?

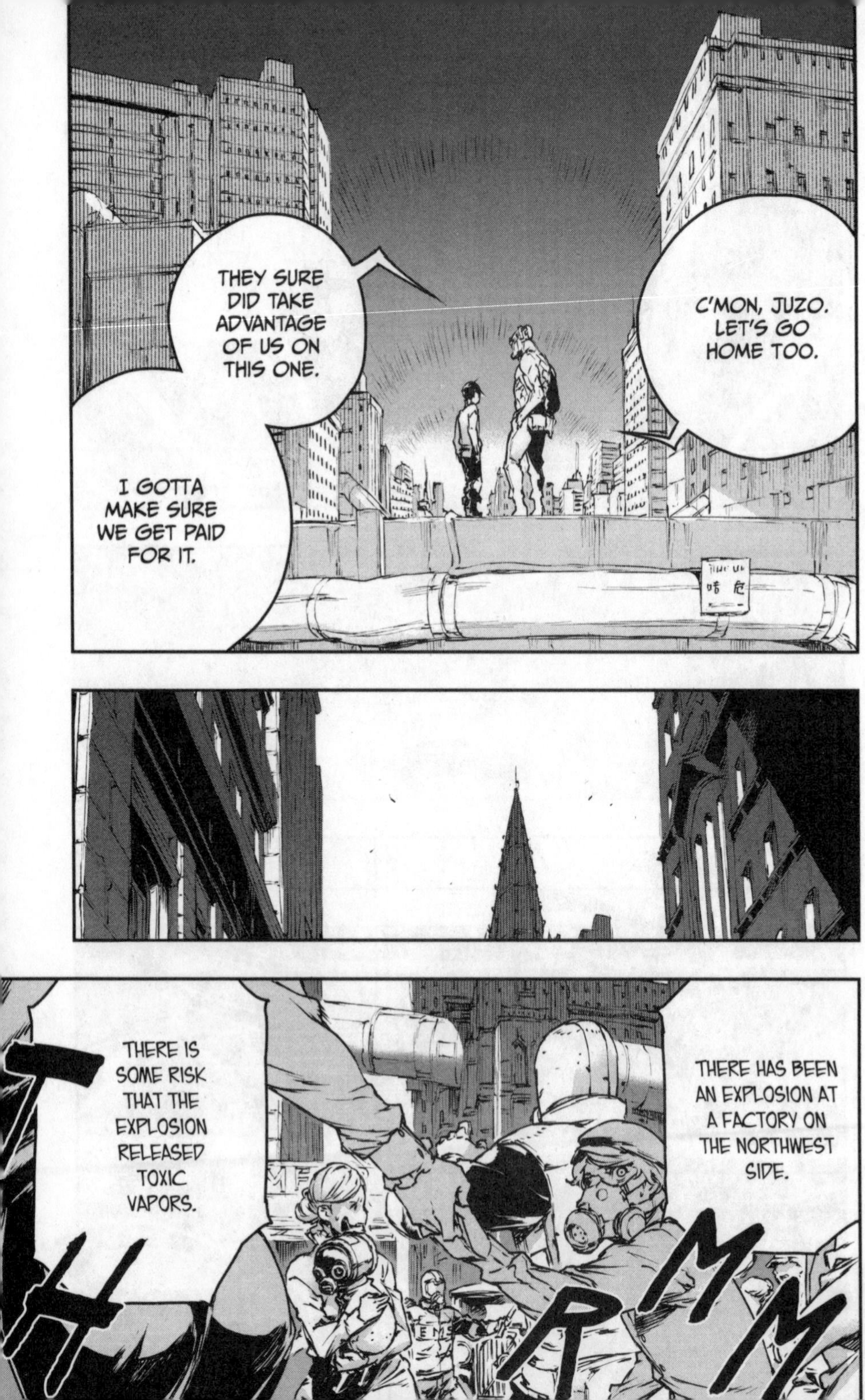
C'MON, JUZO. LET'S GO HOME TOO.
THEY SURE DID TAKE ADVANTAGE OF US ON THIS ONE.
I GOTTA MAKE SURE WE GET PAID FOR IT.
THERE HAS BEEN AN EXPLOSION AT A FACTORY ON THE NORTHWEST SIDE.
THERE IS SOME RISK THAT THE EXPLOSION RELEASED TOXIC VAPORS.
MMRM

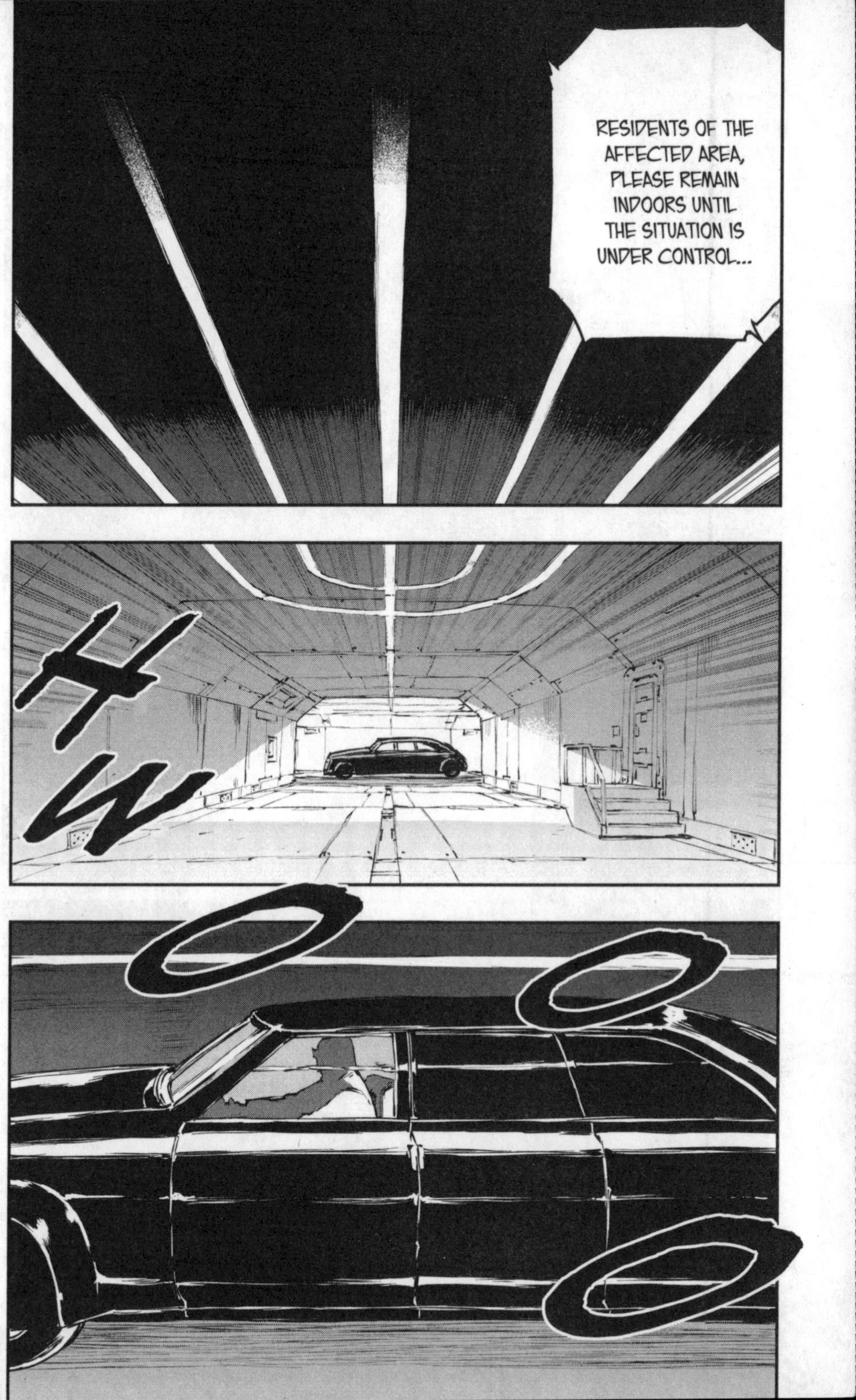
RESIDENTS OF THE AFFECTED AREA, PLEASE REMAIN INDOORS UNTIL THE SITUATION IS UNDER CONTROL...
HWOOOO

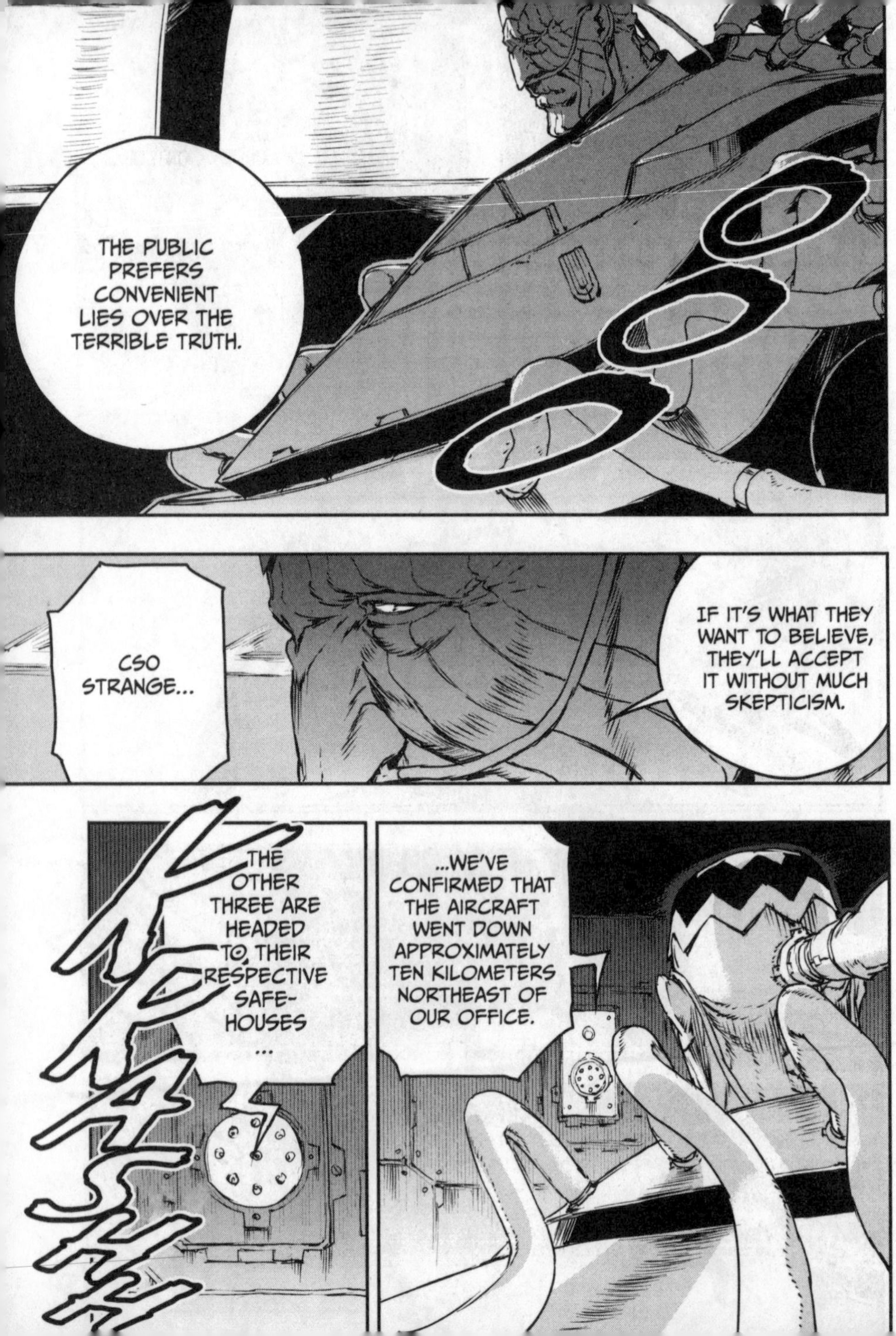
THE PUBLIC PREFERS CONVENIENT LIES OVER THE TERRIBLE TRUTH.
IF IT'S WHAT THEY WANT TO BELIEVE, THEY'LL ACCEPT IT WITHOUT MUCH SKEPTICISM.
CSO STRANGE...
...WE'VE CONFIRMED THAT THE AIRCRAFT WENT DOWN APPROXIMATELY TEN KILOMETERS NORTHEAST OF OUR OFFICE.
THE OTHER THREE ARE HEADED TO THEIR RESPECTIVE SAFE-HOUSES ...

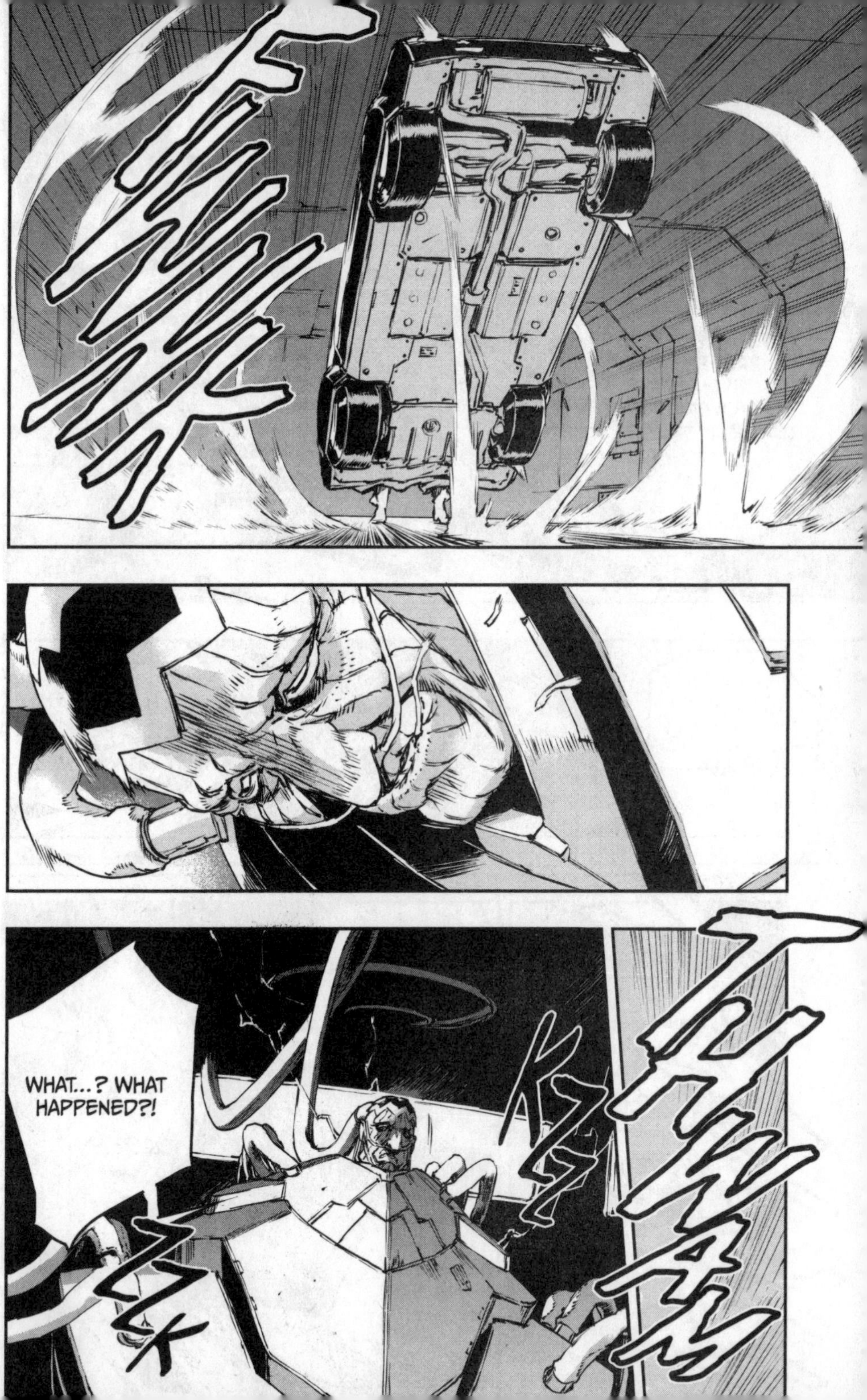
WHAT...? WHAT HAPPENED?!

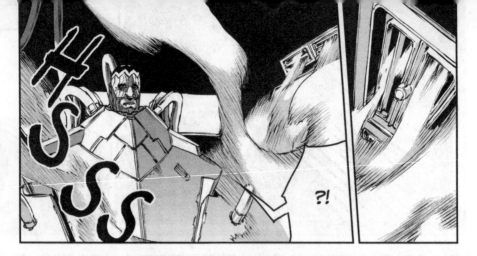

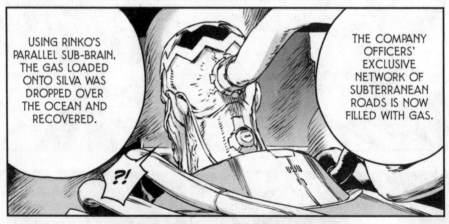

HISSS
?!
THE COMPANY OFFICERS' EXCLUSIVE NETWORK OF SUBTERRANEAN ROADS IS NOW FILLED WITH GAS.
USING RINKO'S PARALLEL SUB-BRAIN, THE GAS LOADED ONTO SILVA WAS DROPPED OVER THE OCEAN AND RECOVERED.
?!
G...
GAS?!
THE CITY'S RULERS FLEEING IN A TIME OF CRISIS. HOW SHAMEFUL.
HACK

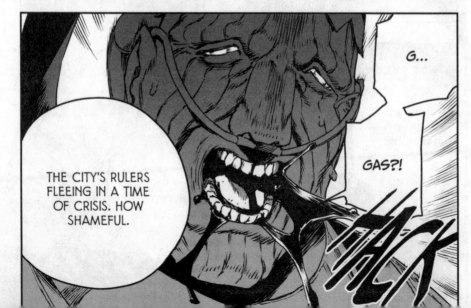

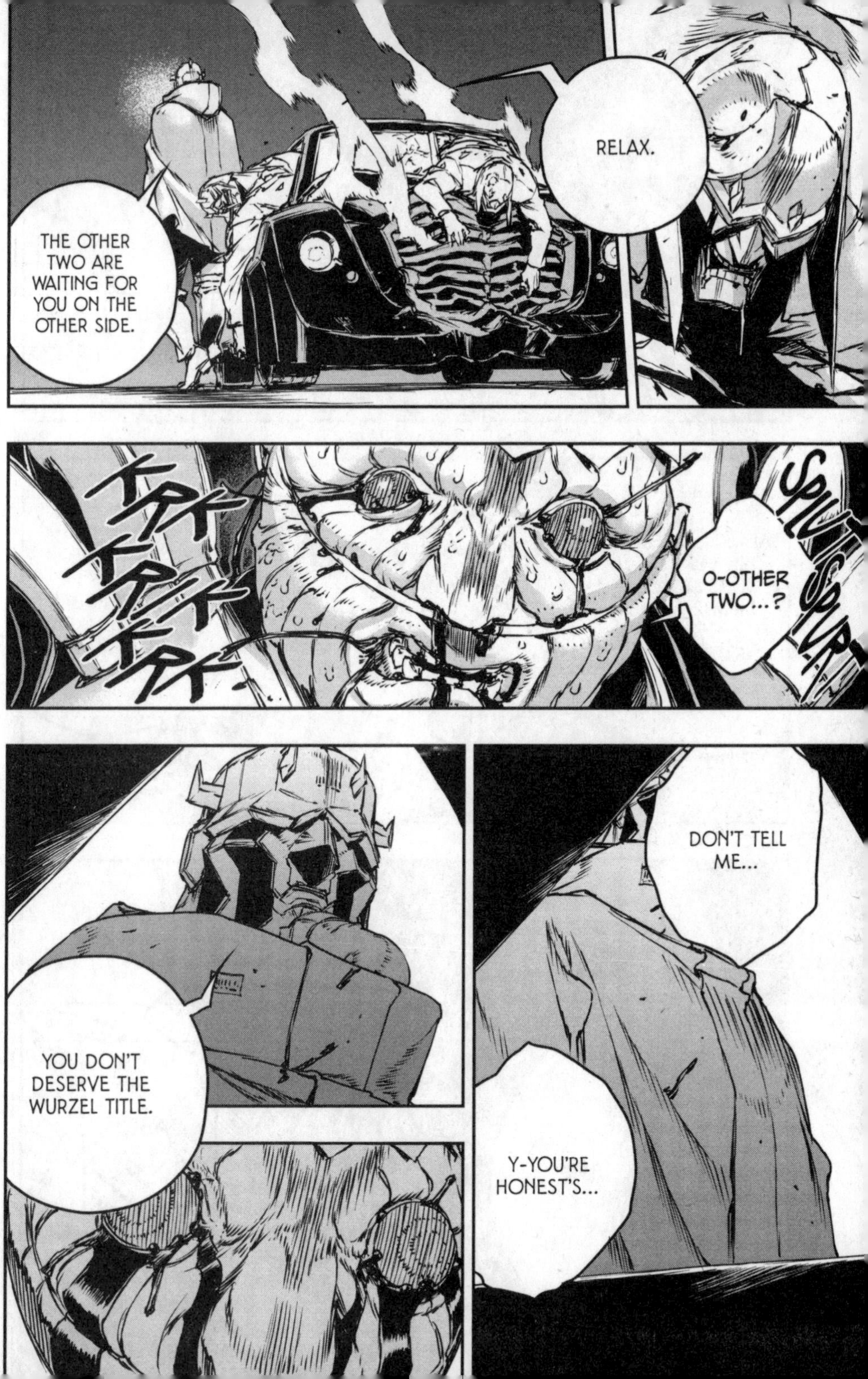
RELAX.
THE OTHER TWO ARE WAITING FOR YOU ON THE OTHER SIDE.
O-OTHER TWO...?
KRK KRIK KRK
DON'T TELL ME...
Y-YOU'RE HONEST'S...
YOU DON'T DESERVE THE WURZEL TITLE.

YOU'LL FADE INTO OBSCURITY DEEP UNDERGROUND.

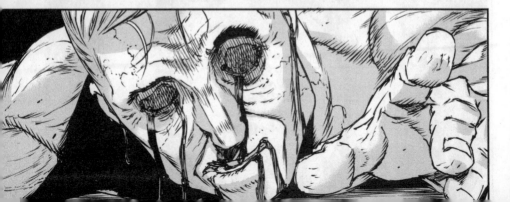

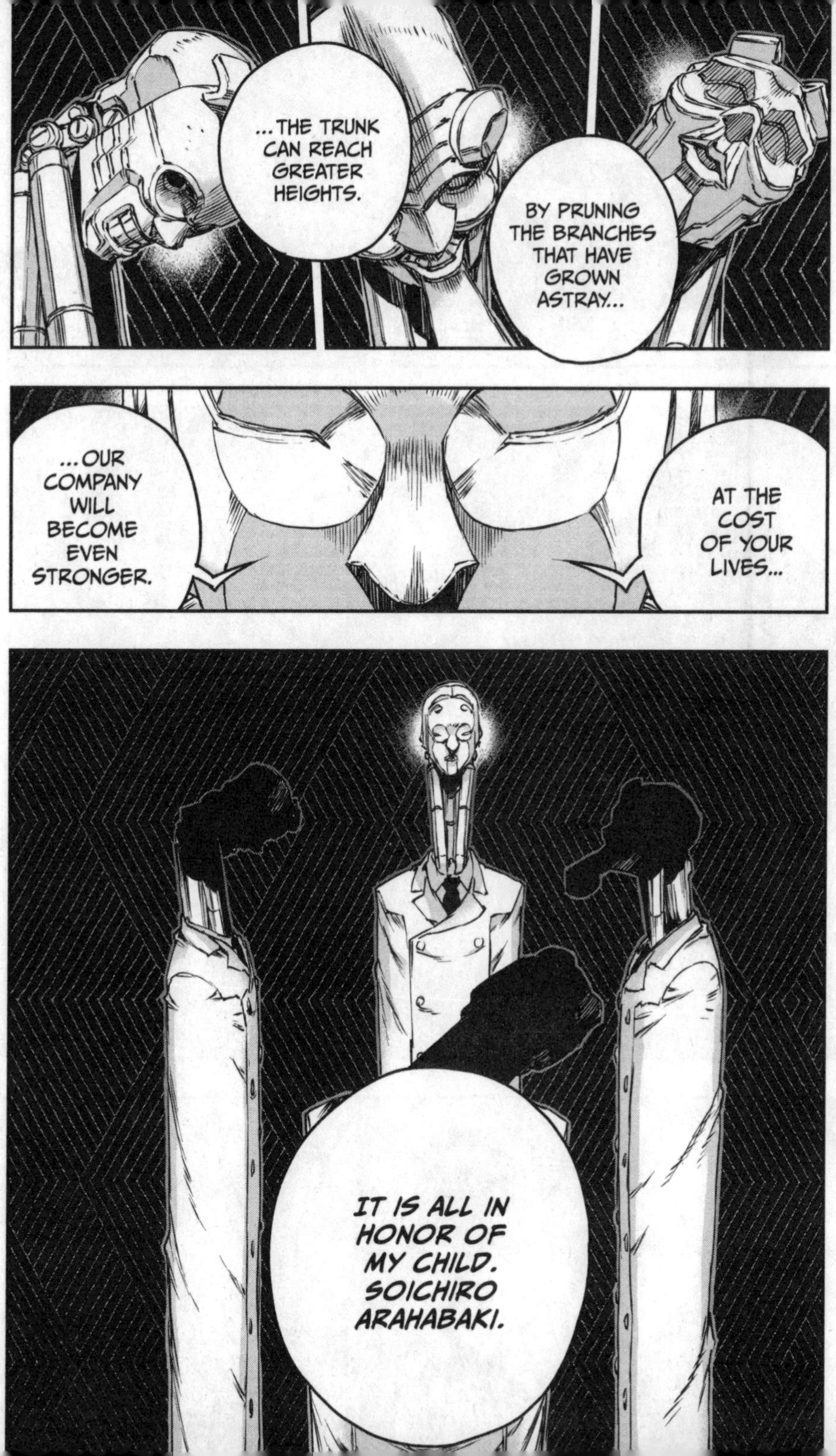
BY PRUNING THE BRANCHES THAT HAVE GROWN ASTRAY...
...THE TRUNK CAN REACH GREATER HEIGHTS.
AT THE COST OF YOUR LIVES...
...OUR COMPANY WILL BECOME EVEN STRONGER.
IT IS ALL IN HONOR OF MY CHILD. SOICHIRO ARAHABAKI.

NO GUNS LIFE

The gunsmoke drifts, the muzzle talks

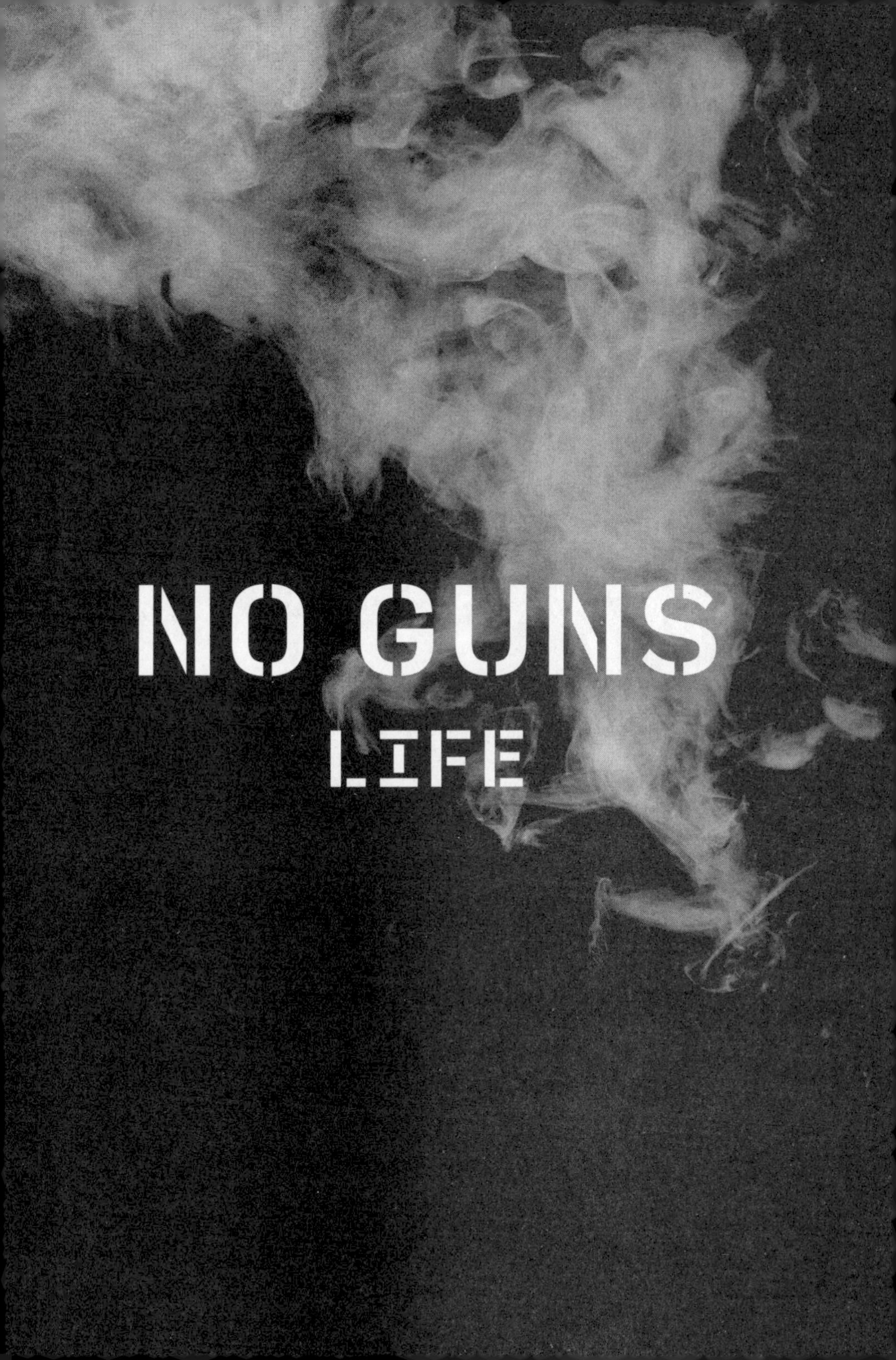
NO GUNS
LIFE

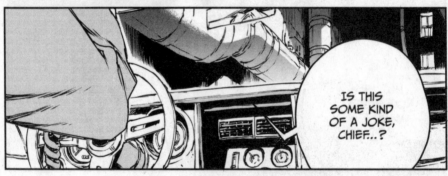

IS THIS SOME KIND OF A JOKE, CHIEF...?

YOU WANT ME TO HELP INUI PICK OUT A CAR?

Chapter 65
Chase

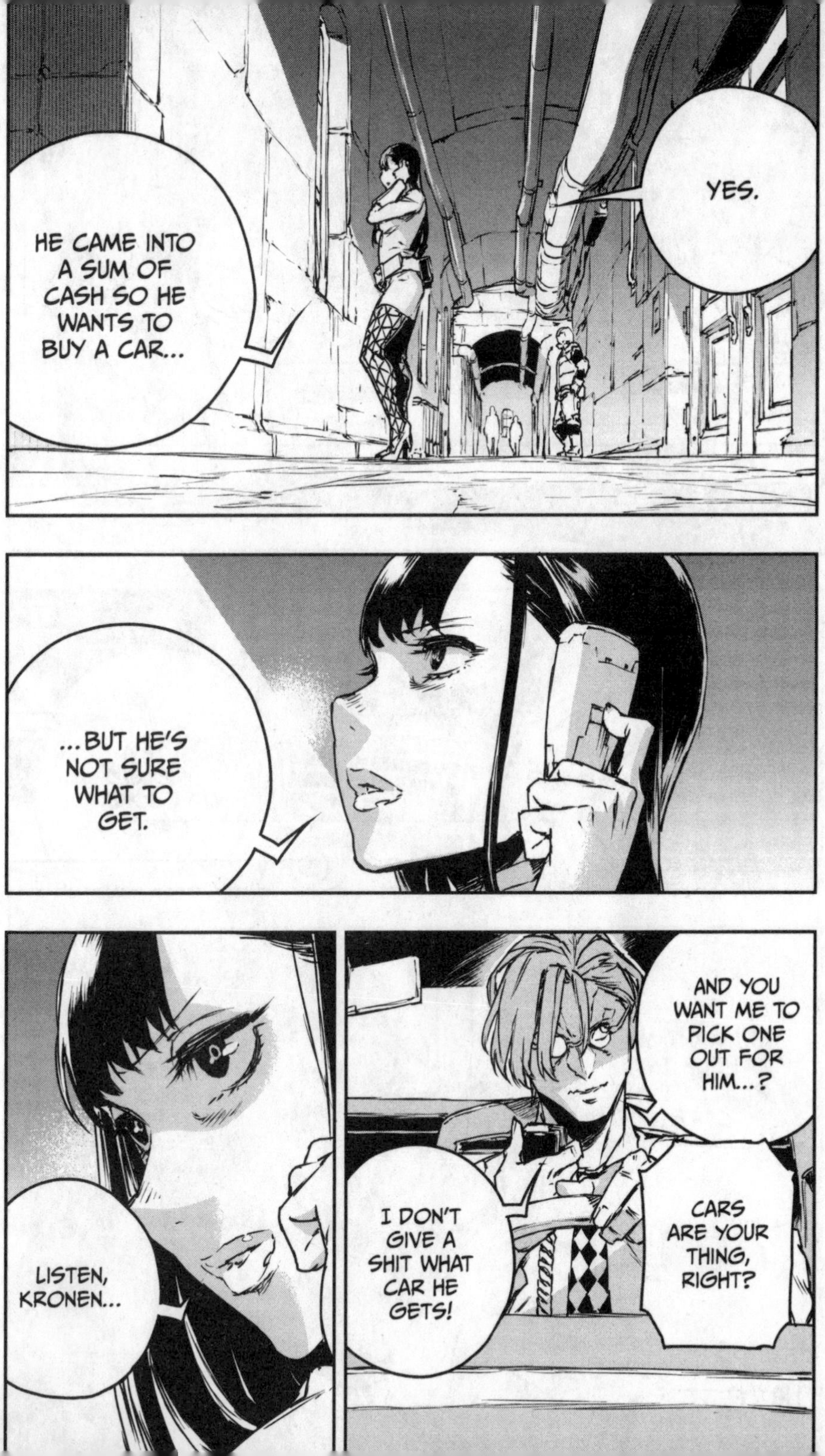
YES.
HE CAME INTO A SUM OF CASH SO HE WANTS TO BUY A CAR...
...BUT HE'S NOT SURE WHAT TO GET.
AND YOU WANT ME TO PICK ONE OUT FOR HIM...?
CARS ARE YOUR THING, RIGHT?
I DON'T GIVE A SHIT WHAT CAR HE GETS!
LISTEN, KRONEN...

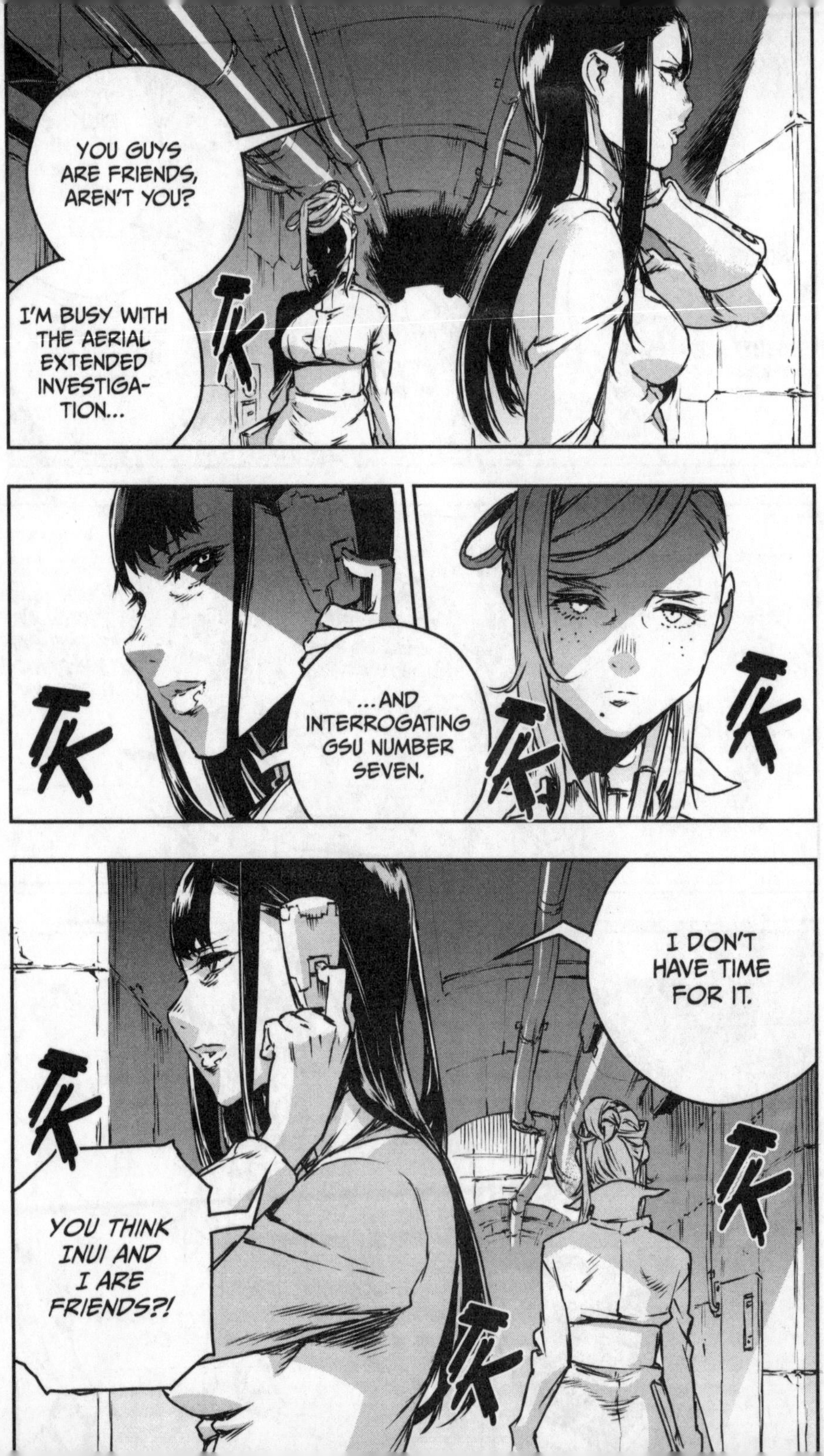
YOU GUYS ARE FRIENDS, AREN'T YOU?
TK
I'M BUSY WITH THE AERIAL EXTENDED INVESTIGA-TION...
TK
TK
...AND INTERROGATING GSU NUMBER SEVEN.
TK
I DON'T HAVE TIME FOR IT.
TK
TK
YOU THINK INUI AND I ARE FRIENDS?!
TK

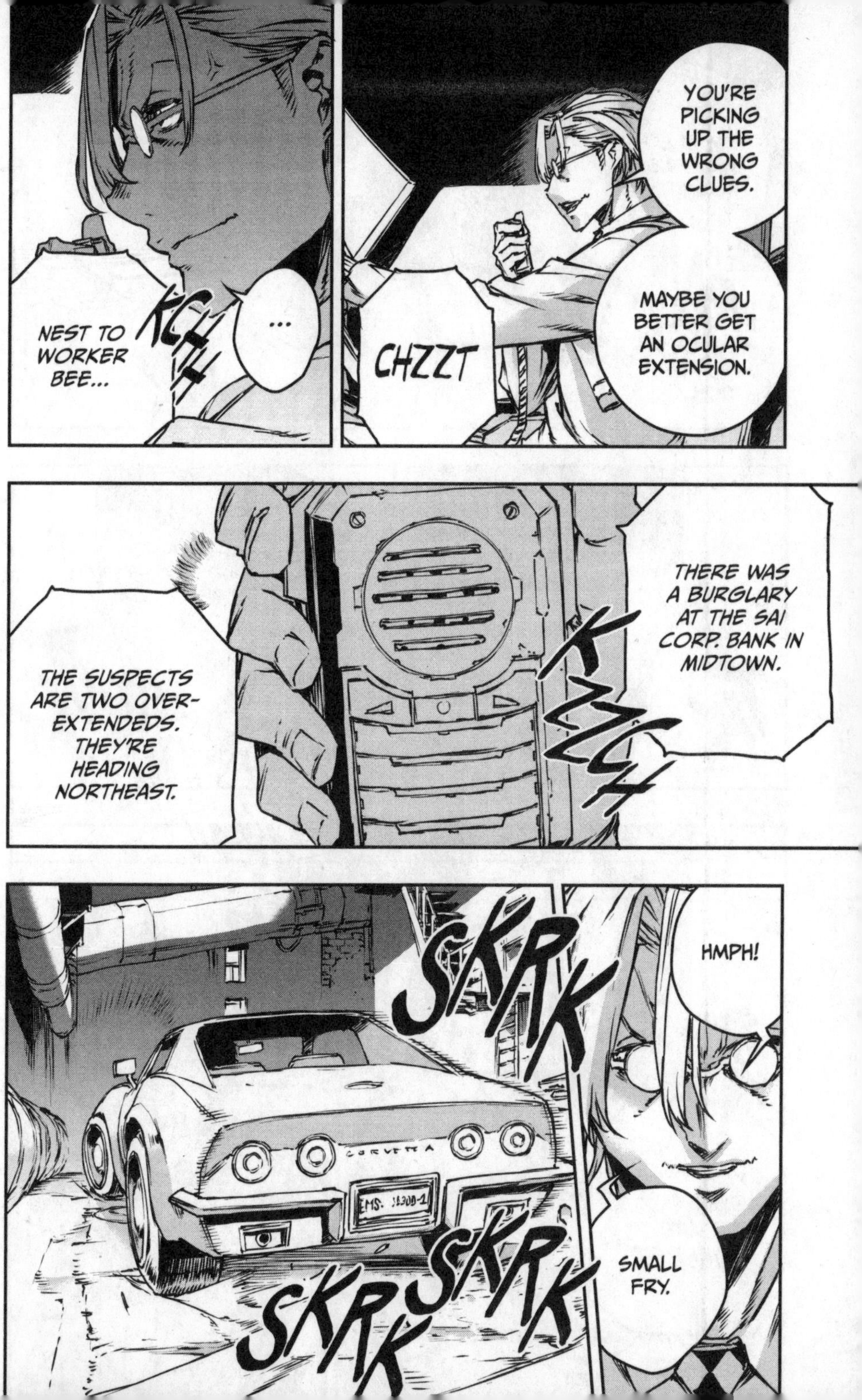
YOU'RE PICKING UP THE WRONG CLUES.
MAYBE YOU BETTER GET AN OCULAR EXTENSION.
CHZZT
...
KCHH
NEST TO WORKER BEE...
THERE WAS A BURGLARY AT THE SAI CORP. BANK IN MIDTOWN.
KZZZCH
THE SUSPECTS ARE TWO OVER-EXTENDEDS. THEY'RE HEADING NORTHEAST.
HMPH!
SKRK
SMALL FRY.
SKRK
SKRK

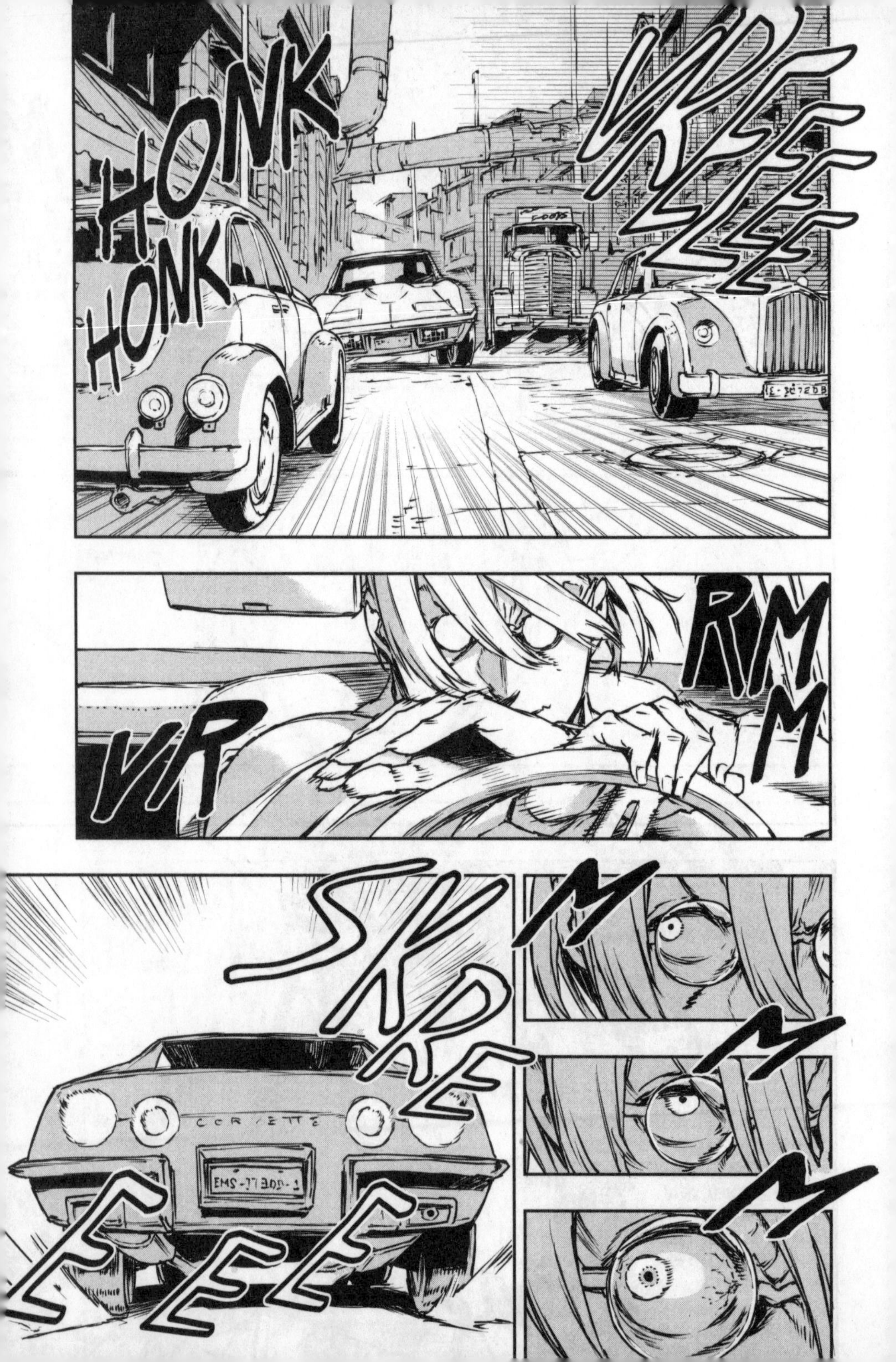
HONK
HONK
RMMM
VR
MMM
SKREEEEE
CORVETTE

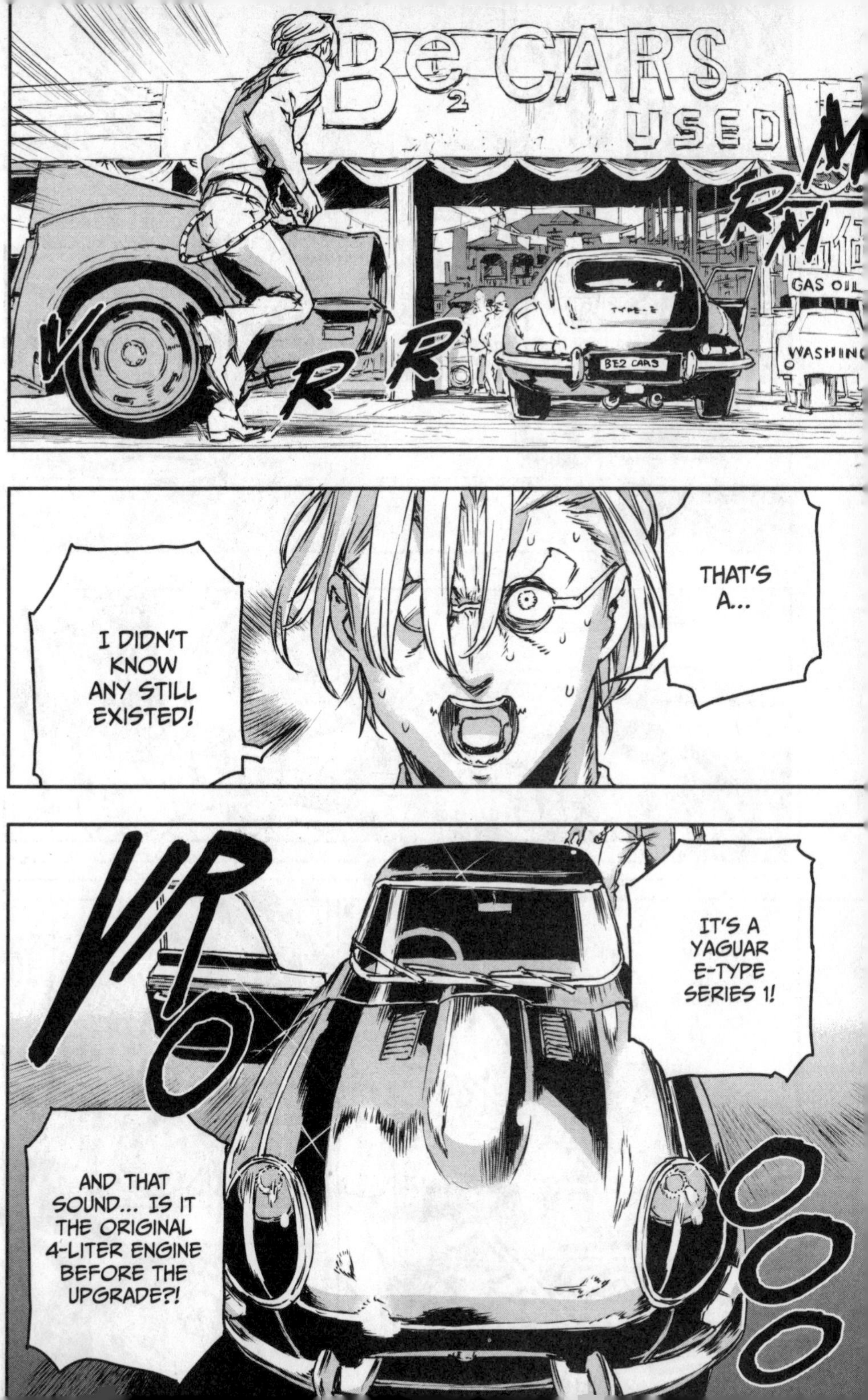
Be2 CARS
USED
GAS OIL
WASHING
BE2 CARS
VRR
RMM
THAT'S A...
I DIDN'T KNOW ANY STILL EXISTED!
IT'S A YAGUAR E-TYPE SERIES 1!
AND THAT SOUND... IS IT THE ORIGINAL 4-LITER ENGINE BEFORE THE UPGRADE?!
VROOOO

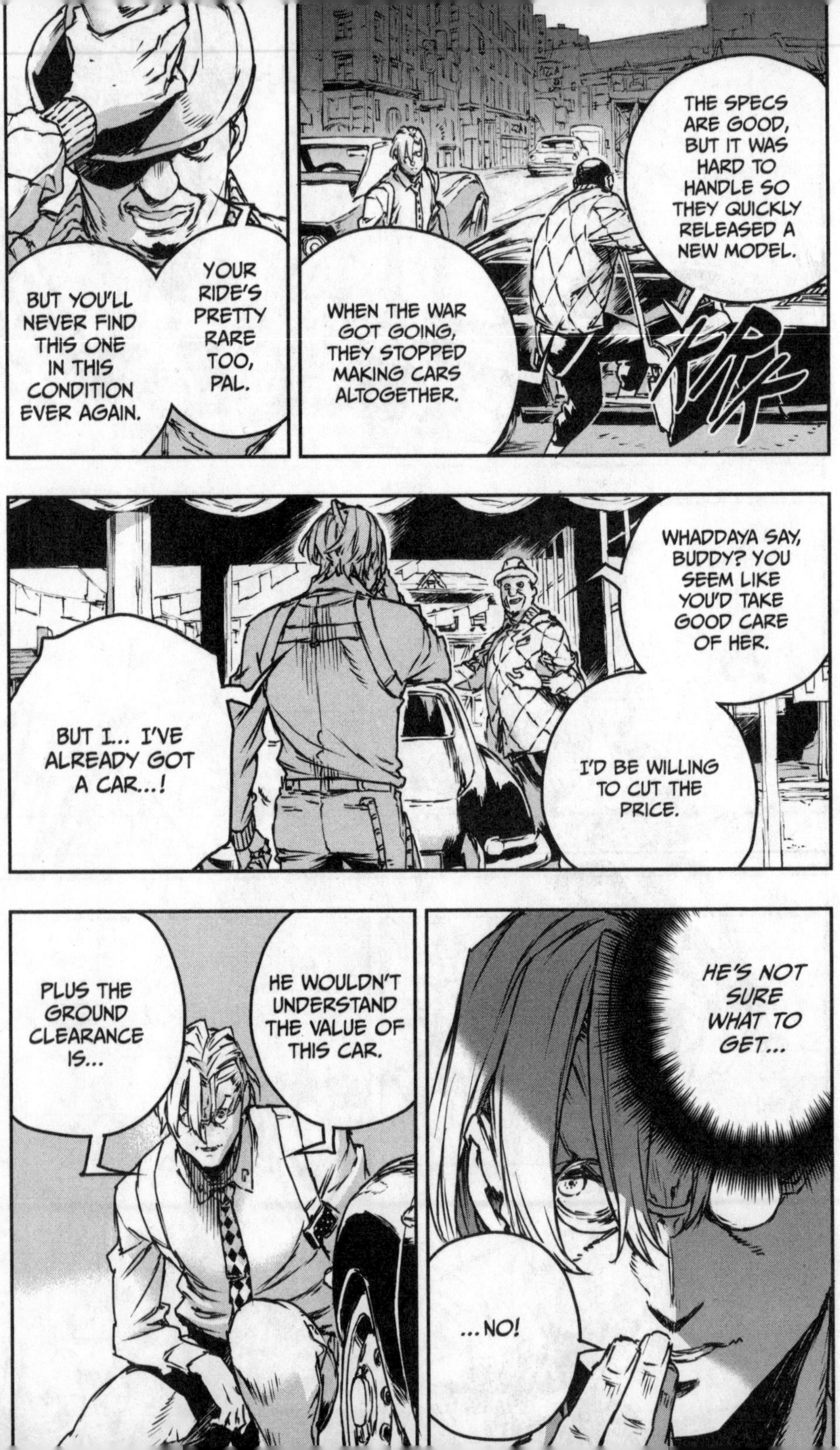
THE SPECS ARE GOOD, BUT IT WAS HARD TO HANDLE SO THEY QUICKLY RELEASED A NEW MODEL.
WHEN THE WAR GOT GOING, THEY STOPPED MAKING CARS ALTOGETHER.
YOUR RIDE'S PRETTY RARE TOO, PAL.
BUT YOU'LL NEVER FIND THIS ONE IN THIS CONDITION EVER AGAIN.
WHADDAYA SAY, BUDDY? YOU SEEM LIKE YOU'D TAKE GOOD CARE OF HER.
I'D BE WILLING TO CUT THE PRICE.
BUT I... I'VE ALREADY GOT A CAR...!
HE'S NOT SURE WHAT TO GET...
...NO!
HE WOULDN'T UNDERSTAND THE VALUE OF THIS CAR.
PLUS THE GROUND CLEARANCE IS...

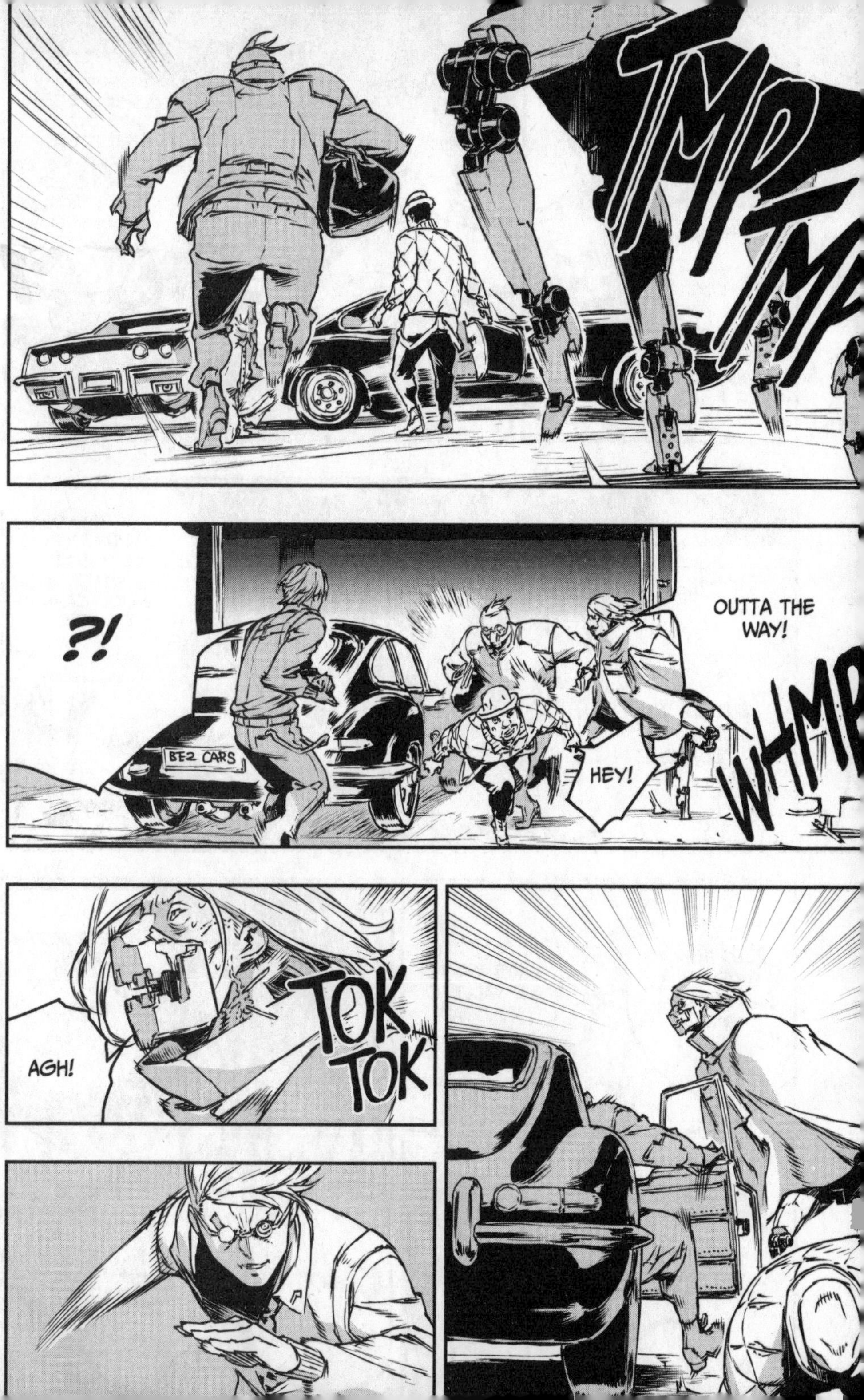
TMP
TMP
OUTTA THE WAY!
WHMP
HEY!
?!
TOK TOK
AGH!

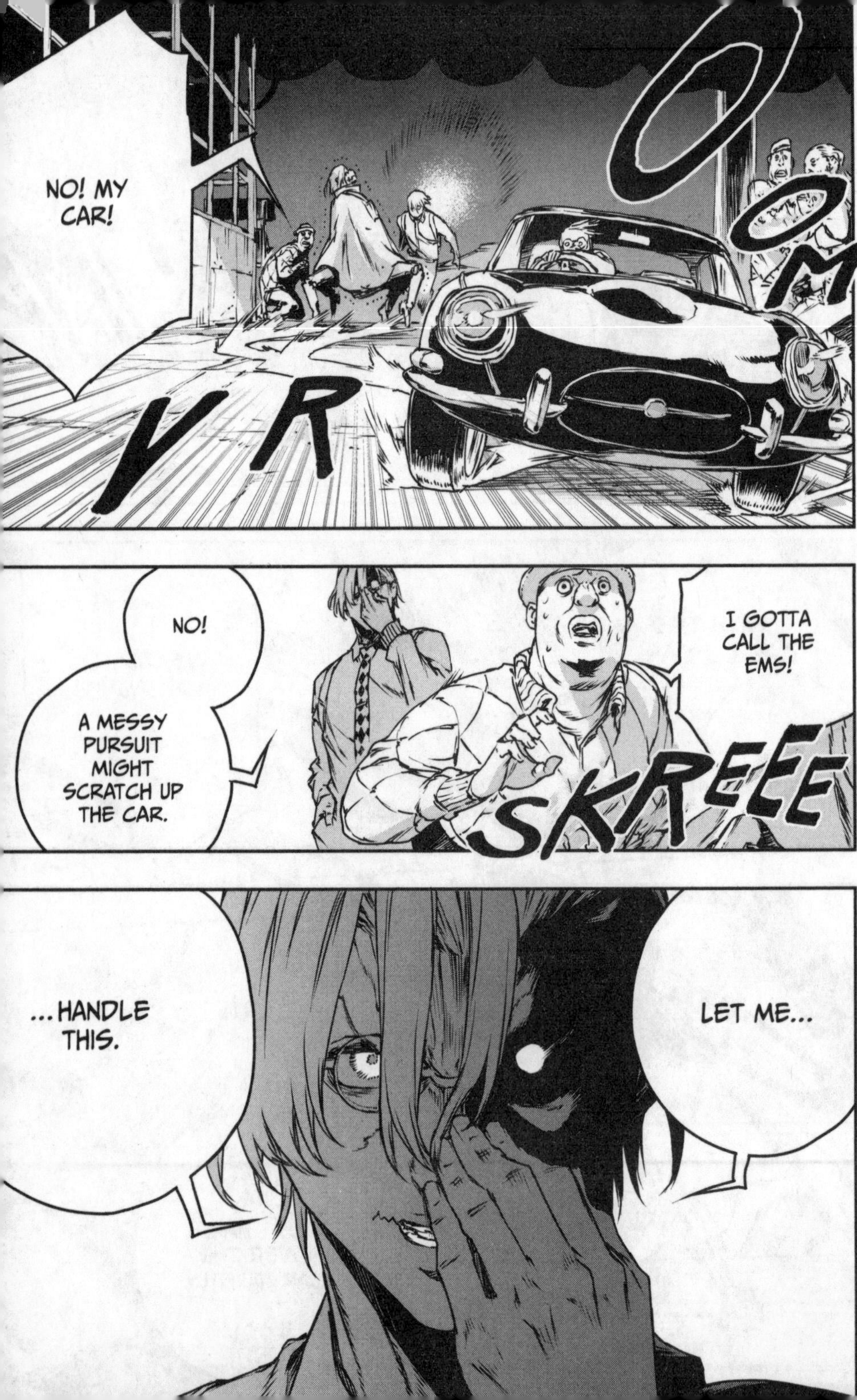
VROOM
NO! MY CAR!
I GOTTA CALL THE EMS!
SKREEE
NO!
A MESSY PURSUIT MIGHT SCRATCH UP THE CAR.
LET ME...
...HANDLE THIS.

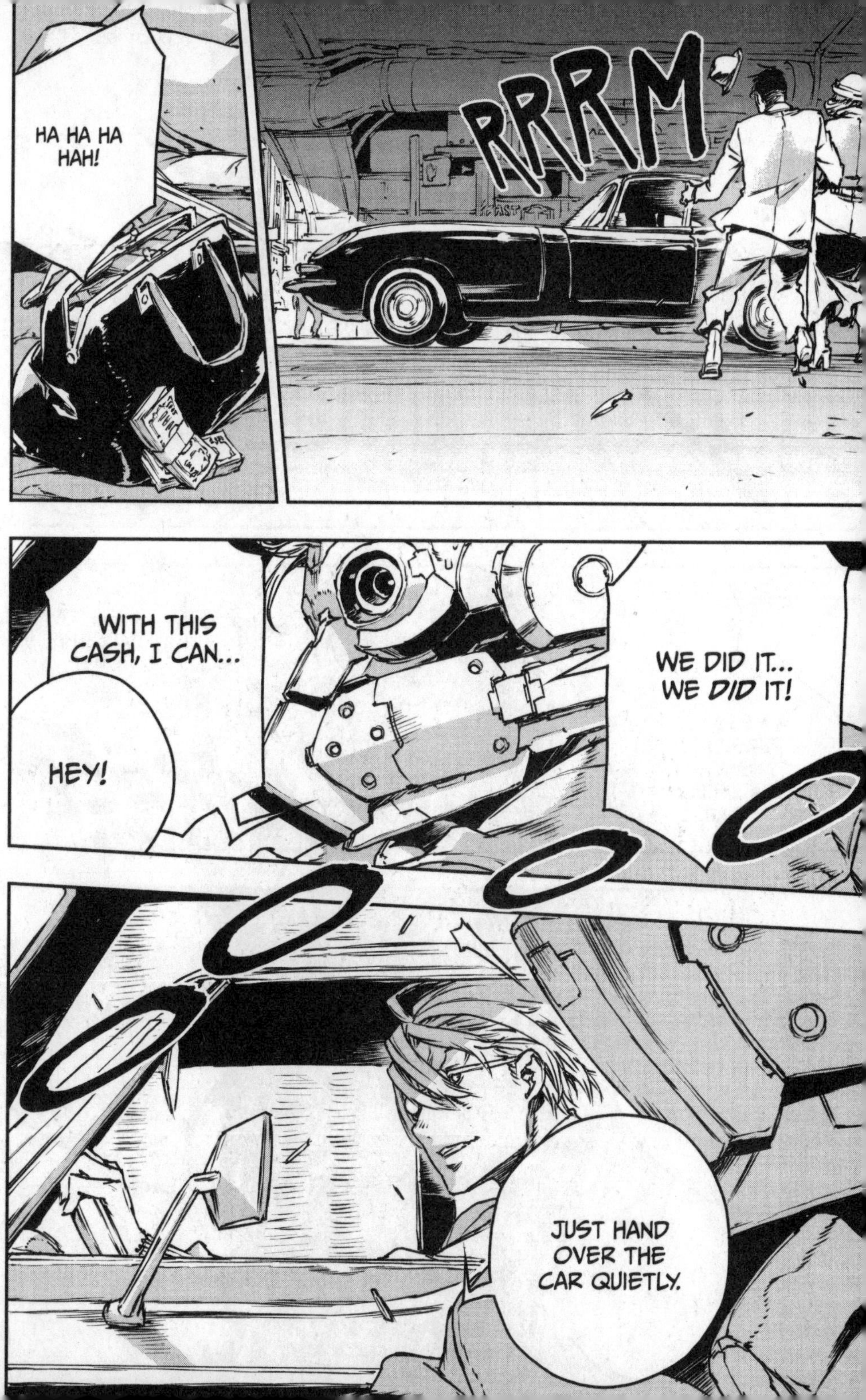
RRRM
HA HA HA HAH!
WE DID IT... WE *DID* IT!
WITH THIS CASH, I CAN...
HEY!
JUST HAND OVER THE CAR QUIETLY.

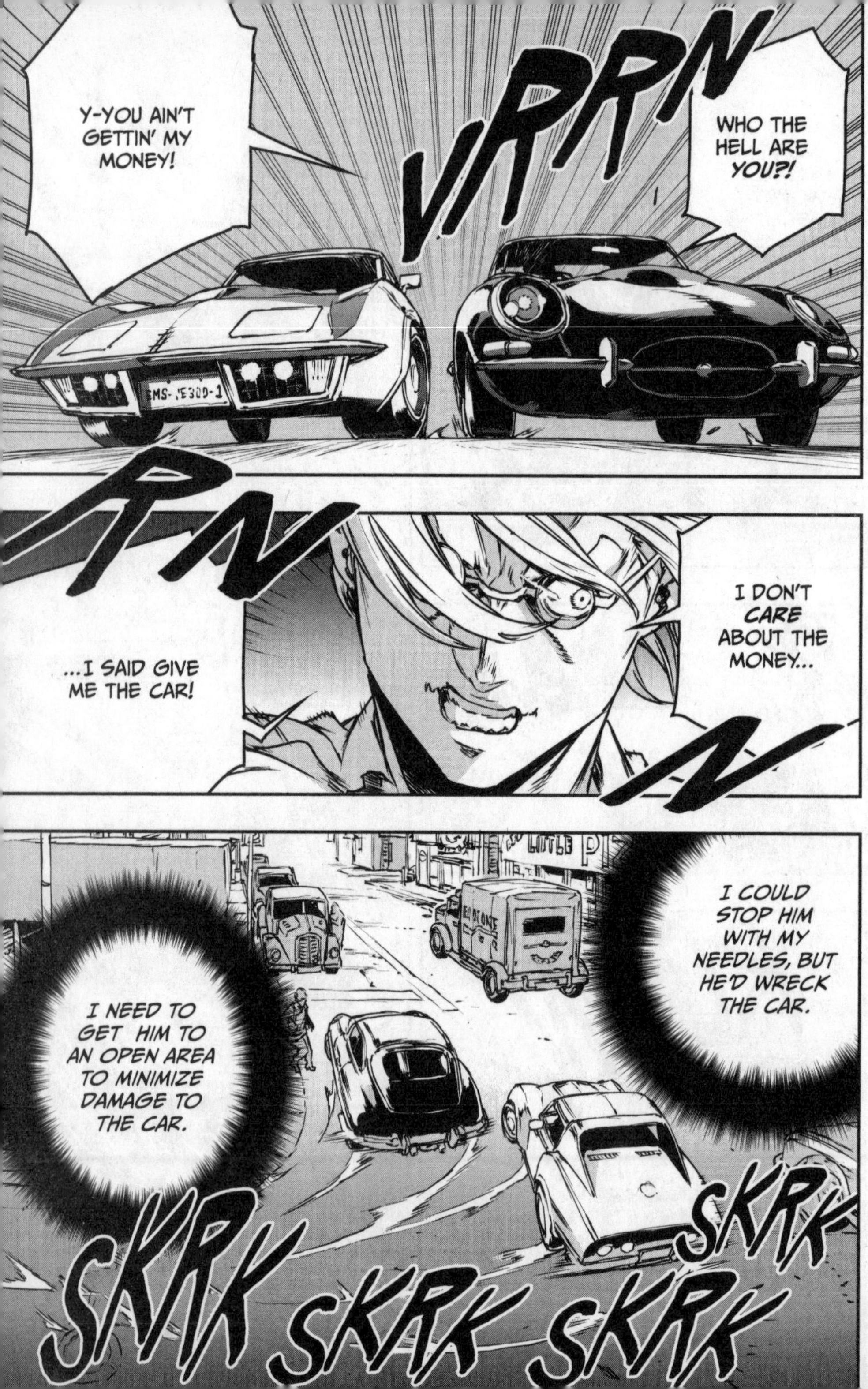
WHO THE HELL ARE YOU?!
Y-YOU AIN'T GETTIN' MY MONEY!
VRRN
RN
N
I DON'T CARE ABOUT THE MONEY...
...I SAID GIVE ME THE CAR!
I COULD STOP HIM WITH MY NEEDLES, BUT HE'D WRECK THE CAR.
I NEED TO GET HIM TO AN OPEN AREA TO MINIMIZE DAMAGE TO THE CAR.
SKRK
SKRK
SKRK
SKRK

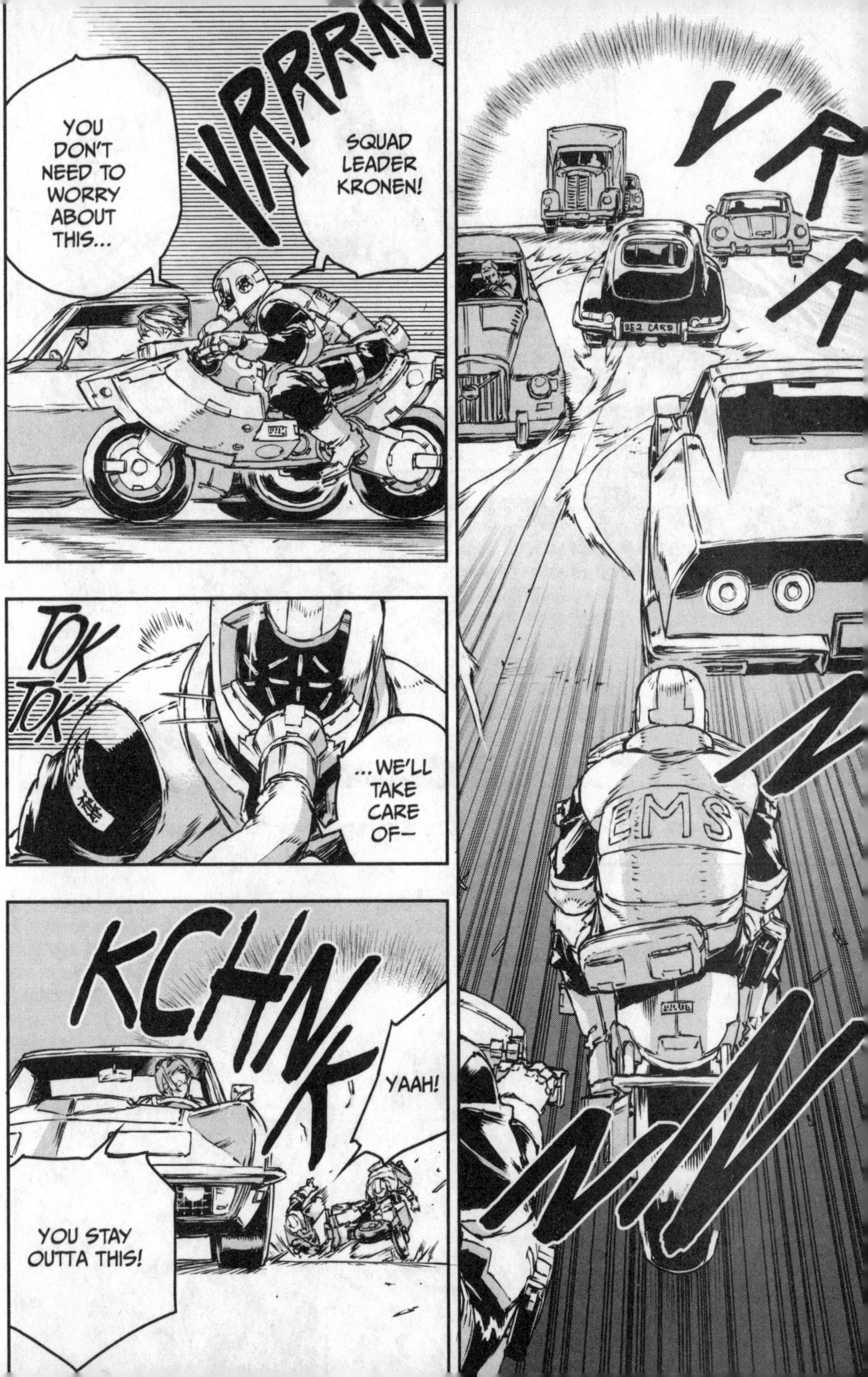
VRRNNNN
EMS
SQUAD LEADER KRONEN!
VRRRN
YOU DON'T NEED TO WORRY ABOUT THIS...
...WE'LL TAKE CARE OF—
TOK TOK
KCHNK
YAAH!
YOU STAY OUTTA THIS!

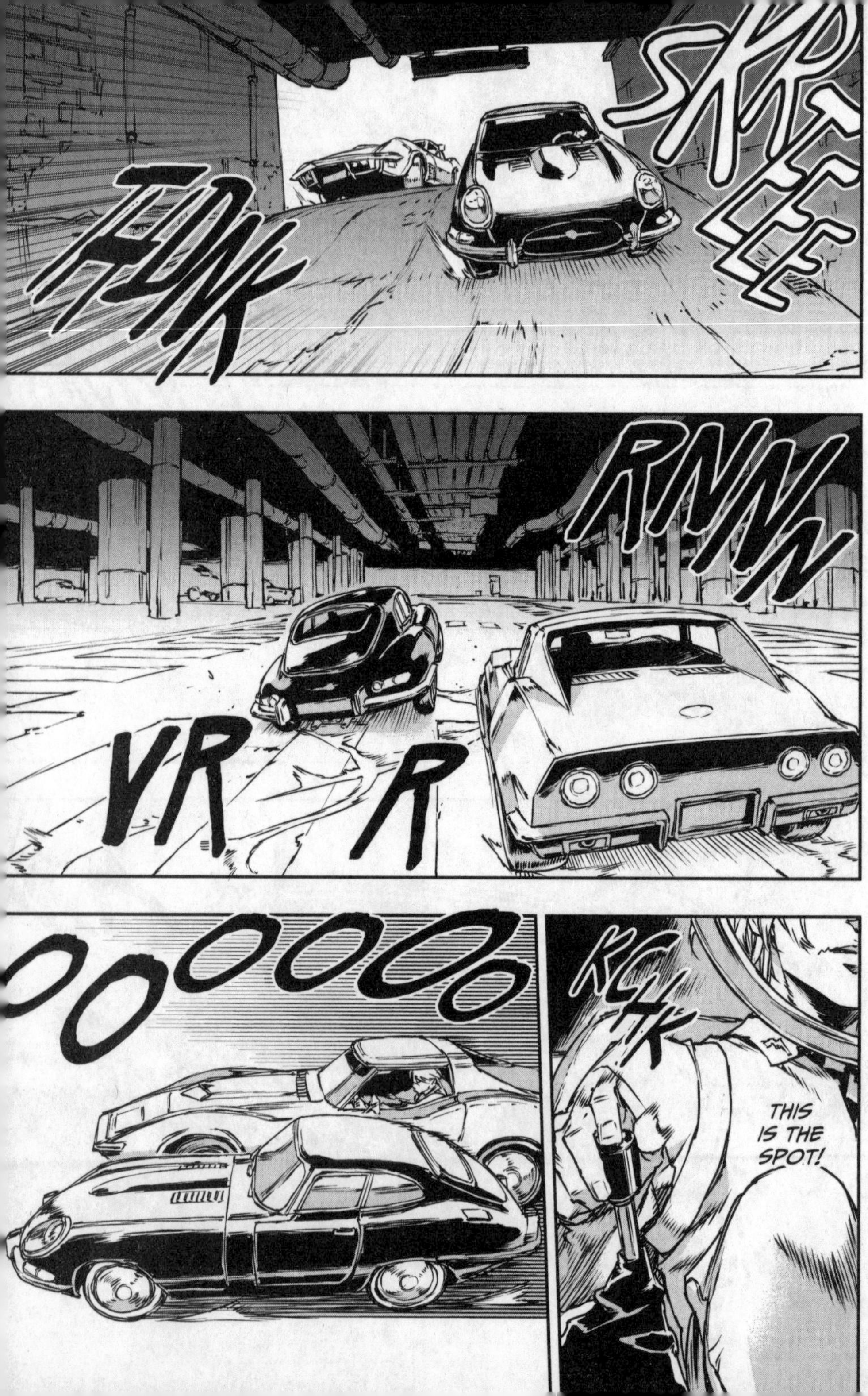
SKREEEE
THUNK
RNNNW
VR R
KCHK
THIS IS THE SPOT!
OOOOOO

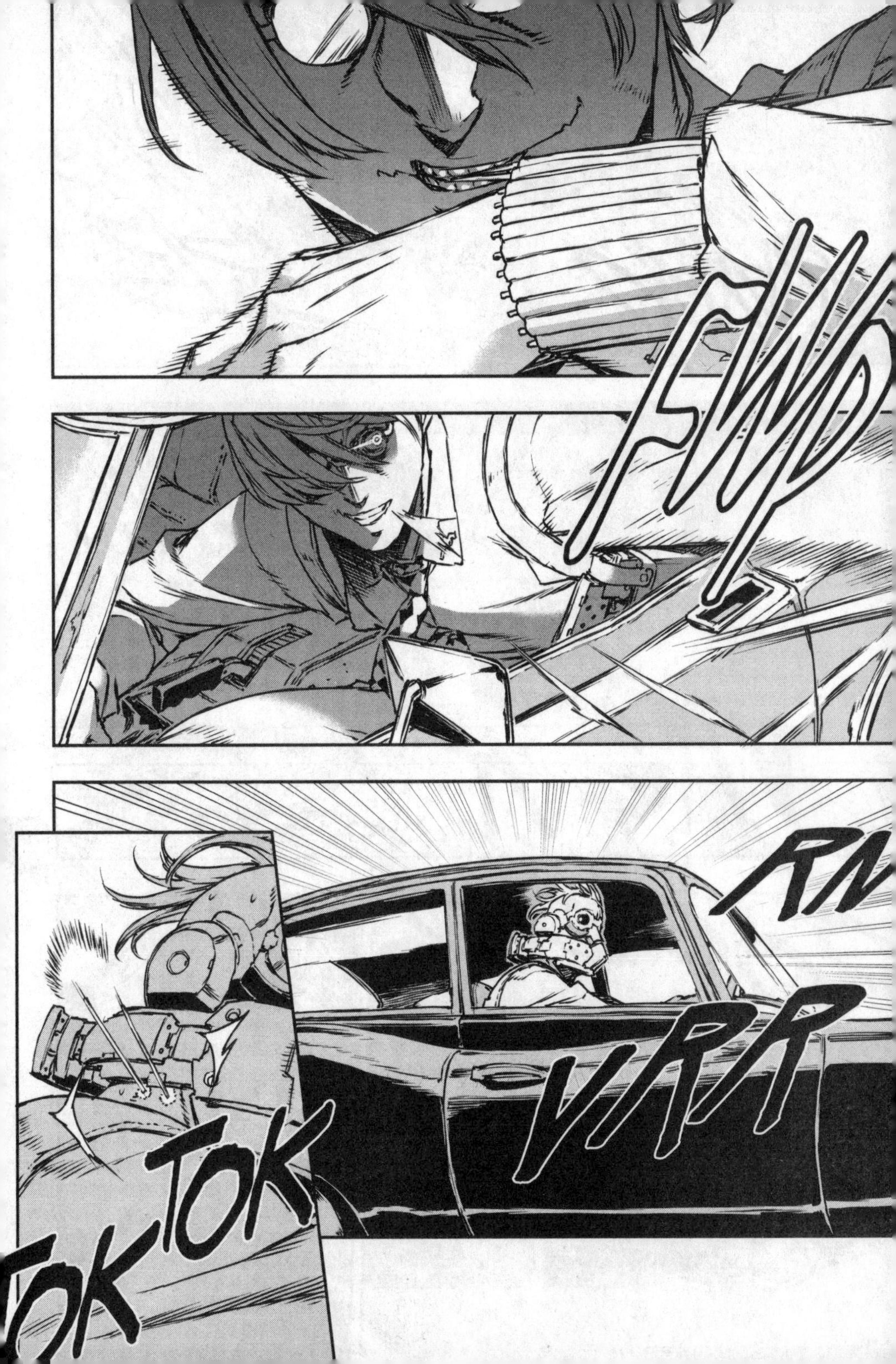
FWP
RN
VRR
TOK TOK

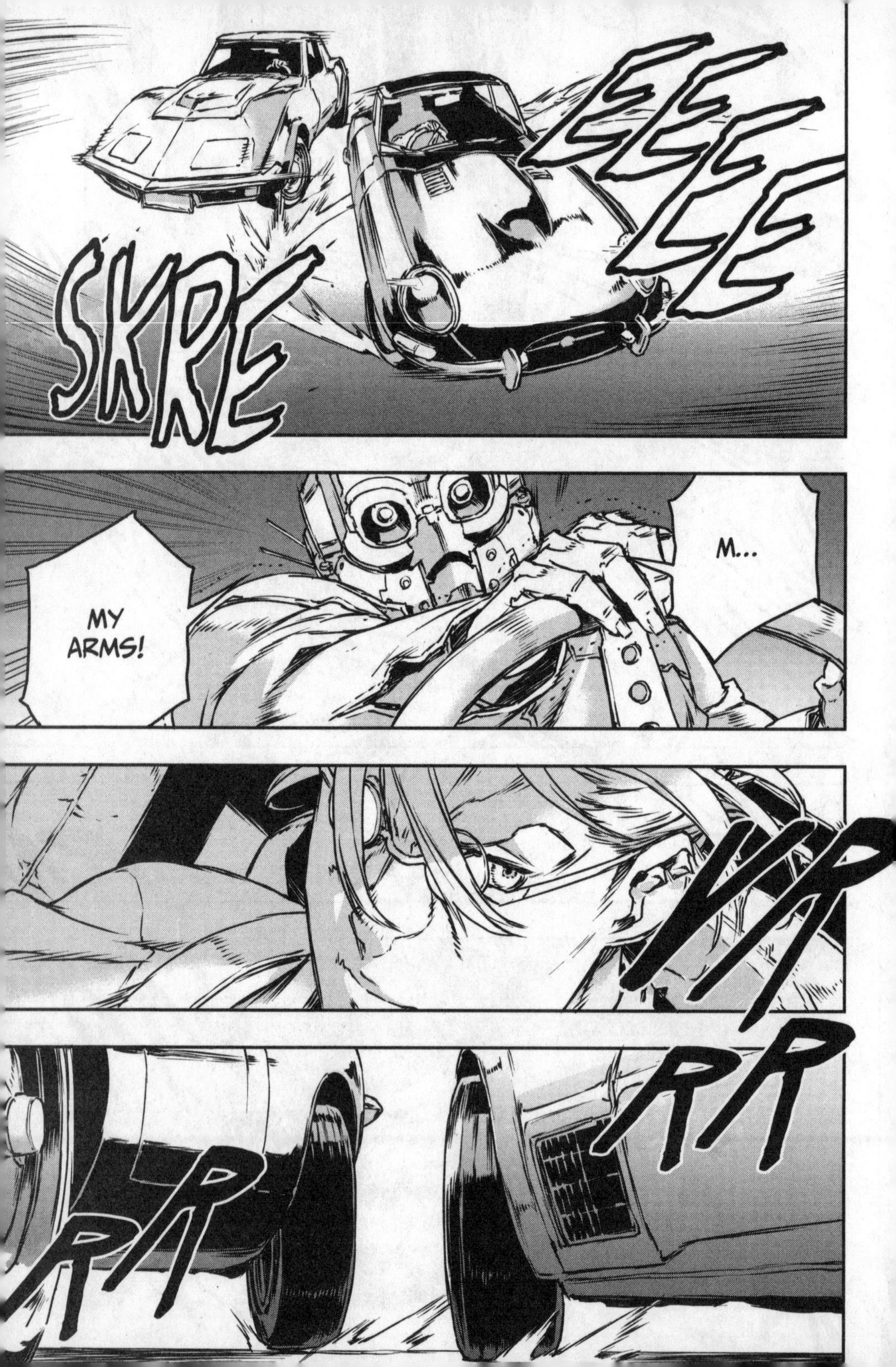

SKRE
EEEEEE
M...
MY ARMS!
VR
RR
RR

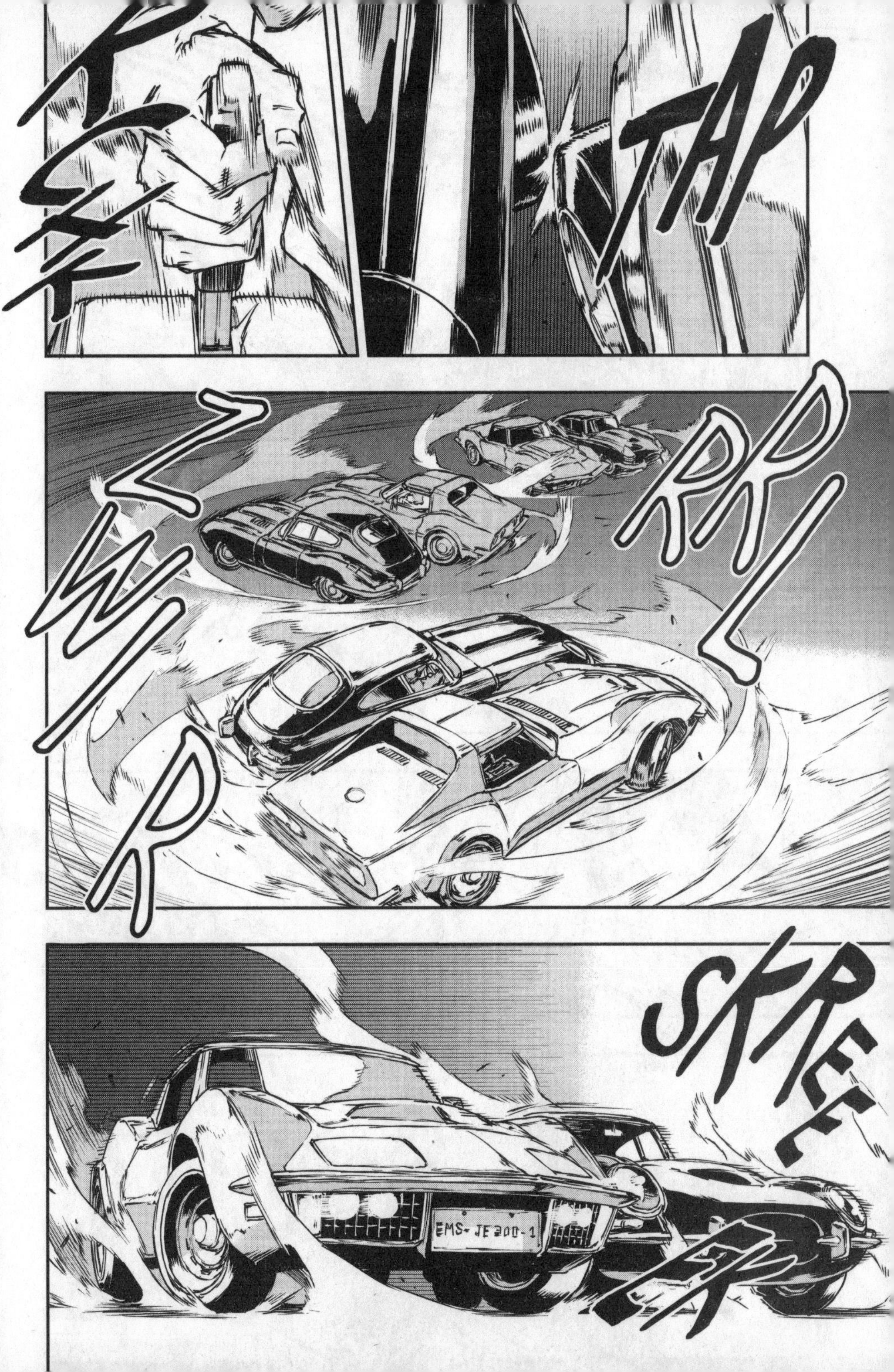
TAP
KSHF
ZWIRRRL
SKREEEK
EMS- JE300-1

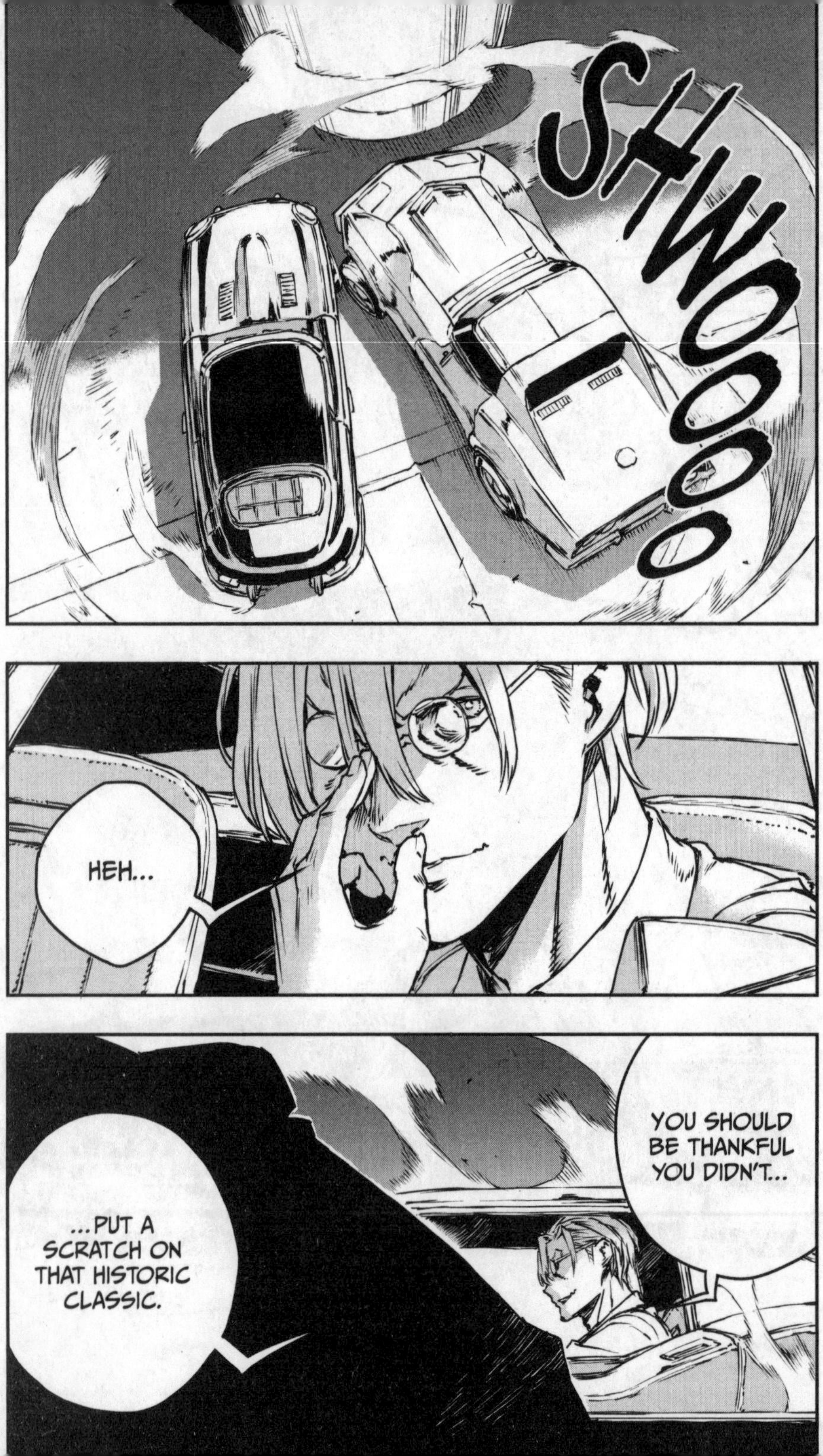
SHWOOOO
HEH...
YOU SHOULD BE THANKFUL YOU DIDN'T...
...PUT A SCRATCH ON THAT HISTORIC CLASSIC.

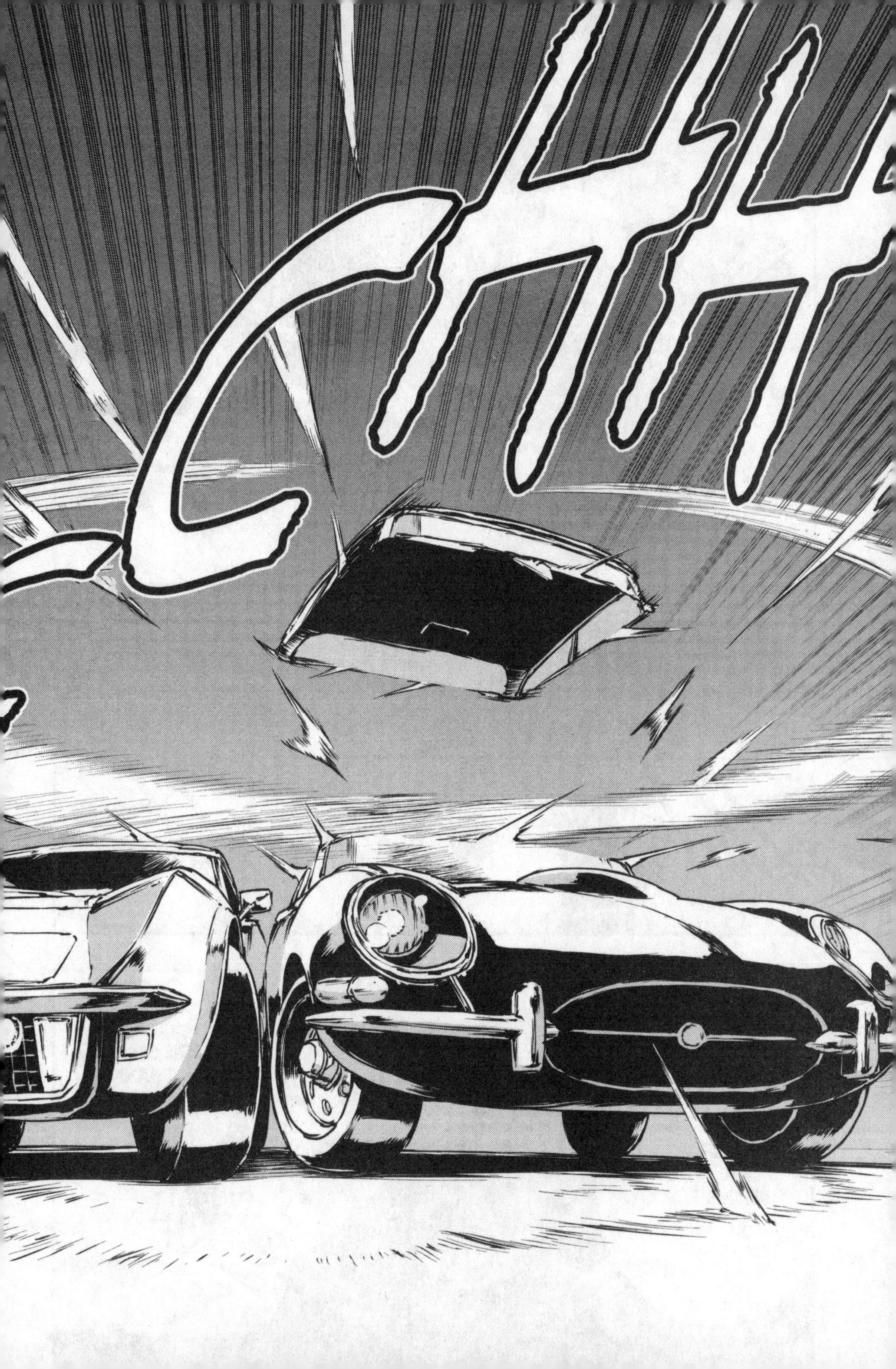
CHH

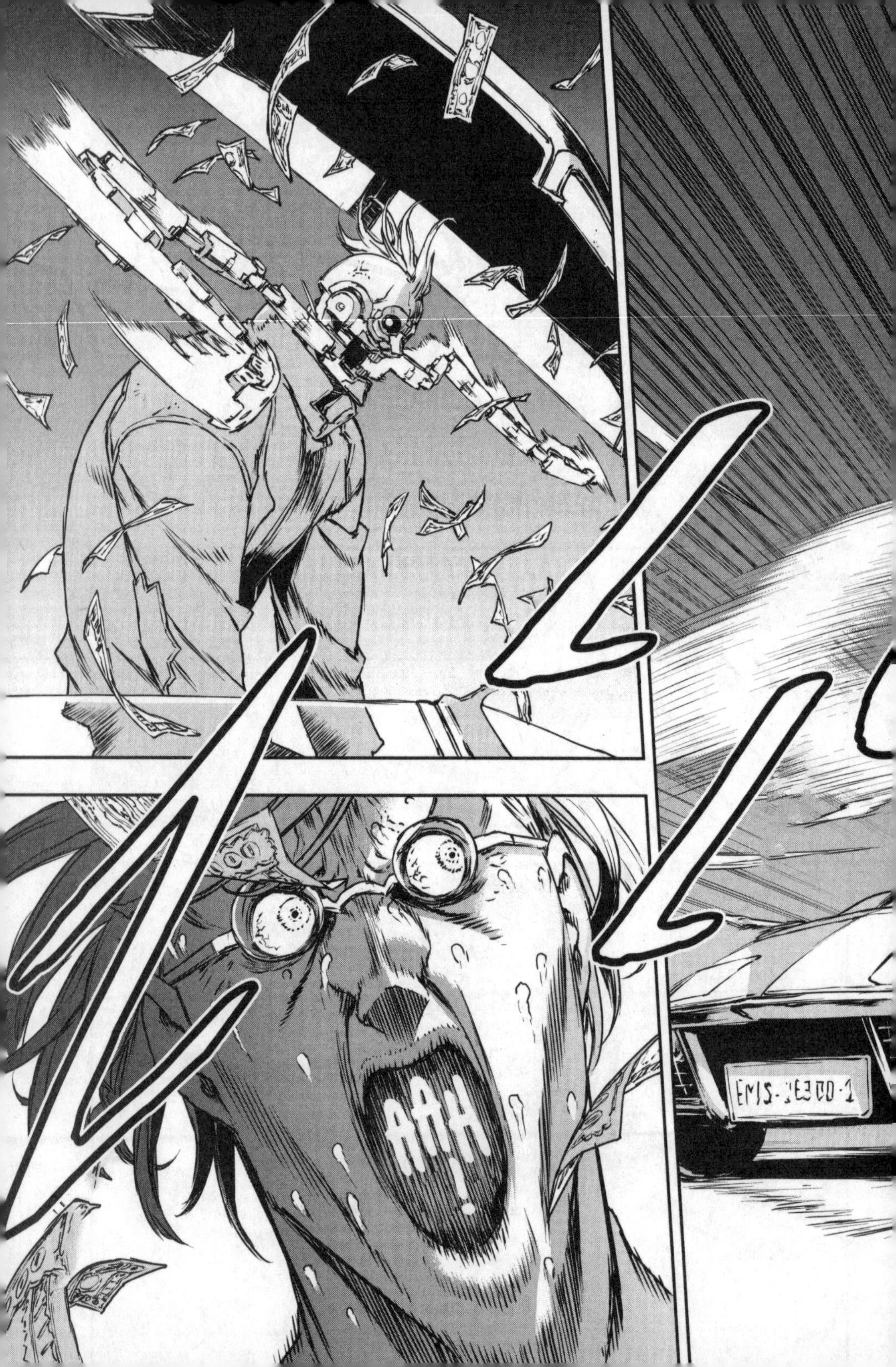
AAH!
EMIS-JE300-1

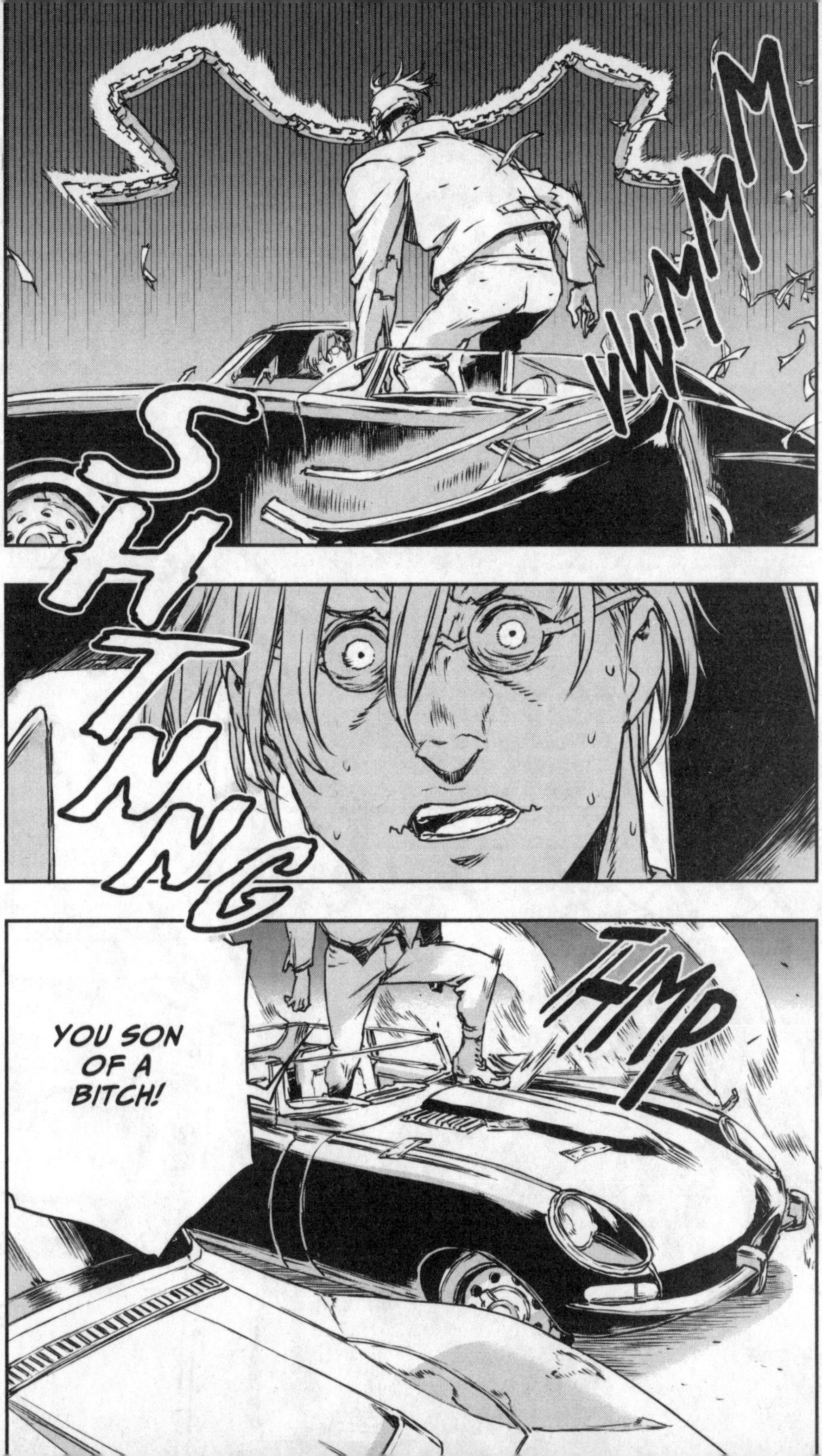
VWMMMM
SHTNNG
THMP
YOU SON OF A BITCH!

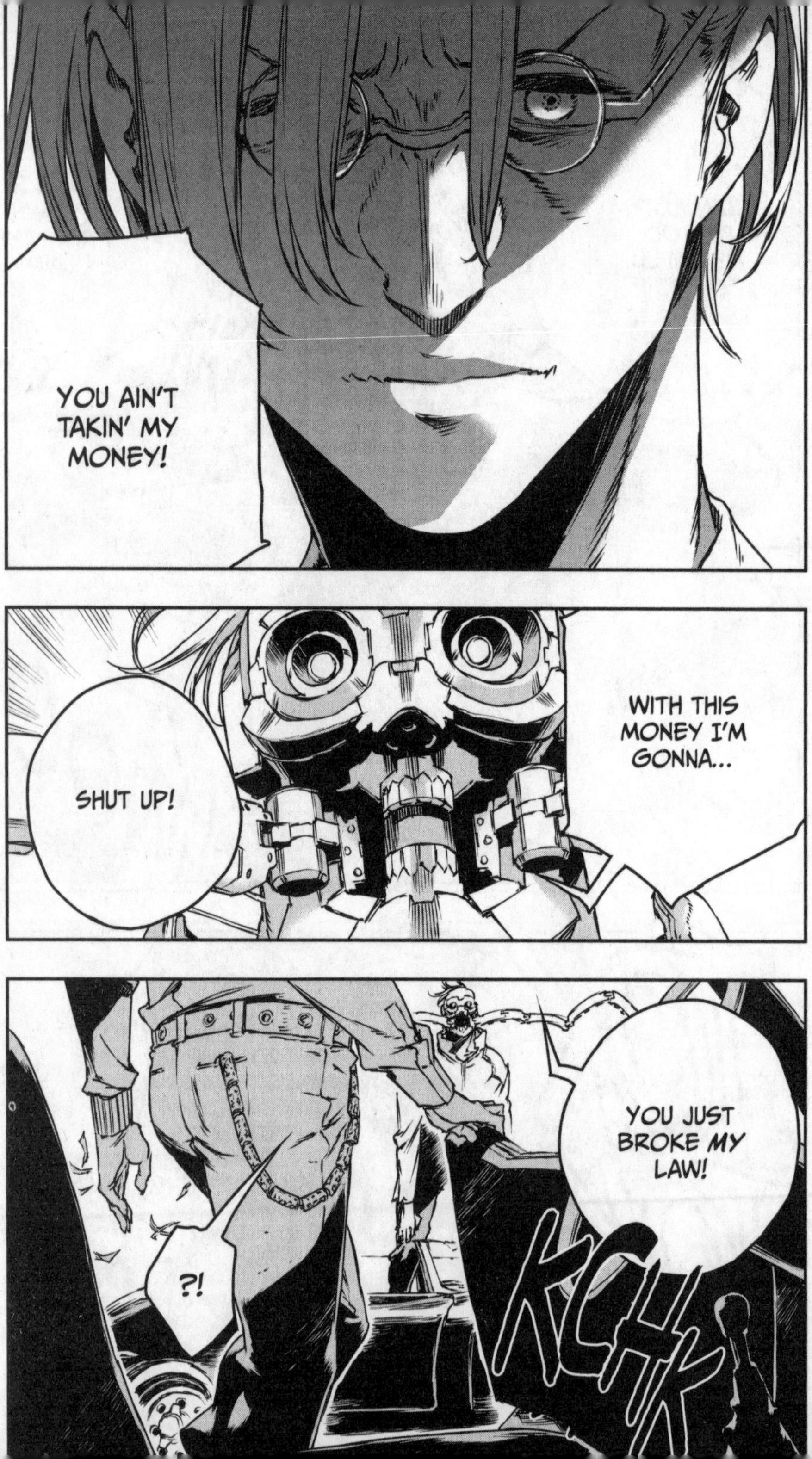
YOU AIN'T TAKIN' MY MONEY!
WITH THIS MONEY I'M GONNA...
SHUT UP!
YOU JUST BROKE MY LAW!
KCHK
?!

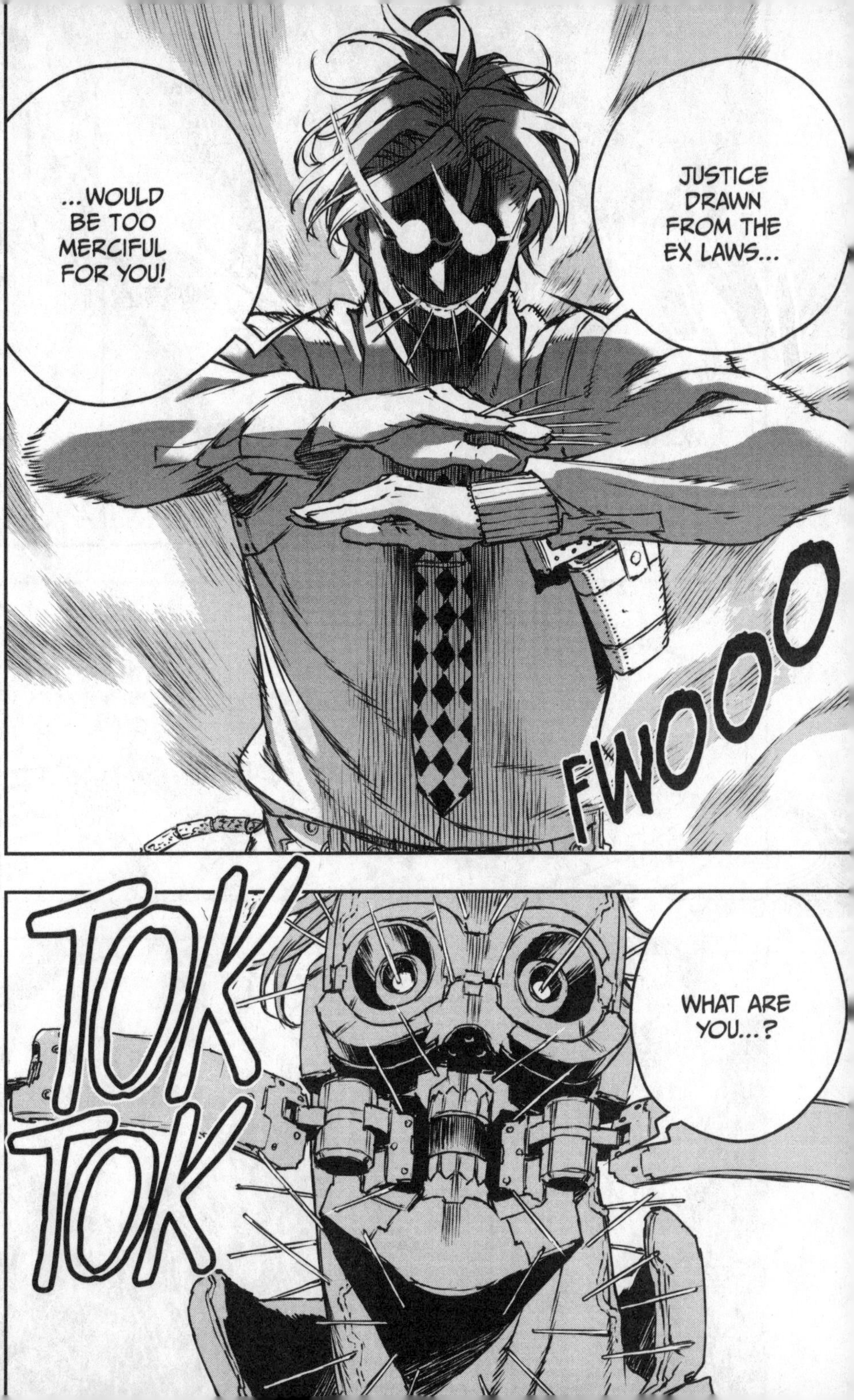
JUSTICE DRAWN FROM THE EX LAWS...
...WOULD BE TOO MERCIFUL FOR YOU!
FWOOO
WHAT ARE YOU...?
TOK TOK

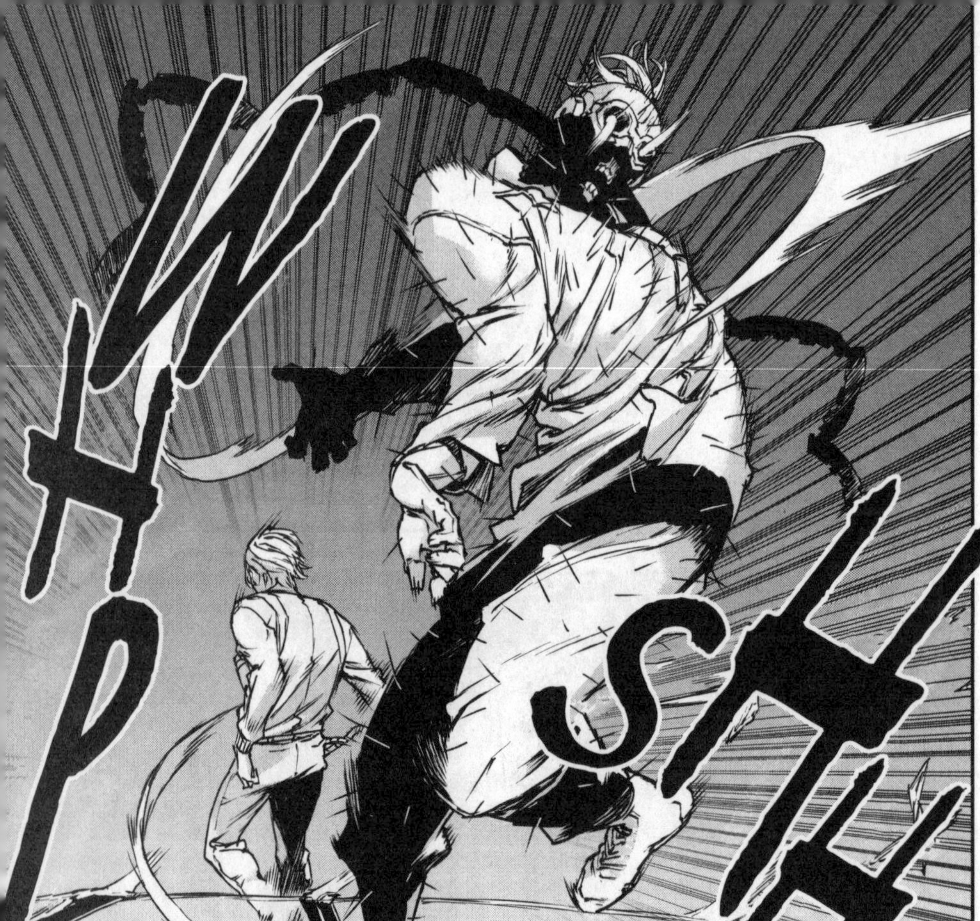
SHHH
WHP

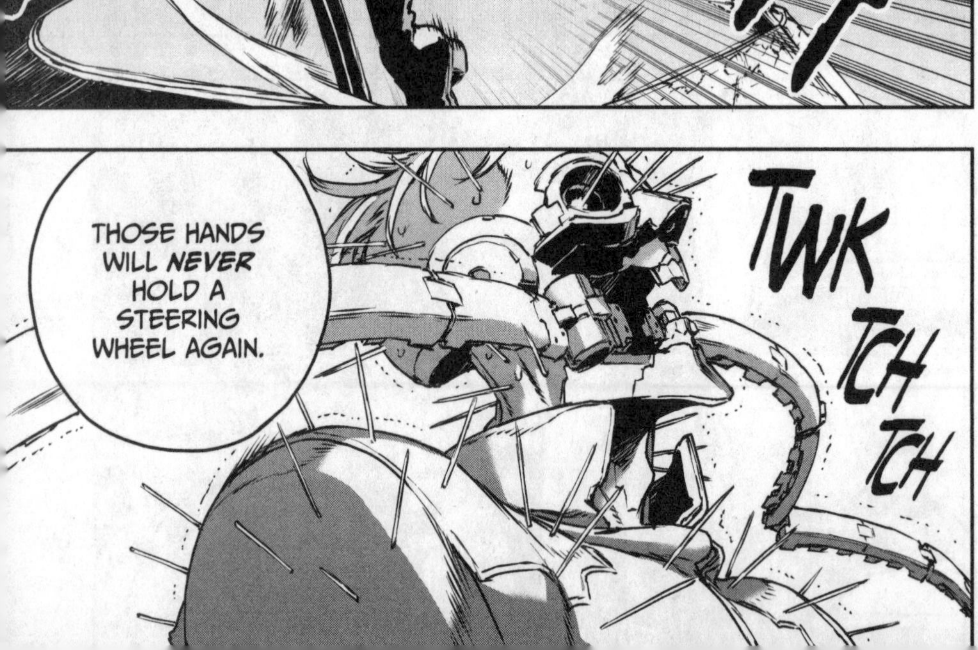
TWK TCH TCH
THOSE HANDS WILL *NEVER* HOLD A STEERING WHEEL AGAIN.

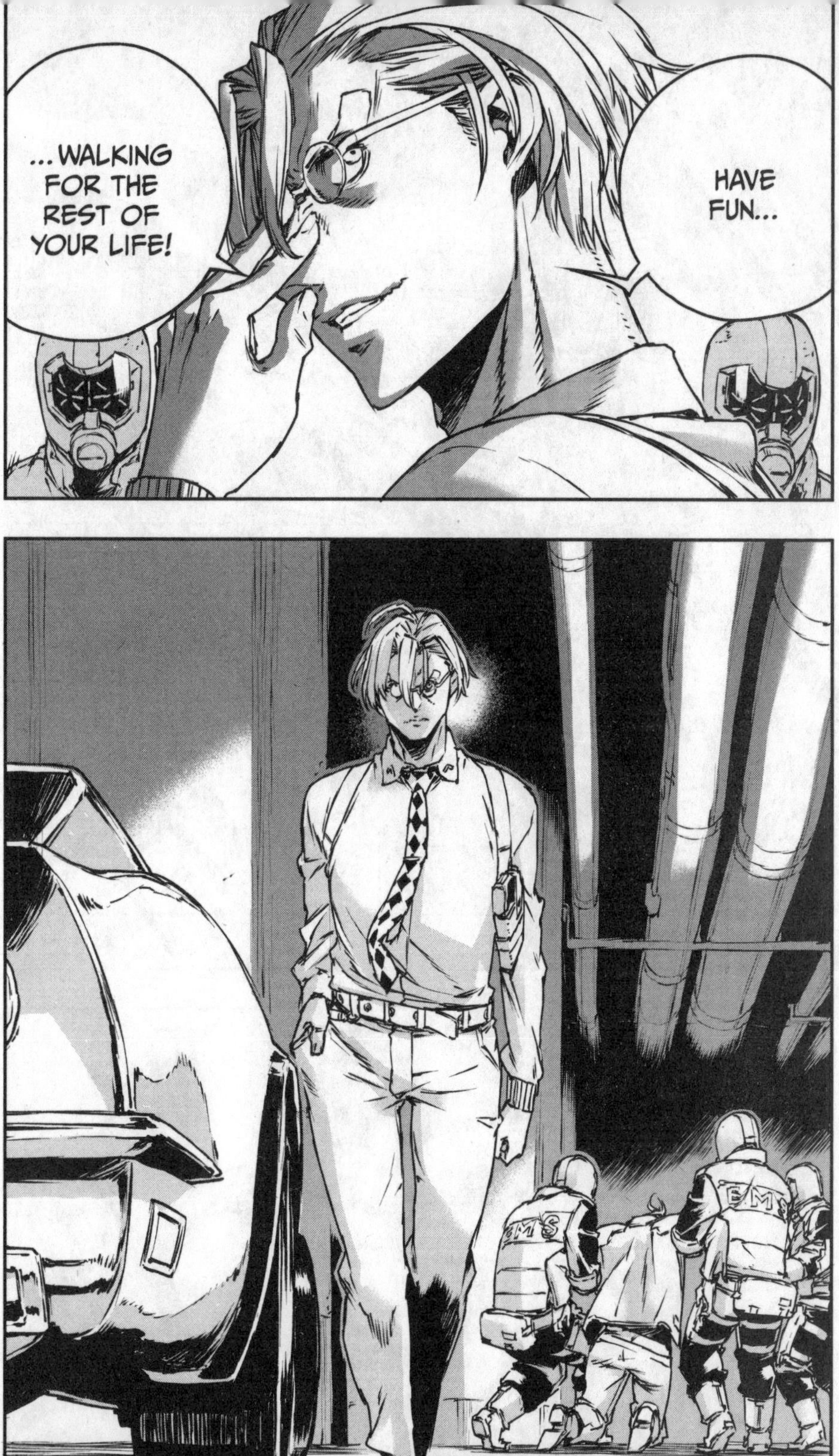
HAVE FUN...
...WALKING FOR THE REST OF YOUR LIFE!
EMS

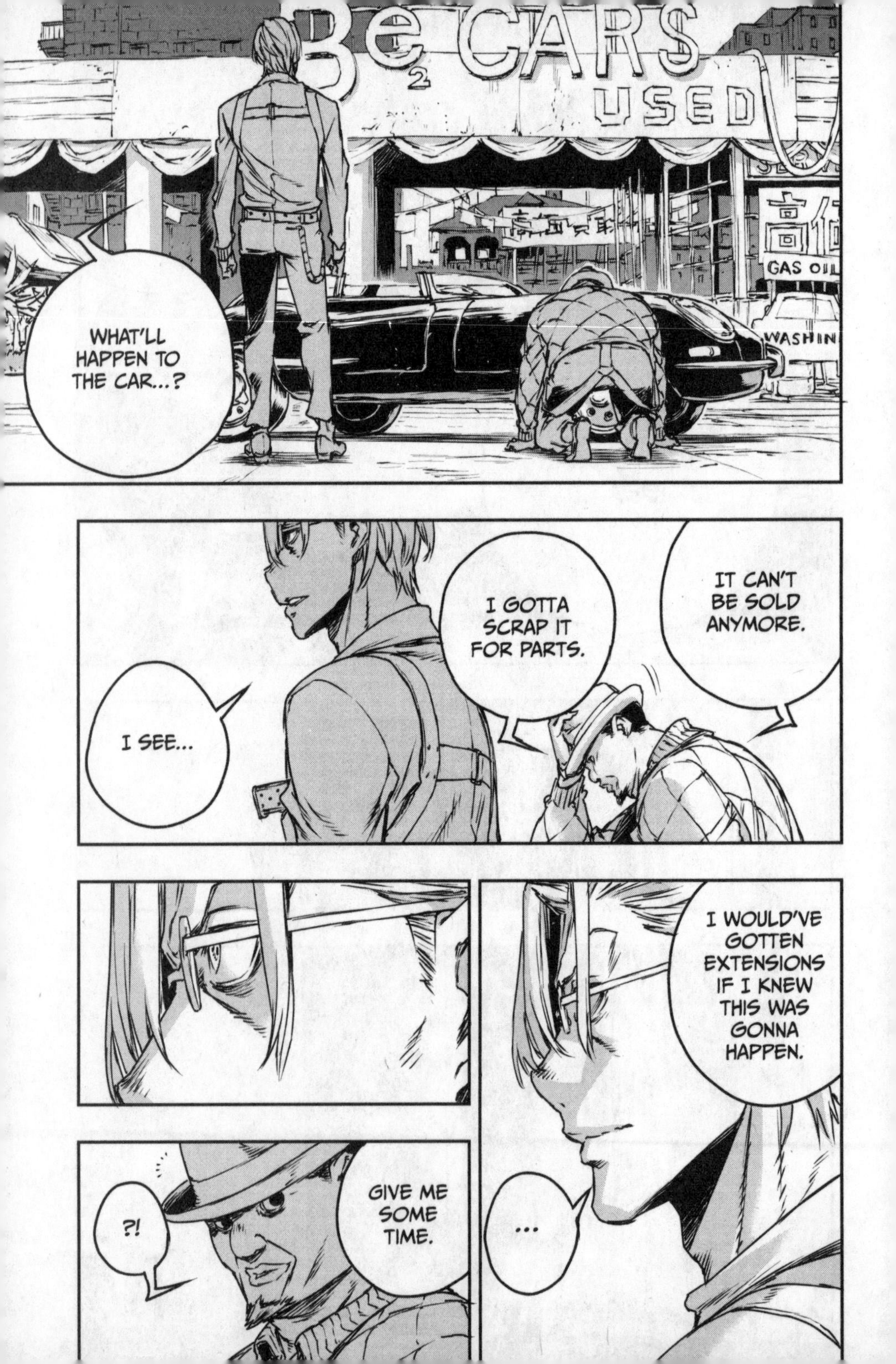
CARS
USED
GAS OIL
WASHIN
WHAT'LL HAPPEN TO THE CAR...?
IT CAN'T BE SOLD ANYMORE.
I GOTTA SCRAP IT FOR PARTS.
I SEE...
I WOULD'VE GOTTEN EXTENSIONS IF I KNEW THIS WAS GONNA HAPPEN.
...
GIVE ME SOME TIME.
?!

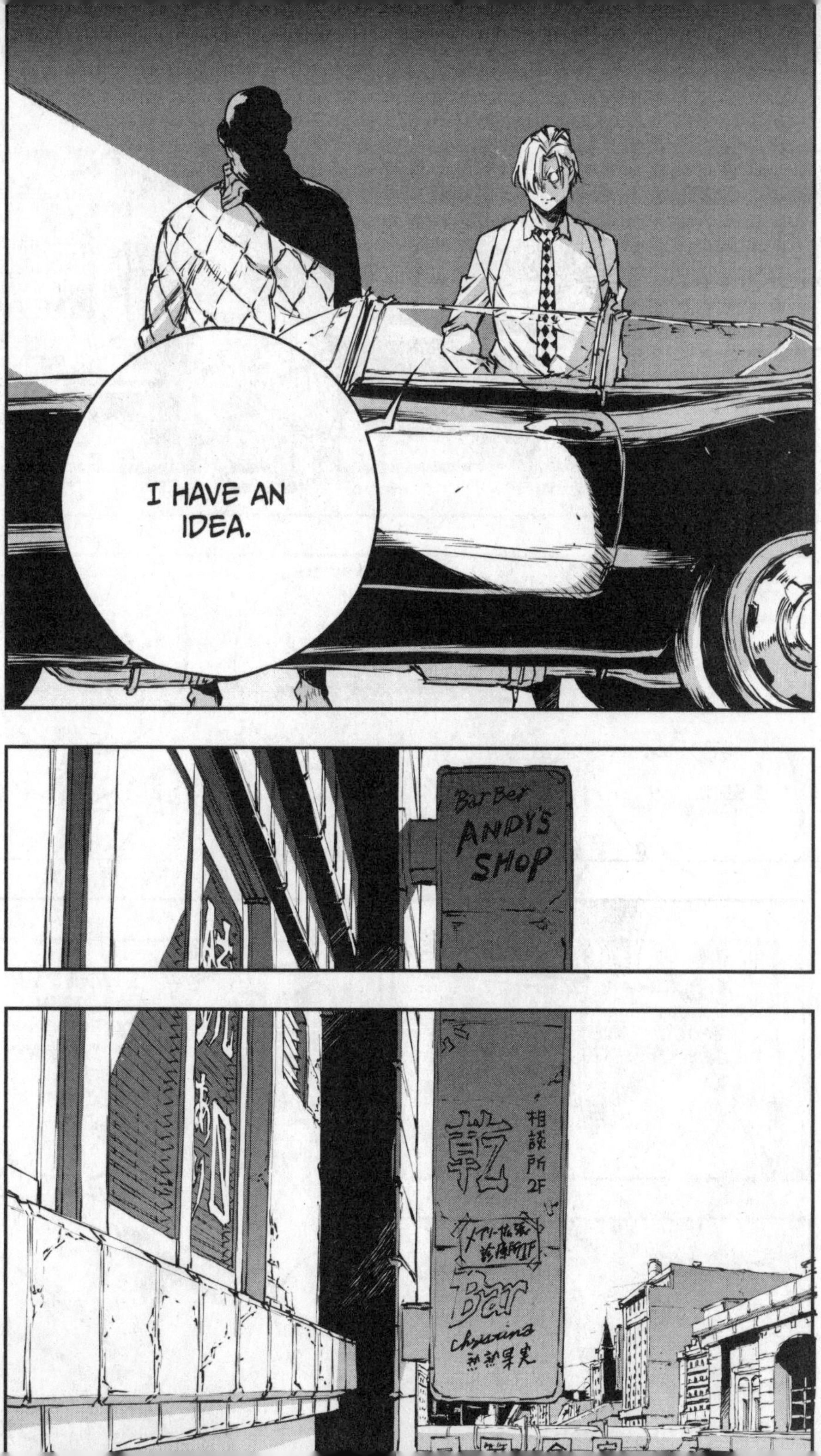
I HAVE AN IDEA.
Bar Ber
ANDY'S SHOP
乾
相談所 2F
Bar
Christina

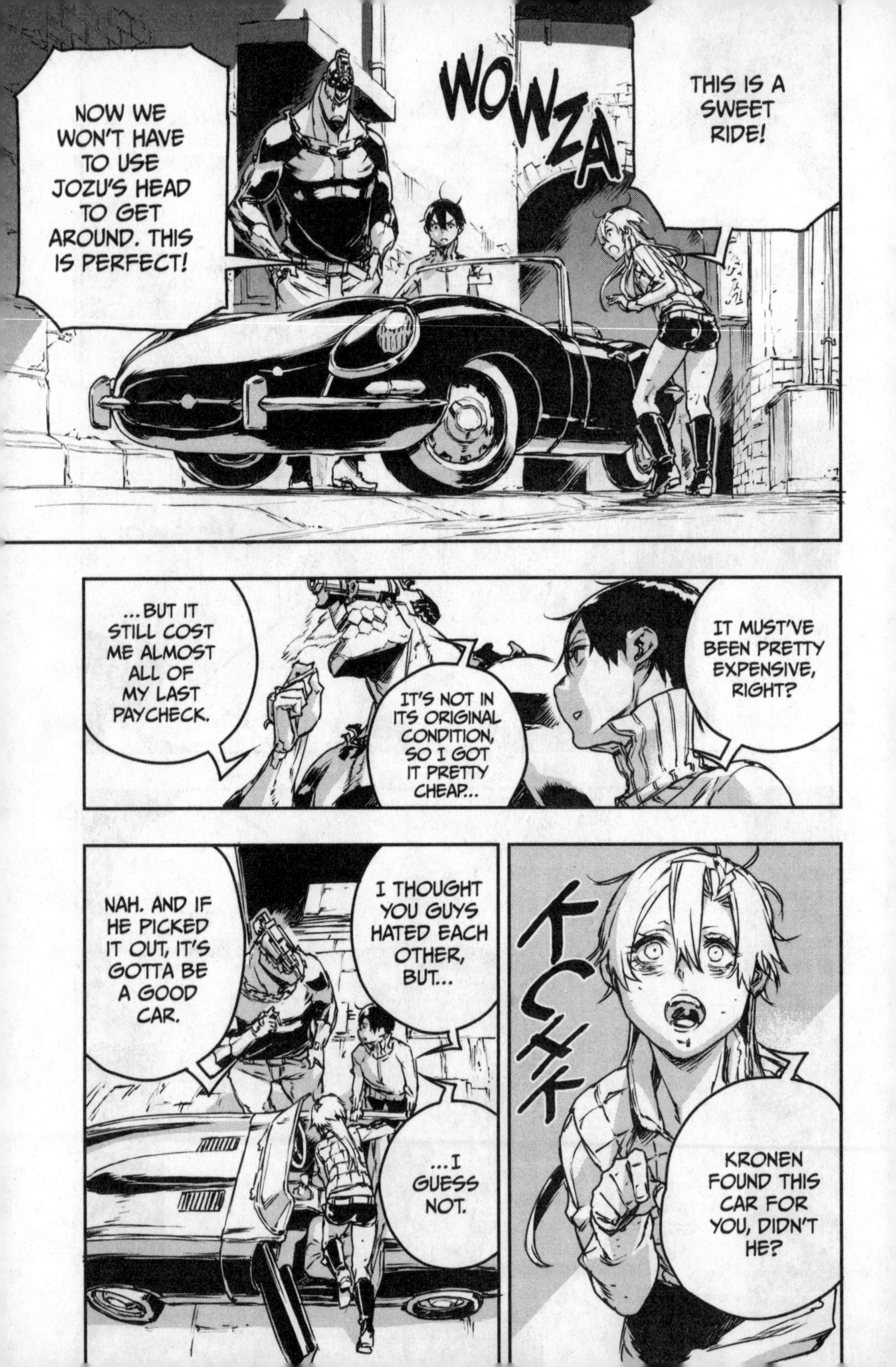
THIS IS A SWEET RIDE!
WOWZA
NOW WE WON'T HAVE TO USE JOZU'S HEAD TO GET AROUND. THIS IS PERFECT!
IT MUST'VE BEEN PRETTY EXPENSIVE, RIGHT?
IT'S NOT IN ITS ORIGINAL CONDITION, SO I GOT IT PRETTY CHEAP...
...BUT IT STILL COST ME ALMOST ALL OF MY LAST PAYCHECK.
KCHK
KRONEN FOUND THIS CAR FOR YOU, DIDN'T HE?
I THOUGHT YOU GUYS HATED EACH OTHER, BUT...
NAH. AND IF HE PICKED IT OUT, IT'S GOTTA BE A GOOD CAR.
...I GUESS NOT.

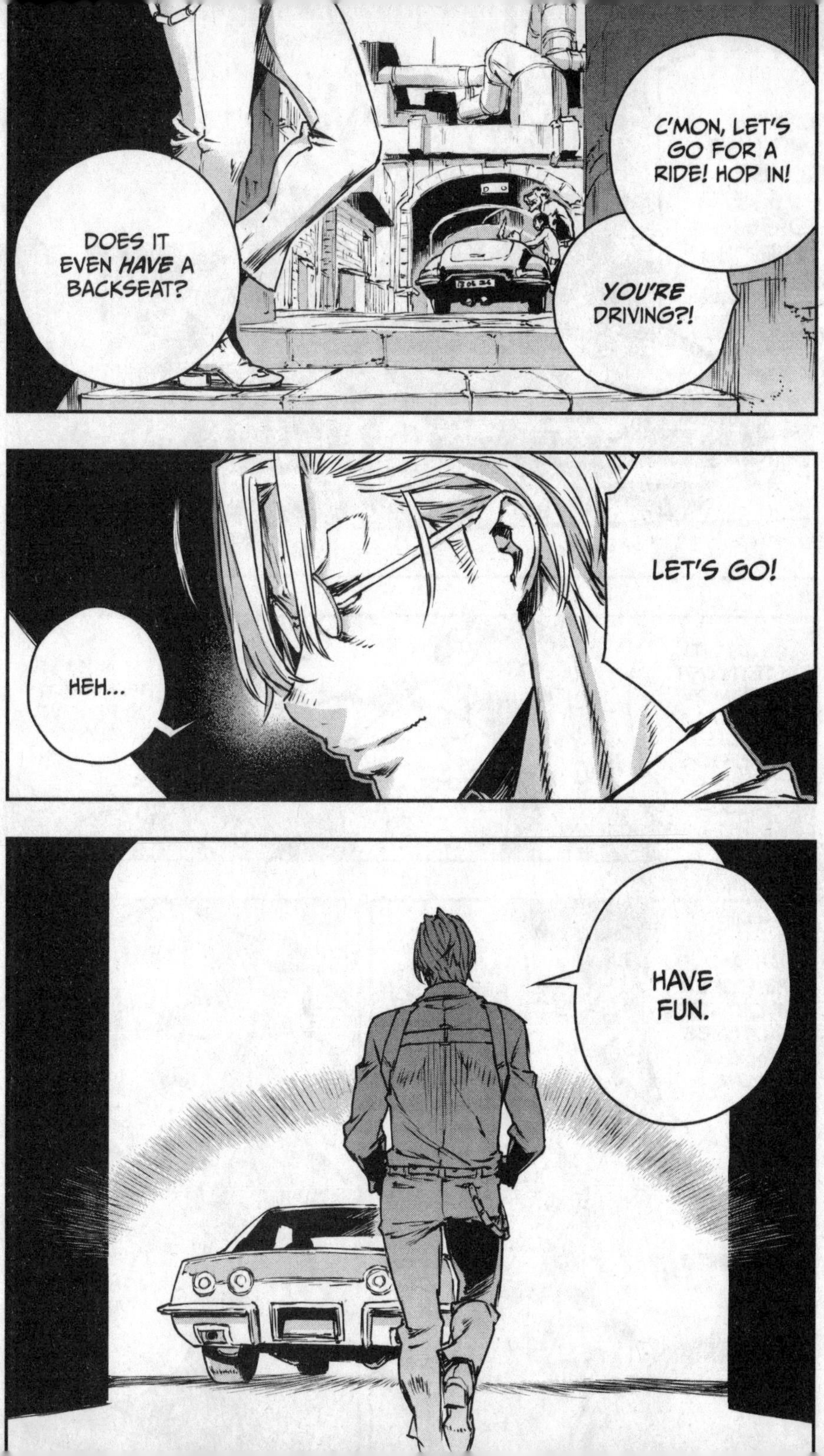
C'MON, LET'S GO FOR A RIDE! HOP IN!
YOU'RE DRIVING?!
DOES IT EVEN *HAVE* A BACKSEAT?
LET'S GO!
HEH...
HAVE FUN.

NO GUNS LIFE

LIFE

The gunsmoke drifts, the muzzle talks

NO GUNS
LIFE

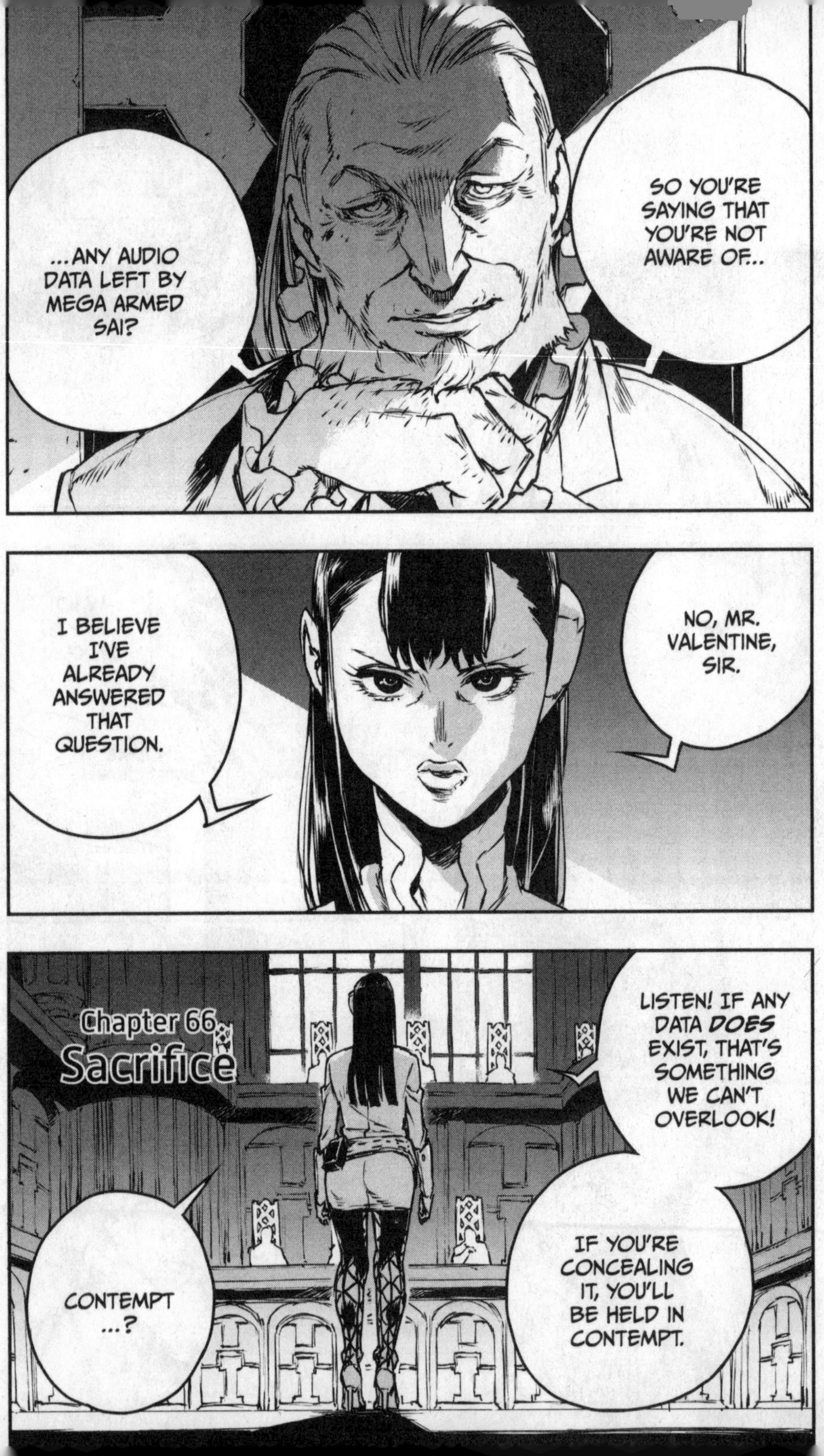
SO YOU'RE SAYING THAT YOU'RE NOT AWARE OF...
...ANY AUDIO DATA LEFT BY MEGA ARMED SAI?
NO, MR. VALENTINE, SIR.
I BELIEVE I'VE ALREADY ANSWERED THAT QUESTION.
LISTEN! IF ANY DATA ***DOES*** EXIST, THAT'S SOMETHING WE CAN'T OVERLOOK!
Chapter 66
Sacrifice
IF YOU'RE CONCEALING IT, YOU'LL BE HELD IN CONTEMPT.
CONTEMPT ...?

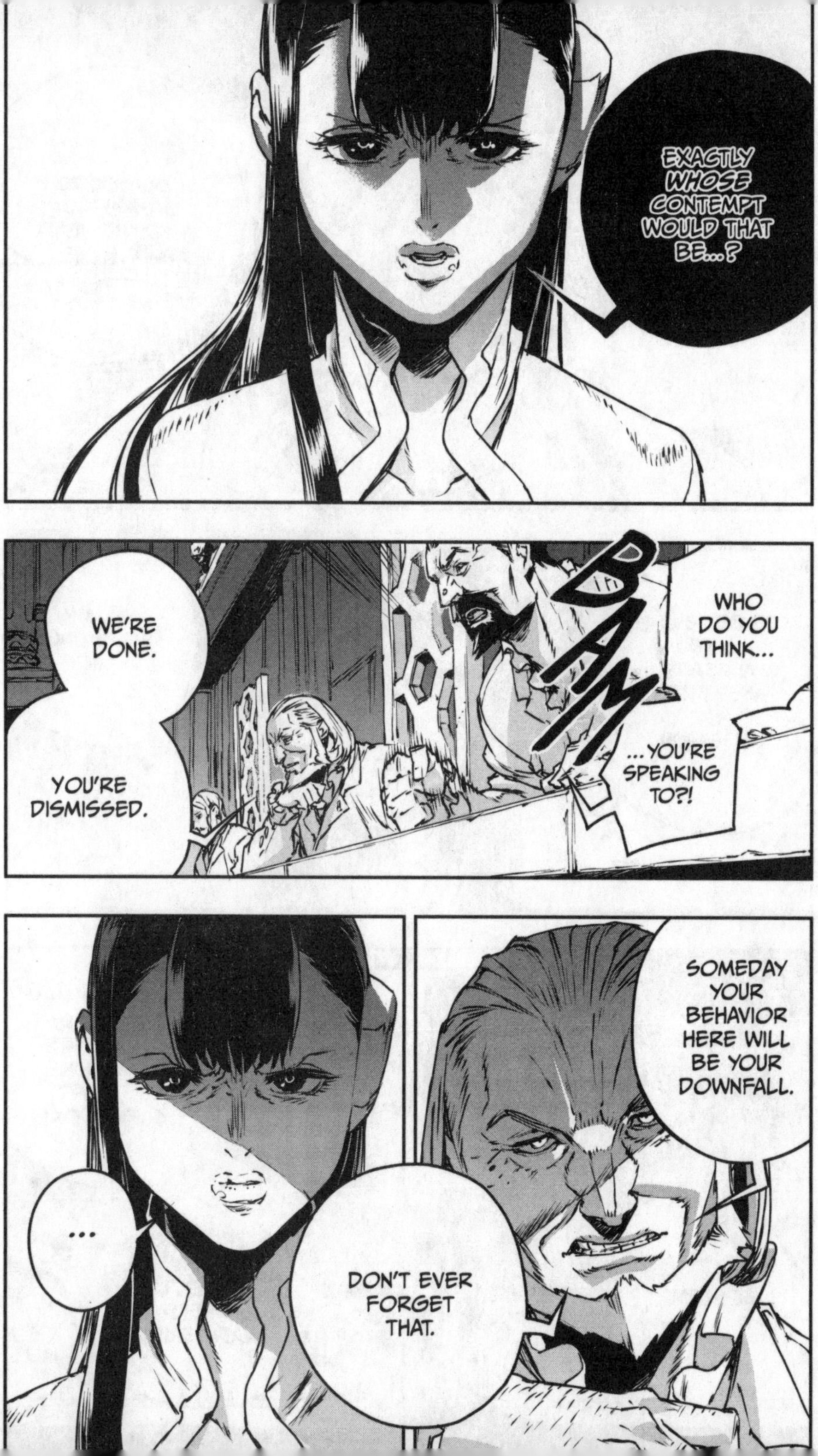
EXACTLY WHOSE CONTEMPT WOULD THAT BE...?
WHO DO YOU THINK...
BAM
...YOU'RE SPEAKING TO?!
WE'RE DONE.
YOU'RE DISMISSED.
SOMEDAY YOUR BEHAVIOR HERE WILL BE YOUR DOWNFALL.
DON'T EVER FORGET THAT.
...

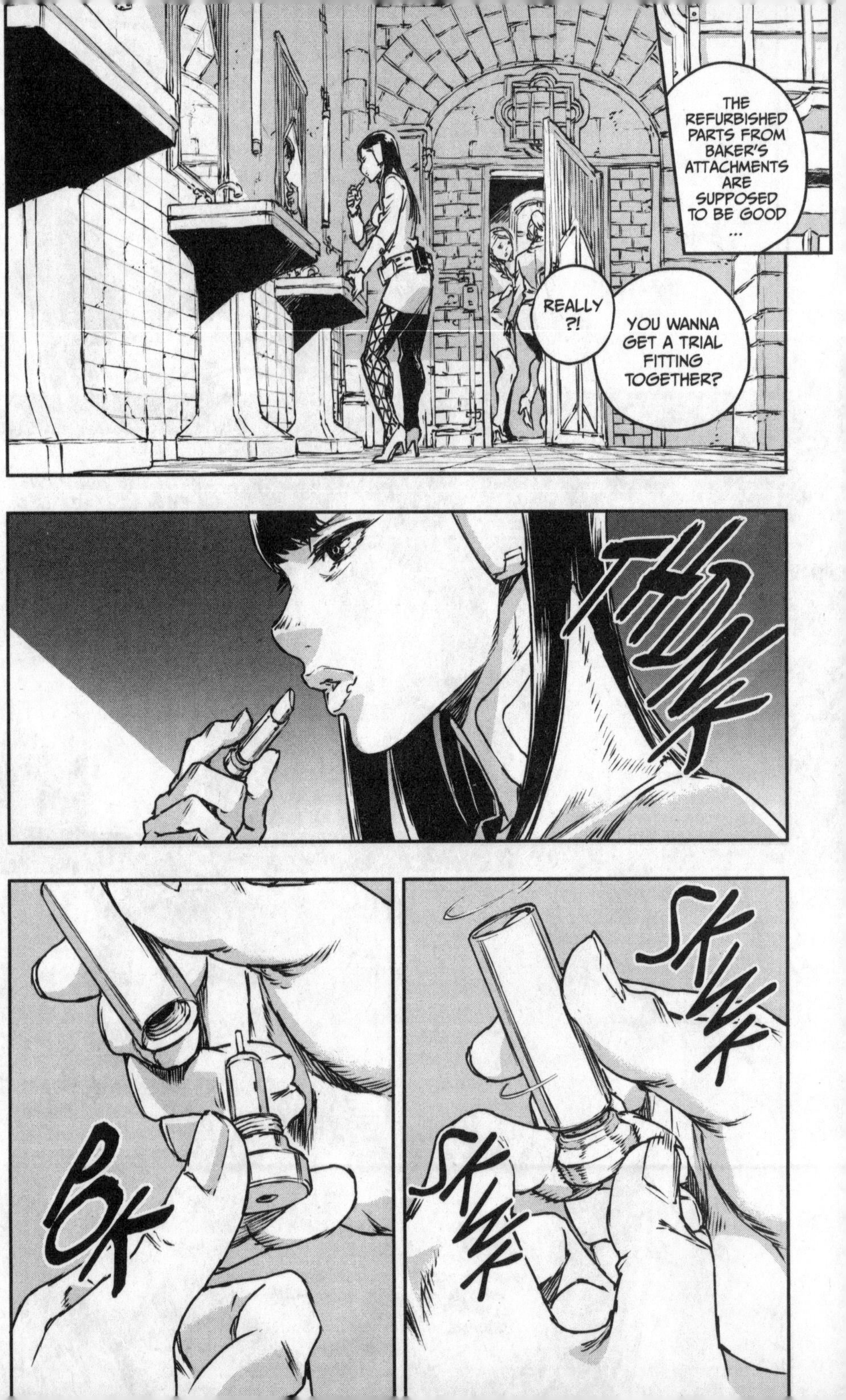
THE REFURBISHED PARTS FROM BAKER'S ATTACHMENTS ARE SUPPOSED TO BE GOOD ...
YOU WANNA GET A TRIAL FITTING TOGETHER?
REALLY ?!
THUNK
SKWK
SKWK
BOK

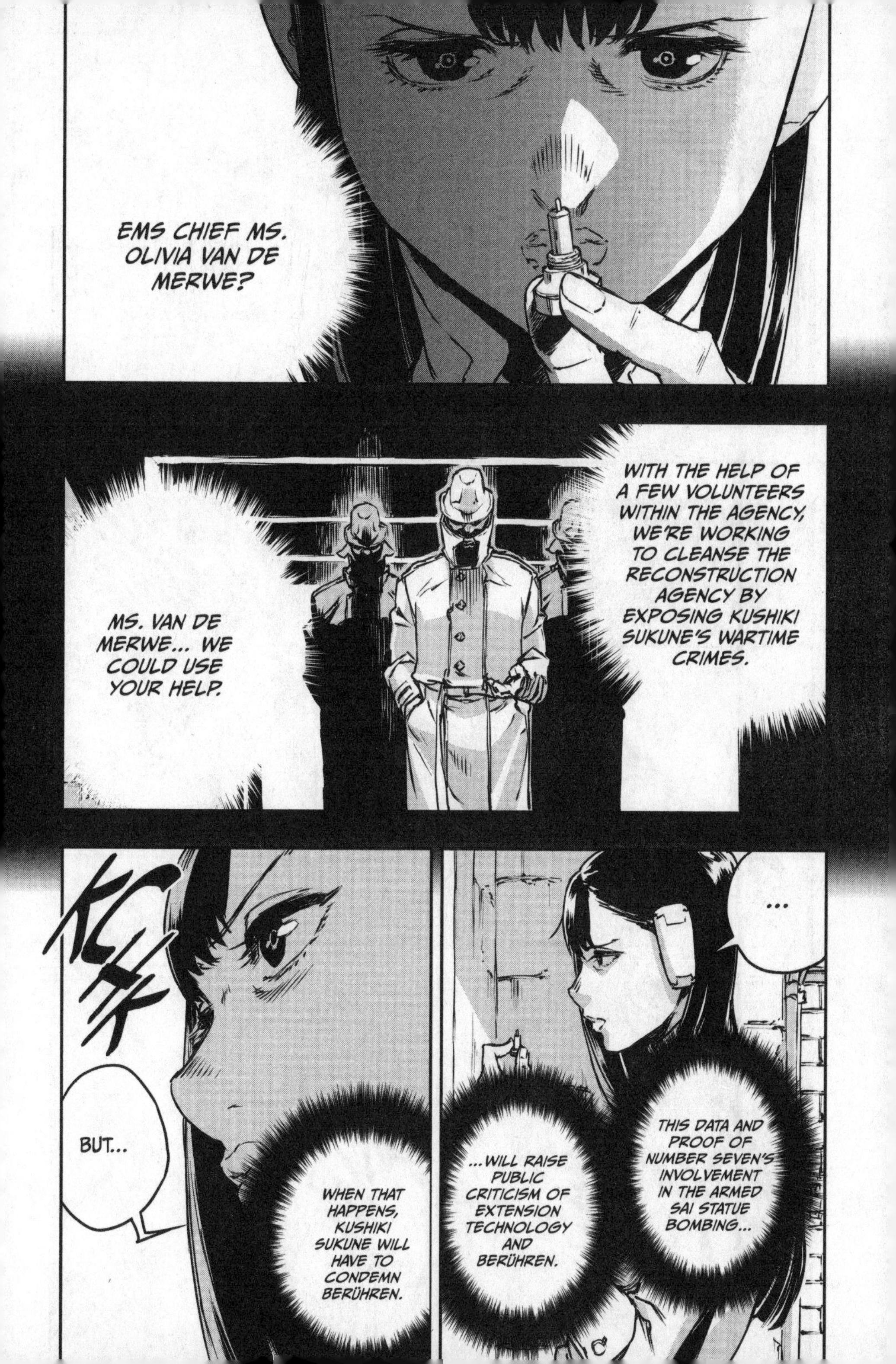
EMS CHIEF MS. OLIVIA VAN DE MERWE?
WITH THE HELP OF A FEW VOLUNTEERS WITHIN THE AGENCY, WE'RE WORKING TO CLEANSE THE RECONSTRUCTION AGENCY BY EXPOSING KUSHIKI SUKUNE'S WARTIME CRIMES.
MS. VAN DE MERWE... WE COULD USE YOUR HELP.
...
THIS DATA AND PROOF OF NUMBER SEVEN'S INVOLVEMENT IN THE ARMED SAI STATUE BOMBING...
...WILL RAISE PUBLIC CRITICISM OF EXTENSION TECHNOLOGY AND BERÜHREN.
KCHK
BUT...
WHEN THAT HAPPENS, KUSHIKI SUKUNE WILL HAVE TO CONDEMN BERÜHREN.

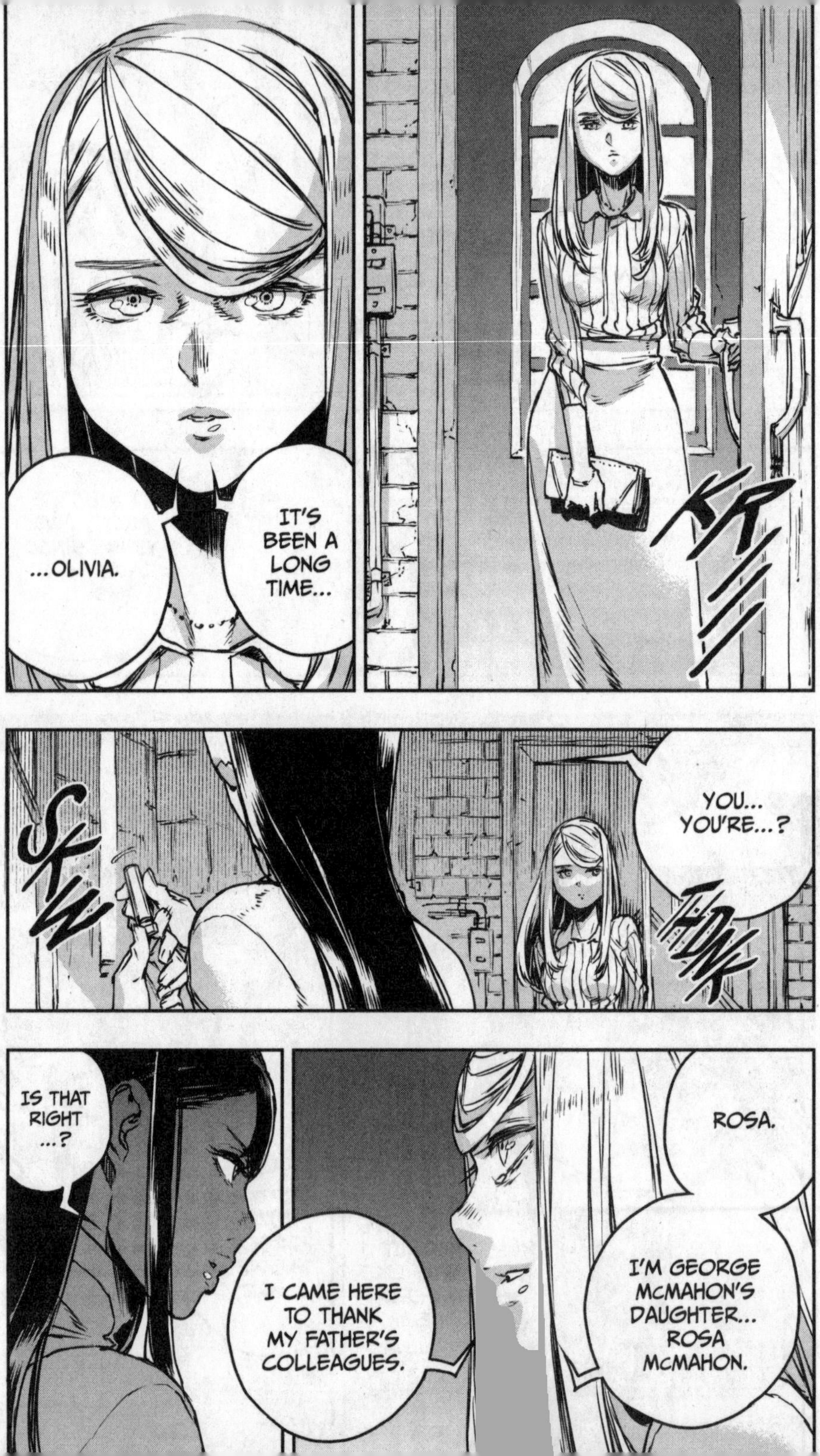
KR
IT'S BEEN A LONG TIME...
...OLIVIA.
YOU... YOU'RE...?
THUNK
SKW
ROSA.
I'M GEORGE McMAHON'S DAUGHTER... ROSA McMAHON.
I CAME HERE TO THANK MY FATHER'S COLLEAGUES.
IS THAT RIGHT ...?

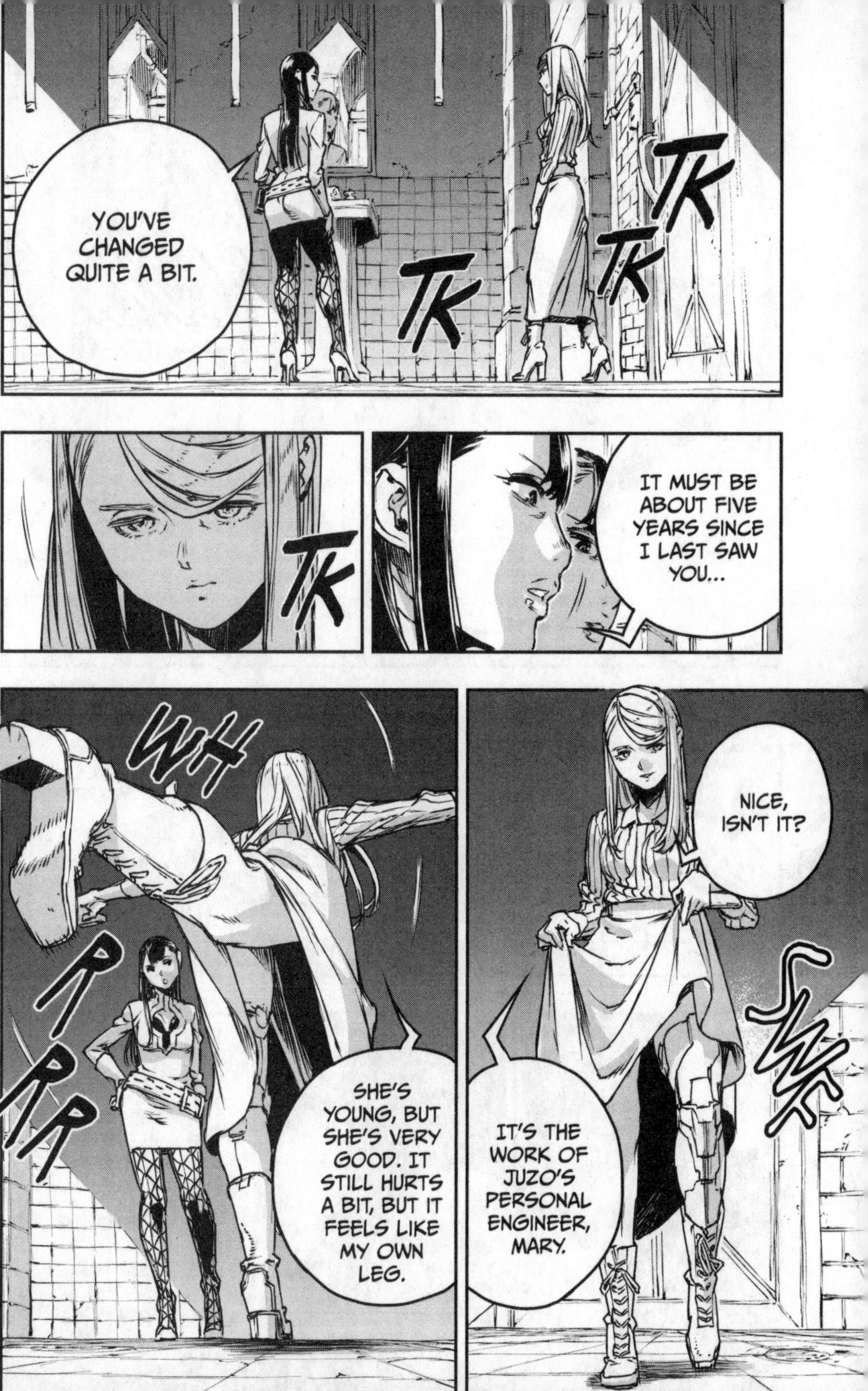
TK
TK
YOU'VE CHANGED QUITE A BIT.
TK
IT MUST BE ABOUT FIVE YEARS SINCE I LAST SAW YOU...
TK
NICE, ISN'T IT?
SWK
IT'S THE WORK OF JUZO'S PERSONAL ENGINEER, MARY.
WH
SHE'S YOUNG, BUT SHE'S VERY GOOD. IT STILL HURTS A BIT, BUT IT FEELS LIKE MY OWN LEG.
RRR

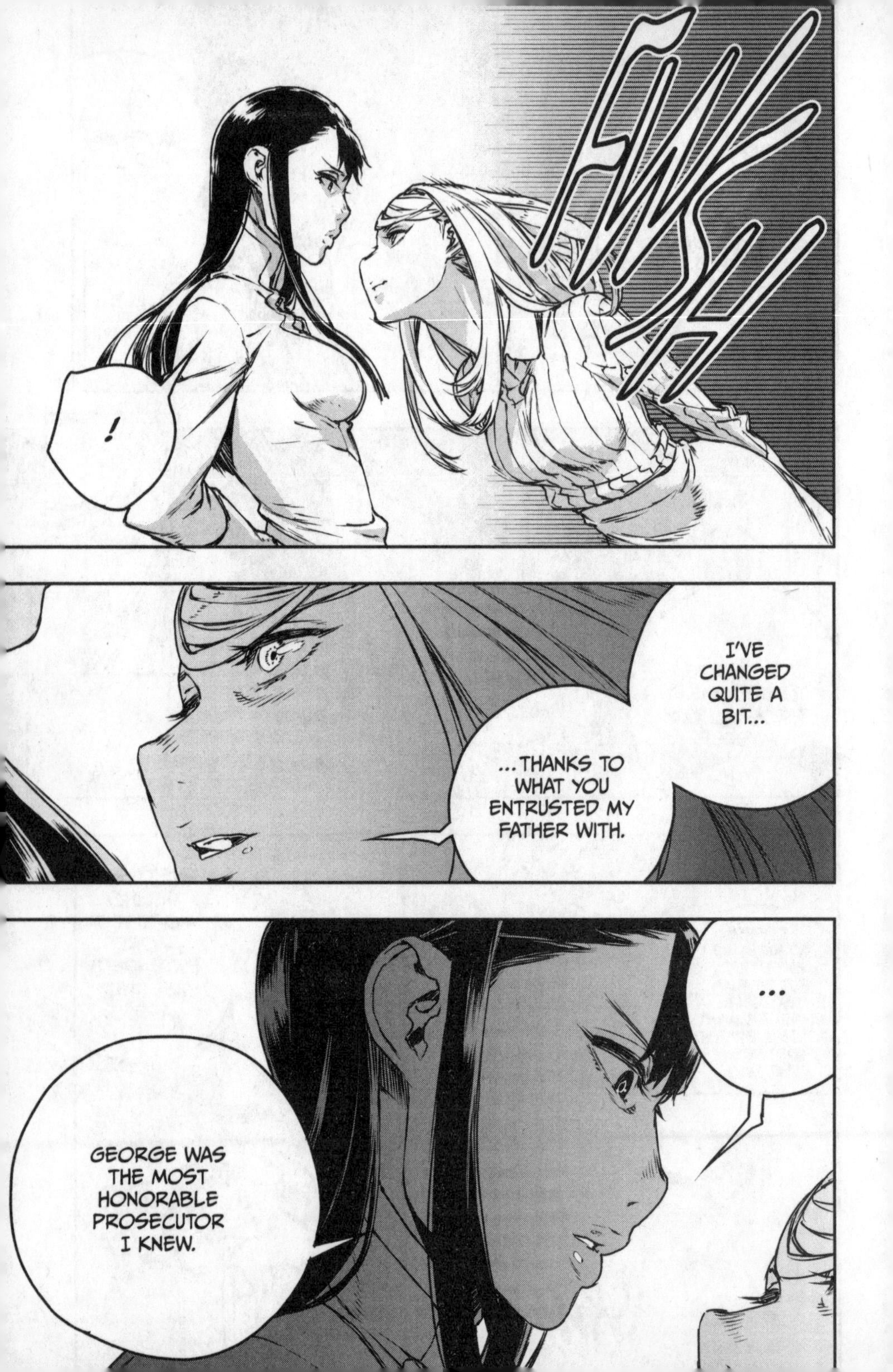
FWSH
!
I'VE CHANGED QUITE A BIT...
...THANKS TO WHAT YOU ENTRUSTED MY FATHER WITH.
...
GEORGE WAS THE MOST HONORABLE PROSECUTOR I KNEW.

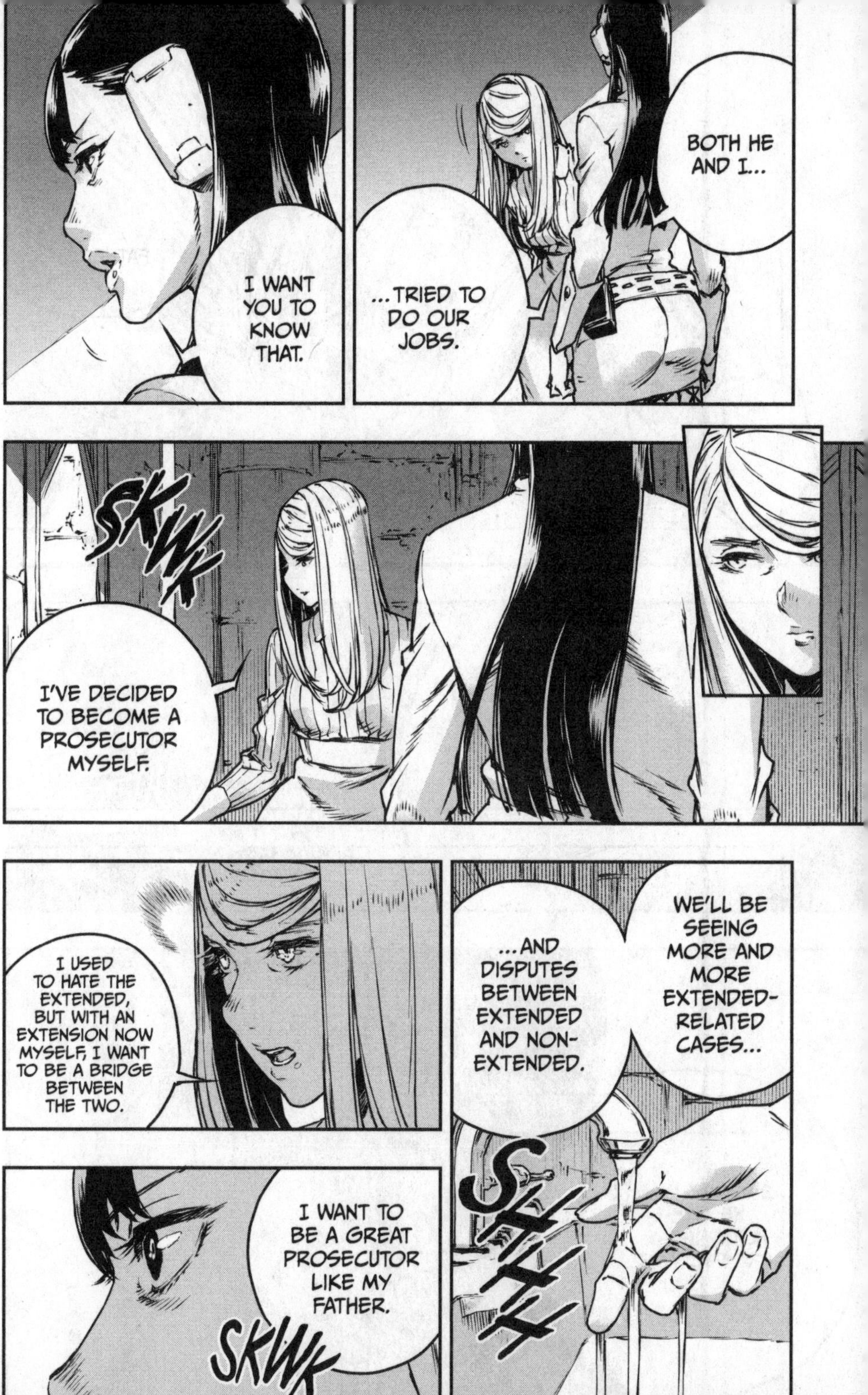
BOTH HE AND I...
...TRIED TO DO OUR JOBS.
I WANT YOU TO KNOW THAT.
SKWK
I'VE DECIDED TO BECOME A PROSECUTOR MYSELF.
WE'LL BE SEEING MORE AND MORE EXTENDED-RELATED CASES...
...AND DISPUTES BETWEEN EXTENDED AND NON-EXTENDED.
SHHHH
I USED TO HATE THE EXTENDED, BUT WITH AN EXTENSION NOW MYSELF, I WANT TO BE A BRIDGE BETWEEN THE TWO.
I WANT TO BE A GREAT PROSECUTOR LIKE MY FATHER.
SKWK

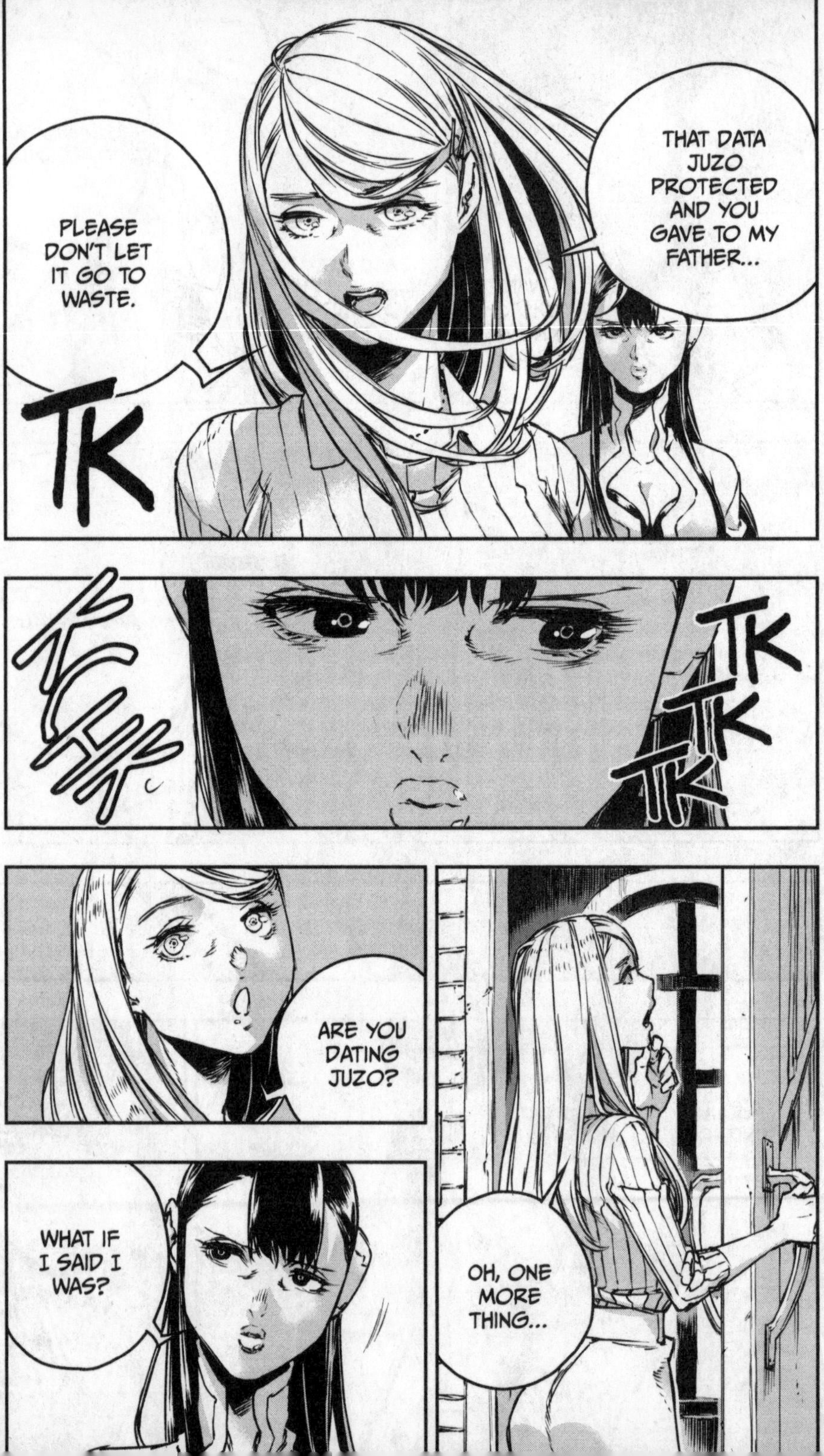
THAT DATA JUZO PROTECTED AND YOU GAVE TO MY FATHER...
PLEASE DON'T LET IT GO TO WASTE.
TK
TK TK TK
KCHK
OH, ONE MORE THING...
ARE YOU DATING JUZO?
WHAT IF I SAID I WAS?

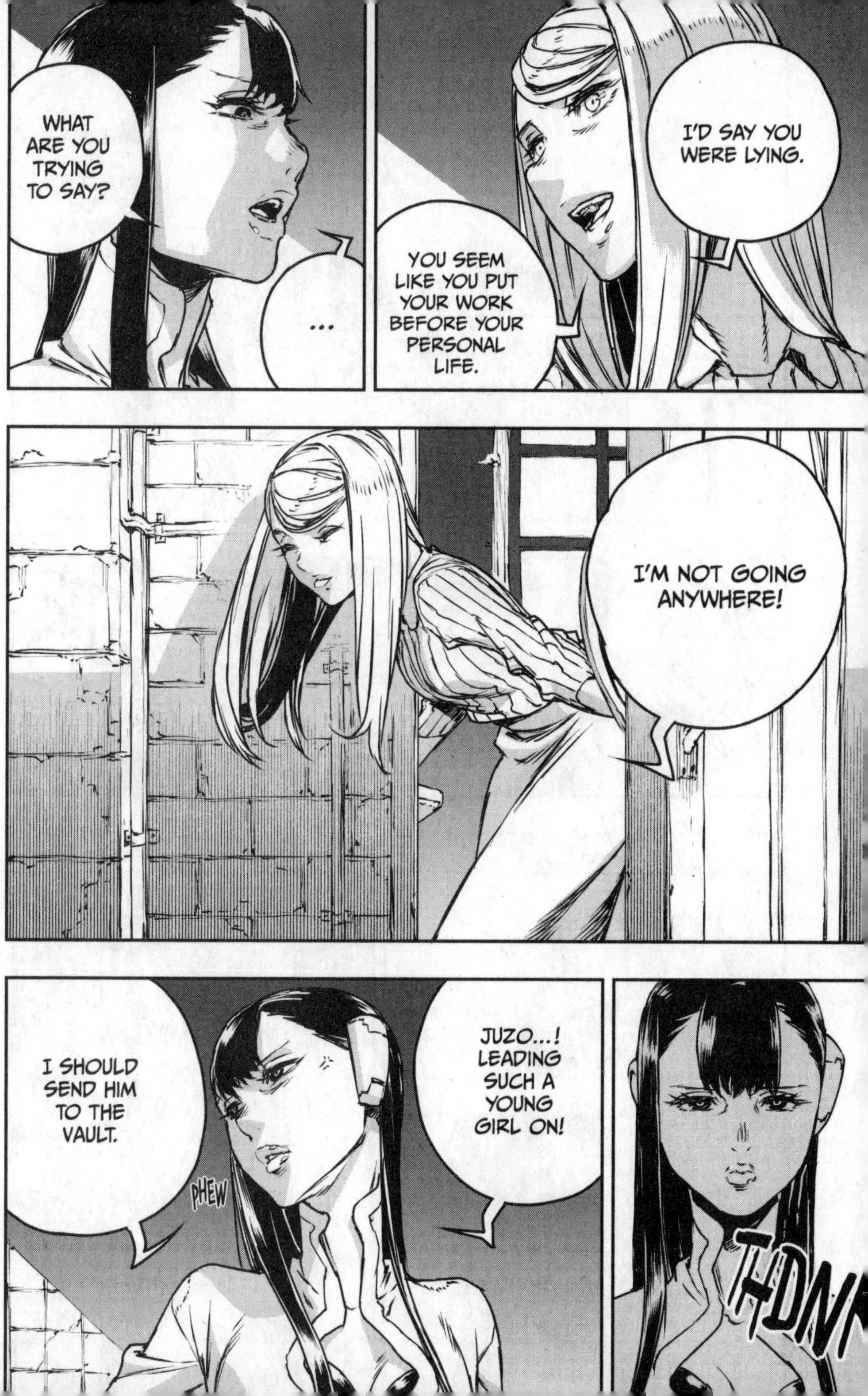
I'D SAY YOU WERE LYING.
YOU SEEM LIKE YOU PUT YOUR WORK BEFORE YOUR PERSONAL LIFE.
WHAT ARE YOU TRYING TO SAY?
...
I'M NOT GOING ANYWHERE!
THDN
JUZO...! LEADING SUCH A YOUNG GIRL ON!
PHEW
I SHOULD SEND HIM TO THE VAULT.

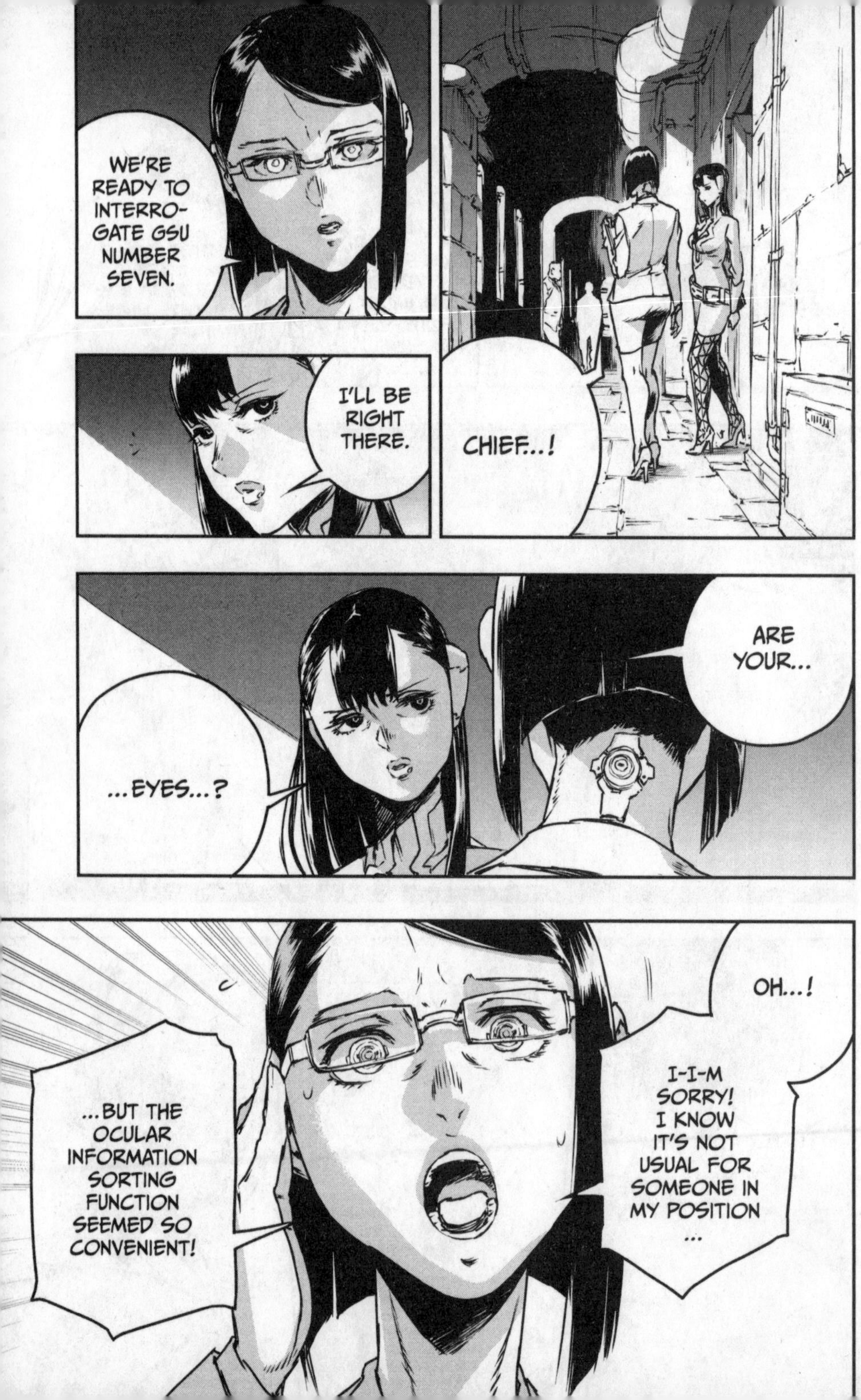
CHIEF...!
WE'RE READY TO INTERRO-GATE GSU NUMBER SEVEN.
I'LL BE RIGHT THERE.
ARE YOUR...
...EYES...?
OH...!
I-I-M SORRY! I KNOW IT'S NOT USUAL FOR SOMEONE IN MY POSITION ...
...BUT THE OCULAR INFORMATION SORTING FUNCTION SEEMED SO CONVENIENT!

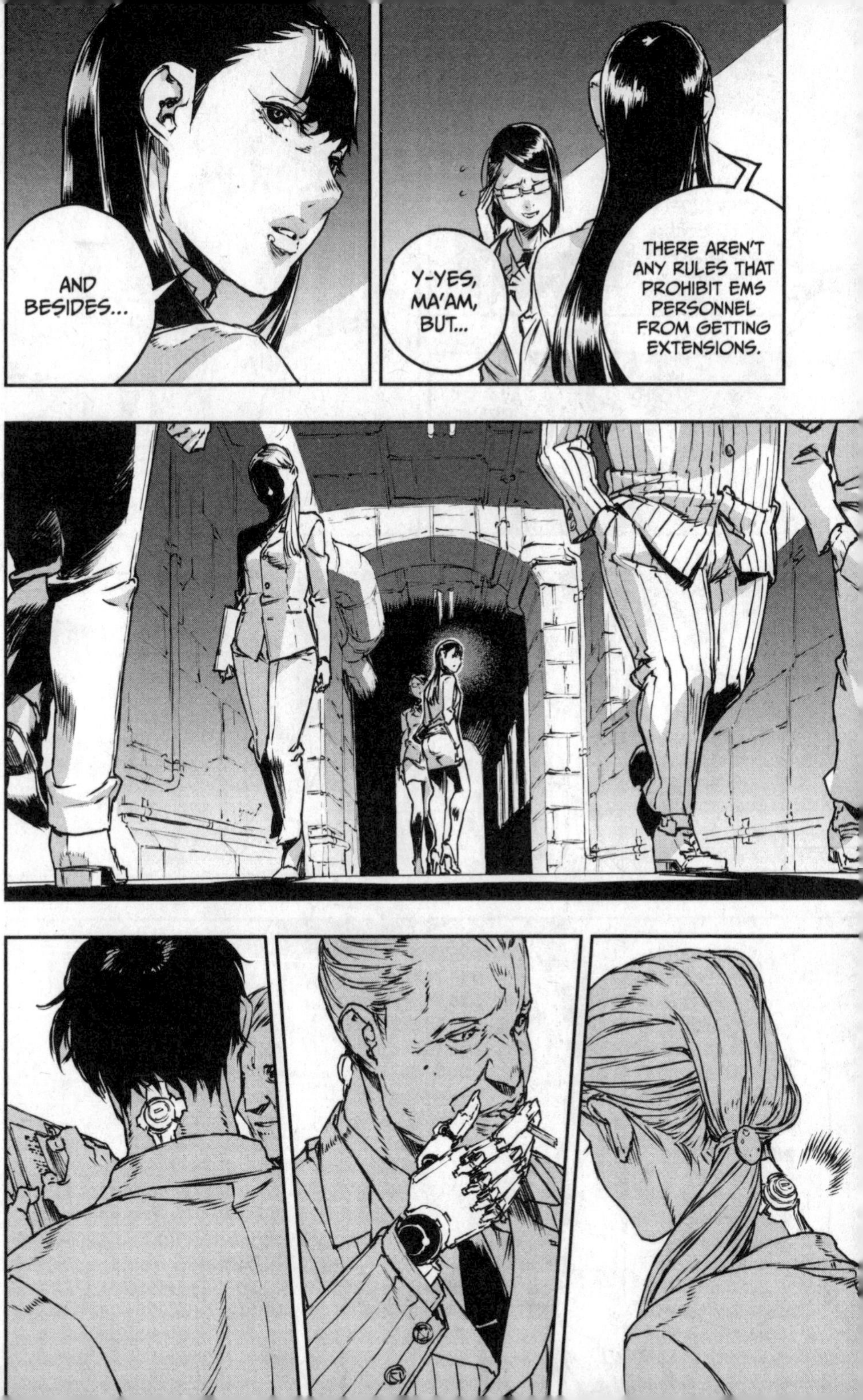
THERE AREN'T ANY RULES THAT PROHIBIT EMS PERSONNEL FROM GETTING EXTENSIONS.
Y-YES, MA'AM, BUT...
AND BESIDES...

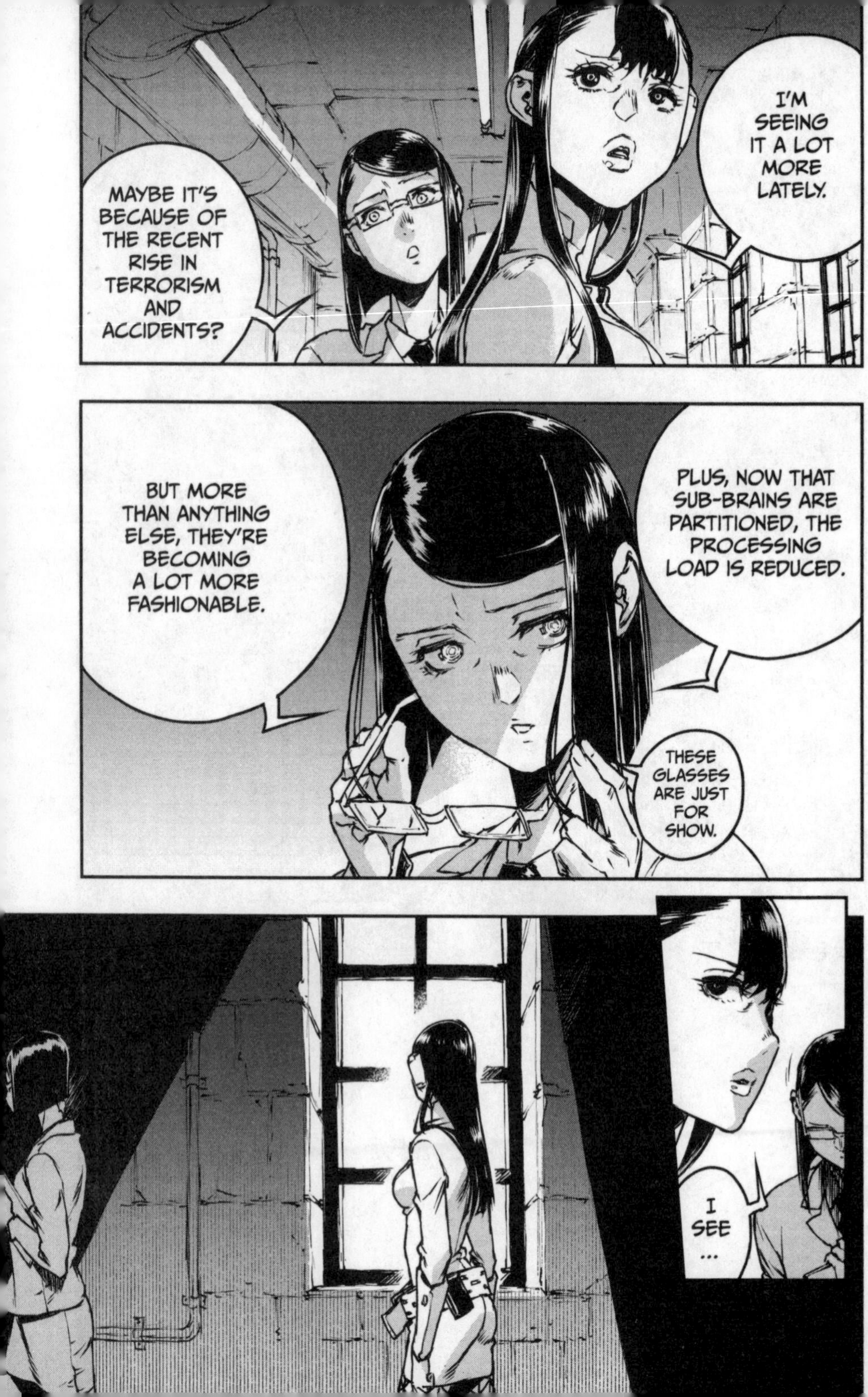
I'M SEEING IT A LOT MORE LATELY.
MAYBE IT'S BECAUSE OF THE RECENT RISE IN TERRORISM AND ACCIDENTS?
PLUS, NOW THAT SUB-BRAINS ARE PARTITIONED, THE PROCESSING LOAD IS REDUCED.
BUT MORE THAN ANYTHING ELSE, THEY'RE BECOMING A LOT MORE FASHIONABLE.
THESE GLASSES ARE JUST FOR SHOW.
I SEE ...

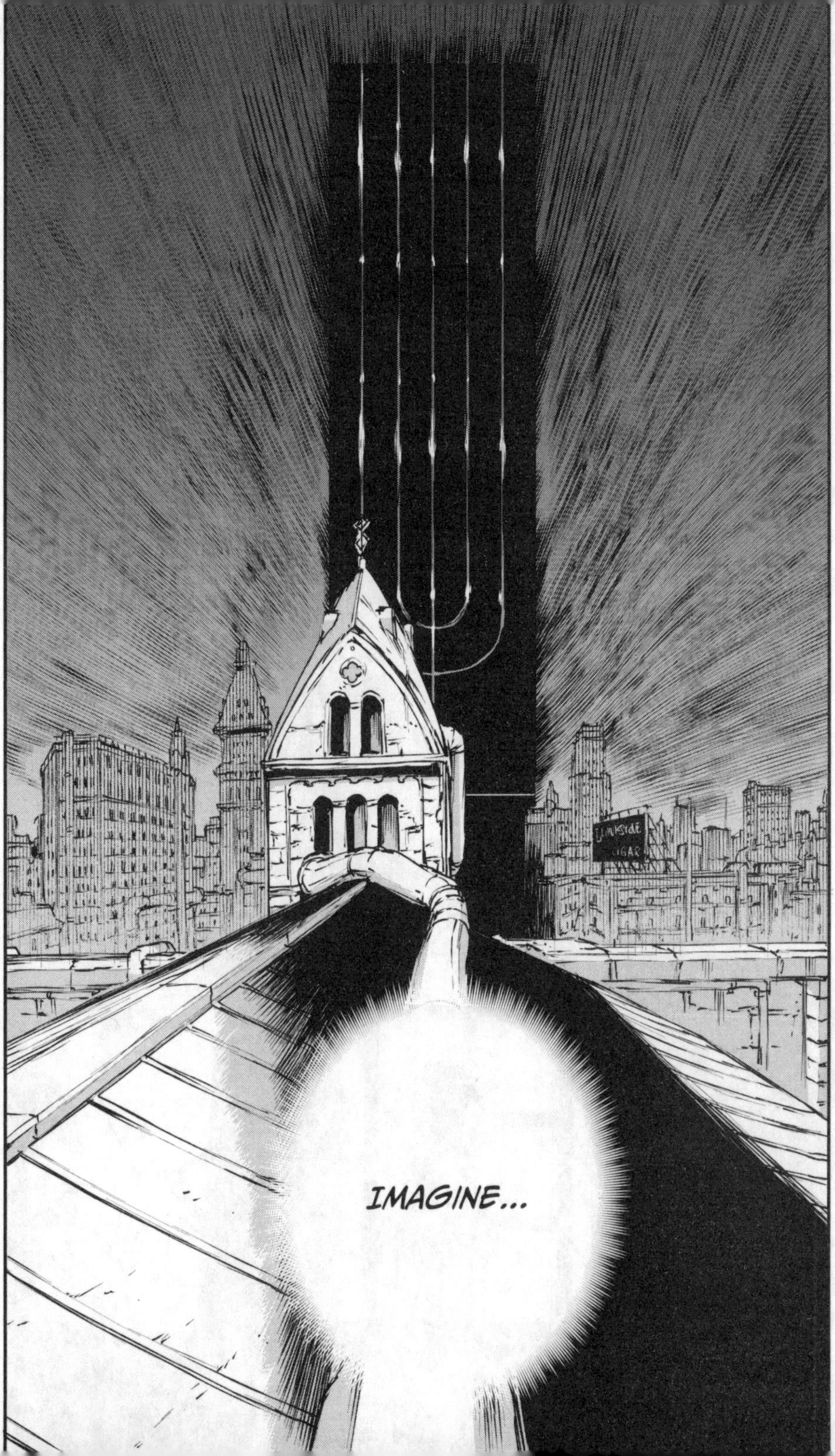
IMAGINE...

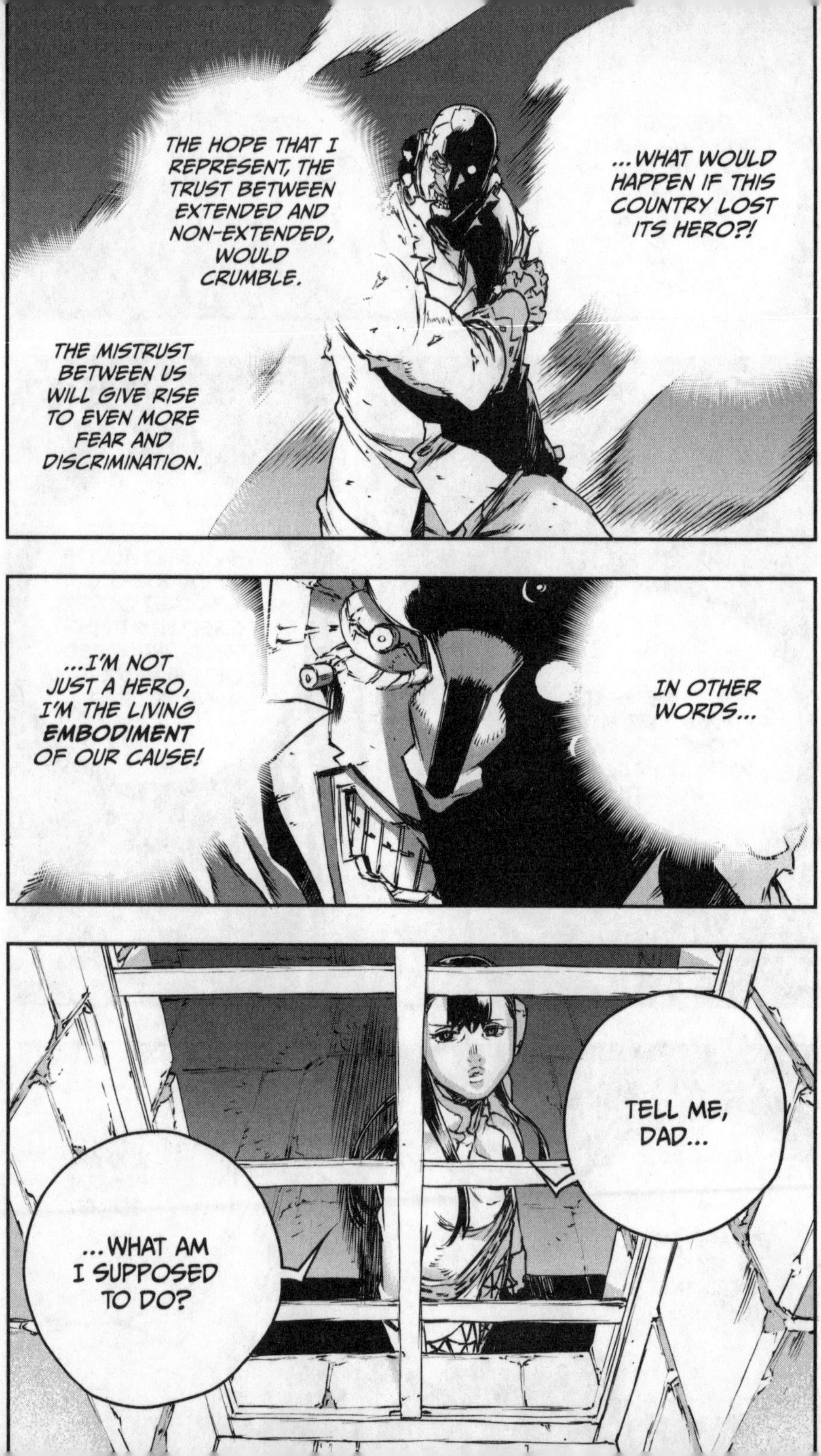
...WHAT WOULD HAPPEN IF THIS COUNTRY LOST ITS HERO?!
THE HOPE THAT I REPRESENT, THE TRUST BETWEEN EXTENDED AND NON-EXTENDED, WOULD CRUMBLE.
THE MISTRUST BETWEEN US WILL GIVE RISE TO EVEN MORE FEAR AND DISCRIMINATION.
IN OTHER WORDS...
...I'M NOT JUST A HERO, I'M THE LIVING **EMBODIMENT** OF OUR CAUSE!
TELL ME, DAD...
...WHAT AM I SUPPOSED TO DO?

IN ORDER TO RELEASE SUISO, WHOM I STAKED THE COMPANY'S FUTURE ON, I NEEDED THE WURZEL'S APPROVAL...

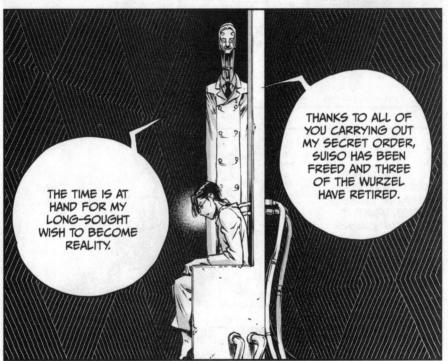

THANKS TO ALL OF YOU CARRYING OUT MY SECRET ORDER, SUISO HAS BEEN FREED AND THREE OF THE WURZEL HAVE RETIRED.

THE TIME IS AT HAND FOR MY LONG-SOUGHT WISH TO BECOME REALITY.

IO... YOU ARE SPECIAL TO ME.

PLEASE STAY BY MY SIDE UNTIL THAT HAPPENS...

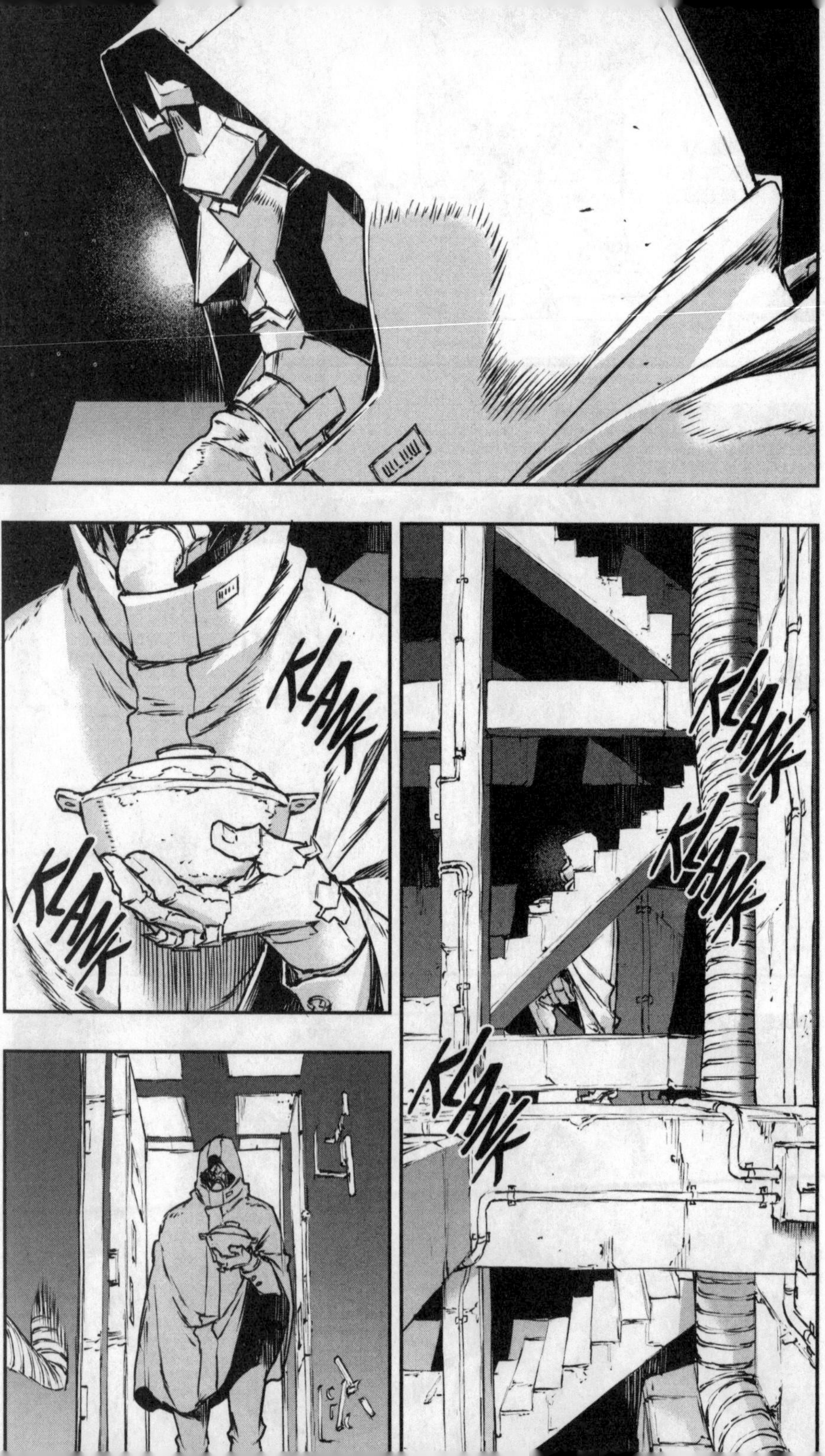
KLANK
KLANK
KLANK
KLANK
KLANK

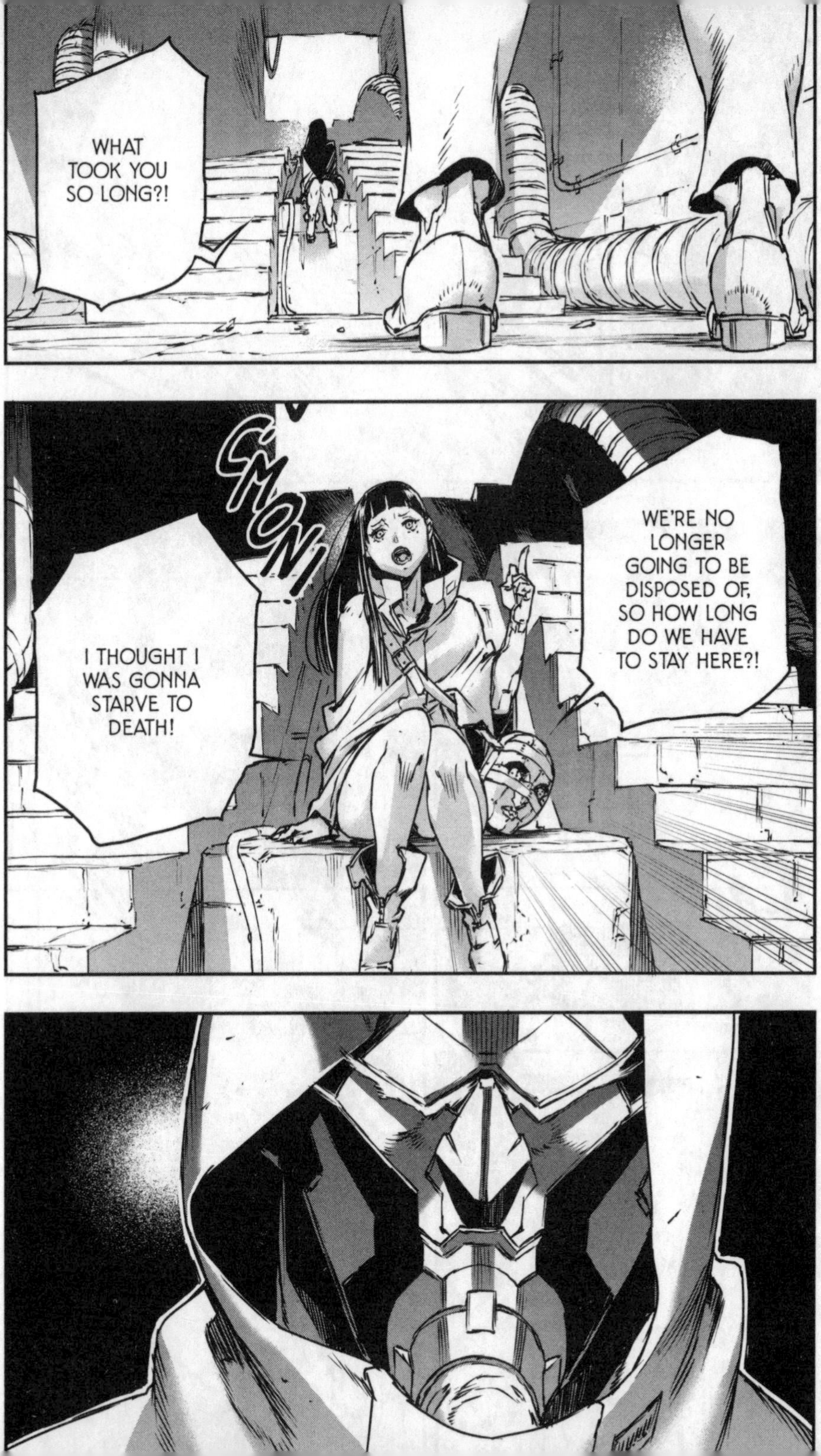
WHAT TOOK YOU SO LONG?!
C'MON!
WE'RE NO LONGER GOING TO BE DISPOSED OF, SO HOW LONG DO WE HAVE TO STAY HERE?!
I THOUGHT I WAS GONNA STARVE TO DEATH!

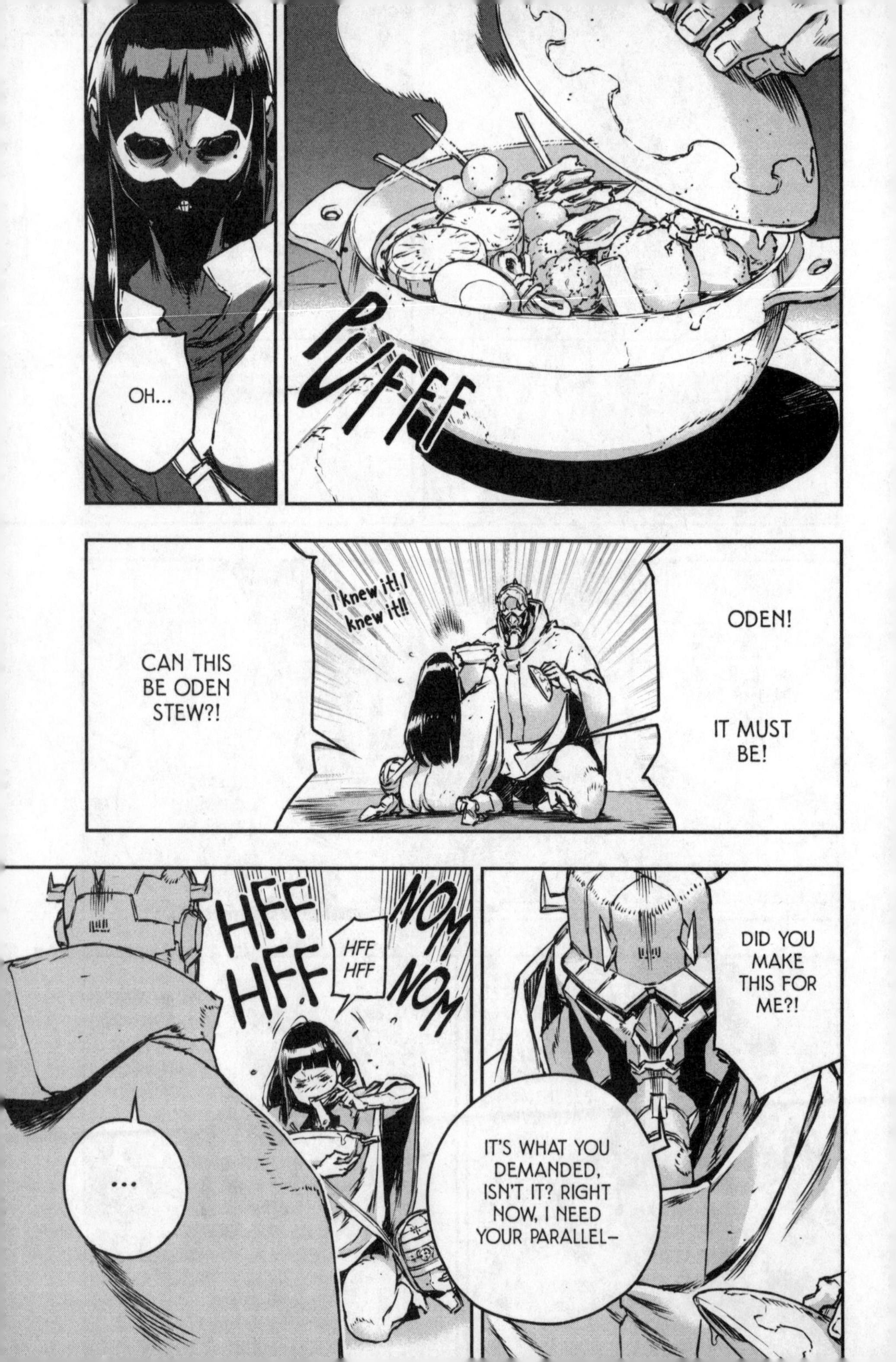
PUFFF
OH...
ODEN!
I knew it! I knew it!!
IT MUST BE!
CAN THIS BE ODEN STEW?!
DID YOU MAKE THIS FOR ME?!
IT'S WHAT YOU DEMANDED, ISN'T IT? RIGHT NOW, I NEED YOUR PARALLEL–
NOM NOM
HFF HFF
HFF HFF
...

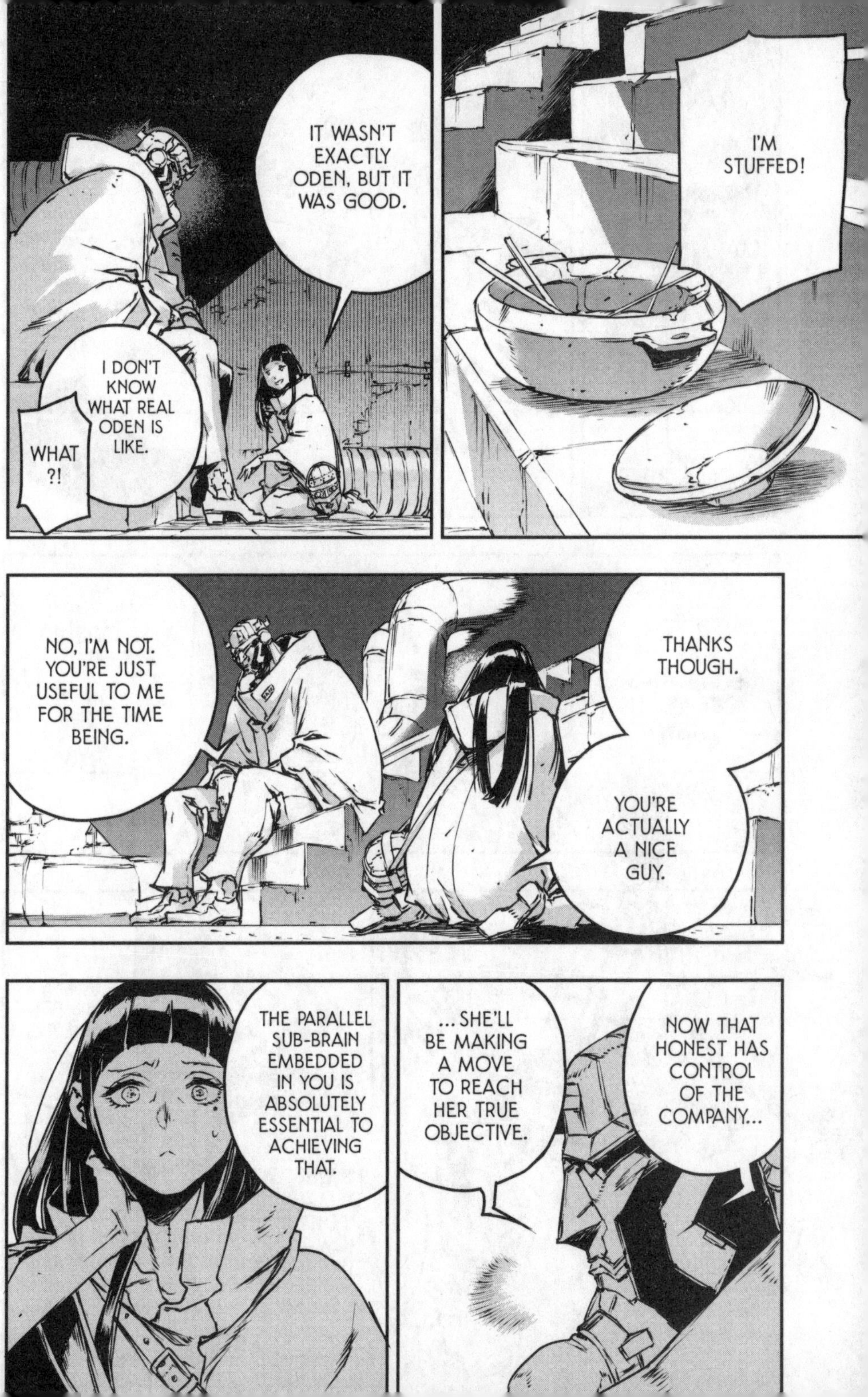
I'M STUFFED!
IT WASN'T EXACTLY ODEN, BUT IT WAS GOOD.
I DON'T KNOW WHAT REAL ODEN IS LIKE.
WHAT?!
THANKS THOUGH.
YOU'RE ACTUALLY A NICE GUY.
NO, I'M NOT. YOU'RE JUST USEFUL TO ME FOR THE TIME BEING.
NOW THAT HONEST HAS CONTROL OF THE COMPANY...
...SHE'LL BE MAKING A MOVE TO REACH HER TRUE OBJECTIVE.
THE PARALLEL SUB-BRAIN EMBEDDED IN YOU IS ABSOLUTELY ESSENTIAL TO ACHIEVING THAT.

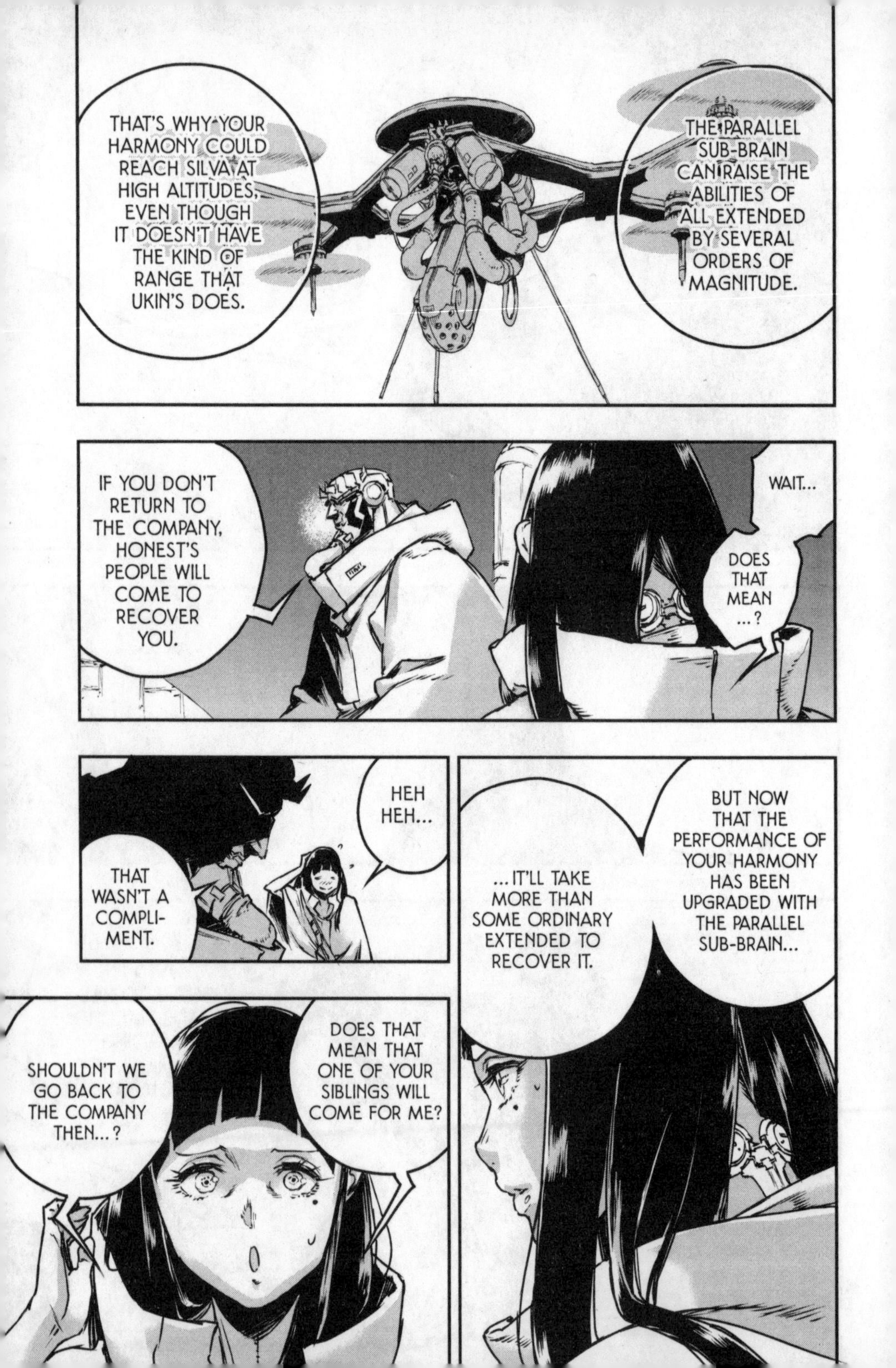
THE PARALLEL SUB-BRAIN CAN RAISE THE ABILITIES OF ALL EXTENDED BY SEVERAL ORDERS OF MAGNITUDE.
THAT'S WHY YOUR HARMONY COULD REACH SILVA AT HIGH ALTITUDES, EVEN THOUGH IT DOESN'T HAVE THE KIND OF RANGE THAT UKIN'S DOES.
WAIT...
DOES THAT MEAN ...?
IF YOU DON'T RETURN TO THE COMPANY, HONEST'S PEOPLE WILL COME TO RECOVER YOU.
BUT NOW THAT THE PERFORMANCE OF YOUR HARMONY HAS BEEN UPGRADED WITH THE PARALLEL SUB-BRAIN...
...IT'LL TAKE MORE THAN SOME ORDINARY EXTENDED TO RECOVER IT.
HEH HEH...
THAT WASN'T A COMPLIMENT.
DOES THAT MEAN THAT ONE OF YOUR SIBLINGS WILL COME FOR ME?
SHOULDN'T WE GO BACK TO THE COMPANY THEN...?

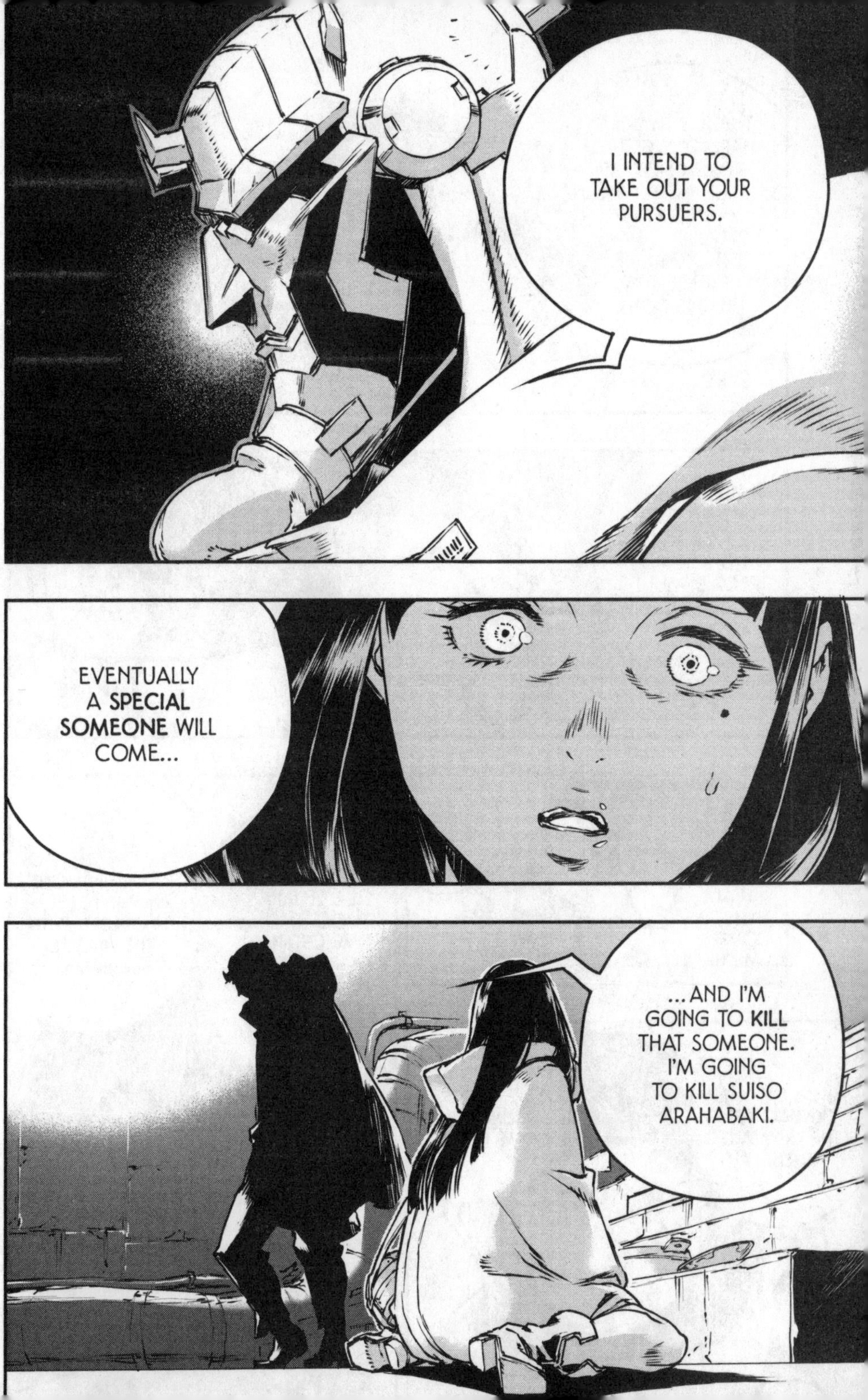

I INTEND TO TAKE OUT YOUR PURSUERS.
EVENTUALLY A **SPECIAL SOMEONE** WILL COME...
...AND I'M GOING TO **KILL** THAT SOMEONE. I'M GOING TO KILL SUISO ARAHABAKI.

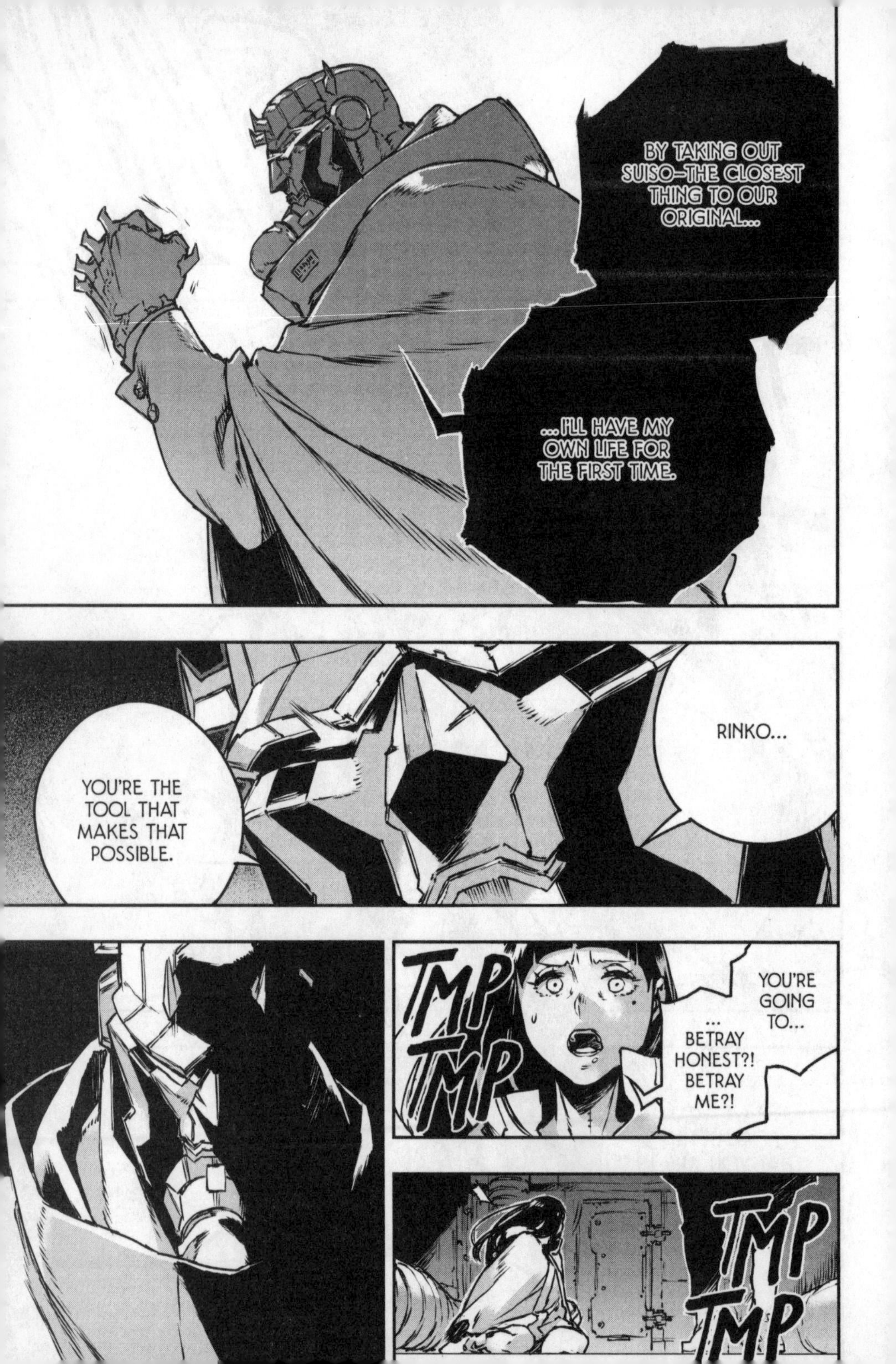
BY TAKING OUT SUISO–THE CLOSEST THING TO OUR ORIGINAL...
...I'LL HAVE MY OWN LIFE FOR THE FIRST TIME.
RINKO...
YOU'RE THE TOOL THAT MAKES THAT POSSIBLE.
YOU'RE GOING TO...
... BETRAY HONEST?! BETRAY ME?!
TMP TMP
TMP TMP

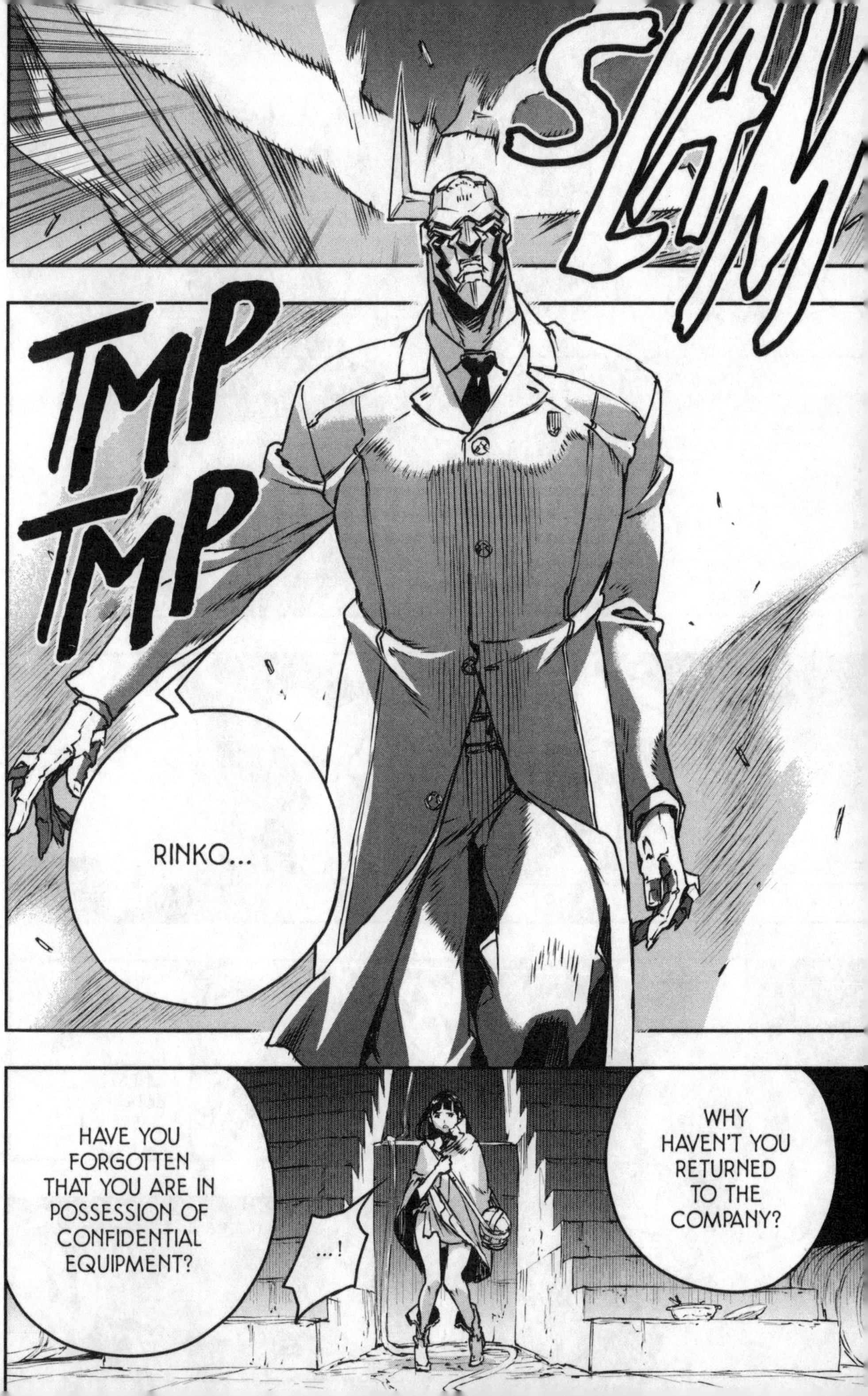
SLAM
TMP TMP
RINKO...
WHY HAVEN'T YOU RETURNED TO THE COMPANY?
...!
HAVE YOU FORGOTTEN THAT YOU ARE IN POSSESSION OF CONFIDENTIAL EQUIPMENT?

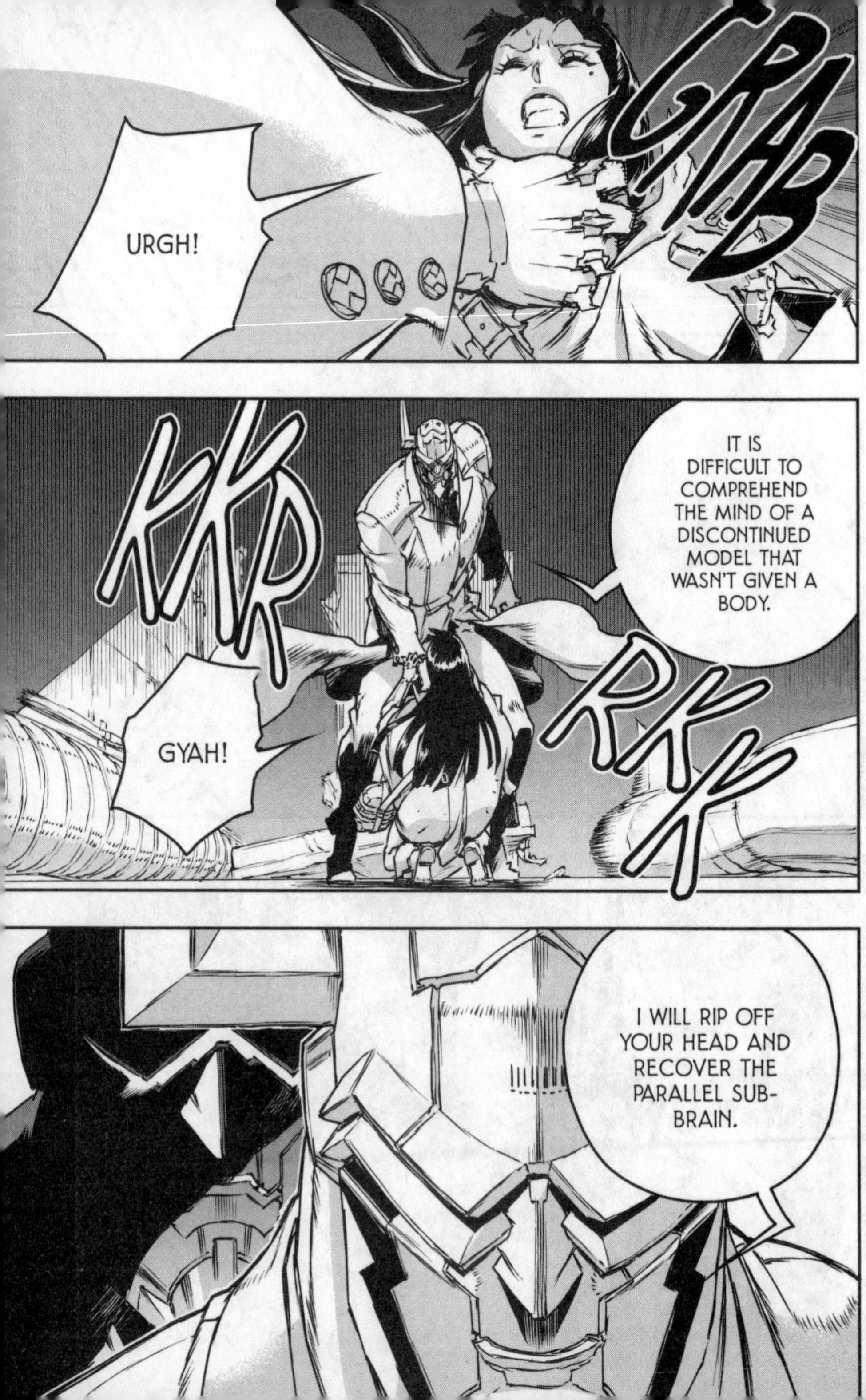
GRAB
URGH!
IT IS DIFFICULT TO COMPREHEND THE MIND OF A DISCONTINUED MODEL THAT WASN'T GIVEN A BODY.
KKR
RKK
GYAH!
I WILL RIP OFF YOUR HEAD AND RECOVER THE PARALLEL SUB-BRAIN.

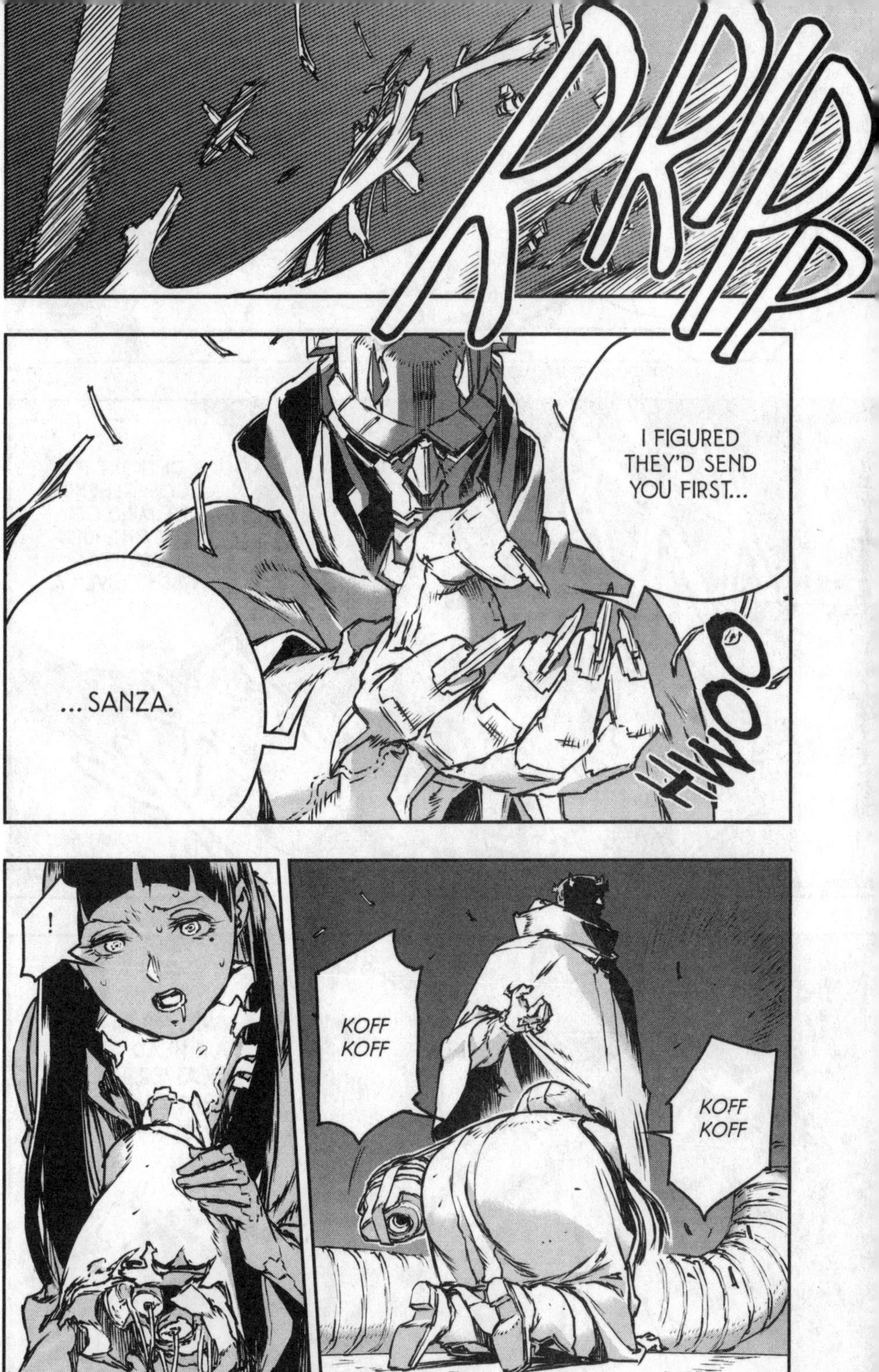
RRIPP
I FIGURED THEY'D SEND YOU FIRST...
...SANZA.
KOFF KOFF
KOFF KOFF
!

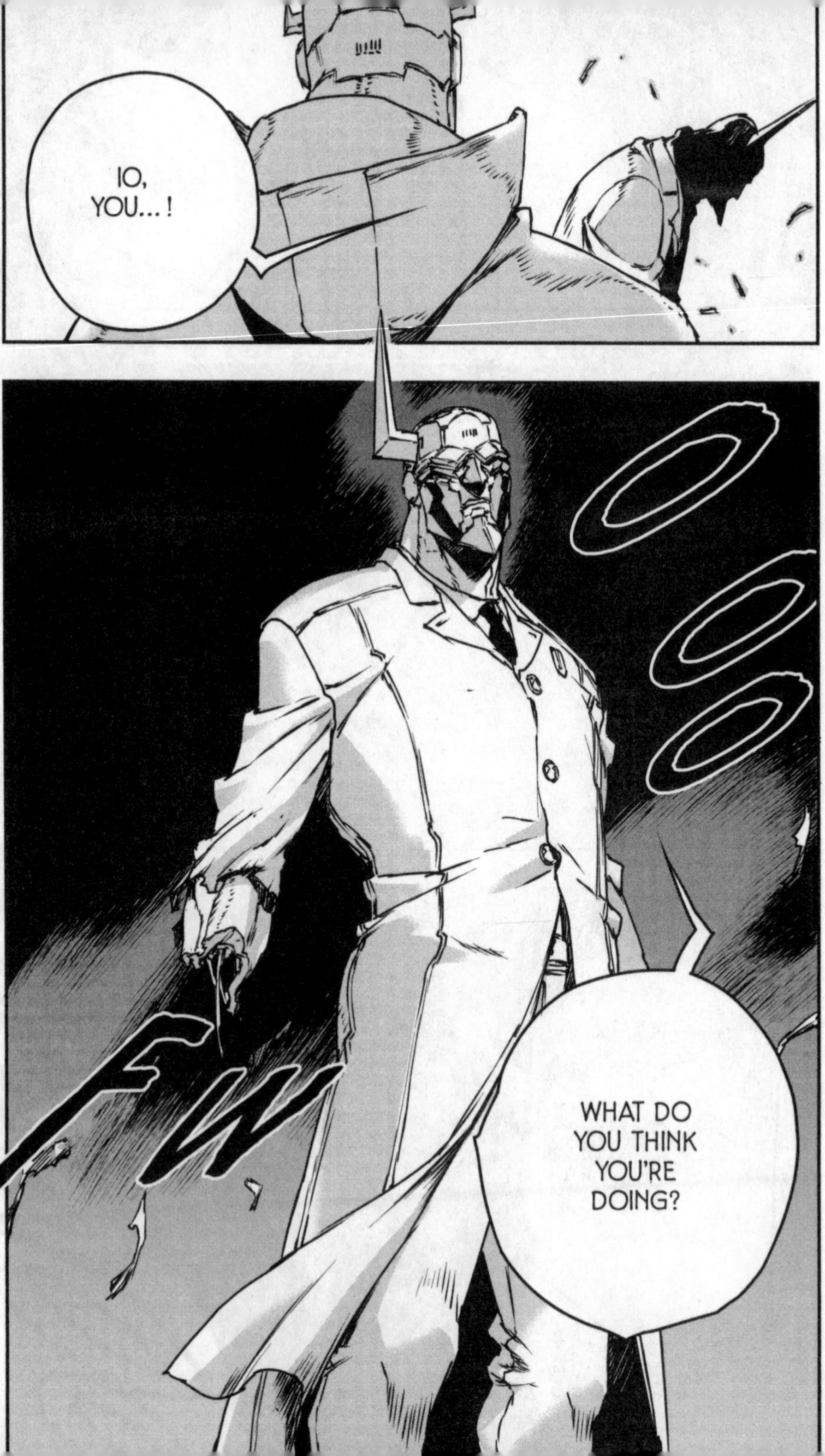
IO, YOU... !
OOO
WHAT DO YOU THINK YOU'RE DOING?
FW

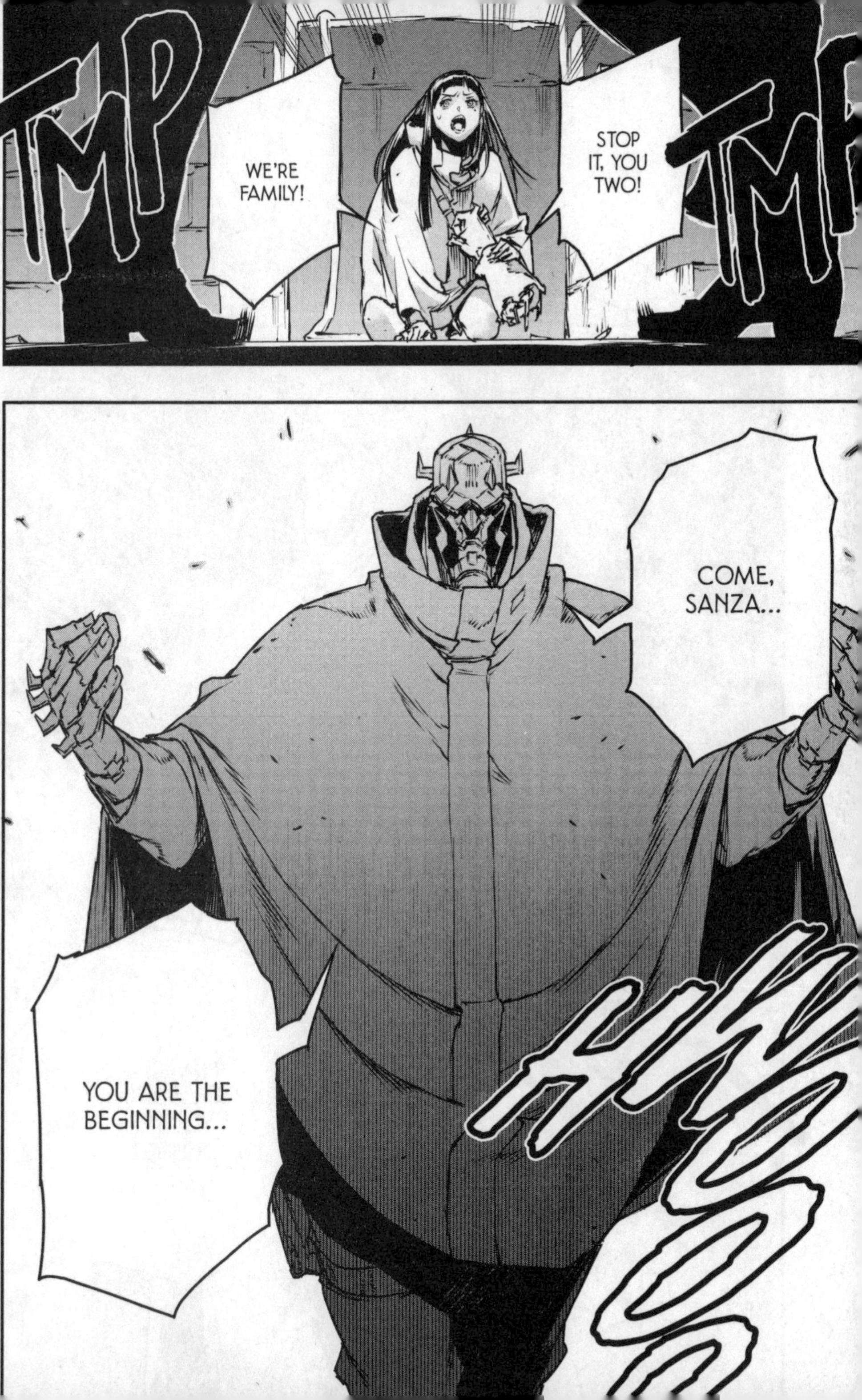
STOP IT, YOU TWO!
WE'RE FAMILY!
TMP
COME, SANZA...
YOU ARE THE BEGINNING...

NO GUNS LIFE

The gunsmoke drifts, the muzzle talks

NO GUNS LIFE

The gunsmoke drifts, the muzzle talks

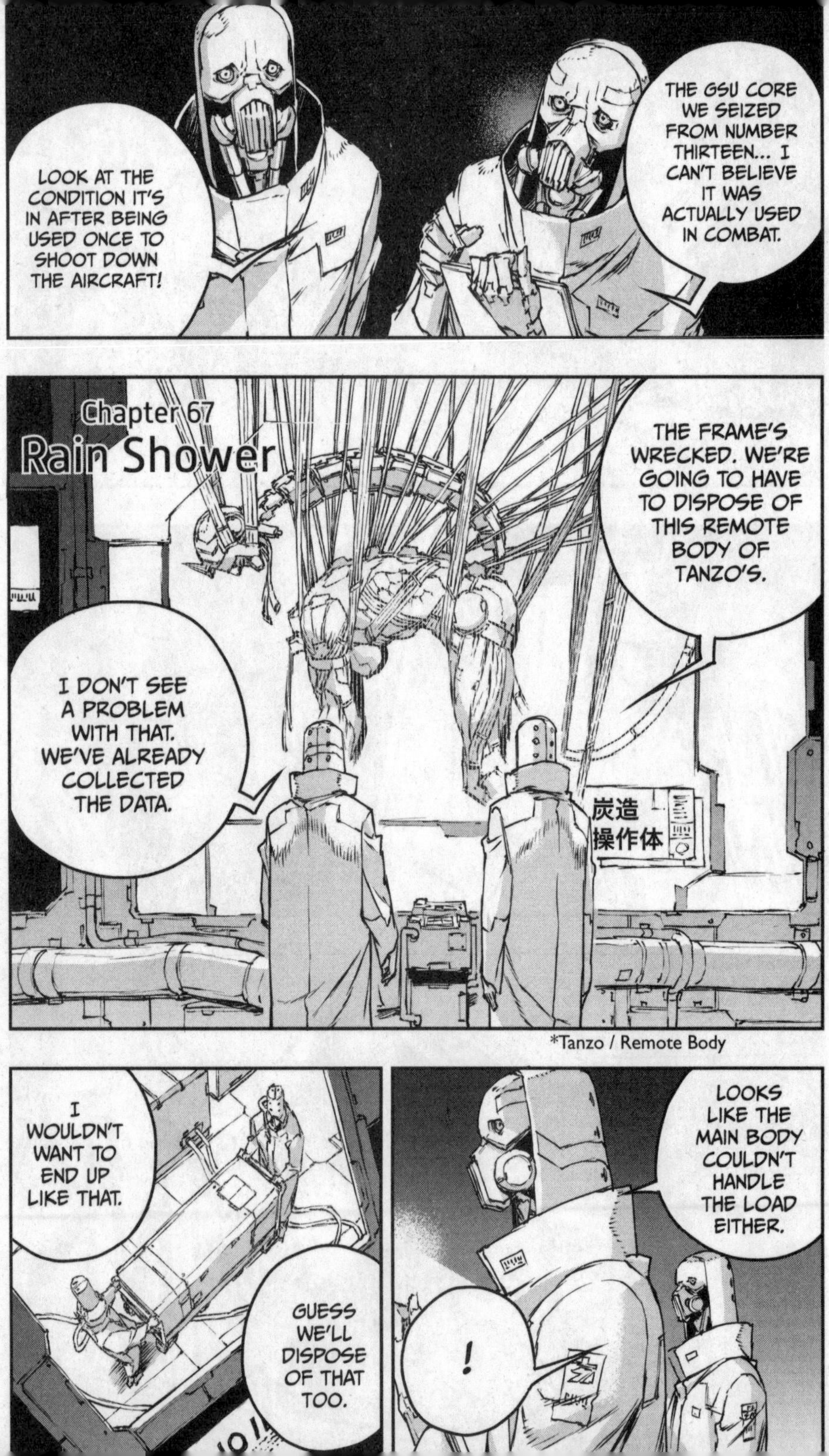
THE GSU CORE WE SEIZED FROM NUMBER THIRTEEN... I CAN'T BELIEVE IT WAS ACTUALLY USED IN COMBAT.
LOOK AT THE CONDITION IT'S IN AFTER BEING USED ONCE TO SHOOT DOWN THE AIRCRAFT!
Chapter 67
Rain Shower
THE FRAME'S WRECKED. WE'RE GOING TO HAVE TO DISPOSE OF THIS REMOTE BODY OF TANZO'S.
炭造
操作体
I DON'T SEE A PROBLEM WITH THAT. WE'VE ALREADY COLLECTED THE DATA.
*Tanzo / Remote Body
LOOKS LIKE THE MAIN BODY COULDN'T HANDLE THE LOAD EITHER.
!
I WOULDN'T WANT TO END UP LIKE THAT.
GUESS WE'LL DISPOSE OF THAT TOO.

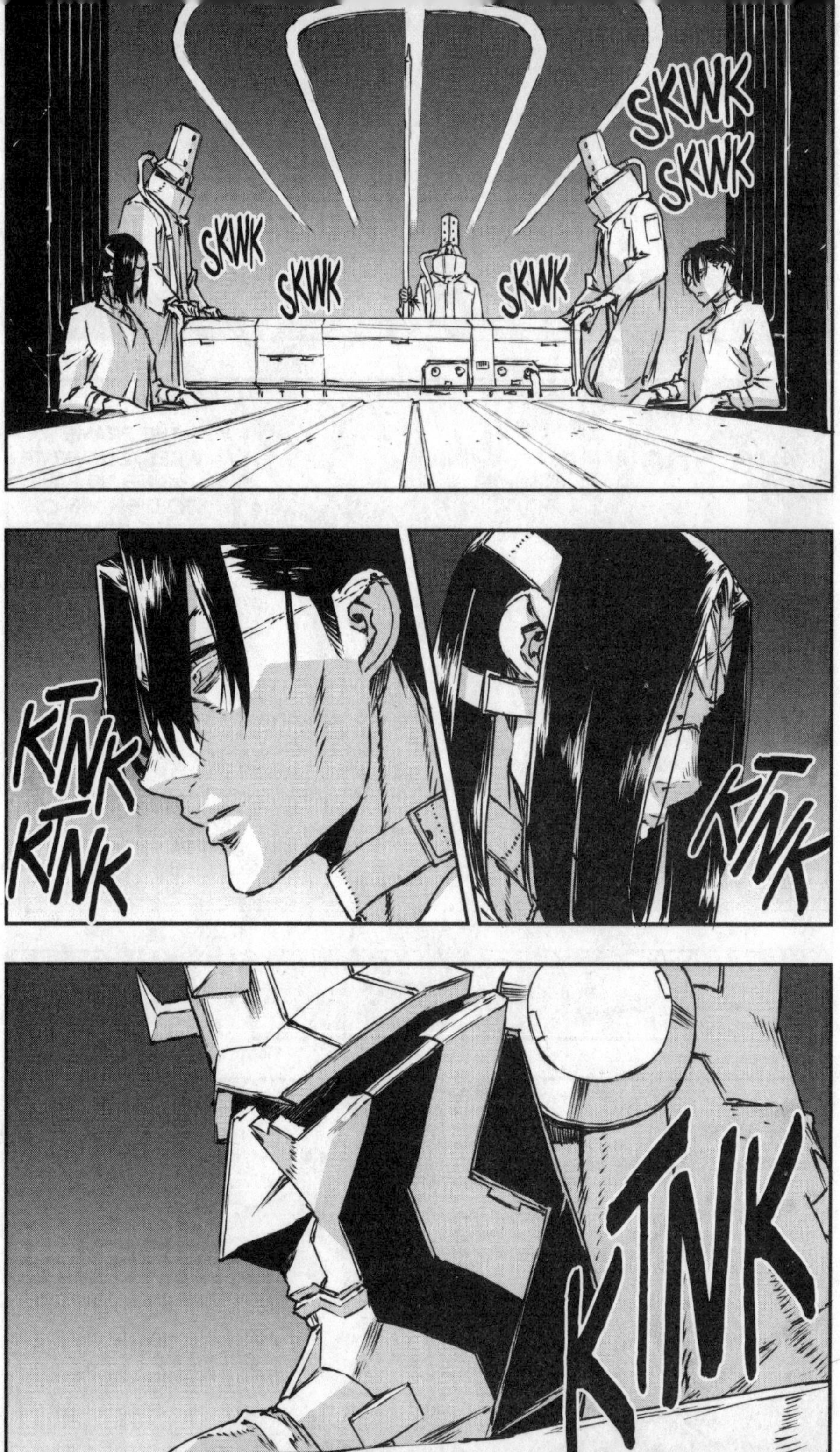
SKWK
SKWK
SKWK
SKWK
SKWK
KTNK
KTNK
KTNK
KTNK

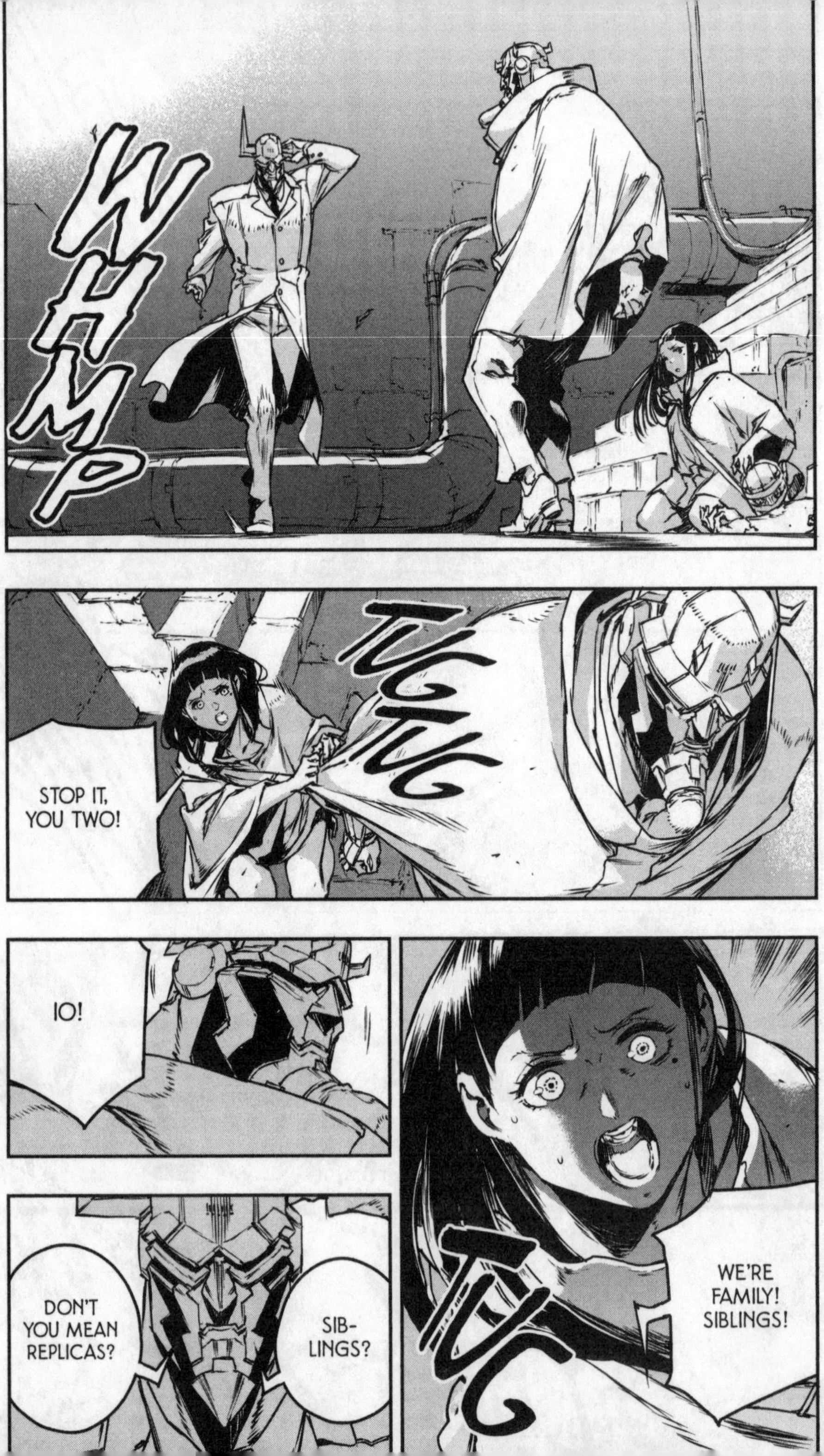
WHMP
TUG TUG
STOP IT, YOU TWO!
WE'RE FAMILY! SIBLINGS!
TUG
IO!
SIB-LINGS?
DON'T YOU MEAN REPLICAS?

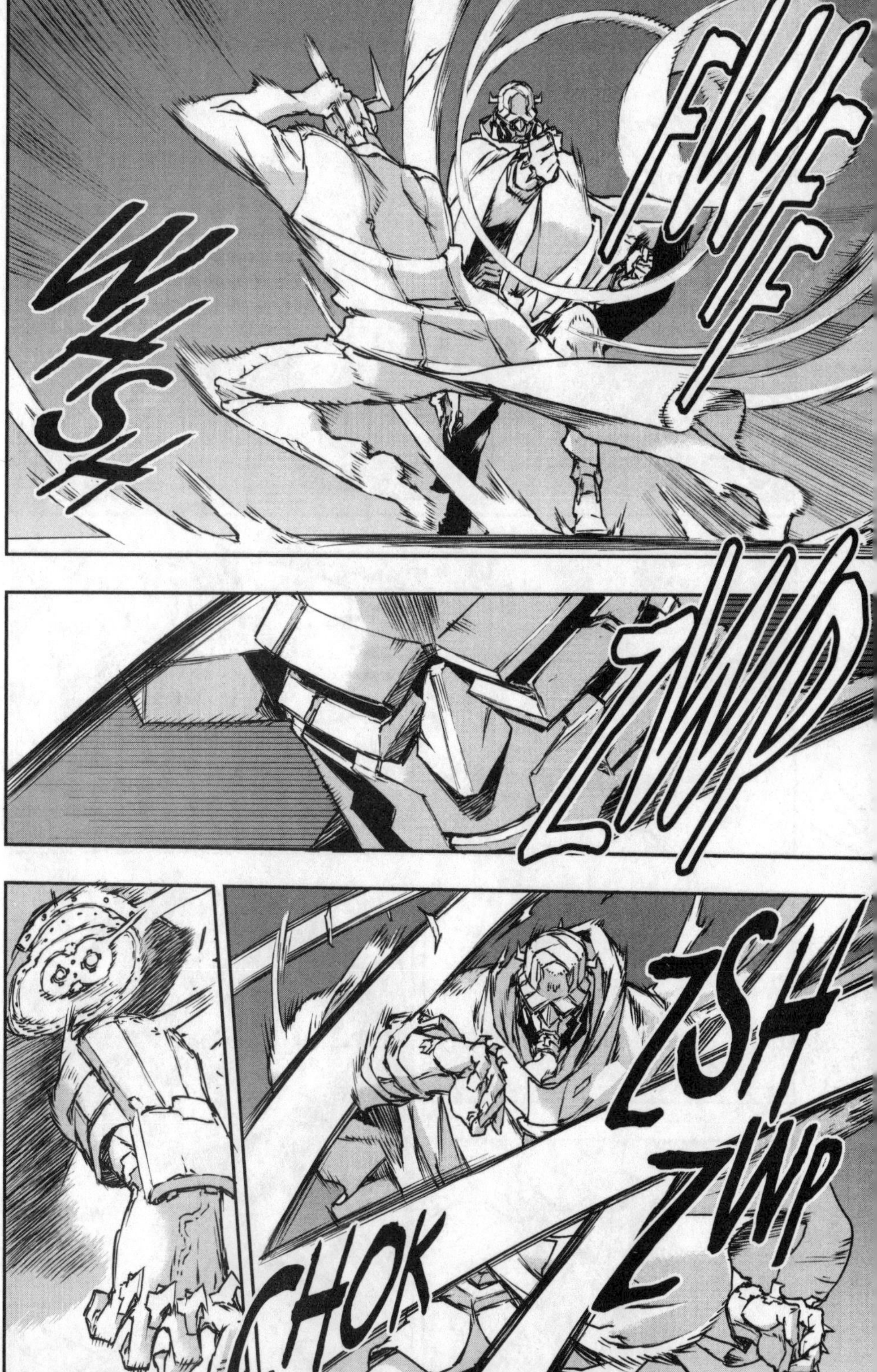
FWFF
WHSH
ZWP
ZSH
ZWP
CHOK

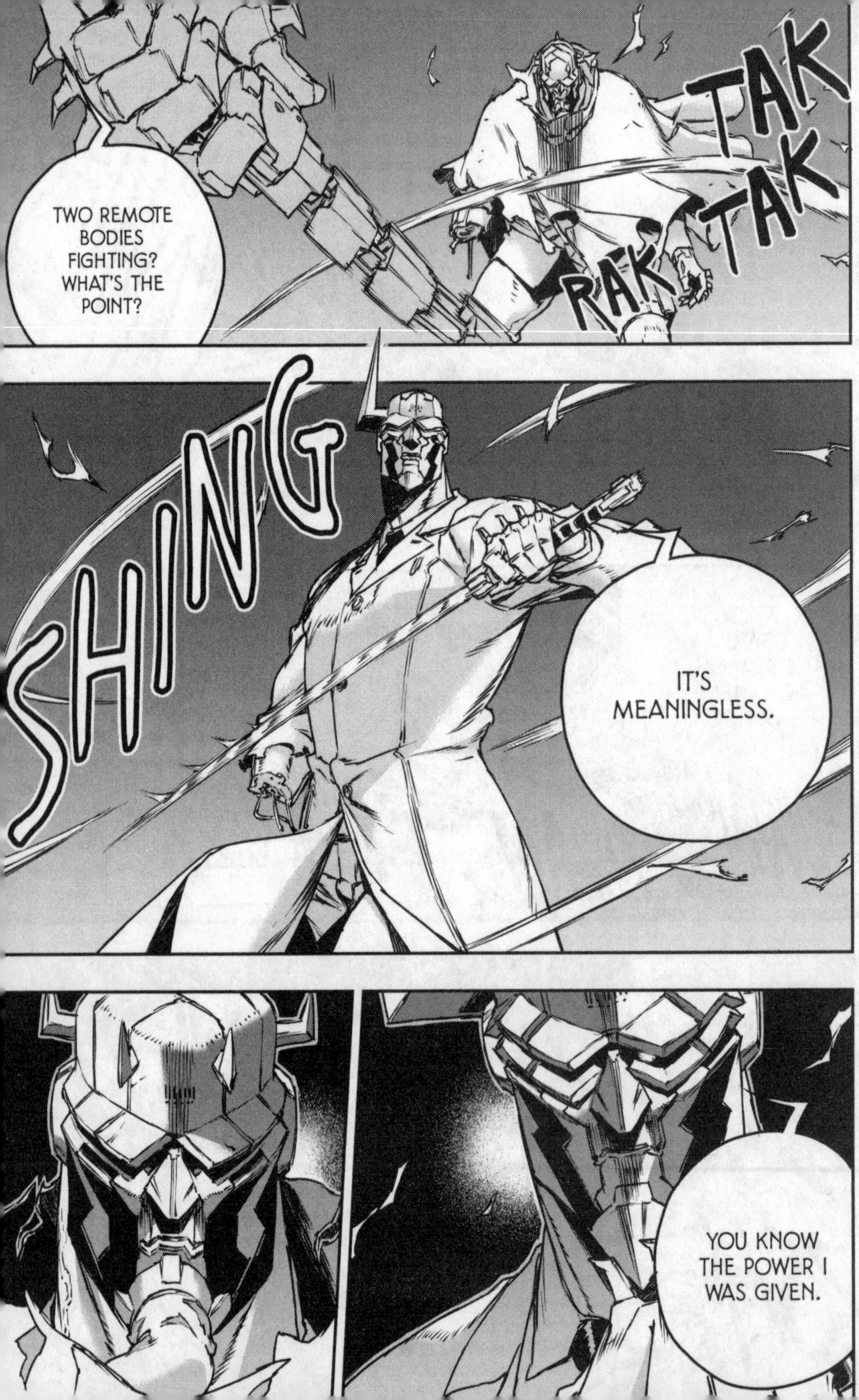
TAK TAK
RAK
TWO REMOTE BODIES FIGHTING? WHAT'S THE POINT?
SHING
IT'S MEANINGLESS.
YOU KNOW THE POWER I WAS GIVEN.

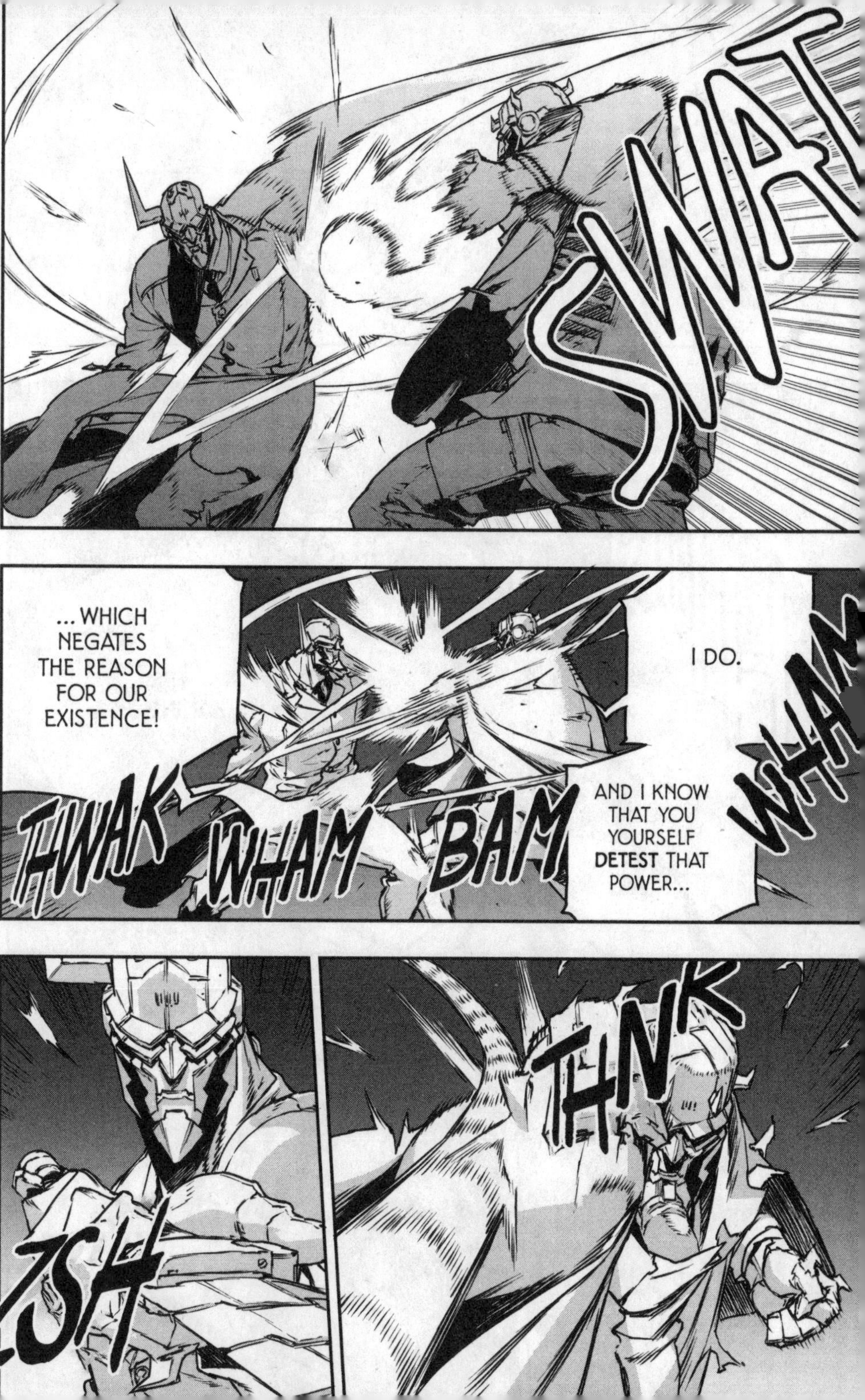
SWAT
WHAM
I DO.
AND I KNOW THAT YOU YOURSELF **DETEST** THAT POWER...
BAM
WHAM
THWAK
...WHICH NEGATES THE REASON FOR OUR EXISTENCE!
THNK
ZSH

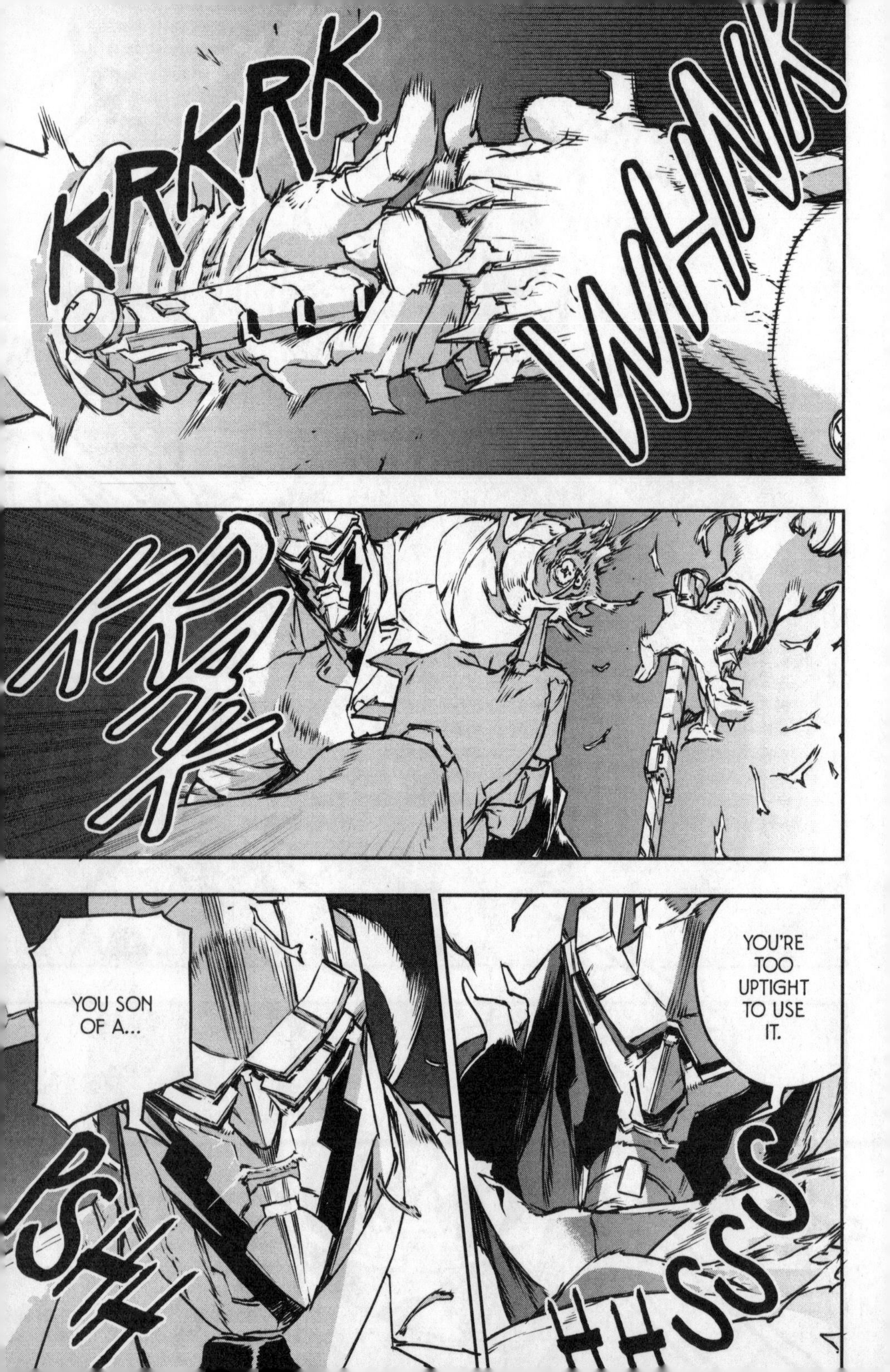
WHNK
KRKRK
KRAK
YOU'RE TOO UPTIGHT TO USE IT.
SSSHH
YOU SON OF A...
PSHH

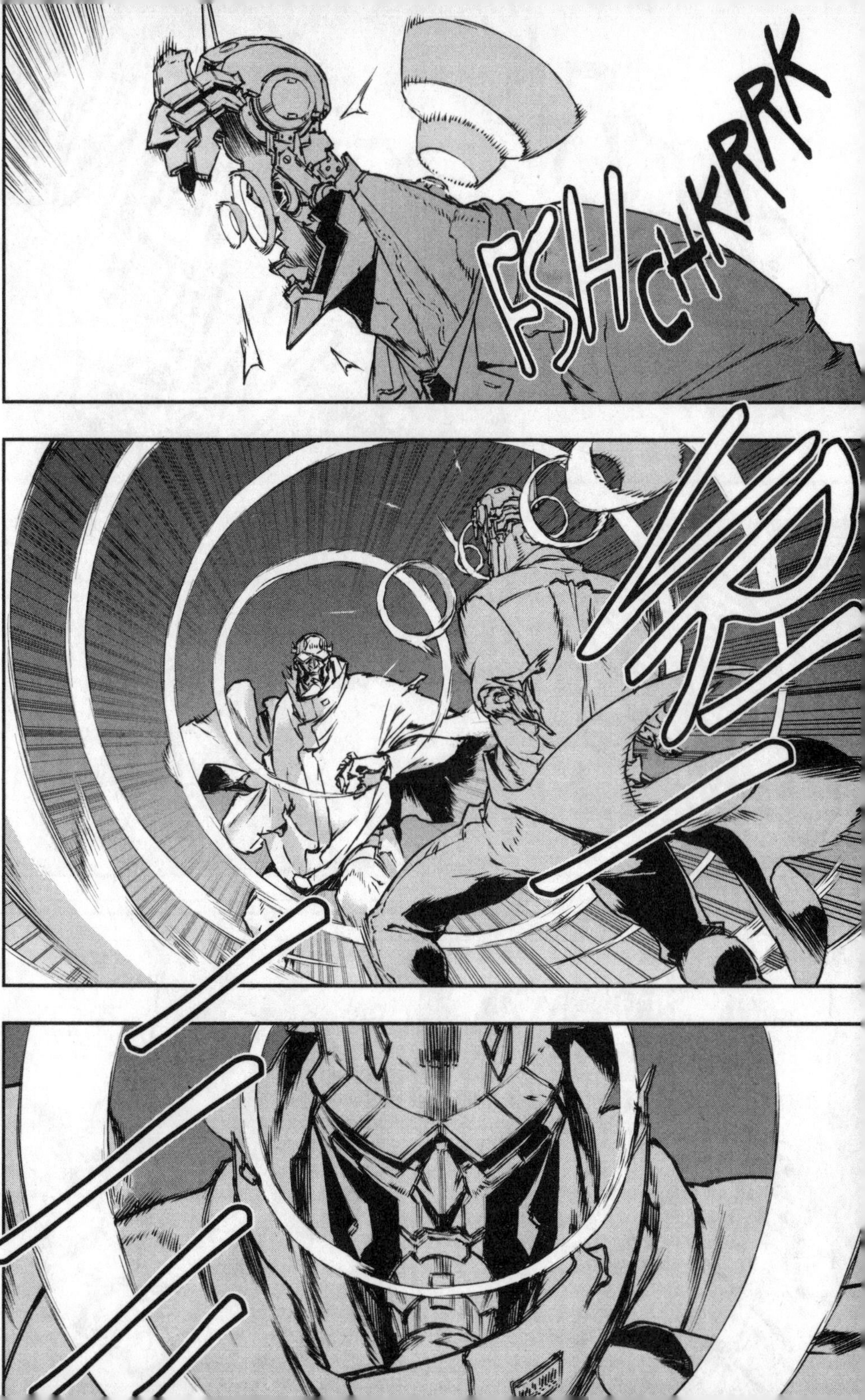
FSH CHKRRK

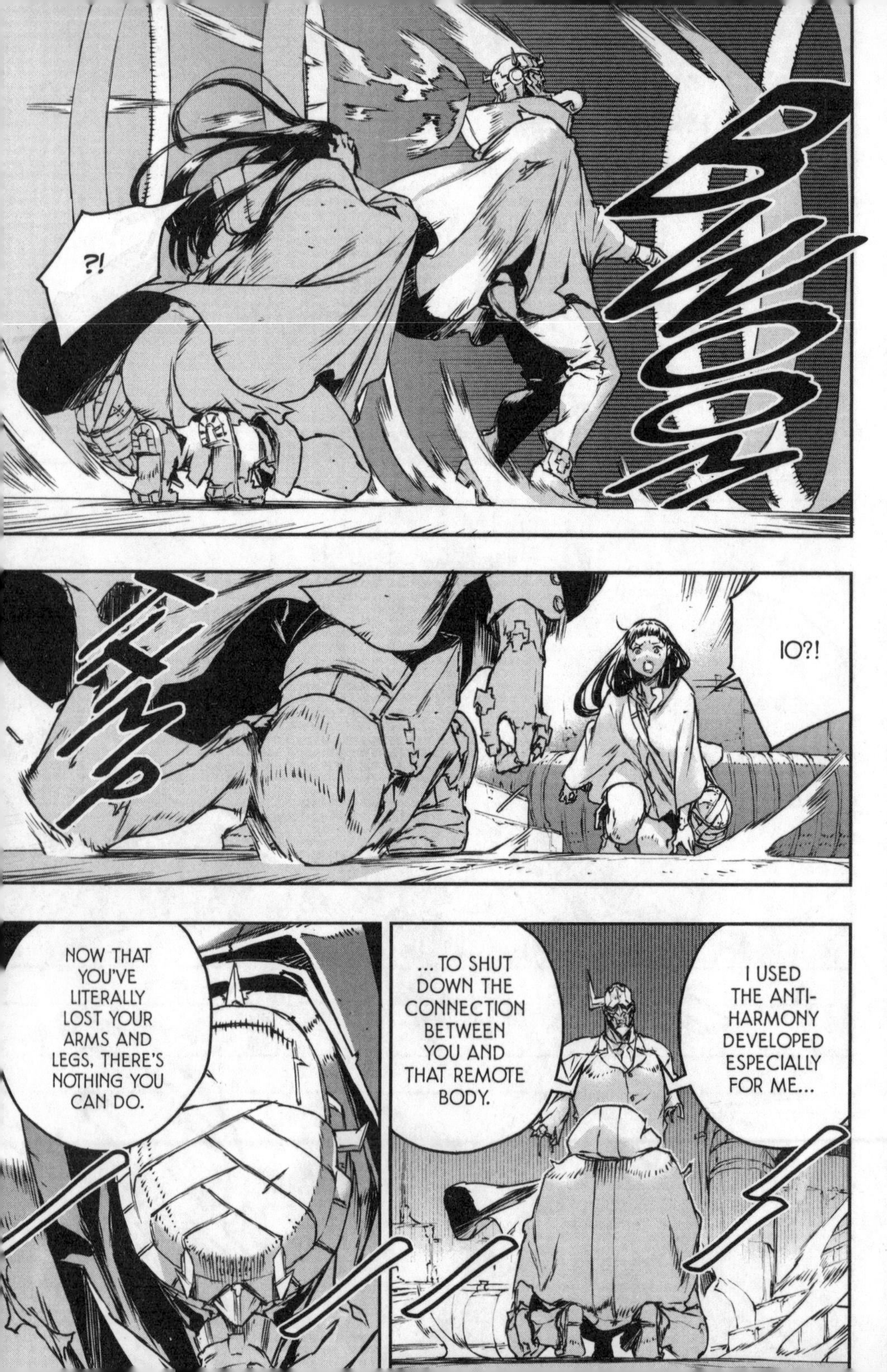
BWOOM
?!
IO?!
THMP
I USED THE ANTI-HARMONY DEVELOPED ESPECIALLY FOR ME...
... TO SHUT DOWN THE CONNECTION BETWEEN YOU AND THAT REMOTE BODY.
NOW THAT YOU'VE LITERALLY LOST YOUR ARMS AND LEGS, THERE'S NOTHING YOU CAN DO.

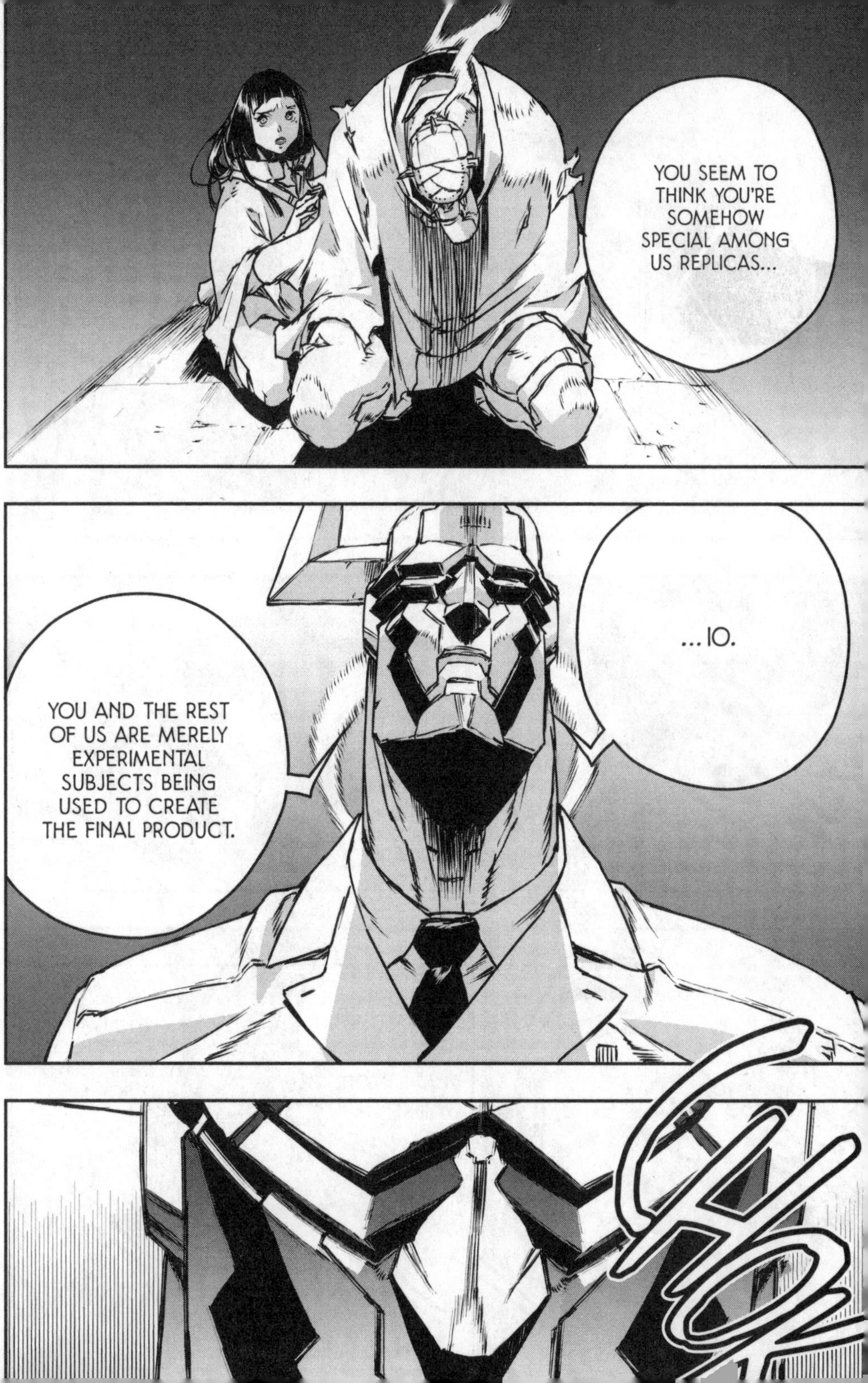
YOU SEEM TO THINK YOU'RE SOMEHOW SPECIAL AMONG US REPLICAS...
...IO.
YOU AND THE REST OF US ARE MERELY EXPERIMENTAL SUBJECTS BEING USED TO CREATE THE FINAL PRODUCT.

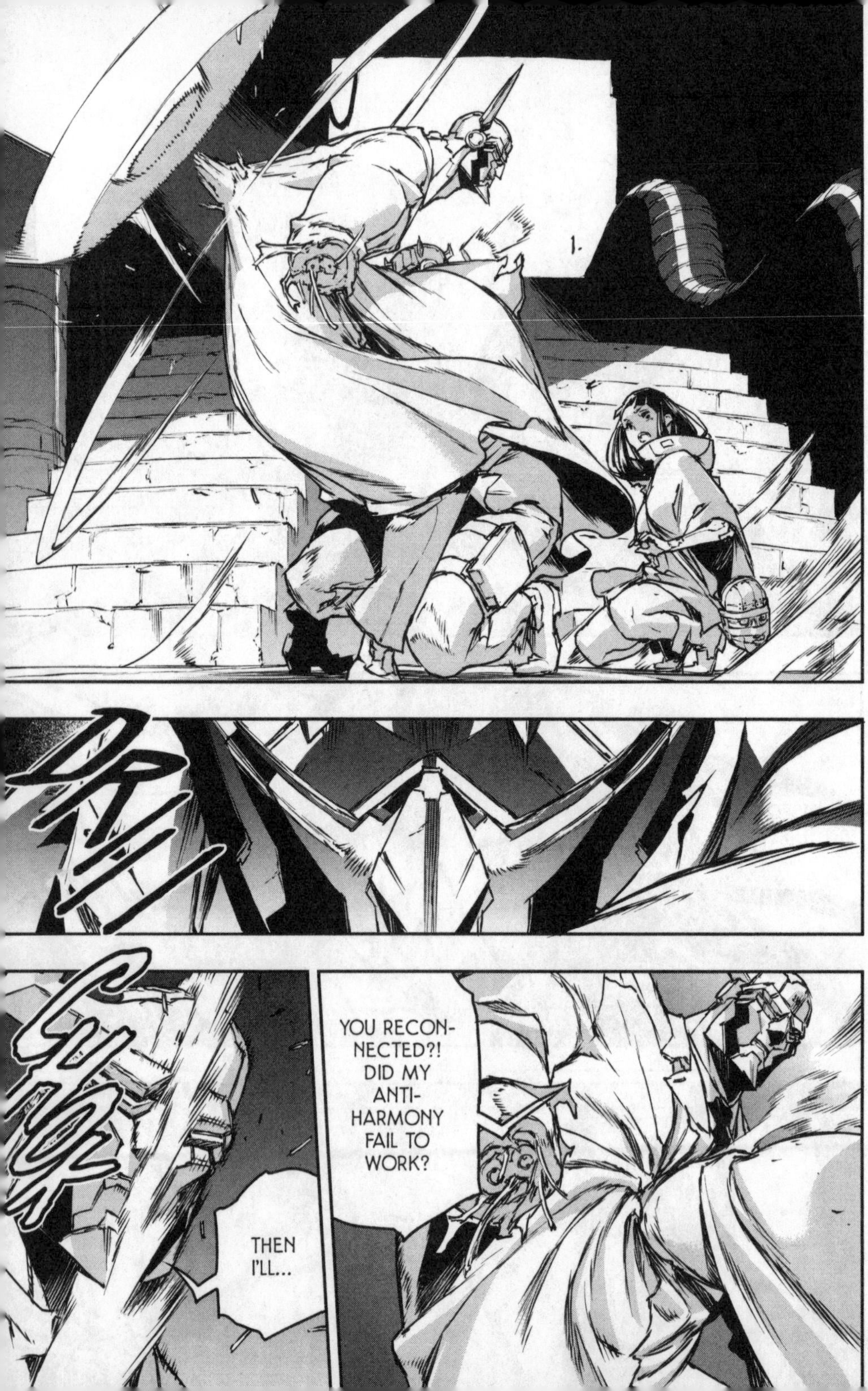
YOU RECONNECTED?! DID MY ANTI-HARMONY FAIL TO WORK?
THEN I'LL...

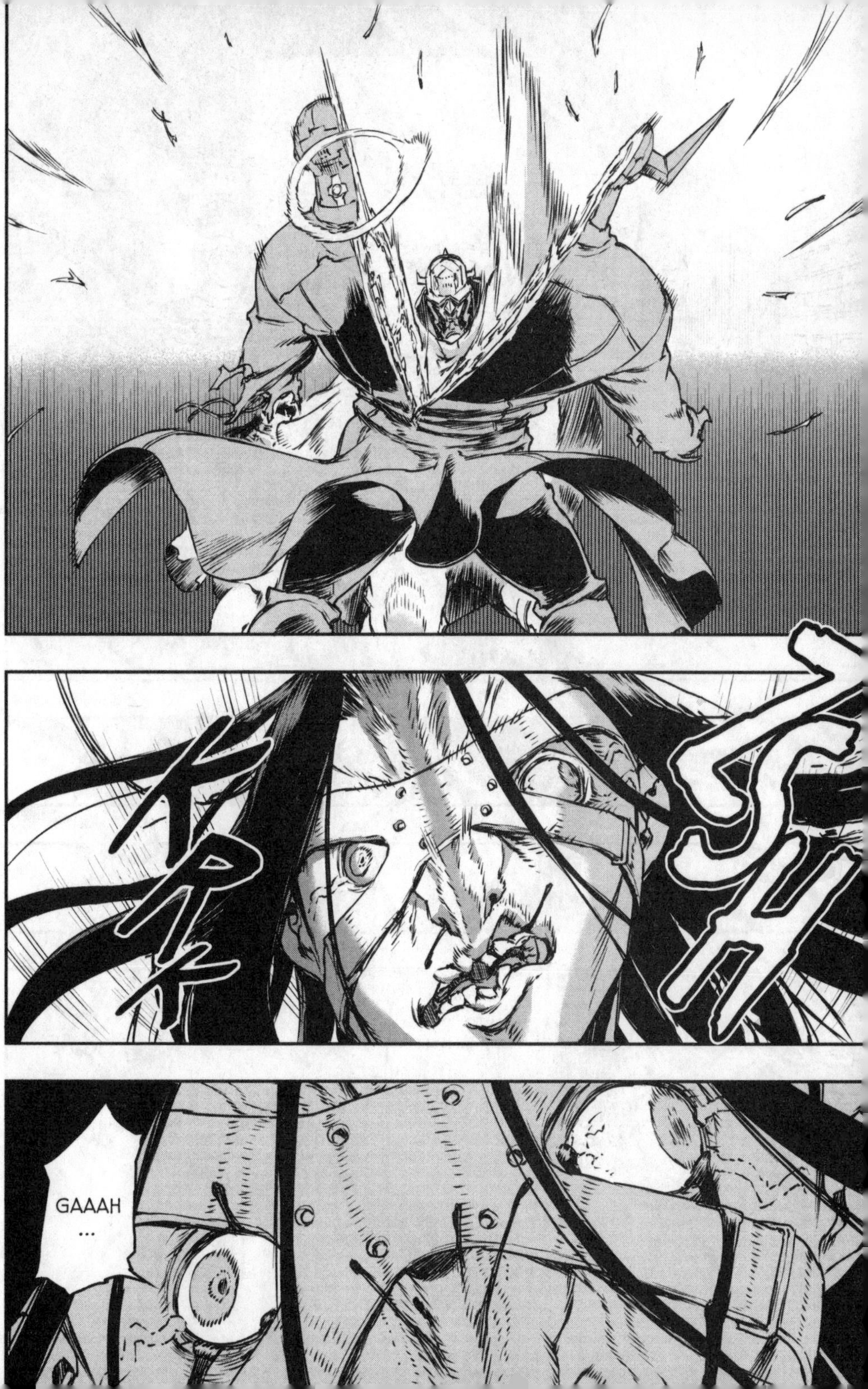
KRK
GAAAH ...

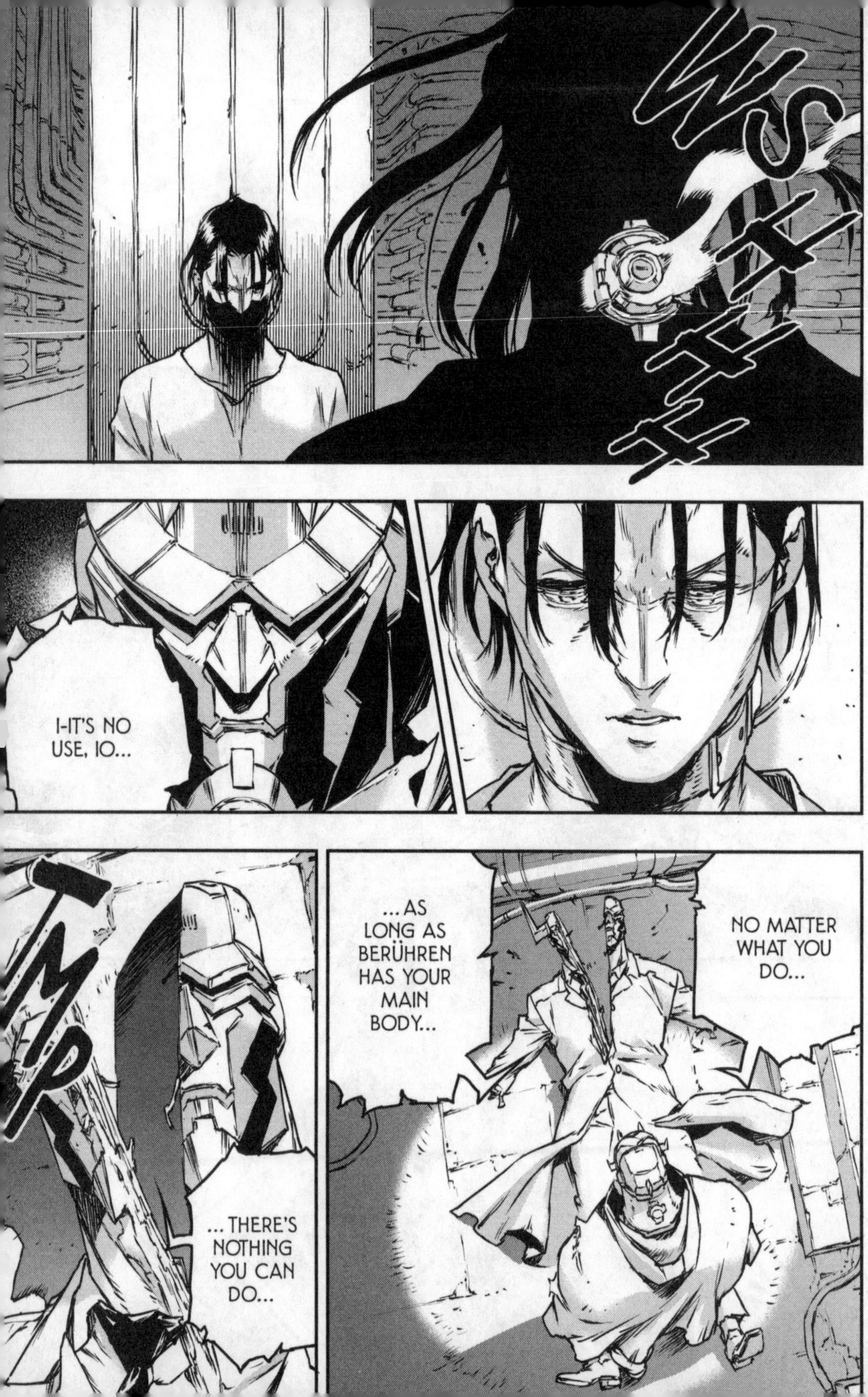
WSHHHH
I-IT'S NO USE, IO...
NO MATTER WHAT YOU DO...
...AS LONG AS BERÜHREN HAS YOUR MAIN BODY...
TMP
...THERE'S NOTHING YOU CAN DO...

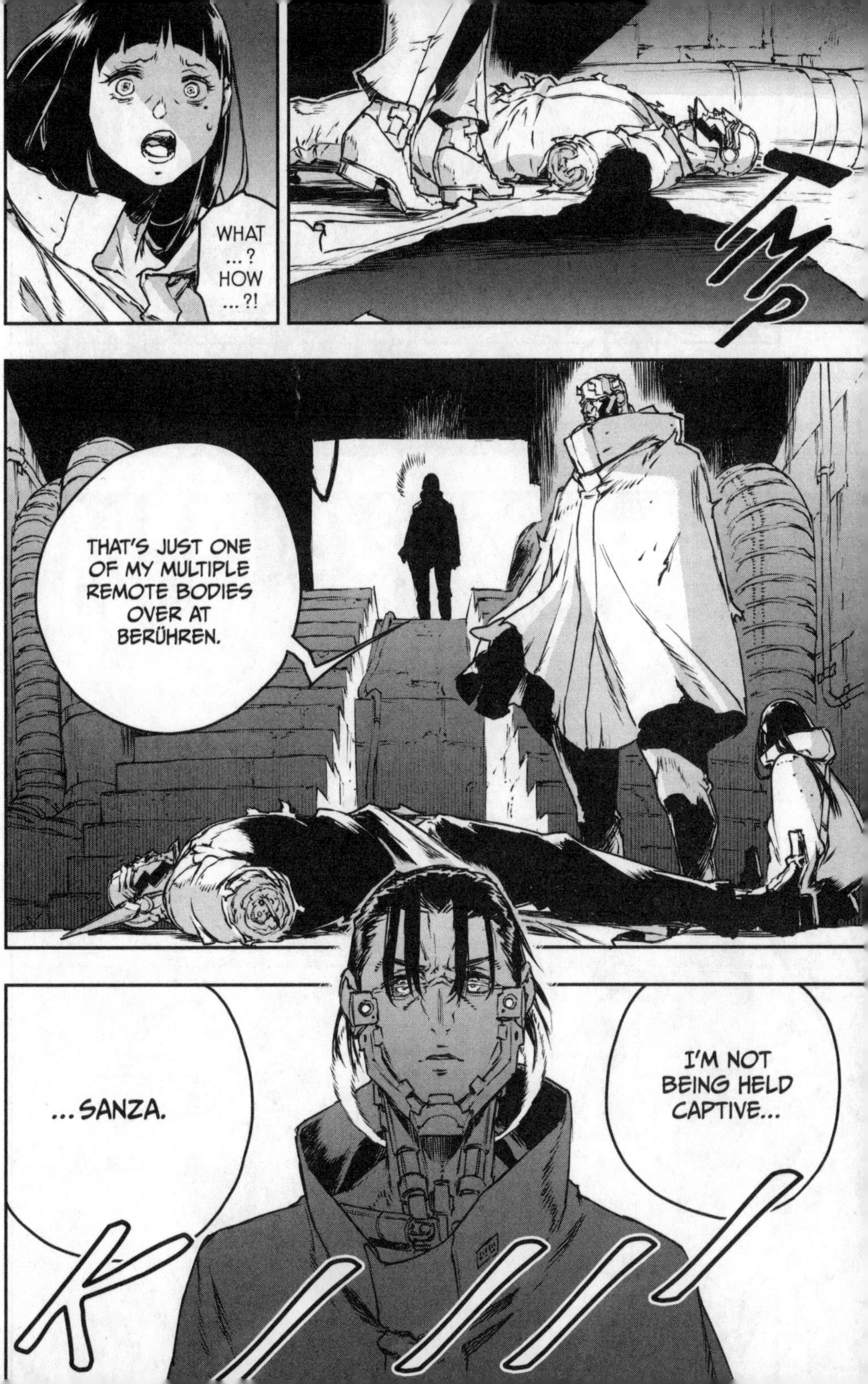
TMP
WHAT ...? HOW ...?!
THAT'S JUST ONE OF MY MULTIPLE REMOTE BODIES OVER AT BERÜHREN.
I'M NOT BEING HELD CAPTIVE...
...SANZA.

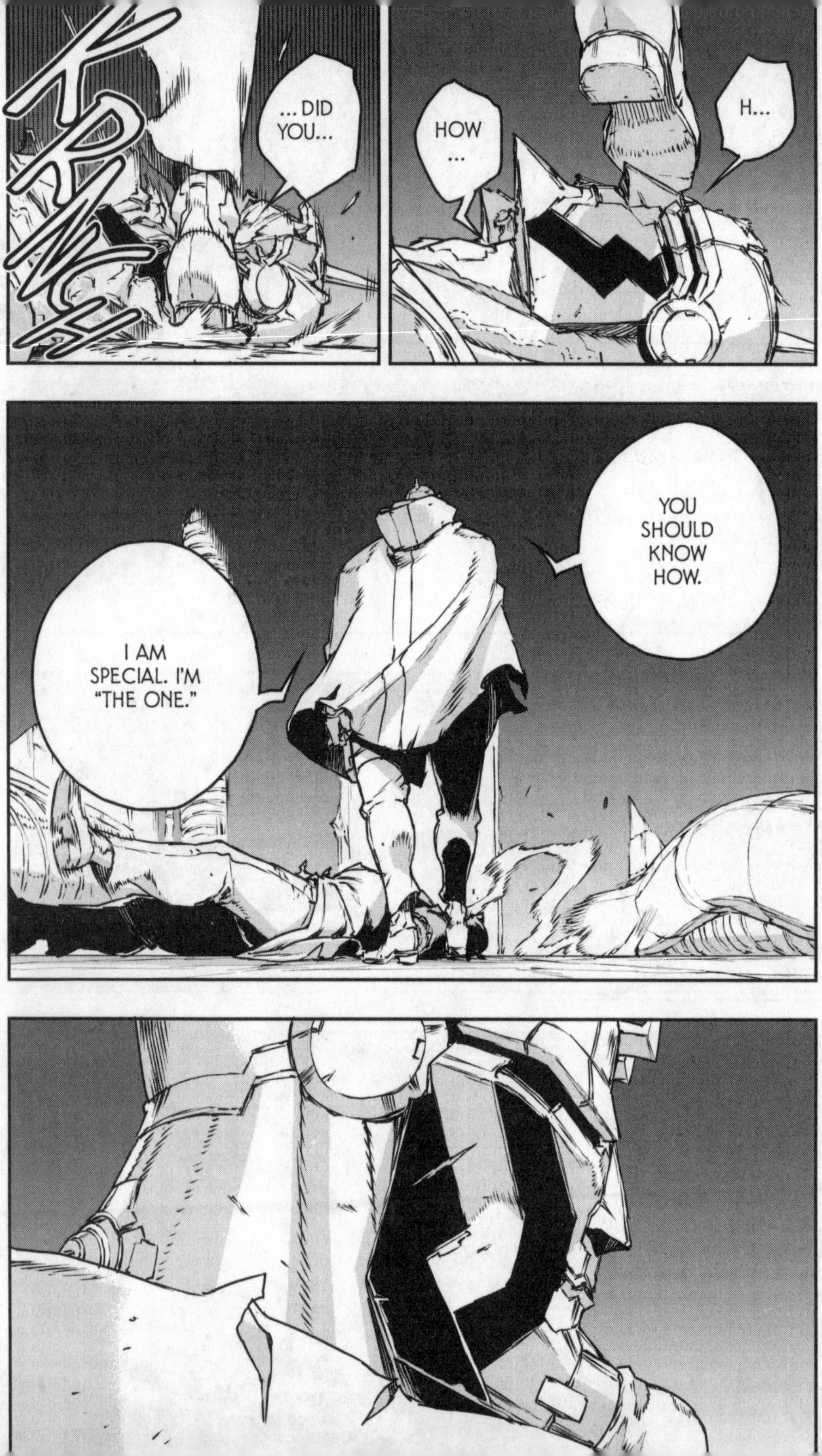
H...
HOW ...
... DID YOU...
KRNCH
YOU SHOULD KNOW HOW.
I AM SPECIAL. I'M "THE ONE."

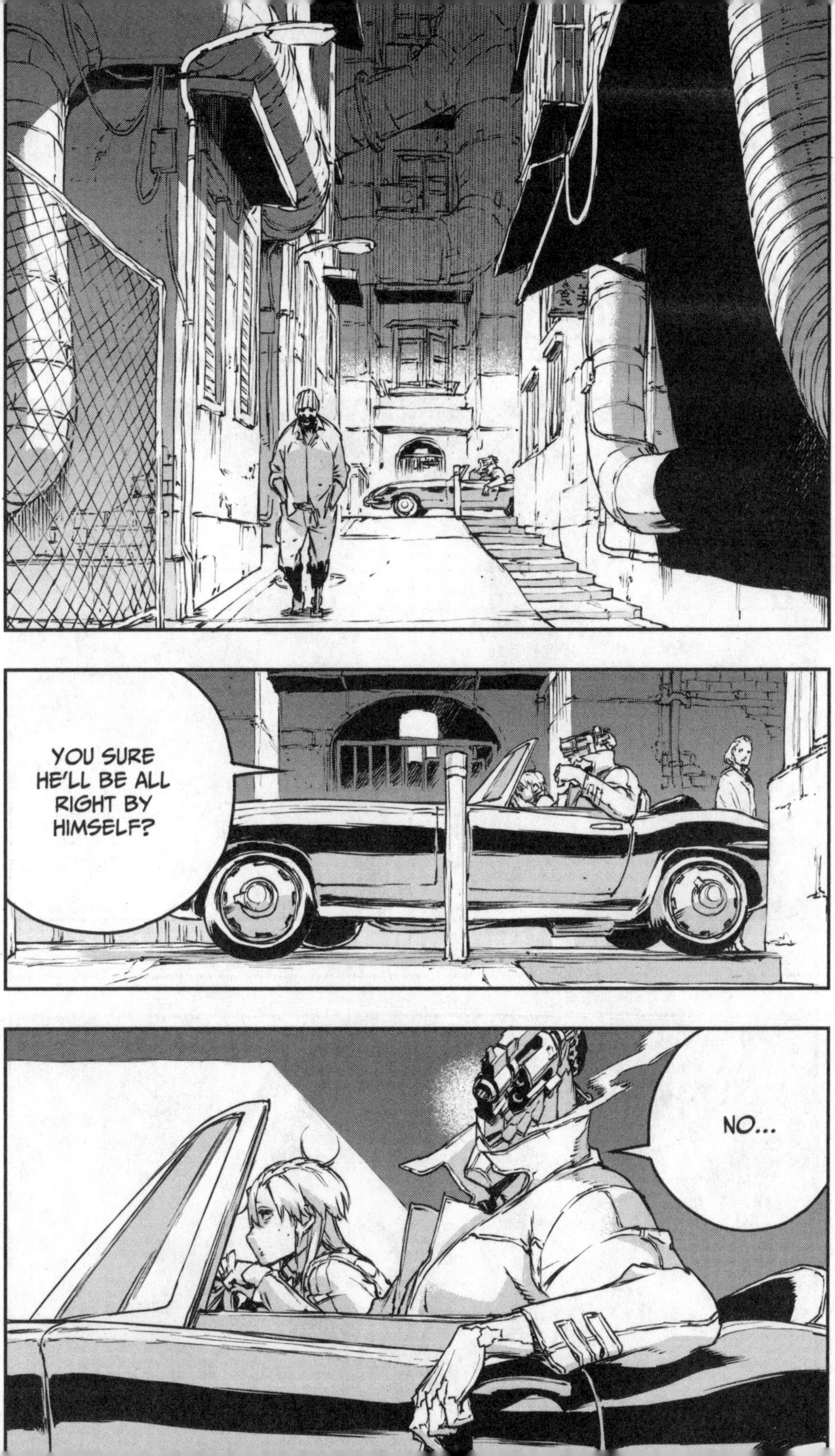
YOU SURE HE'LL BE ALL RIGHT BY HIMSELF?
NO...

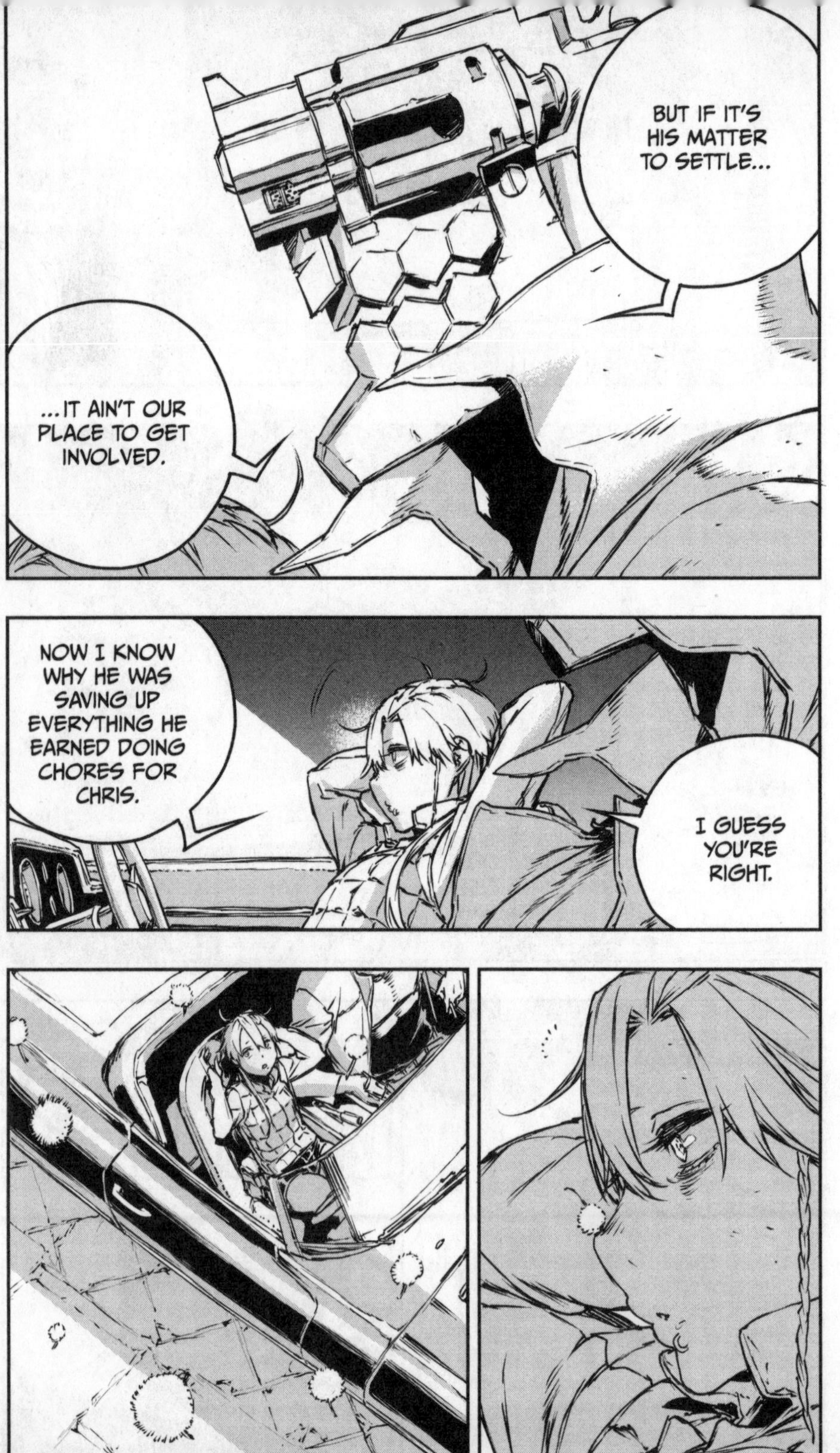
BUT IF IT'S HIS MATTER TO SETTLE...
...IT AIN'T OUR PLACE TO GET INVOLVED.
NOW I KNOW WHY HE WAS SAVING UP EVERYTHING HE EARNED DOING CHORES FOR CHRIS.
I GUESS YOU'RE RIGHT.

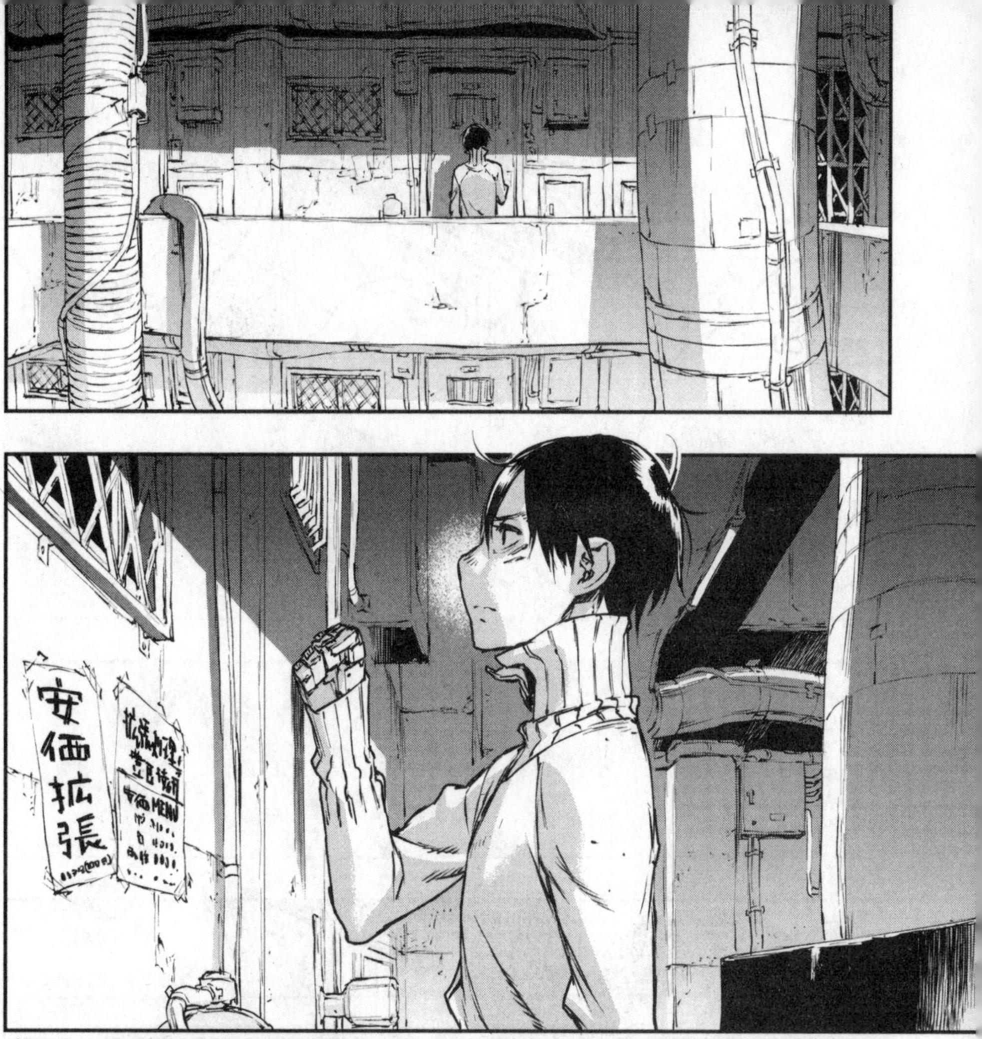
安価拡張
MENU
*Discount Extensions *Extension Repair

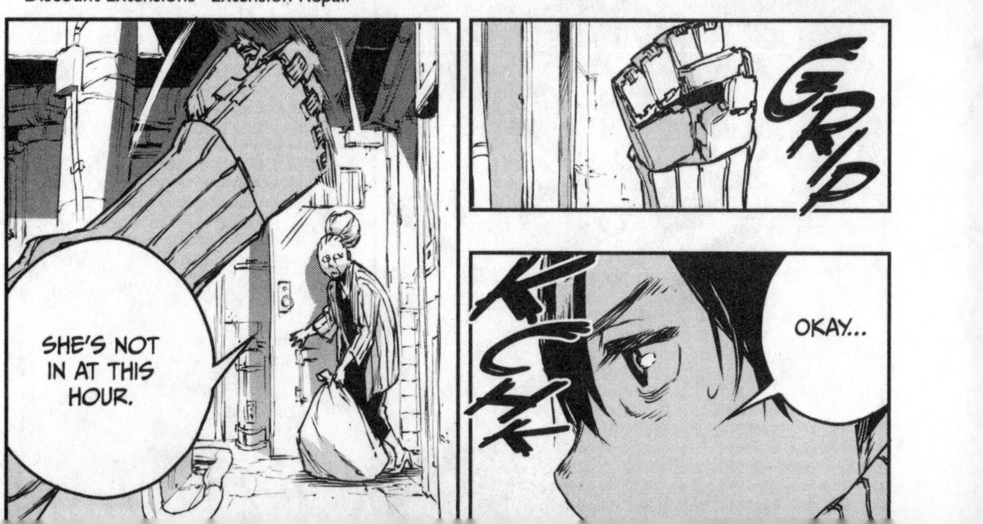
GRIP
KTCHK
OKAY...
SHE'S NOT IN AT THIS HOUR.

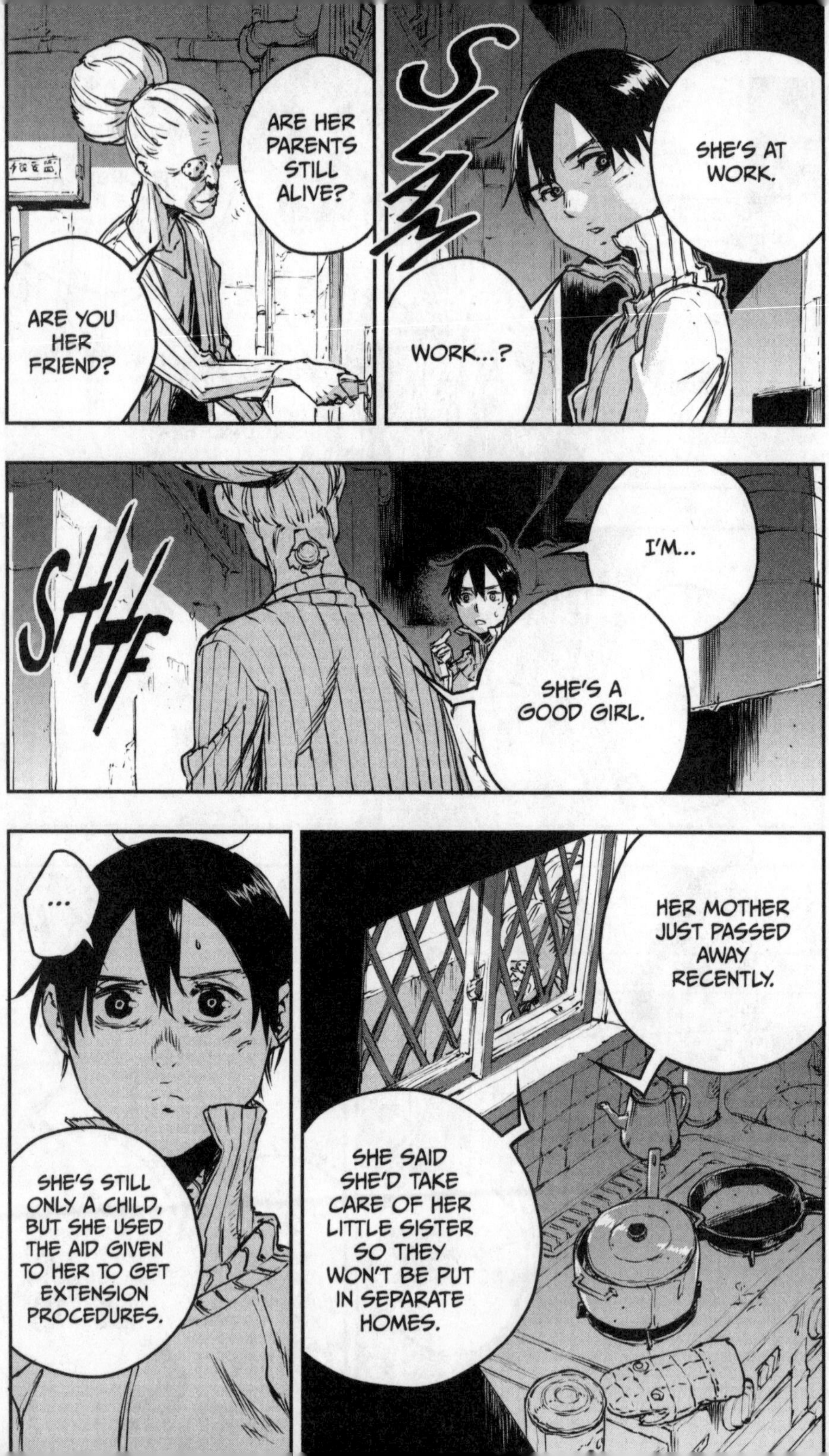
SHE'S AT WORK.
SLAM
WORK...?
ARE HER PARENTS STILL ALIVE?
ARE YOU HER FRIEND?
I'M...
SHE'S A GOOD GIRL.
SHHF
HER MOTHER JUST PASSED AWAY RECENTLY.
SHE SAID SHE'D TAKE CARE OF HER LITTLE SISTER SO THEY WON'T BE PUT IN SEPARATE HOMES.
...
SHE'S STILL ONLY A CHILD, BUT SHE USED THE AID GIVEN TO HER TO GET EXTENSION PROCEDURES.

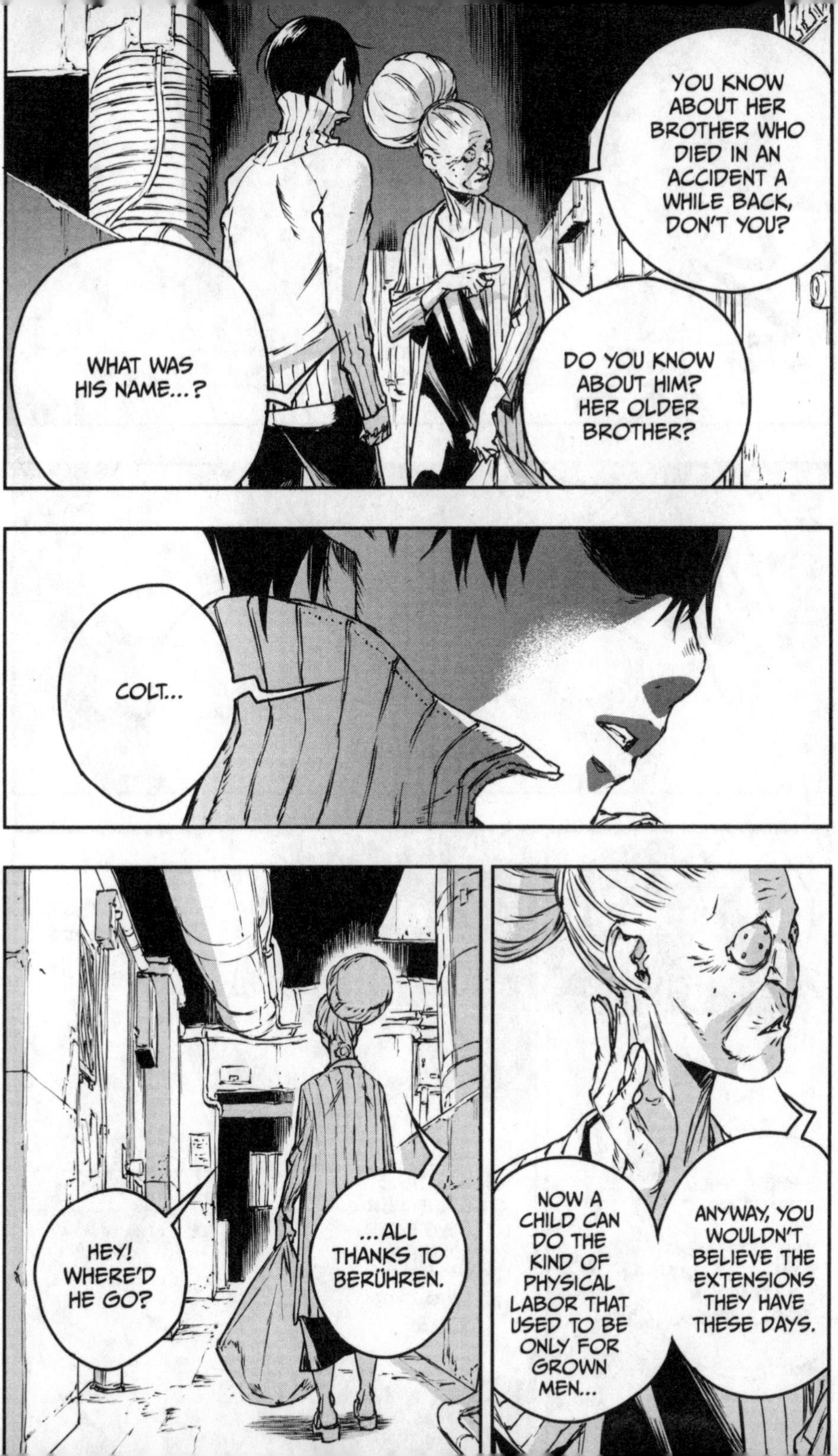
YOU KNOW ABOUT HER BROTHER WHO DIED IN AN ACCIDENT A WHILE BACK, DON'T YOU?
DO YOU KNOW ABOUT HIM? HER OLDER BROTHER?
WHAT WAS HIS NAME...?
COLT...
ANYWAY, YOU WOULDN'T BELIEVE THE EXTENSIONS THEY HAVE THESE DAYS.
NOW A CHILD CAN DO THE KIND OF PHYSICAL LABOR THAT USED TO BE ONLY FOR GROWN MEN...
...ALL THANKS TO BERÜHREN.
HEY! WHERE'D HE GO?

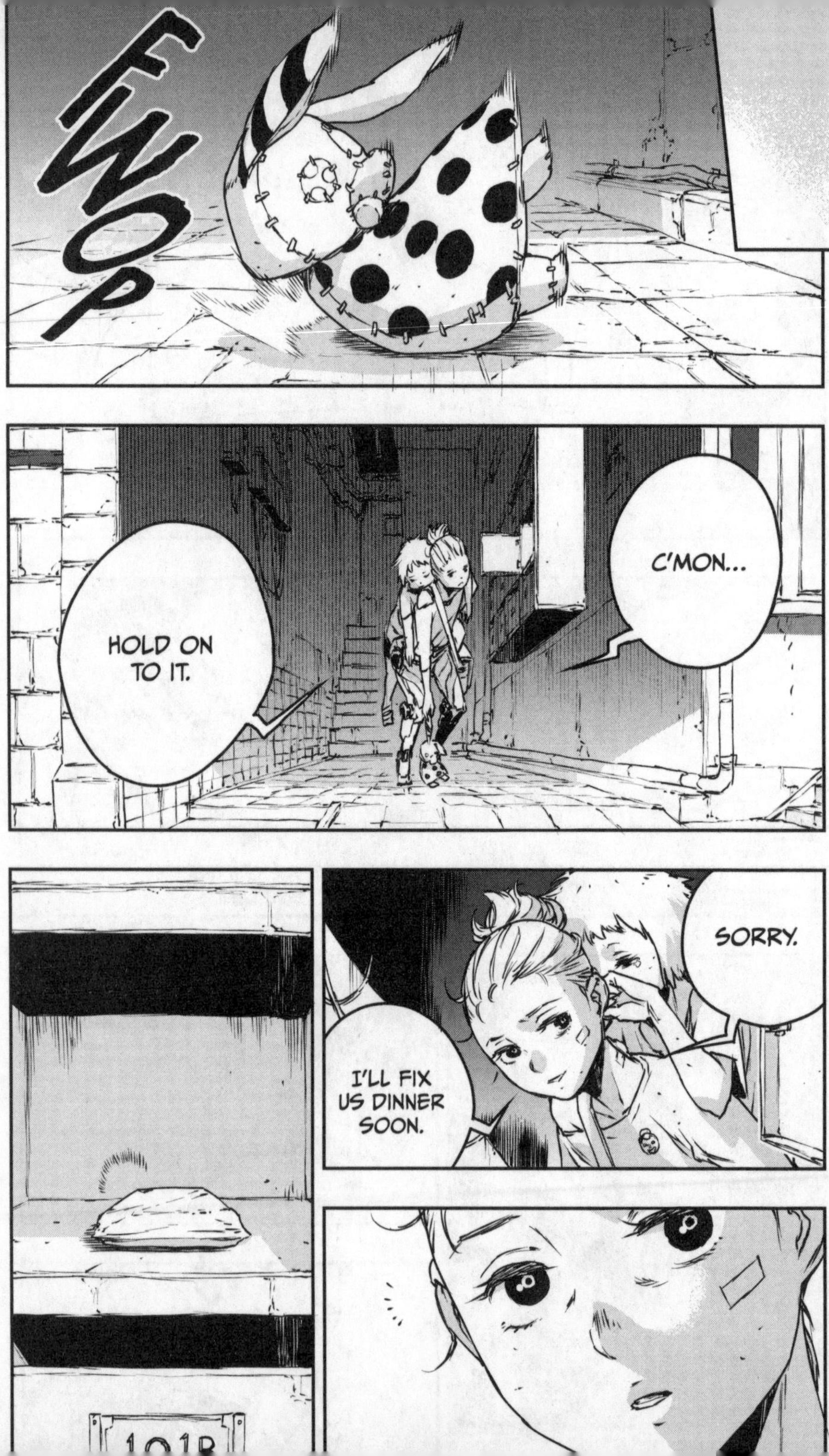
FWOP
C'MON...
HOLD ON TO IT.
SORRY.
I'LL FIX US DINNER SOON.

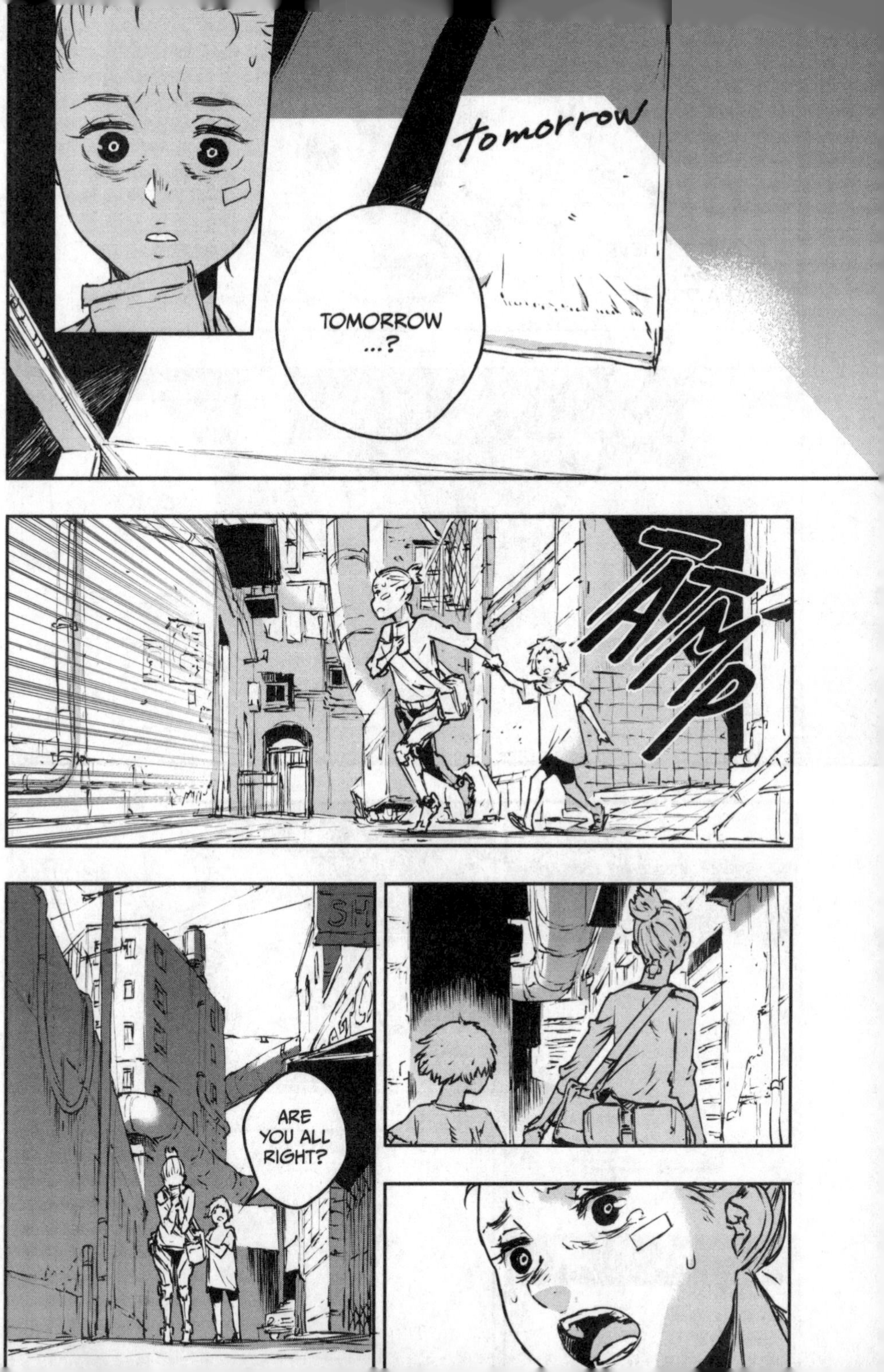
tomorrow
TOMORROW ...?
TAMP
ARE YOU ALL RIGHT?

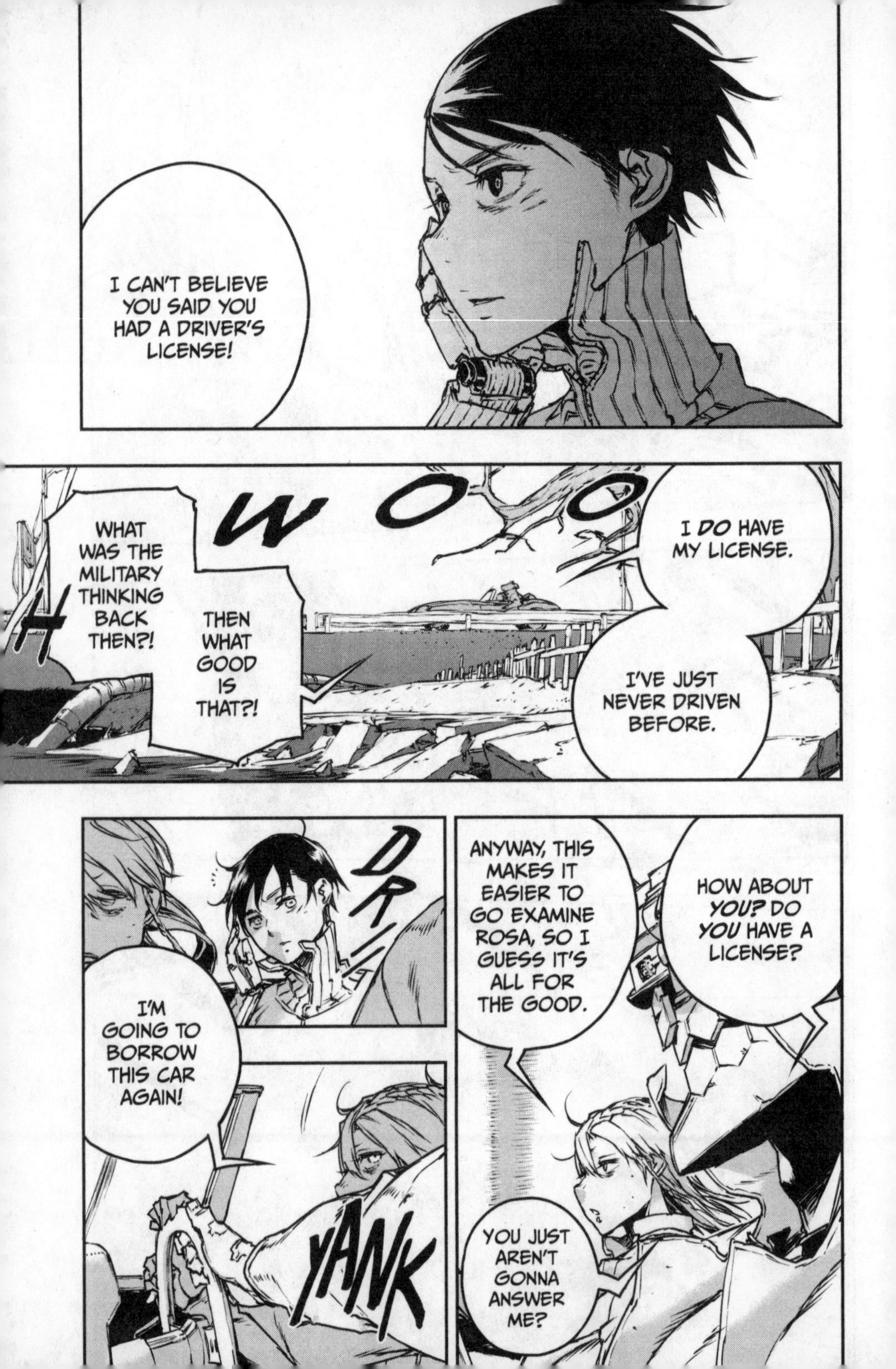

I CAN'T BELIEVE YOU SAID YOU HAD A DRIVER'S LICENSE!
I *DO* HAVE MY LICENSE.
I'VE JUST NEVER DRIVEN BEFORE.
WOOH
THEN WHAT GOOD IS THAT?!
WHAT WAS THE MILITARY THINKING BACK THEN?!
HOW ABOUT *YOU?* DO *YOU* HAVE A LICENSE?
ANYWAY, THIS MAKES IT EASIER TO GO EXAMINE ROSA, SO I GUESS IT'S ALL FOR THE GOOD.
YOU JUST AREN'T GONNA ANSWER ME?
DR
I'M GOING TO BORROW THIS CAR AGAIN!
YANK

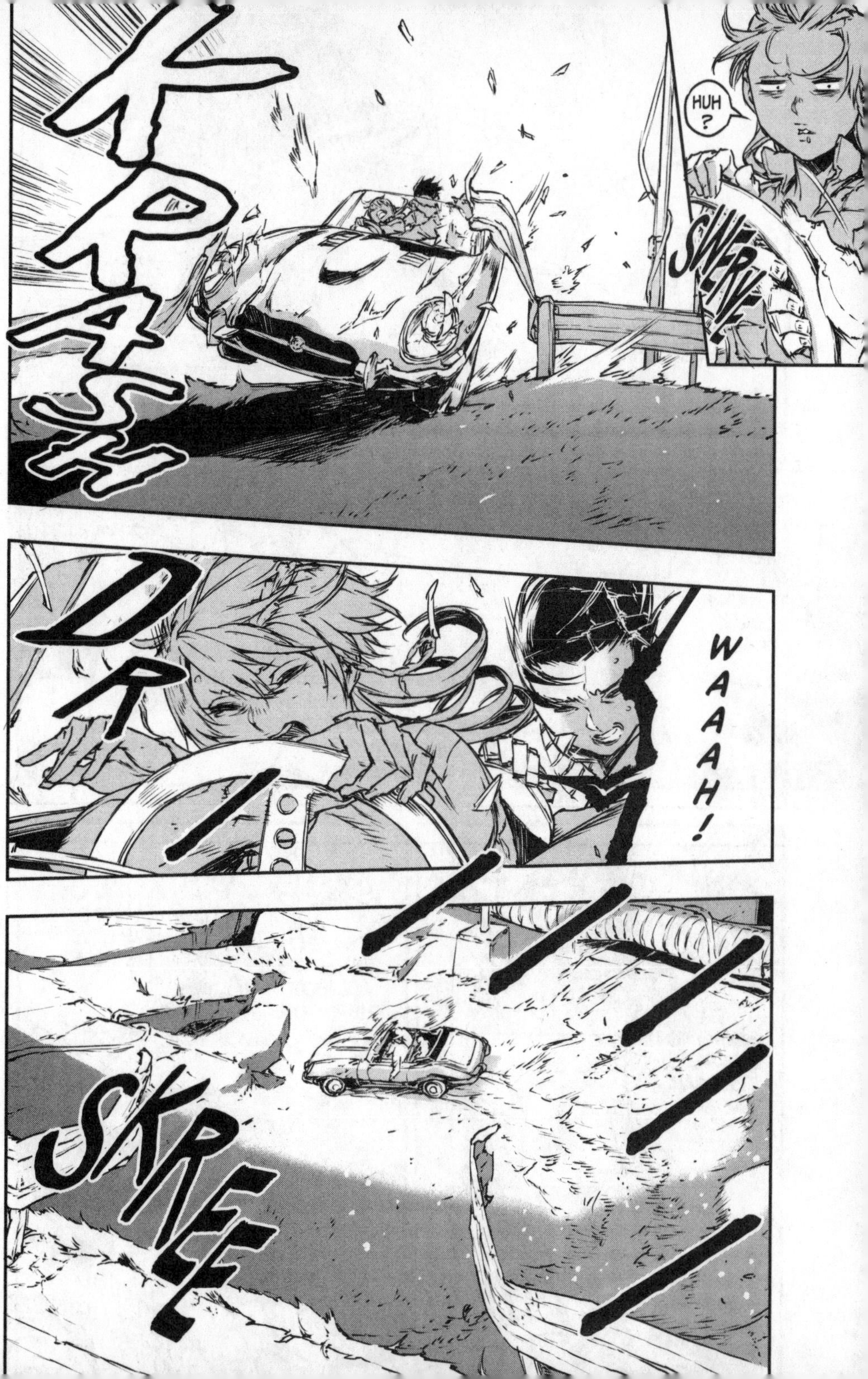
HUH?
SWERV
KRASH
WAAAAH!
DR
SKREE

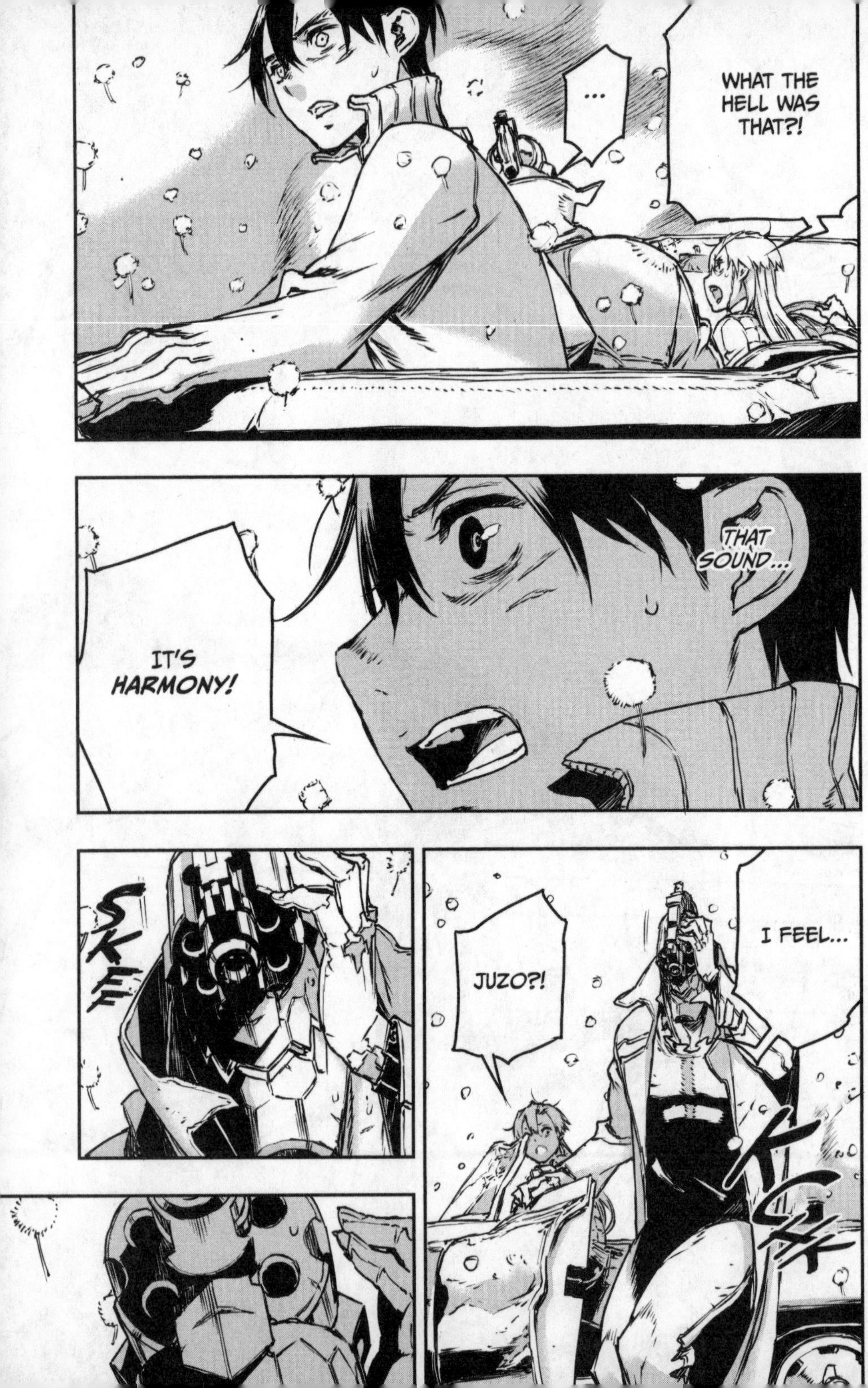
WHAT THE HELL WAS THAT?!
...
THAT SOUND...
IT'S HARMONY!
I FEEL...
KCHK
JUZO?!
SKEF

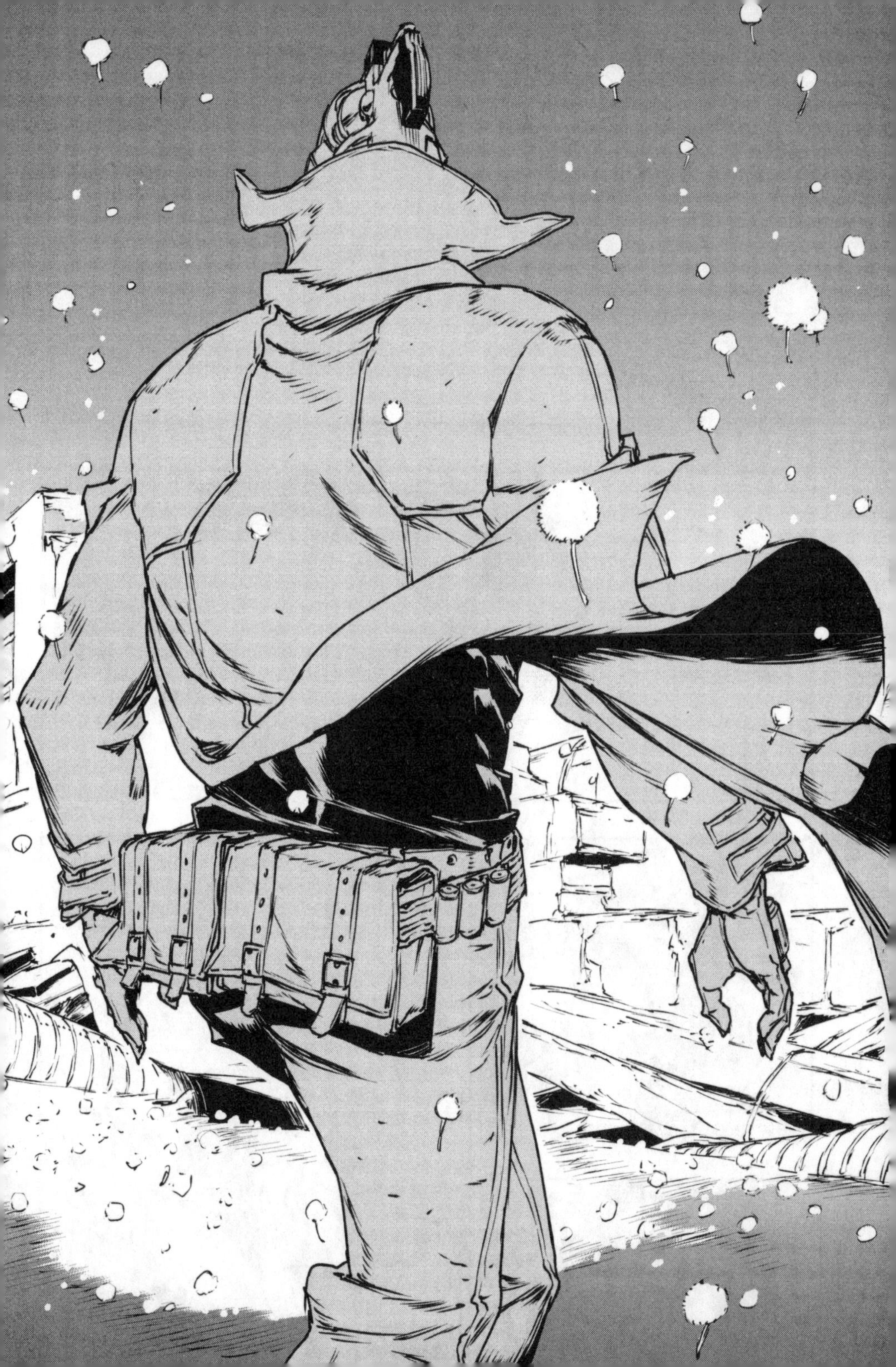

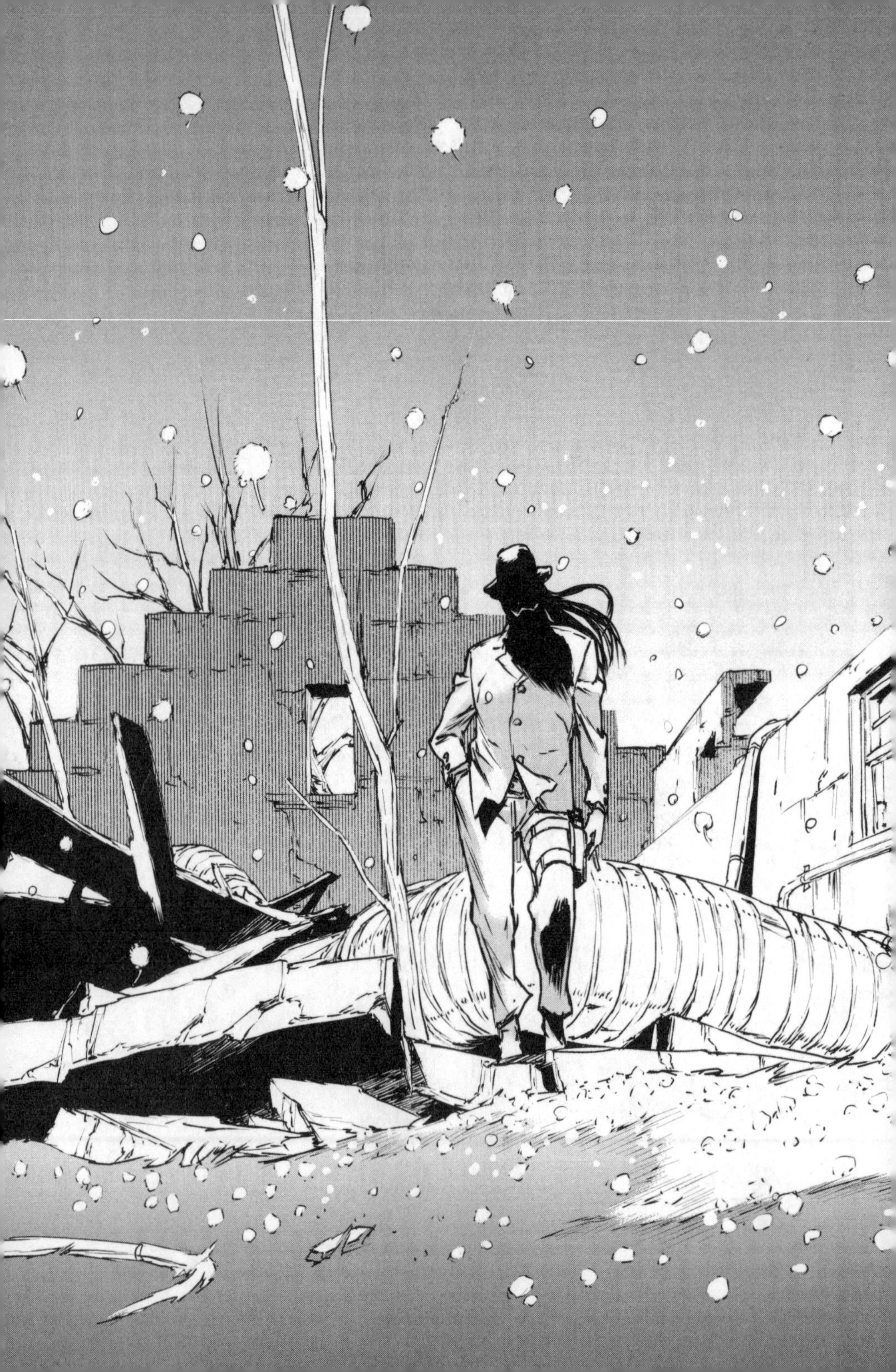

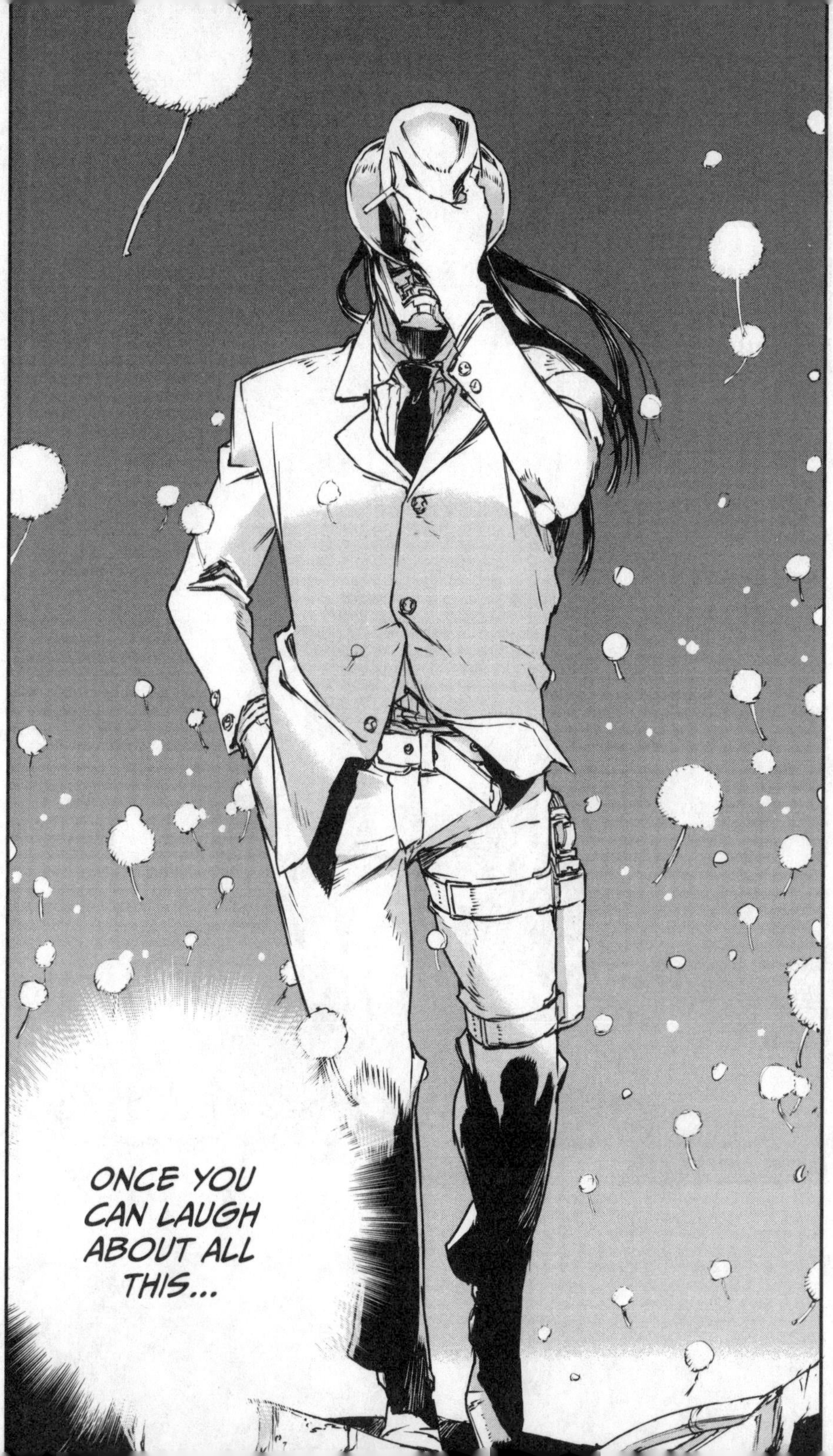
ONCE YOU CAN LAUGH ABOUT ALL THIS...

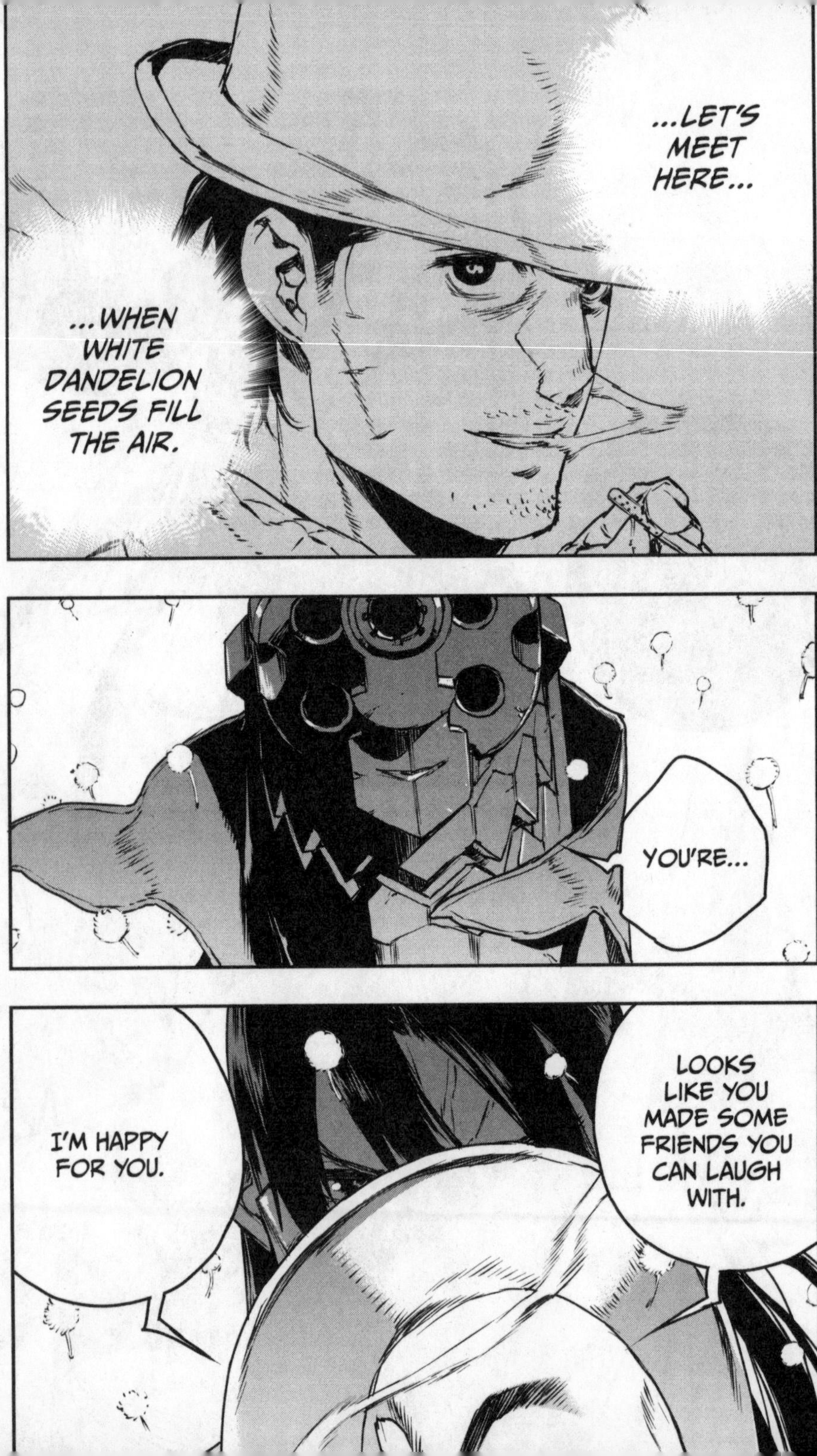
...LET'S MEET HERE...
...WHEN WHITE DANDELION SEEDS FILL THE AIR.
YOU'RE...
LOOKS LIKE YOU MADE SOME FRIENDS YOU CAN LAUGH WITH.
I'M HAPPY FOR YOU.

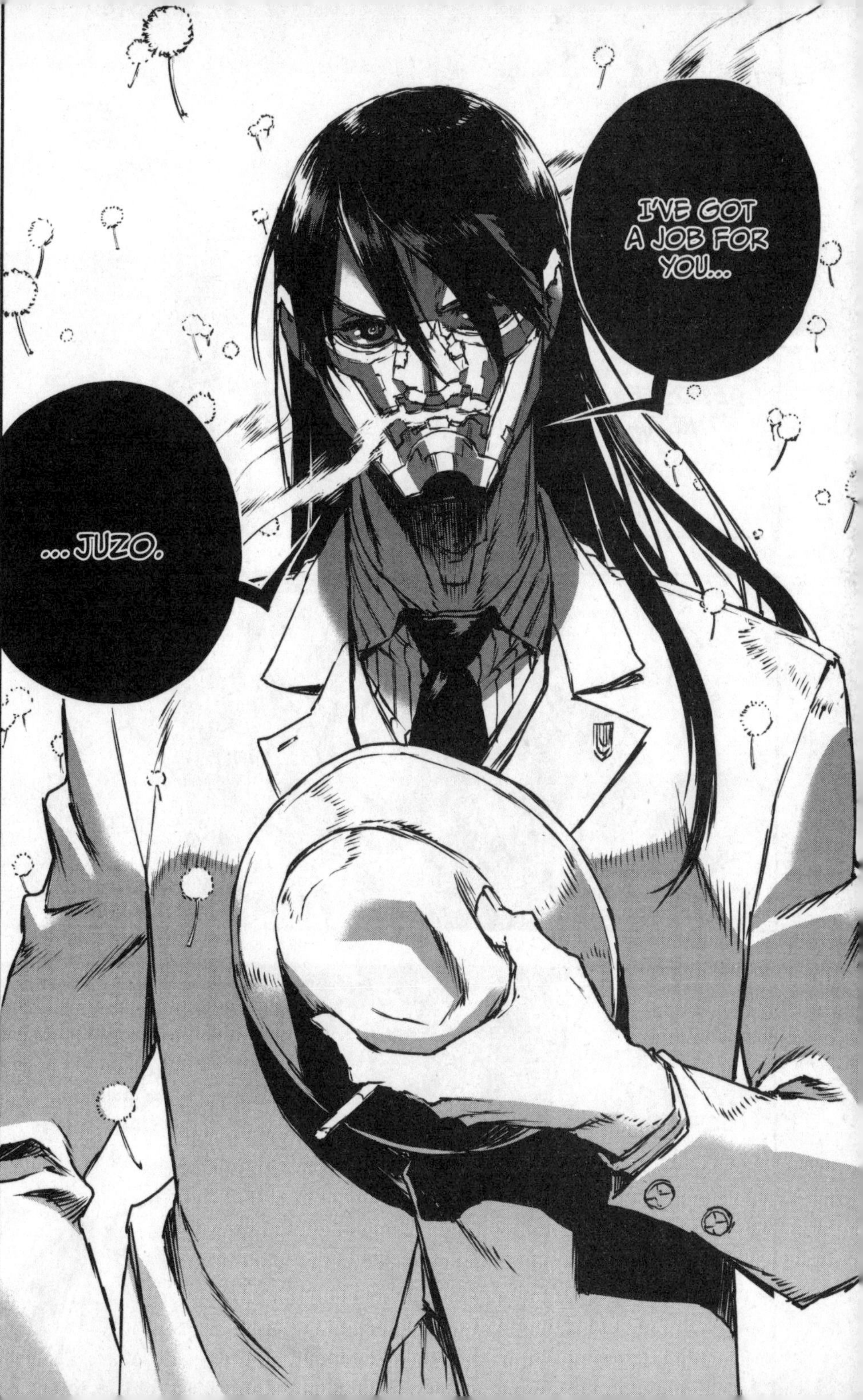
I'VE GOT A JOB FOR YOU...
...JUZO.

NO GUNS LIFE

The gunsmoke drifts, the muzzle talks

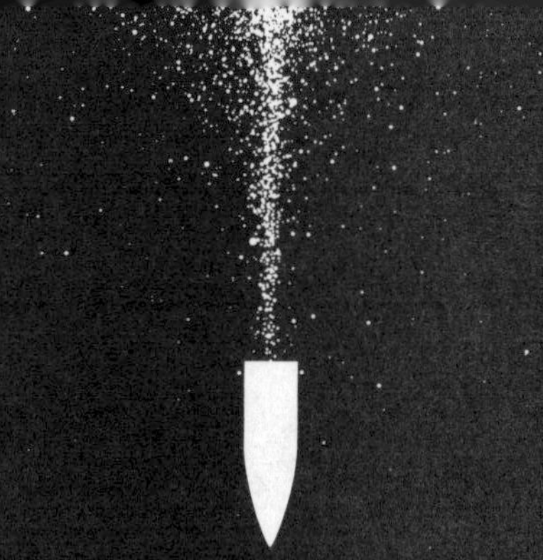

NO GUNS LIFE

The gunsmoke drifts, the muzzle talks

Chapter 68
Partner

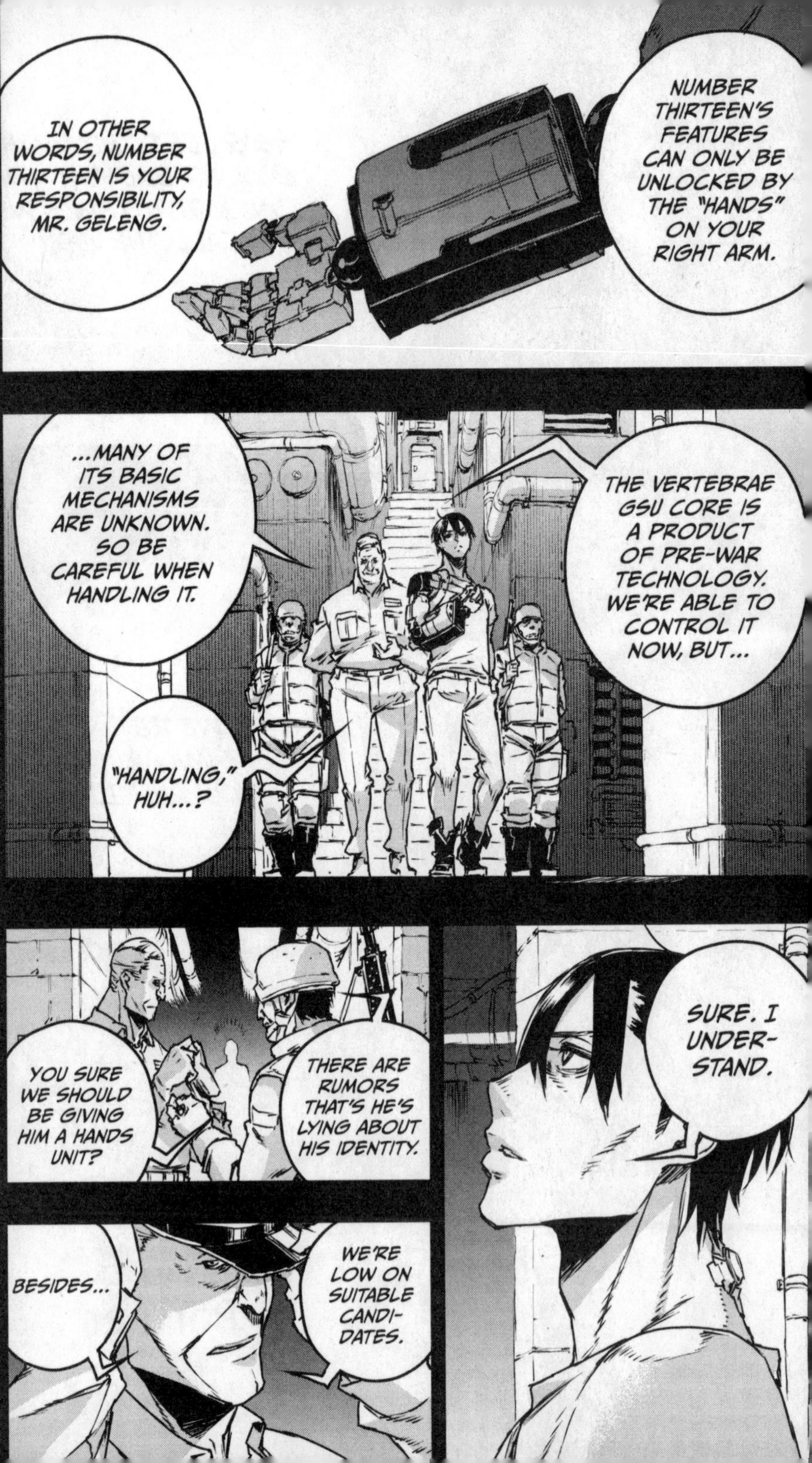
NUMBER THIRTEEN'S FEATURES CAN ONLY BE UNLOCKED BY THE "HANDS" ON YOUR RIGHT ARM.
IN OTHER WORDS, NUMBER THIRTEEN IS YOUR RESPONSIBILITY, MR. GELENG.
THE VERTEBRAE GSU CORE IS A PRODUCT OF PRE-WAR TECHNOLOGY. WE'RE ABLE TO CONTROL IT NOW, BUT...
...MANY OF ITS BASIC MECHANISMS ARE UNKNOWN. SO BE CAREFUL WHEN HANDLING IT.
"HANDLING," HUH...?
SURE. I UNDER-STAND.
THERE ARE RUMORS THAT'S HE'S LYING ABOUT HIS IDENTITY.
YOU SURE WE SHOULD BE GIVING HIM A HANDS UNIT?
BESIDES...
WE'RE LOW ON SUITABLE CANDI-DATES.

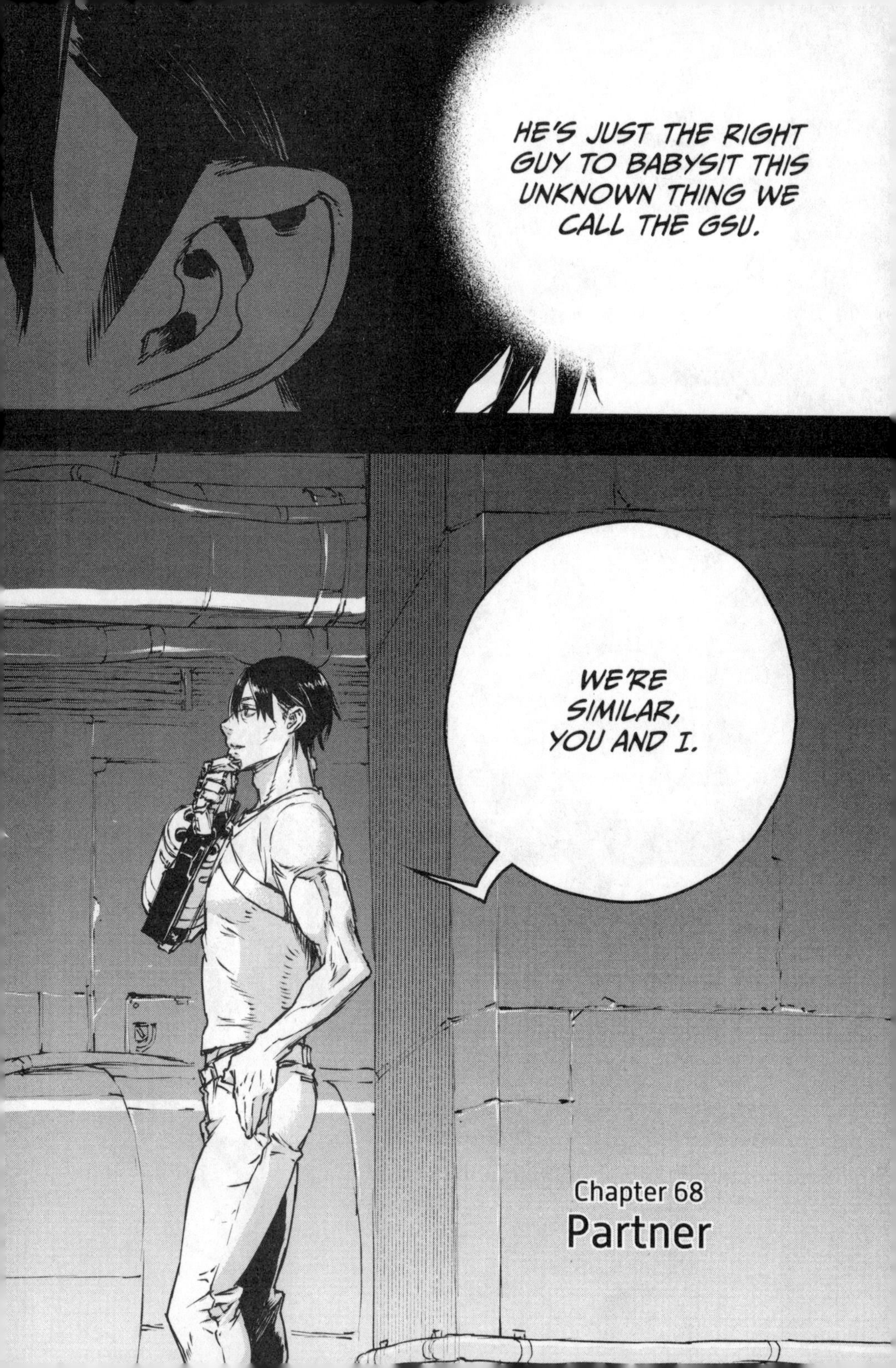
HE'S JUST THE RIGHT GUY TO BABYSIT THIS UNKNOWN THING WE CALL THE GSU.
WE'RE SIMILAR, YOU AND I.
Chapter 68
Partner

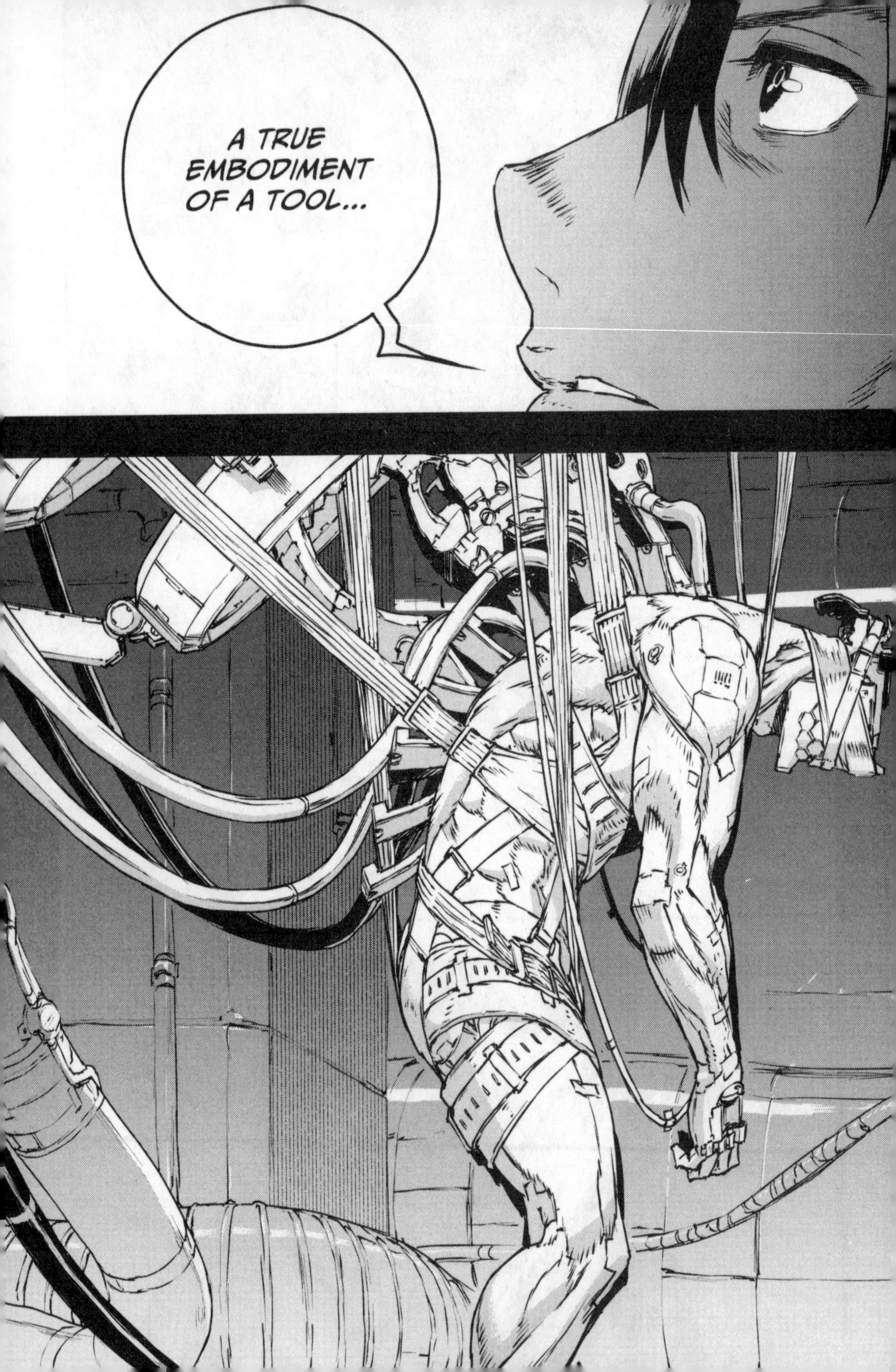
A TRUE EMBODIMENT OF A TOOL...

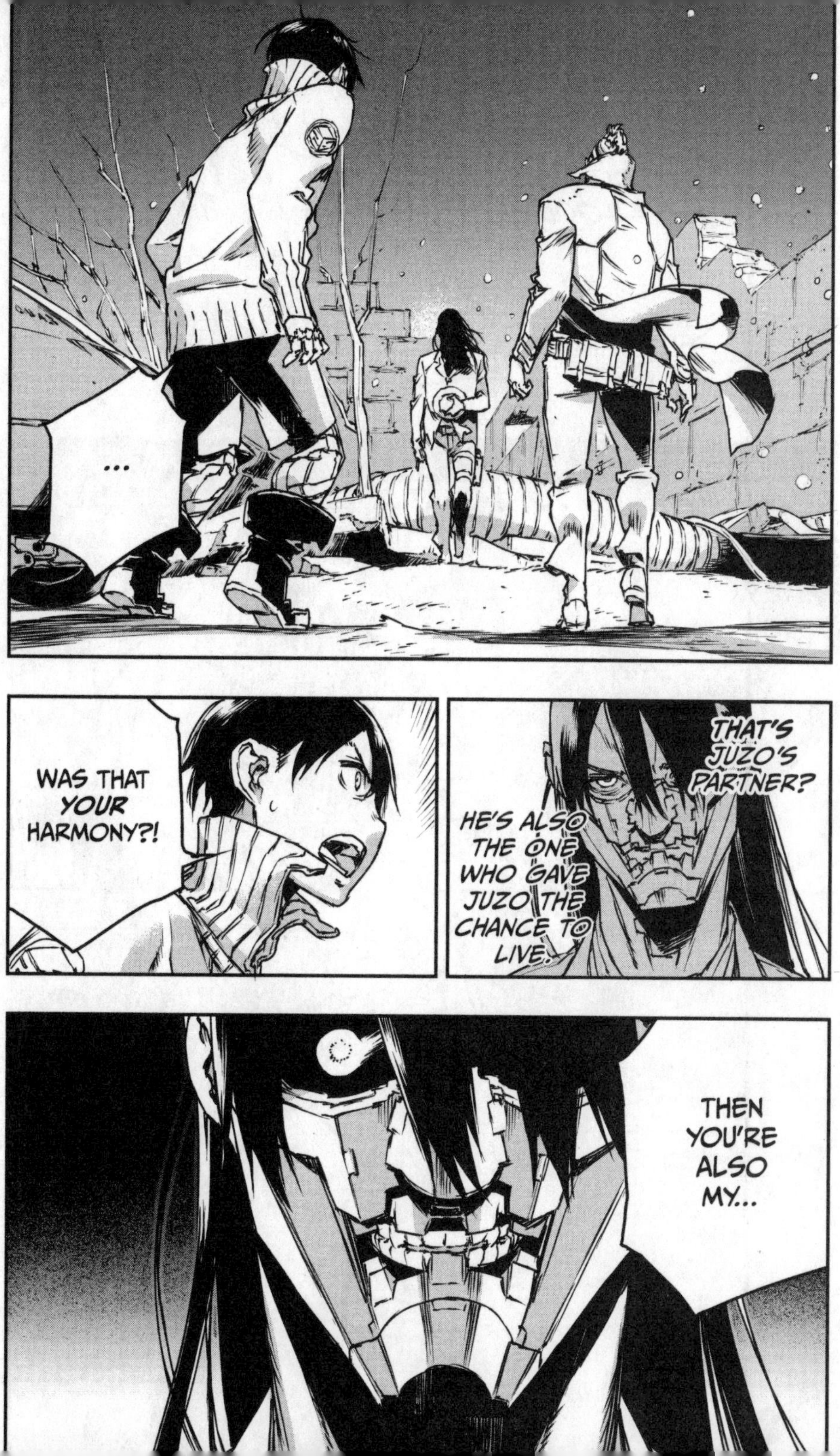
...
THAT'S JUZO'S PARTNER?
HE'S ALSO THE ONE WHO GAVE JUZO THE CHANCE TO LIVE.
WAS THAT YOUR HARMONY?!
THEN YOU'RE ALSO MY...

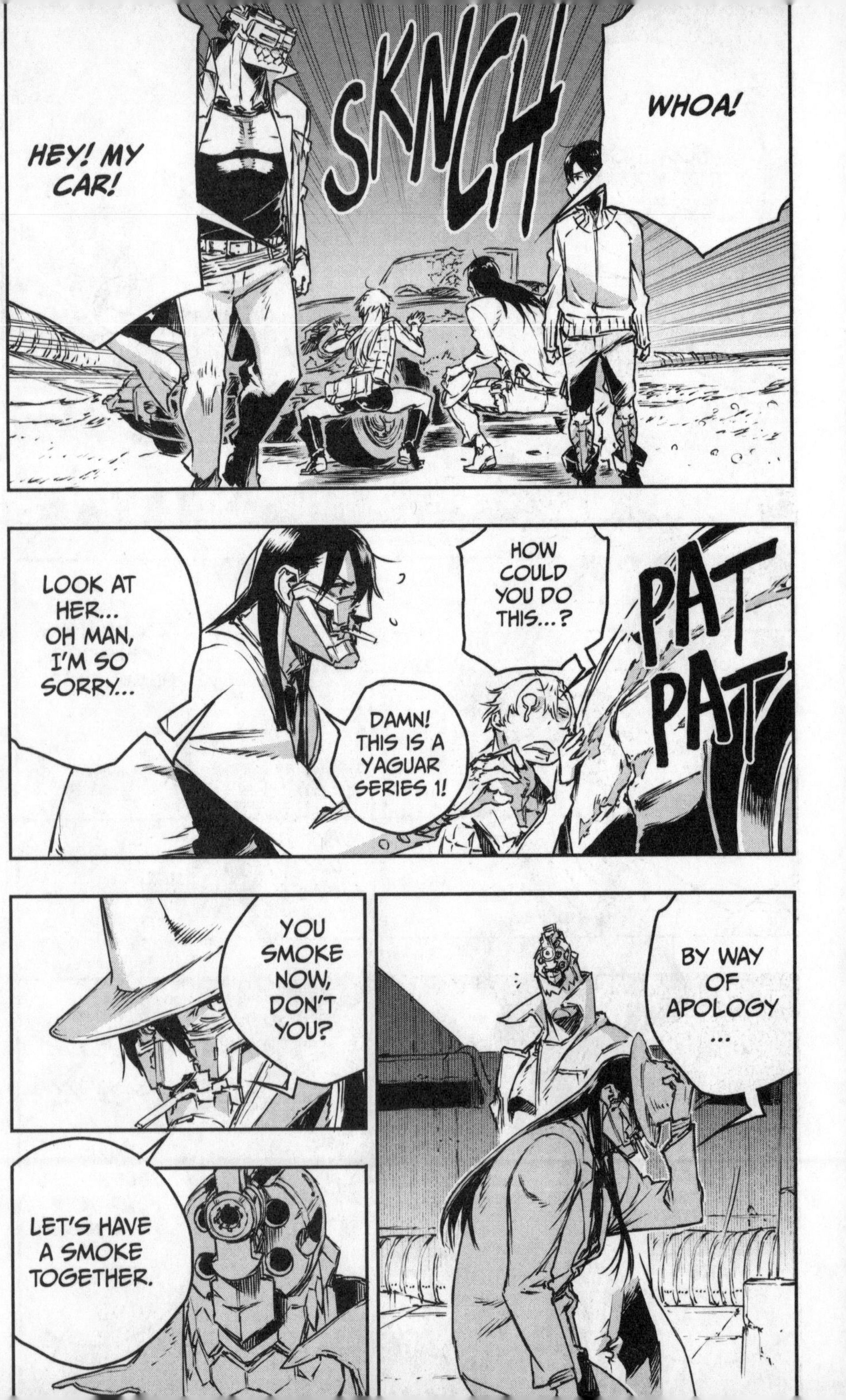
WHOA!
SKNCH
HEY! MY CAR!
PAT PAT
HOW COULD YOU DO THIS...?
LOOK AT HER... OH MAN, I'M SO SORRY...
DAMN! THIS IS A YAGUAR SERIES 1!
BY WAY OF APOLOGY...
YOU SMOKE NOW, DON'T YOU?
LET'S HAVE A SMOKE TOGETHER.

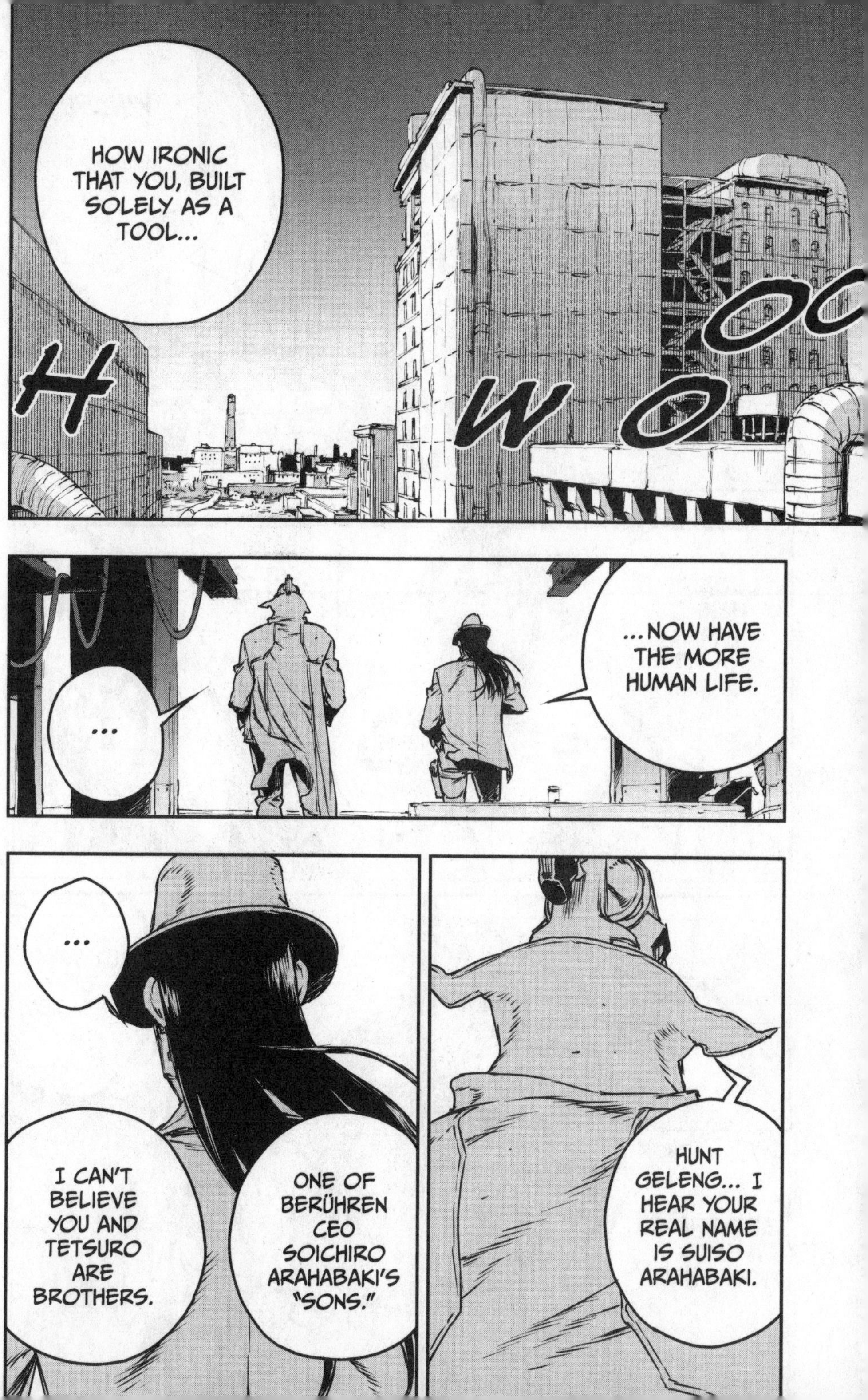
HOW IRONIC THAT YOU, BUILT SOLELY AS A TOOL...
HWOOOO
...NOW HAVE THE MORE HUMAN LIFE.
...
HUNT GELENG... I HEAR YOUR REAL NAME IS SUISO ARAHABAKI.
...
ONE OF BERÜHREN CEO SOICHIRO ARAHABAKI'S "SONS."
I CAN'T BELIEVE YOU AND TETSURO ARE BROTHERS.

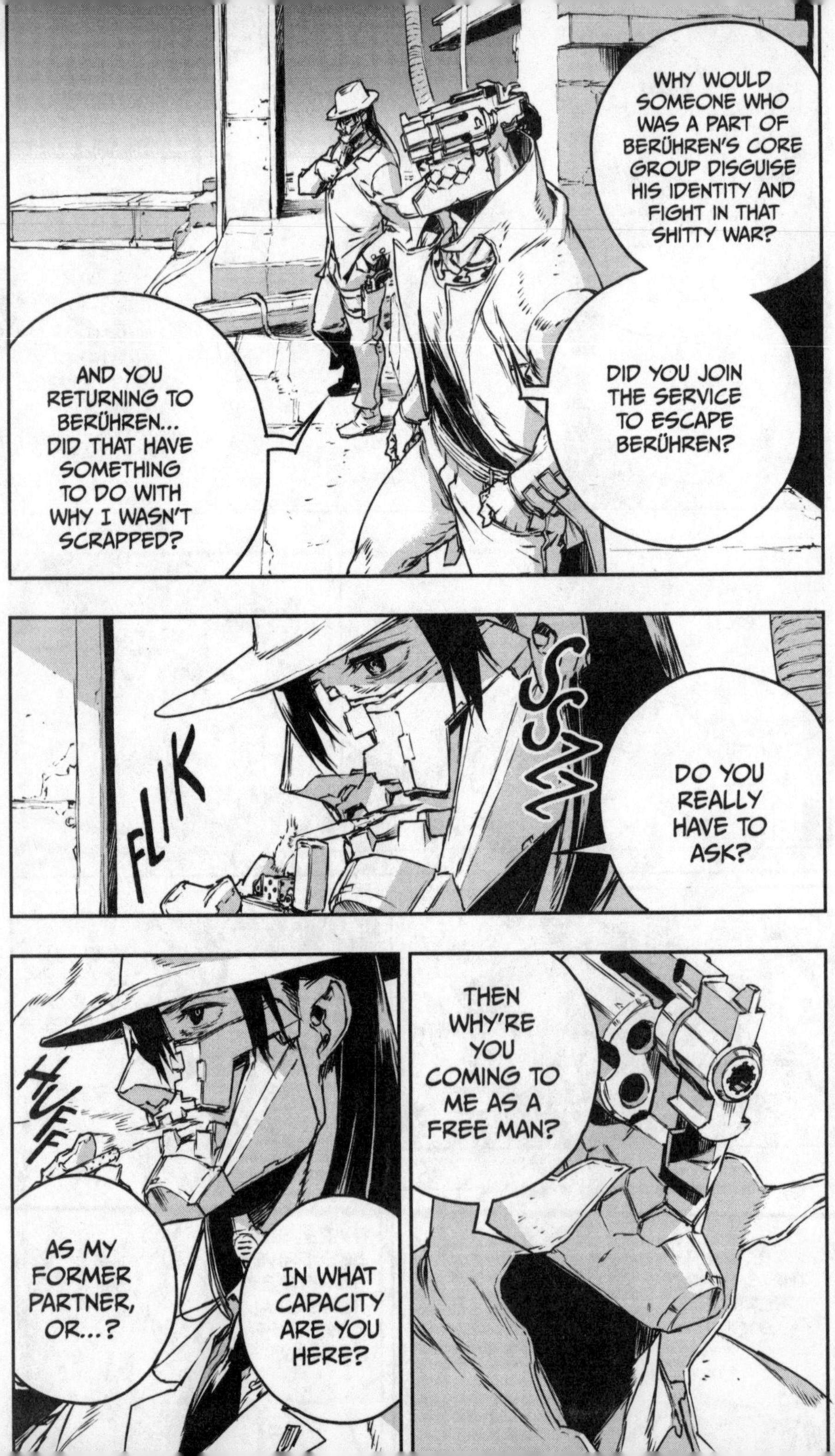
WHY WOULD SOMEONE WHO WAS A PART OF BERÜHREN'S CORE GROUP DISGUISE HIS IDENTITY AND FIGHT IN THAT SHITTY WAR?
DID YOU JOIN THE SERVICE TO ESCAPE BERÜHREN?
AND YOU RETURNING TO BERÜHREN... DID THAT HAVE SOMETHING TO DO WITH WHY I WASN'T SCRAPPED?
DO YOU REALLY HAVE TO ASK?
FLIK
THEN WHY'RE YOU COMING TO ME AS A FREE MAN?
HUFF
IN WHAT CAPACITY ARE YOU HERE?
AS MY FORMER PARTNER, OR...?

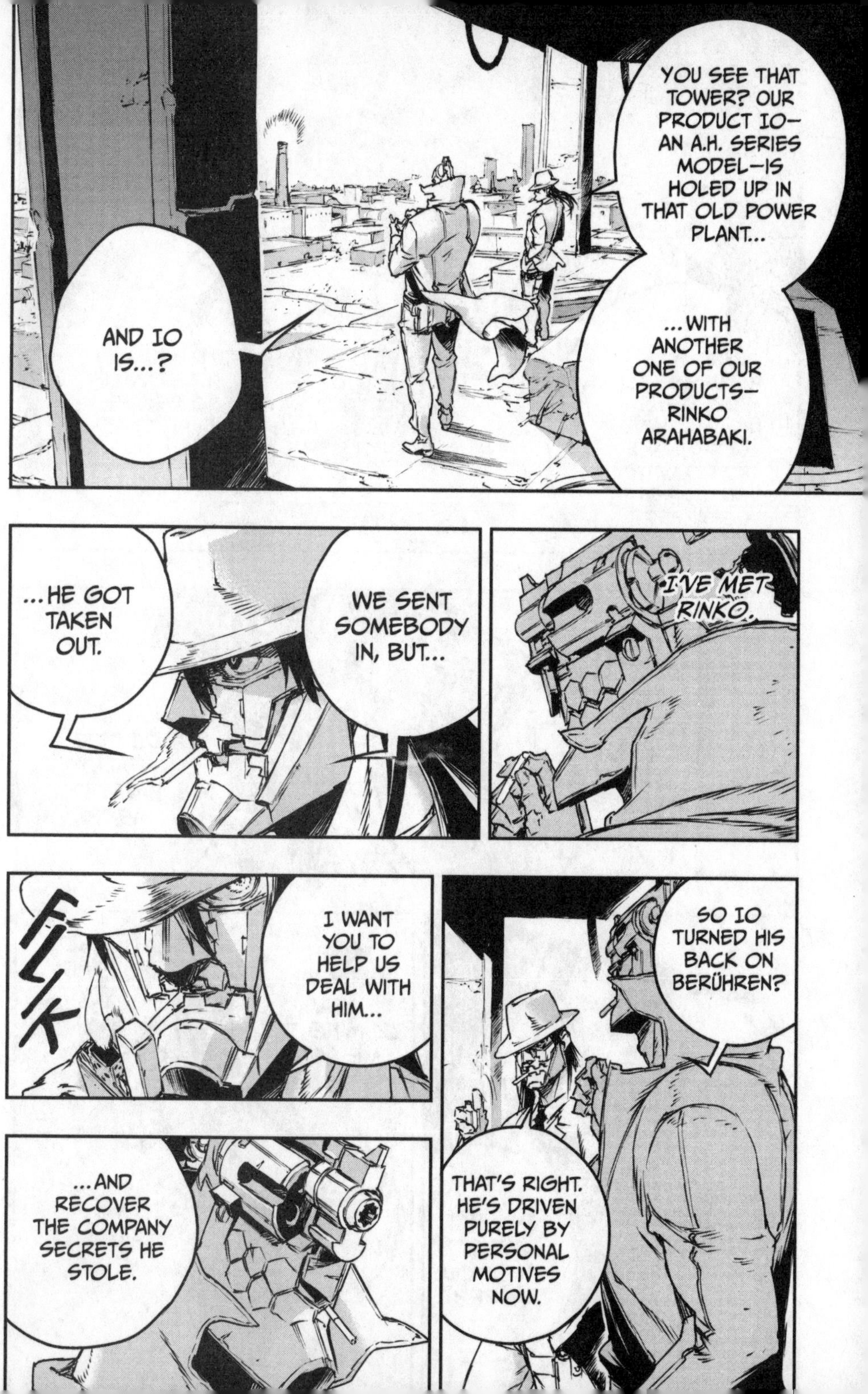
YOU SEE THAT TOWER? OUR PRODUCT IO— AN A.H. SERIES MODEL—IS HOLED UP IN THAT OLD POWER PLANT...
...WITH ANOTHER ONE OF OUR PRODUCTS— RINKO ARAHABAKI.
AND IO IS...?
I'VE MET RINKO.
WE SENT SOMEBODY IN, BUT...
...HE GOT TAKEN OUT.
SO IO TURNED HIS BACK ON BERÜHREN?
THAT'S RIGHT. HE'S DRIVEN PURELY BY PERSONAL MOTIVES NOW.
FLIK
I WANT YOU TO HELP US DEAL WITH HIM...
...AND RECOVER THE COMPANY SECRETS HE STOLE.

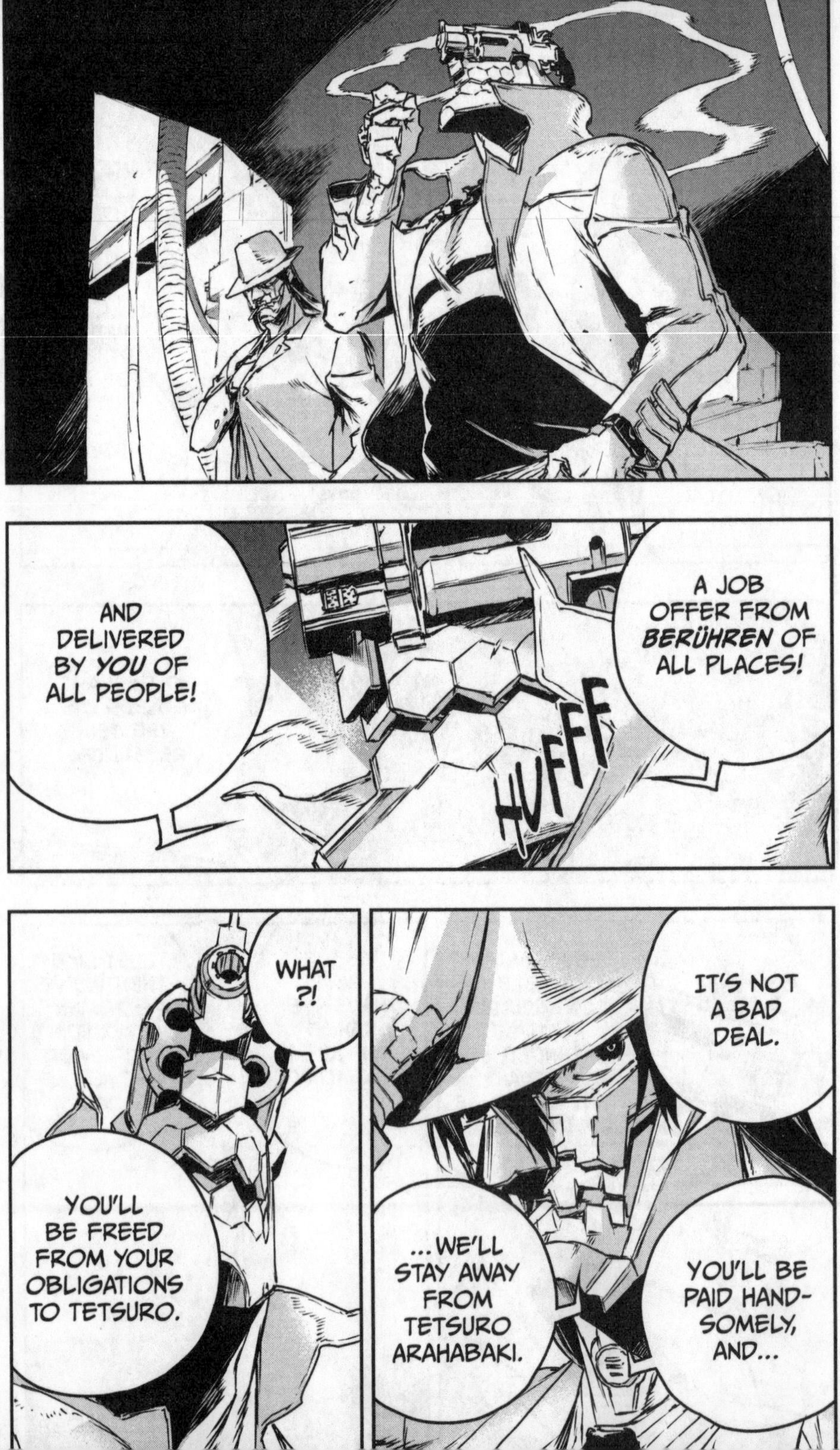
A JOB OFFER FROM BERÜHREN OF ALL PLACES!
HUFFF
AND DELIVERED BY YOU OF ALL PEOPLE!
IT'S NOT A BAD DEAL.
YOU'LL BE PAID HAND-SOMELY, AND...
...WE'LL STAY AWAY FROM TETSURO ARAHABAKI.
WHAT?!
YOU'LL BE FREED FROM YOUR OBLIGATIONS TO TETSURO.

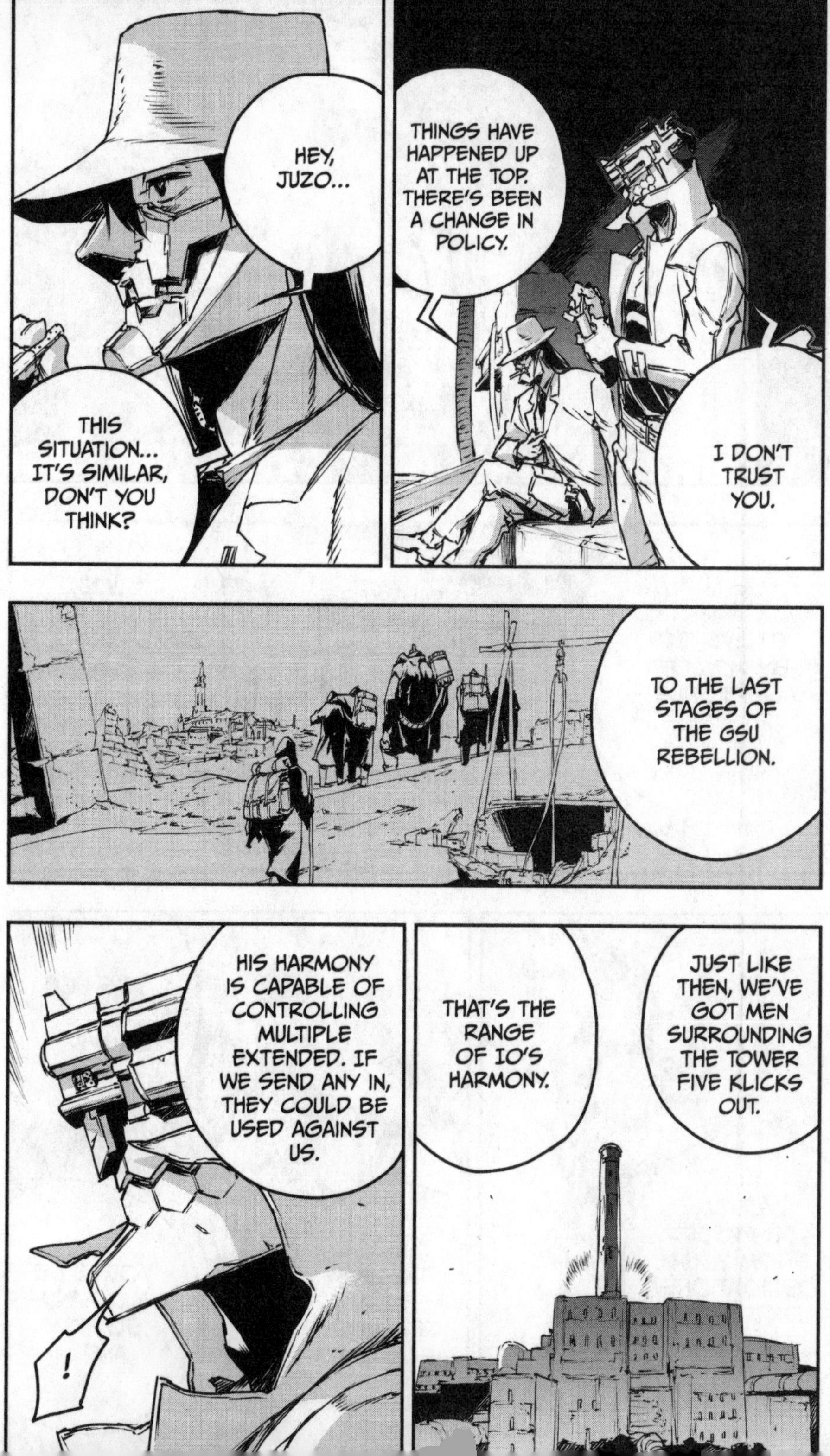
THINGS HAVE HAPPENED UP AT THE TOP. THERE'S BEEN A CHANGE IN POLICY.
I DON'T TRUST YOU.
HEY, JUZO...
THIS SITUATION... IT'S SIMILAR, DON'T YOU THINK?
TO THE LAST STAGES OF THE GSU REBELLION.
JUST LIKE THEN, WE'VE GOT MEN SURROUNDING THE TOWER FIVE KLICKS OUT.
THAT'S THE RANGE OF IO'S HARMONY.
HIS HARMONY IS CAPABLE OF CONTROLLING MULTIPLE EXTENDED. IF WE SEND ANY IN, THEY COULD BE USED AGAINST US.
!

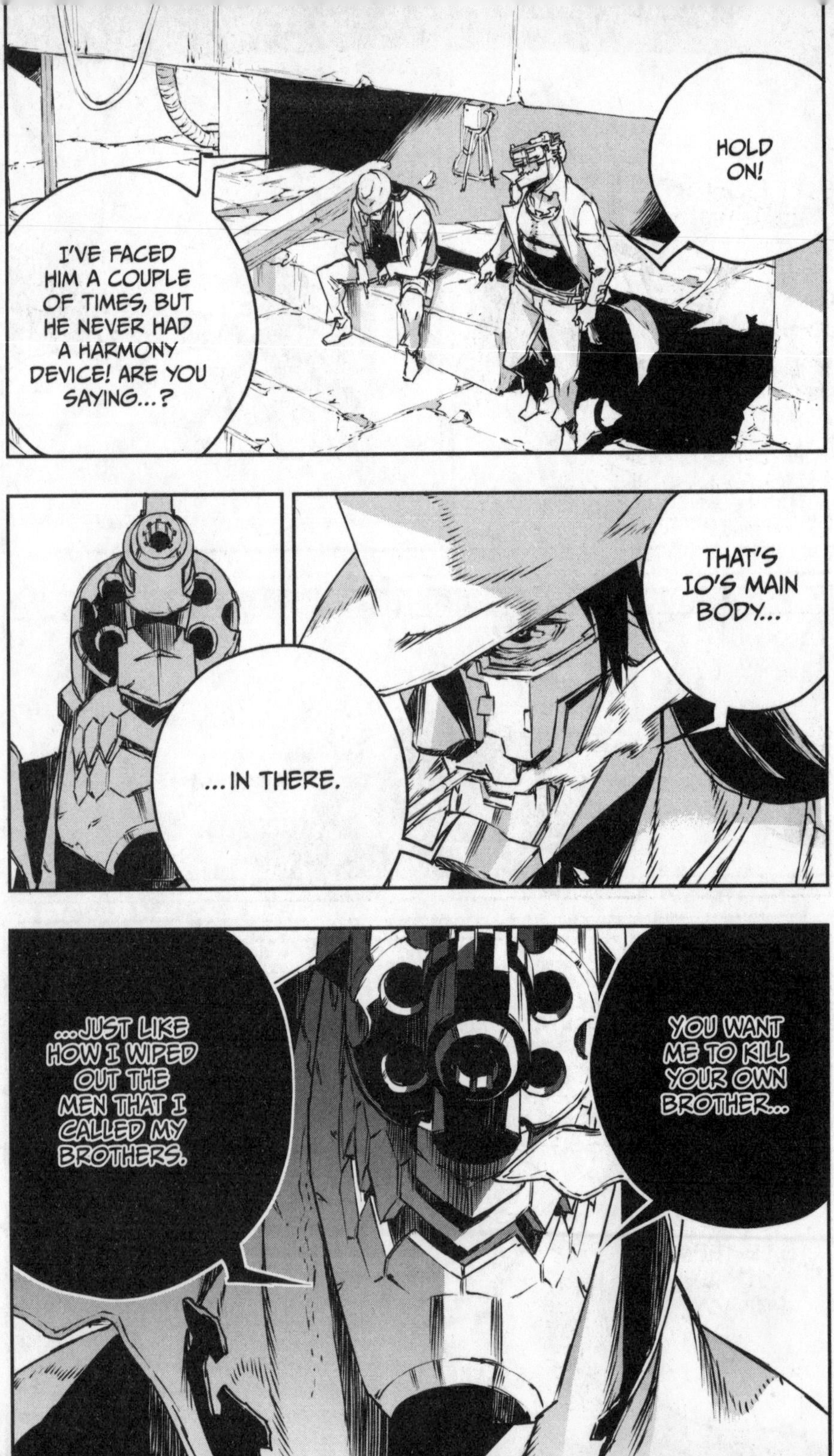
HOLD ON!
I'VE FACED HIM A COUPLE OF TIMES, BUT HE NEVER HAD A HARMONY DEVICE! ARE YOU SAYING...?
THAT'S IO'S MAIN BODY...
...IN THERE.
YOU WANT ME TO KILL YOUR OWN BROTHER...
...JUST LIKE HOW I WIPED OUT THE MEN THAT I CALLED MY BROTHERS.

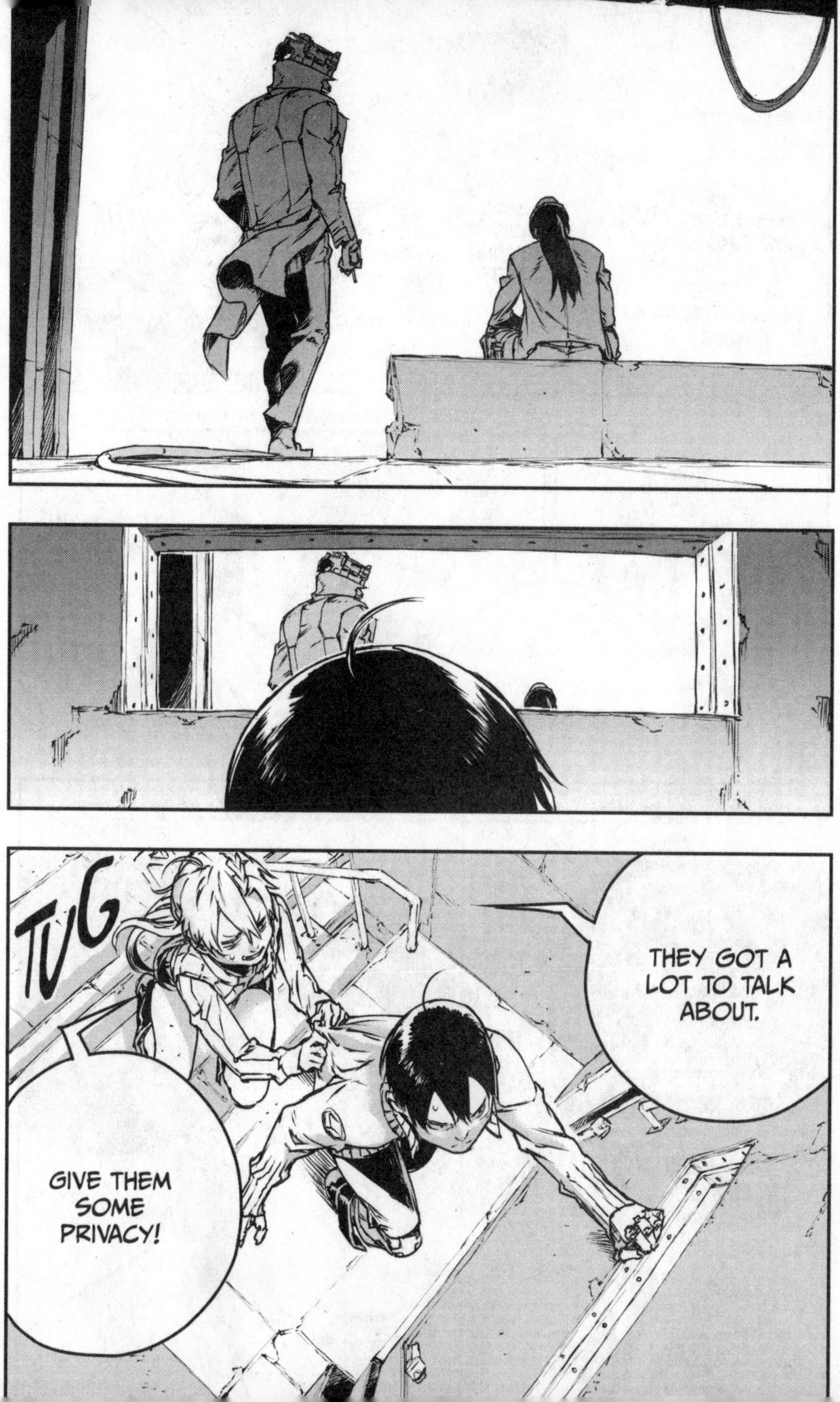
THEY GOT A LOT TO TALK ABOUT.
TUG
GIVE THEM SOME PRIVACY!

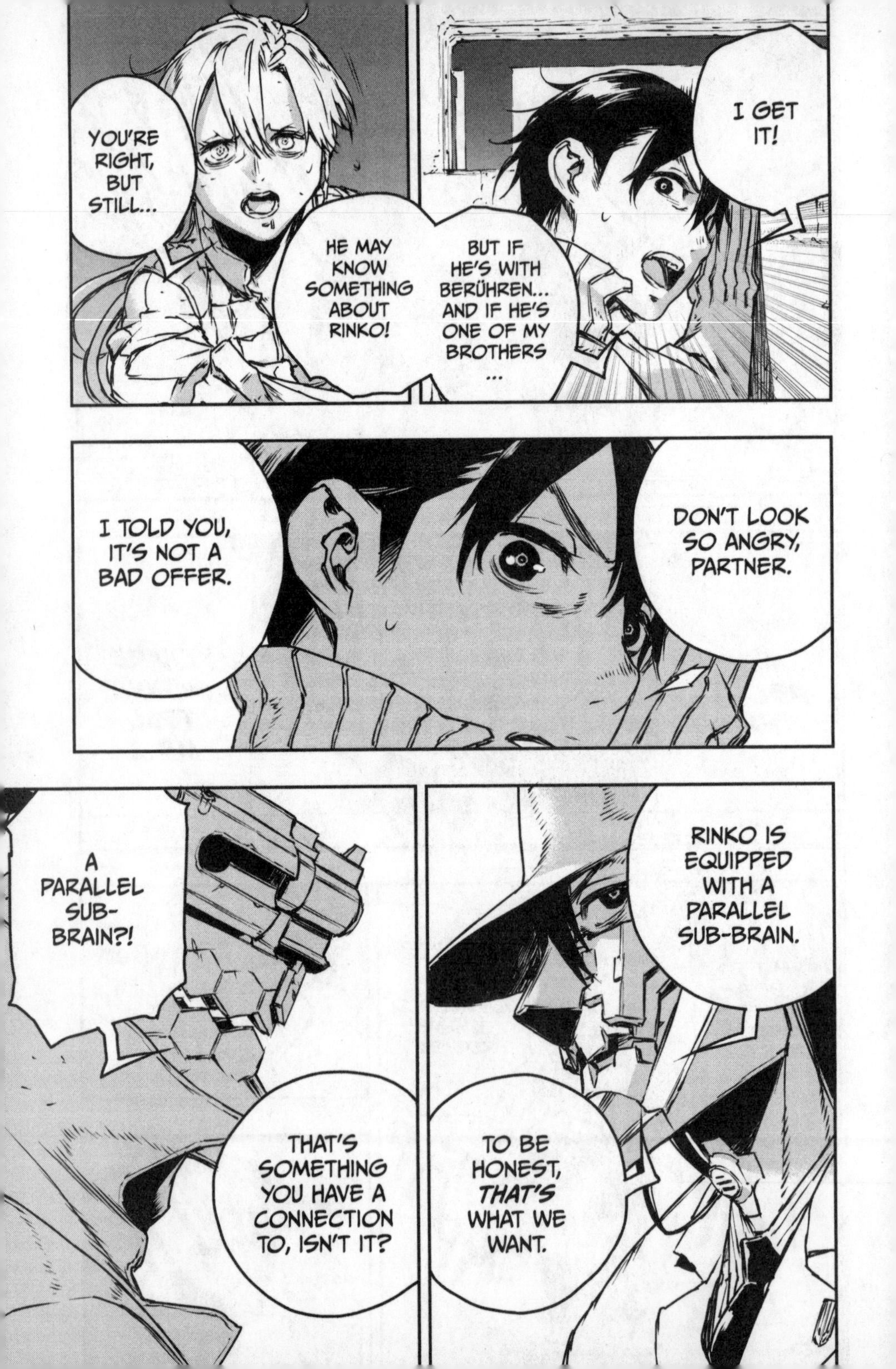
I GET IT!
BUT IF HE'S WITH BERÜHREN... AND IF HE'S ONE OF MY BROTHERS ...
HE MAY KNOW SOMETHING ABOUT RINKO!
YOU'RE RIGHT, BUT STILL...
DON'T LOOK SO ANGRY, PARTNER.
I TOLD YOU, IT'S NOT A BAD OFFER.
RINKO IS EQUIPPED WITH A PARALLEL SUB-BRAIN.
TO BE HONEST, *THAT'S* WHAT WE WANT.
A PARALLEL SUB-BRAIN?!
THAT'S SOMETHING YOU HAVE A CONNECTION TO, ISN'T IT?

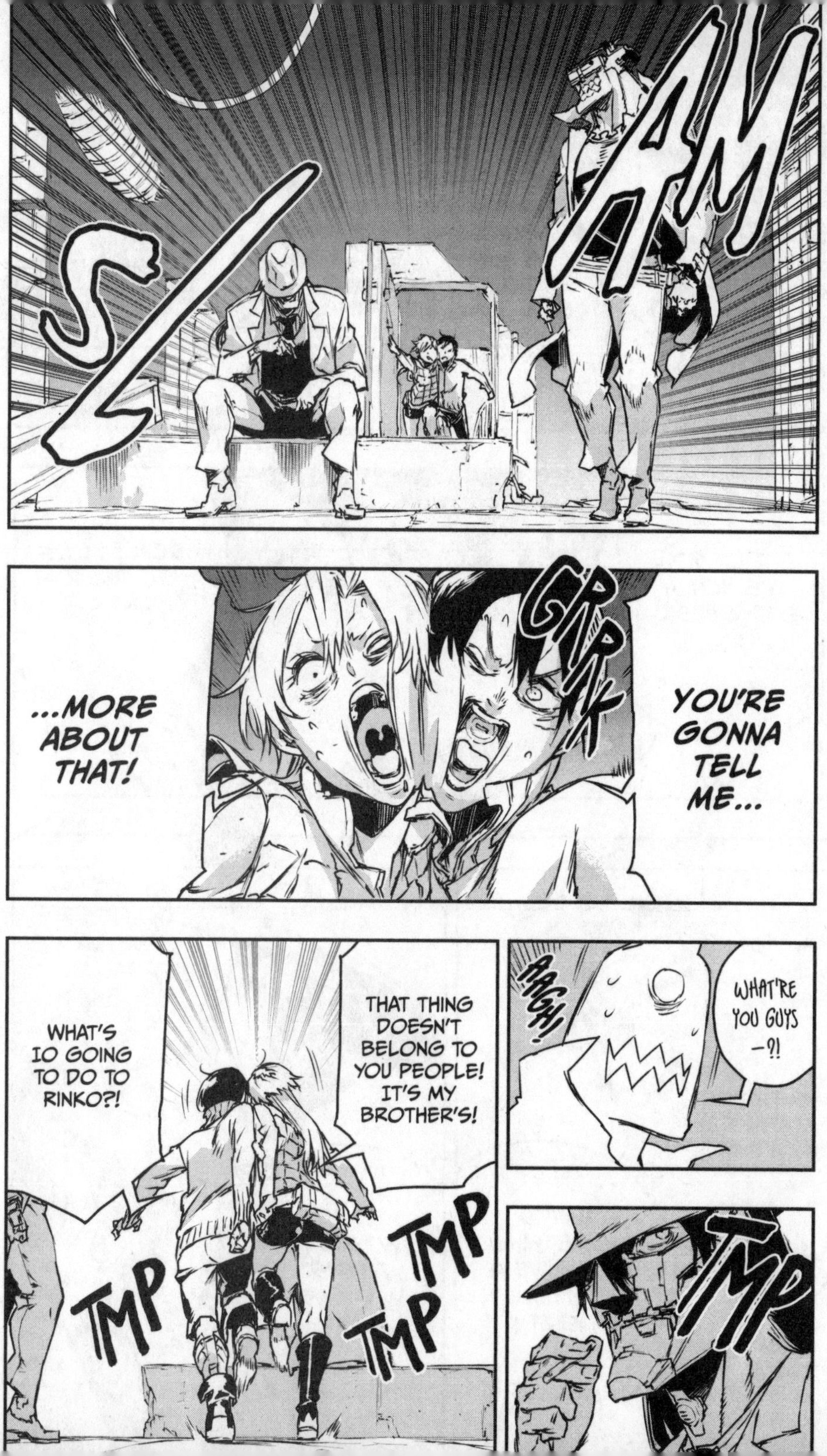
SLAM
YOU'RE GONNA TELL ME...
GRRK
...MORE ABOUT THAT!
WHAT'RE YOU GUYS —?!
AAGH!
TMP
THAT THING DOESN'T BELONG TO YOU PEOPLE! IT'S MY BROTHER'S!
WHAT'S IO GOING TO DO TO RINKO?!
TMP
TMP
TMP
TMP

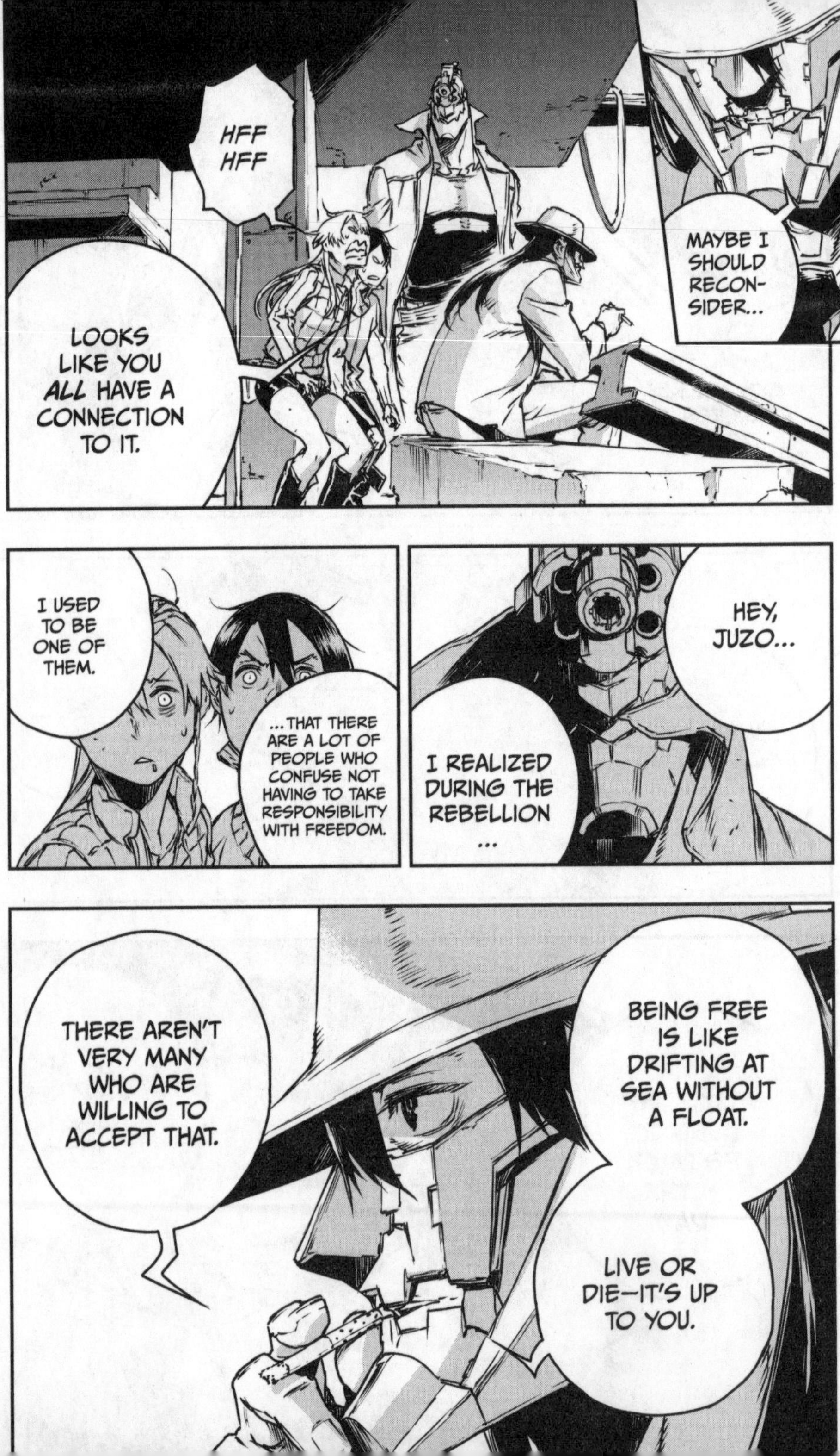
MAYBE I SHOULD RECON-SIDER...
HFF HFF
LOOKS LIKE YOU *ALL* HAVE A CONNECTION TO IT.
HEY, JUZO...
I REALIZED DURING THE REBELLION ...
...THAT THERE ARE A LOT OF PEOPLE WHO CONFUSE NOT HAVING TO TAKE RESPONSIBILITY WITH FREEDOM.
I USED TO BE ONE OF THEM.
BEING FREE IS LIKE DRIFTING AT SEA WITHOUT A FLOAT.
LIVE OR DIE—IT'S UP TO YOU.
THERE AREN'T VERY MANY WHO ARE WILLING TO ACCEPT THAT.

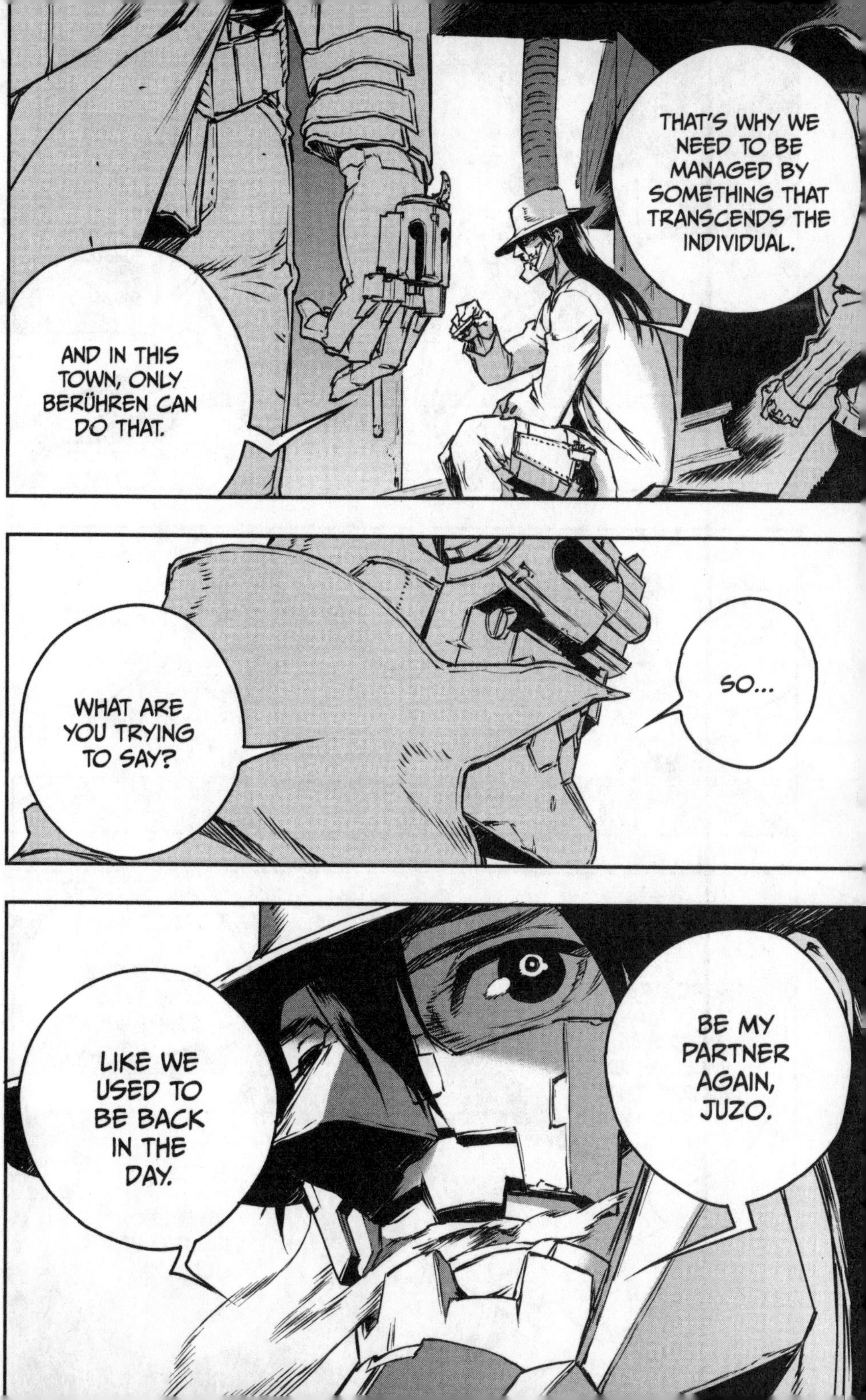
THAT'S WHY WE NEED TO BE MANAGED BY SOMETHING THAT TRANSCENDS THE INDIVIDUAL.
AND IN THIS TOWN, ONLY BERÜHREN CAN DO THAT.
SO...
WHAT ARE YOU TRYING TO SAY?
BE MY PARTNER AGAIN, JUZO.
LIKE WE USED TO BE BACK IN THE DAY.

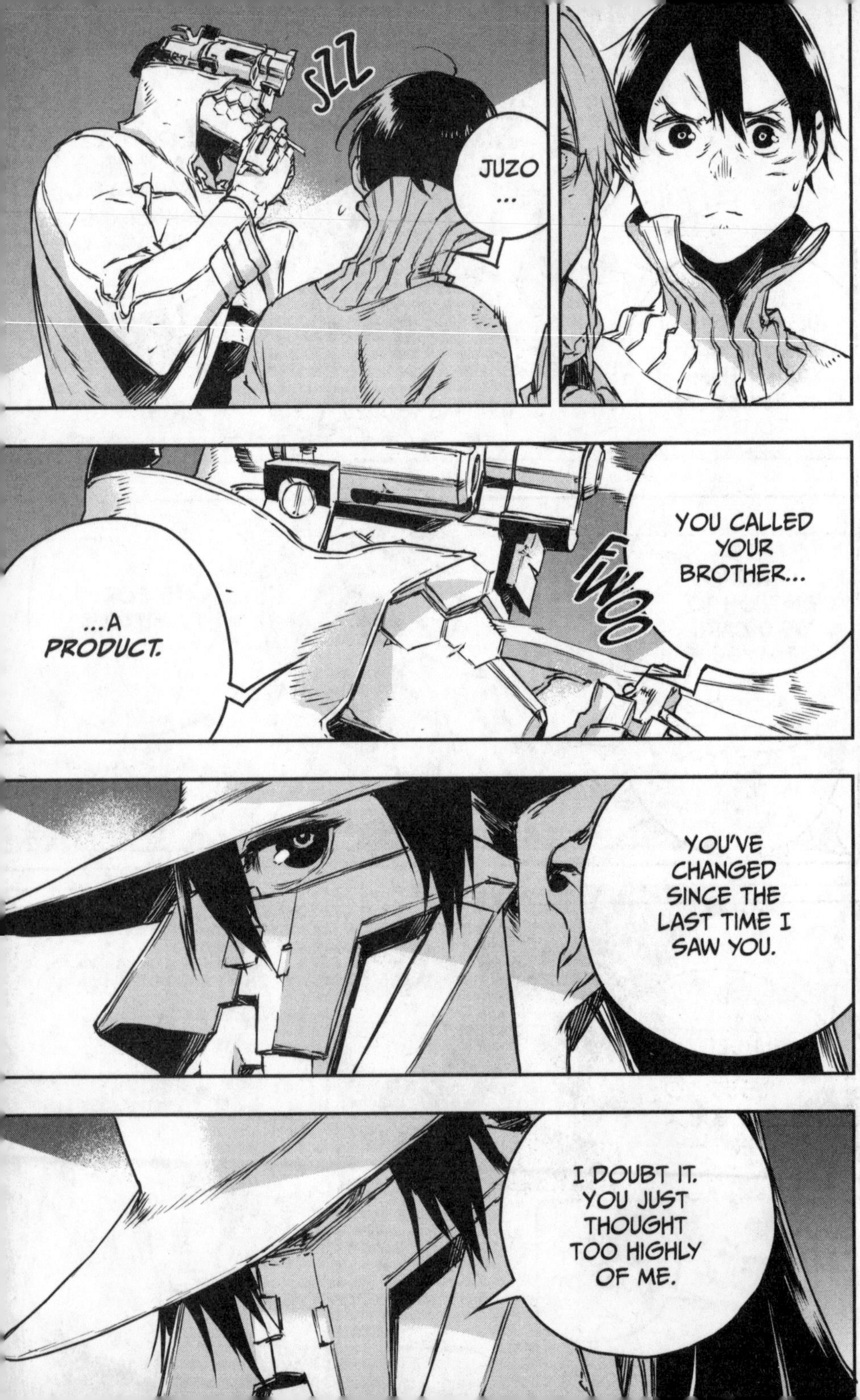
SZZ
JUZO ...
YOU CALLED YOUR BROTHER...
FWOO
...A PRODUCT.
YOU'VE CHANGED SINCE THE LAST TIME I SAW YOU.
I DOUBT IT. YOU JUST THOUGHT TOO HIGHLY OF ME.

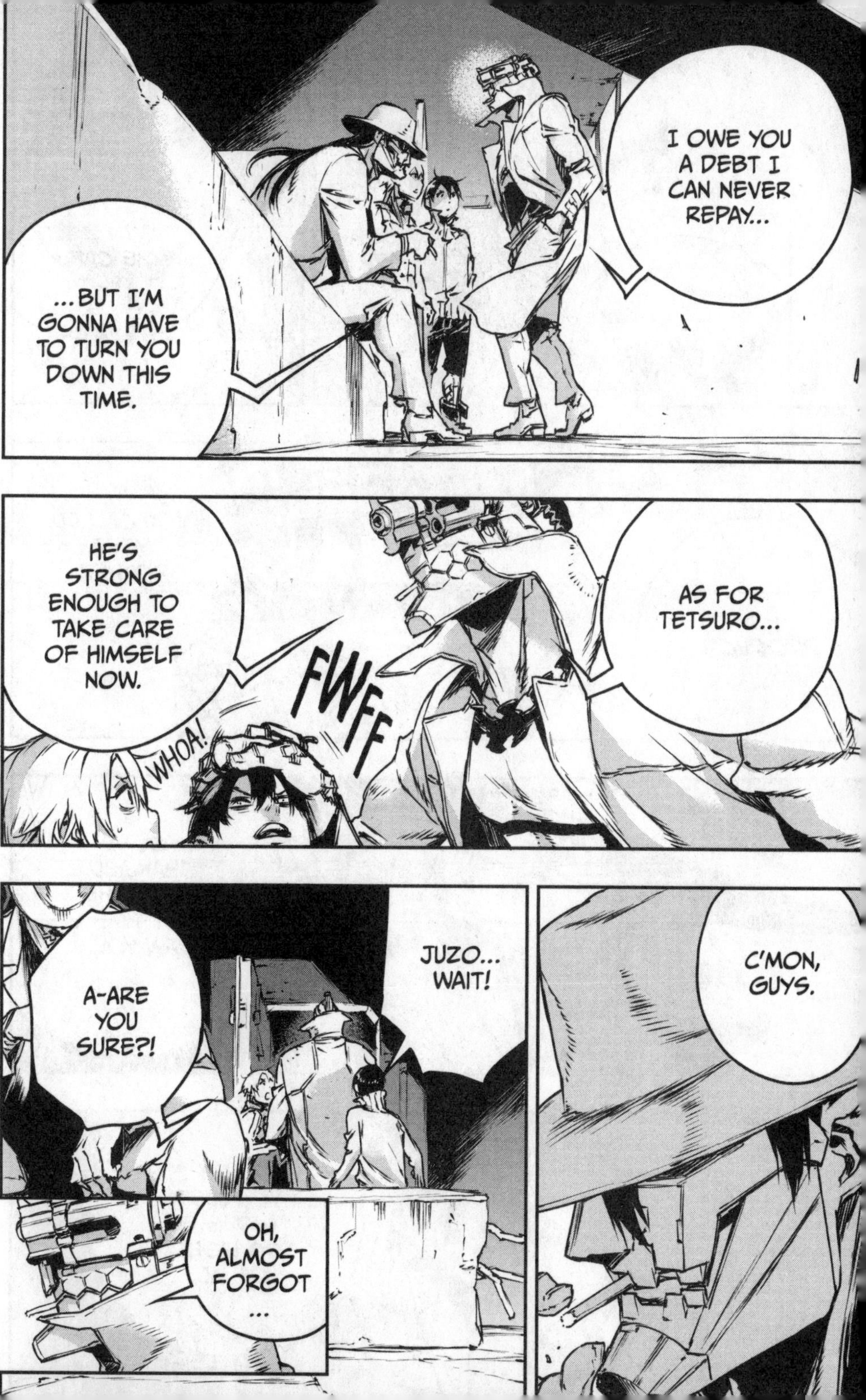
I OWE YOU A DEBT I CAN NEVER REPAY...
...BUT I'M GONNA HAVE TO TURN YOU DOWN THIS TIME.
AS FOR TETSURO...
HE'S STRONG ENOUGH TO TAKE CARE OF HIMSELF NOW.
FWFF
WHOA!
C'MON, GUYS.
JUZO... WAIT!
A-ARE YOU SURE?!
OH, ALMOST FORGOT ...

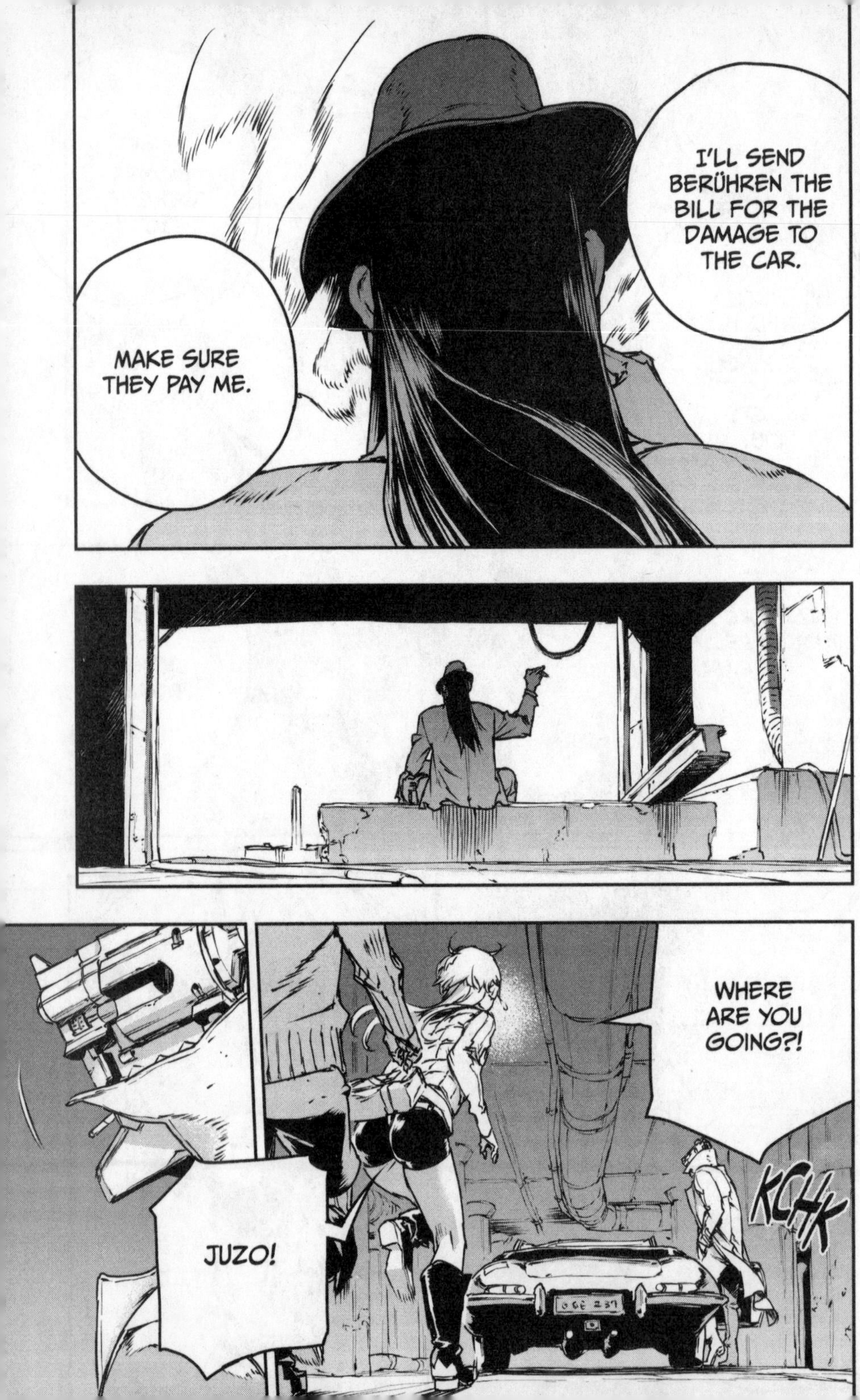
I'LL SEND BERÜHREN THE BILL FOR THE DAMAGE TO THE CAR.
MAKE SURE THEY PAY ME.
WHERE ARE YOU GOING?!
KCHK
JUZO!

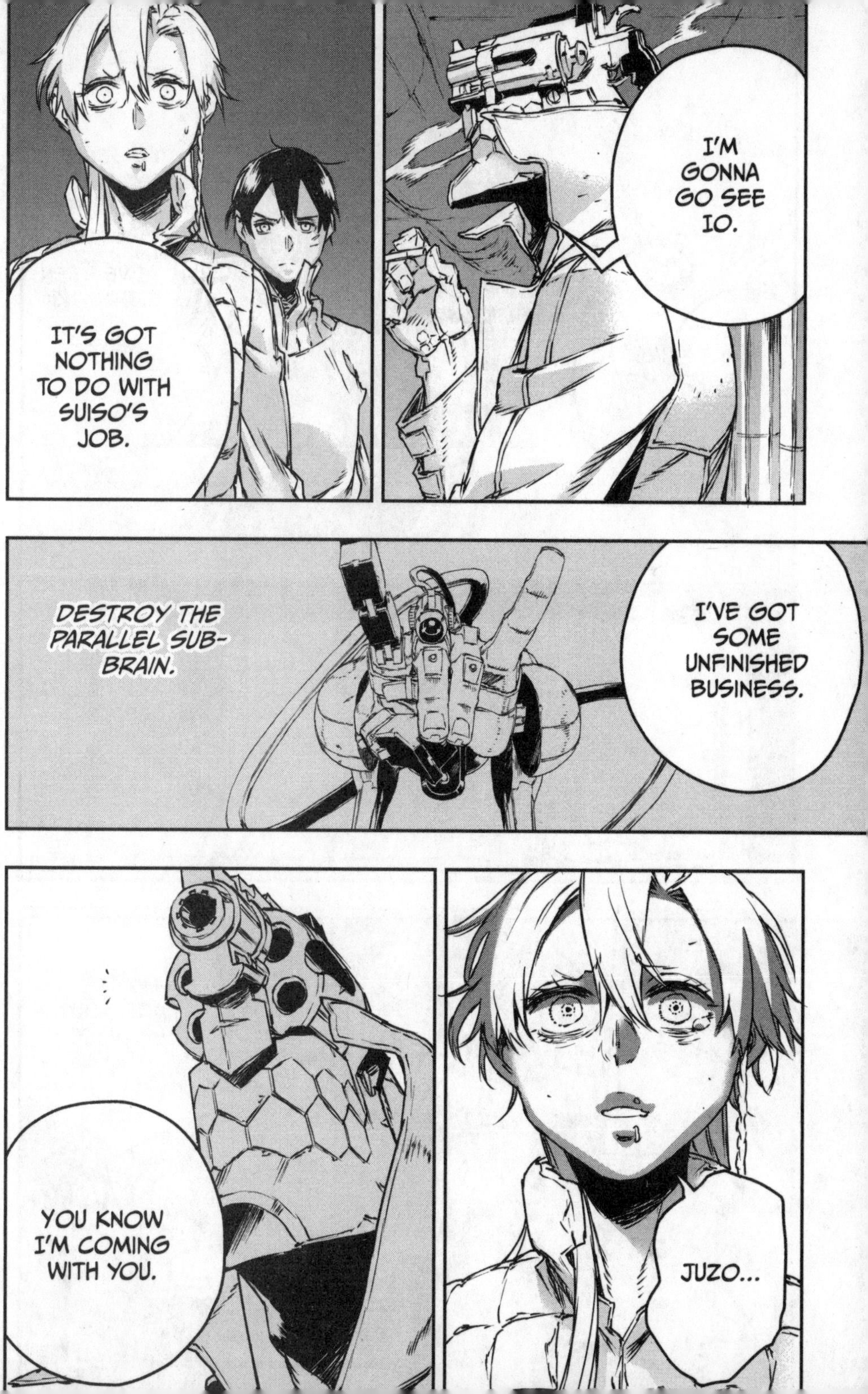
I'M GONNA GO SEE IO.
IT'S GOT NOTHING TO DO WITH SUISO'S JOB.
I'VE GOT SOME UNFINISHED BUSINESS.
DESTROY THE PARALLEL SUB-BRAIN.
JUZO...
YOU KNOW I'M COMING WITH YOU.

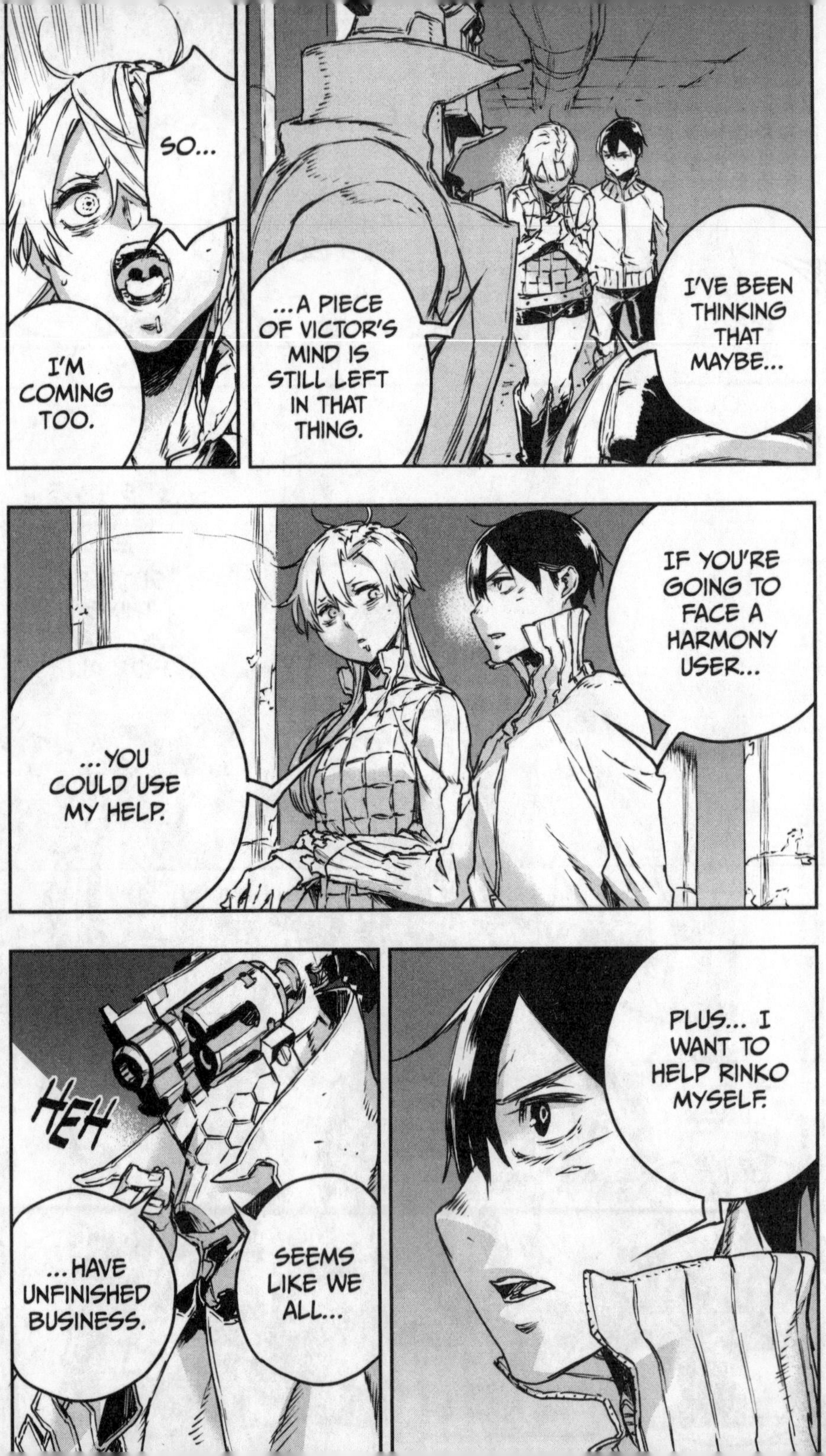
I'VE BEEN THINKING THAT MAYBE...
...A PIECE OF VICTOR'S MIND IS STILL LEFT IN THAT THING.
SO...
I'M COMING TOO.
IF YOU'RE GOING TO FACE A HARMONY USER...
...YOU COULD USE MY HELP.
PLUS... I WANT TO HELP RINKO MYSELF.
HEH
SEEMS LIKE WE ALL...
...HAVE UNFINISHED BUSINESS.

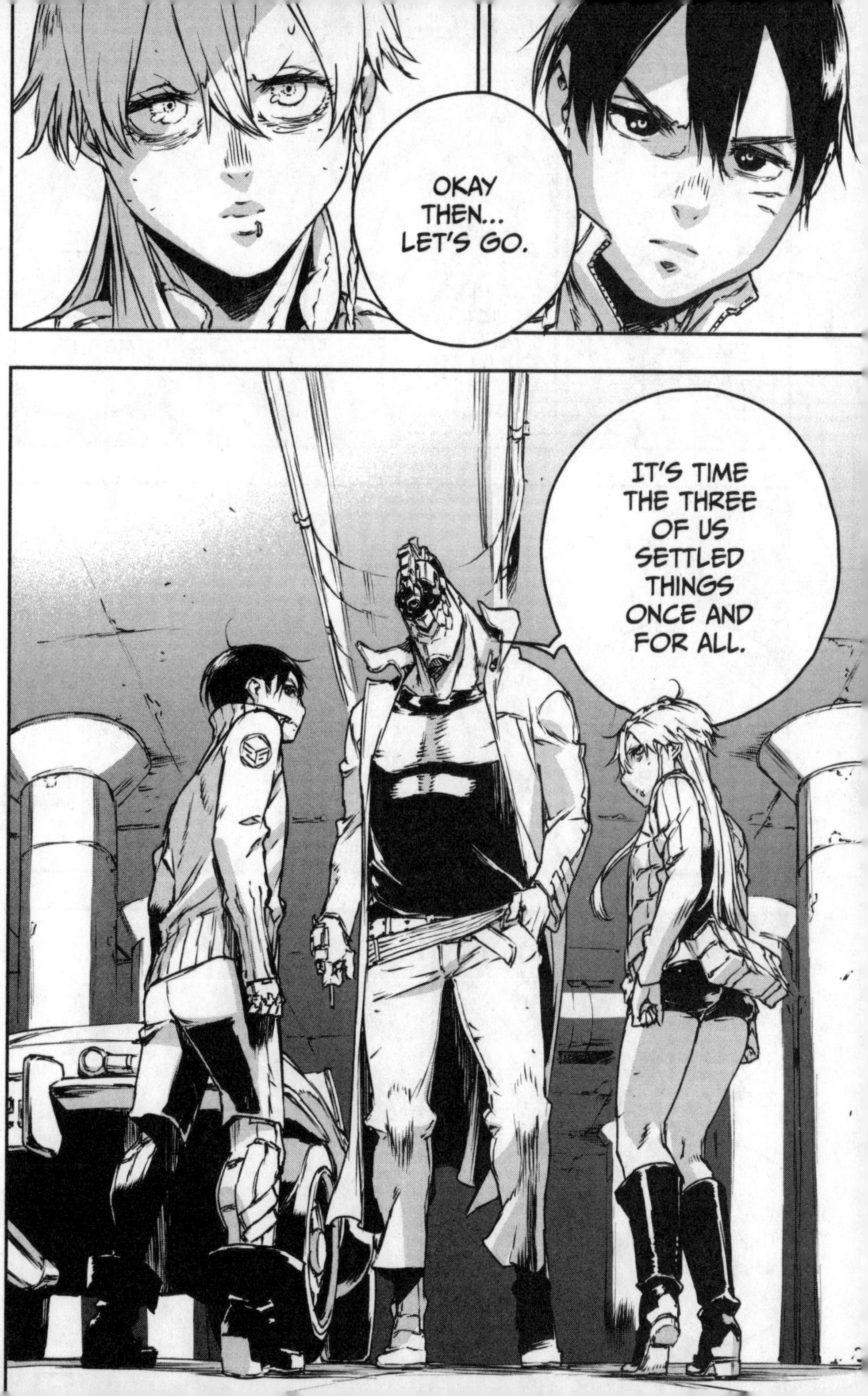
OKAY THEN... LET'S GO.
IT'S TIME THE THREE OF US SETTLED THINGS ONCE AND FOR ALL.

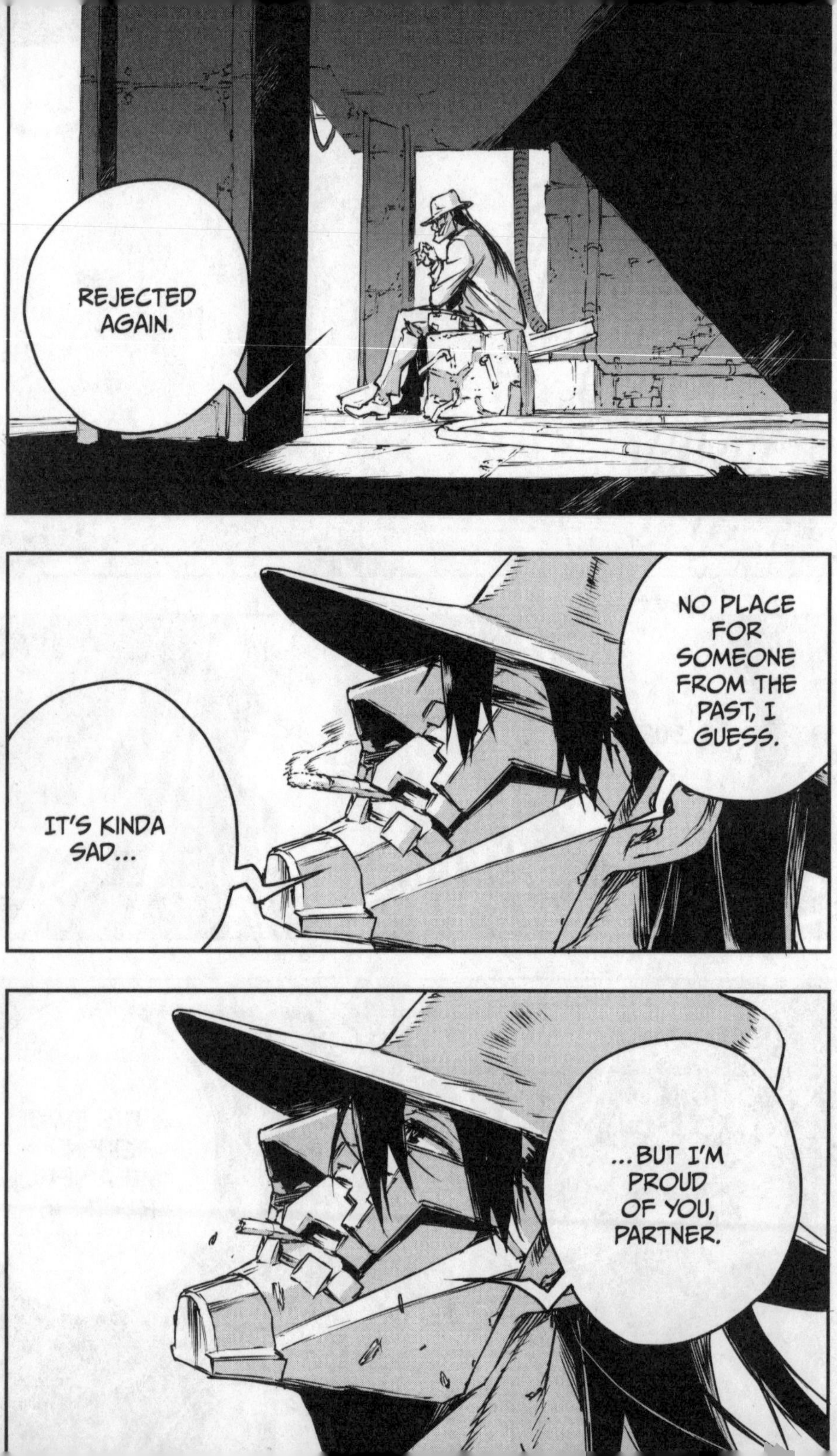
REJECTED AGAIN.
NO PLACE FOR SOMEONE FROM THE PAST, I GUESS.
IT'S KINDA SAD...
...BUT I'M PROUD OF YOU, PARTNER.

I GUESS...

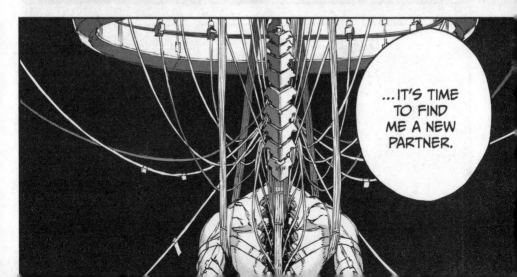

...IT'S TIME TO FIND ME A NEW PARTNER.

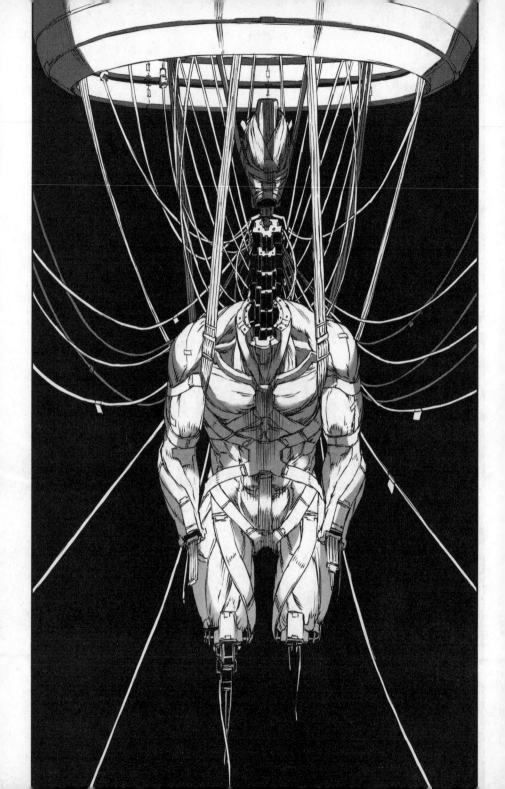

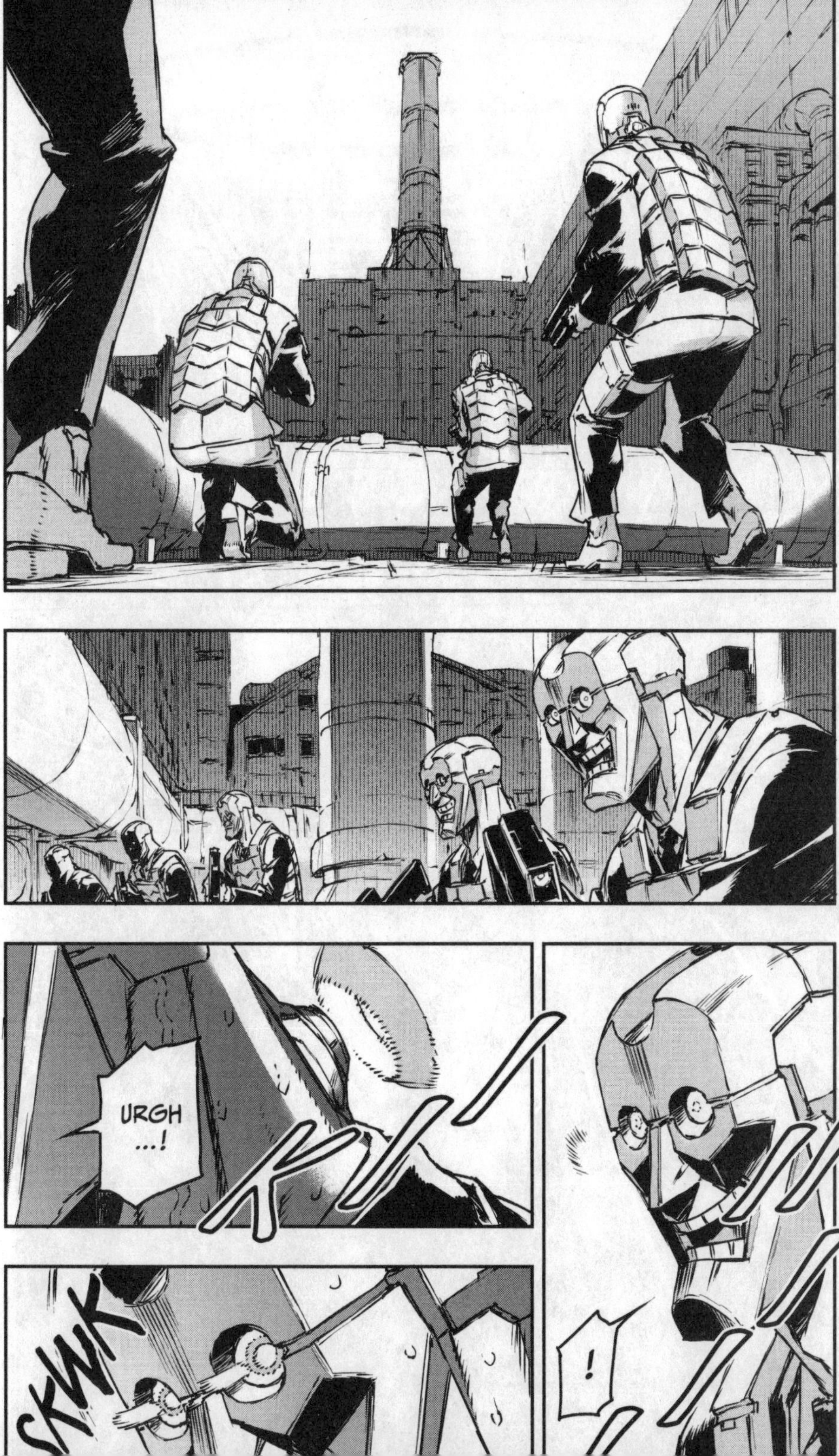
!
URGH ...!
SKWK

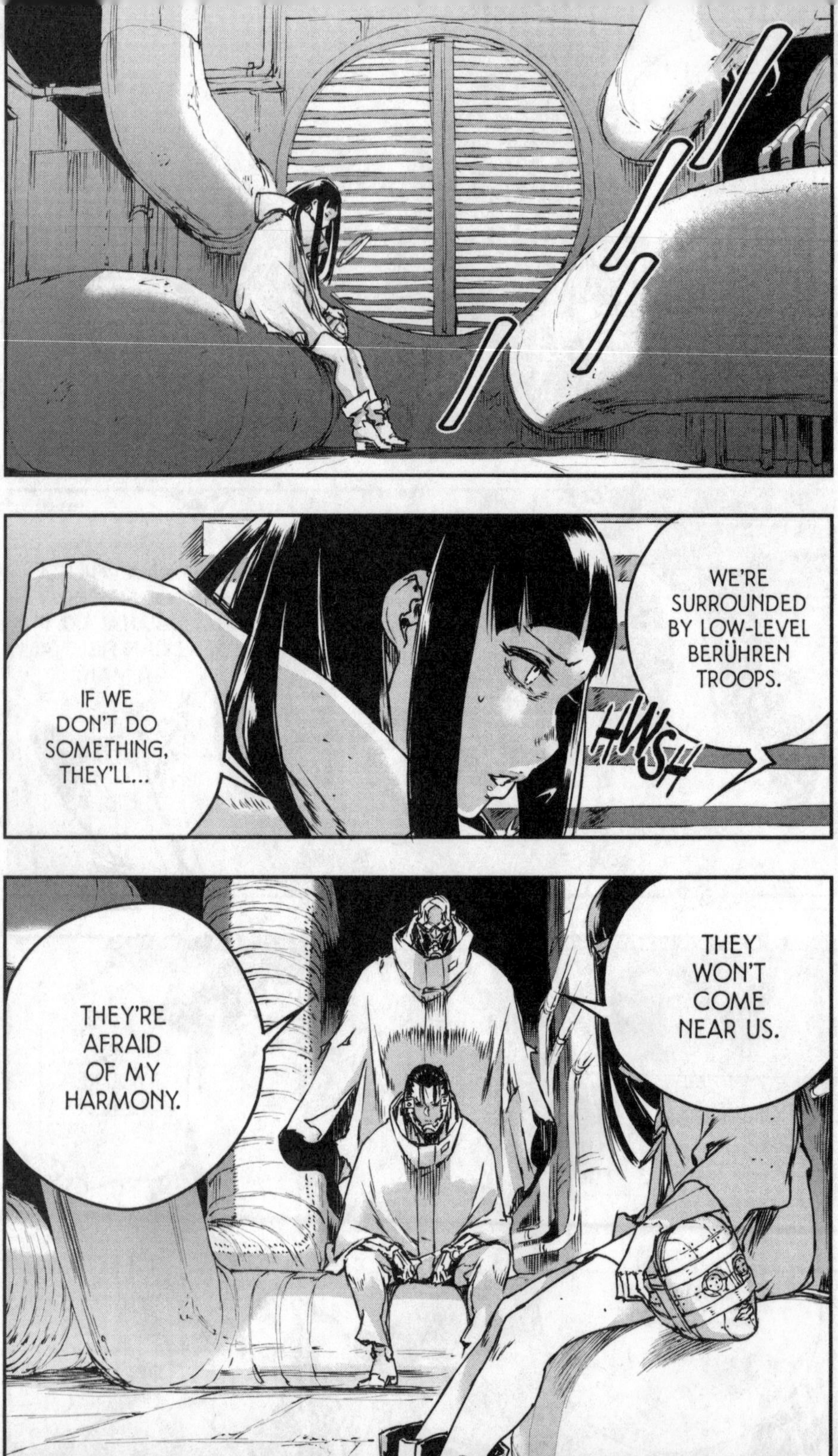
WE'RE SURROUNDED BY LOW-LEVEL BERÜHREN TROOPS.
HWSH
IF WE DON'T DO SOMETHING, THEY'LL...
THEY WON'T COME NEAR US.
THEY'RE AFRAID OF MY HARMONY.

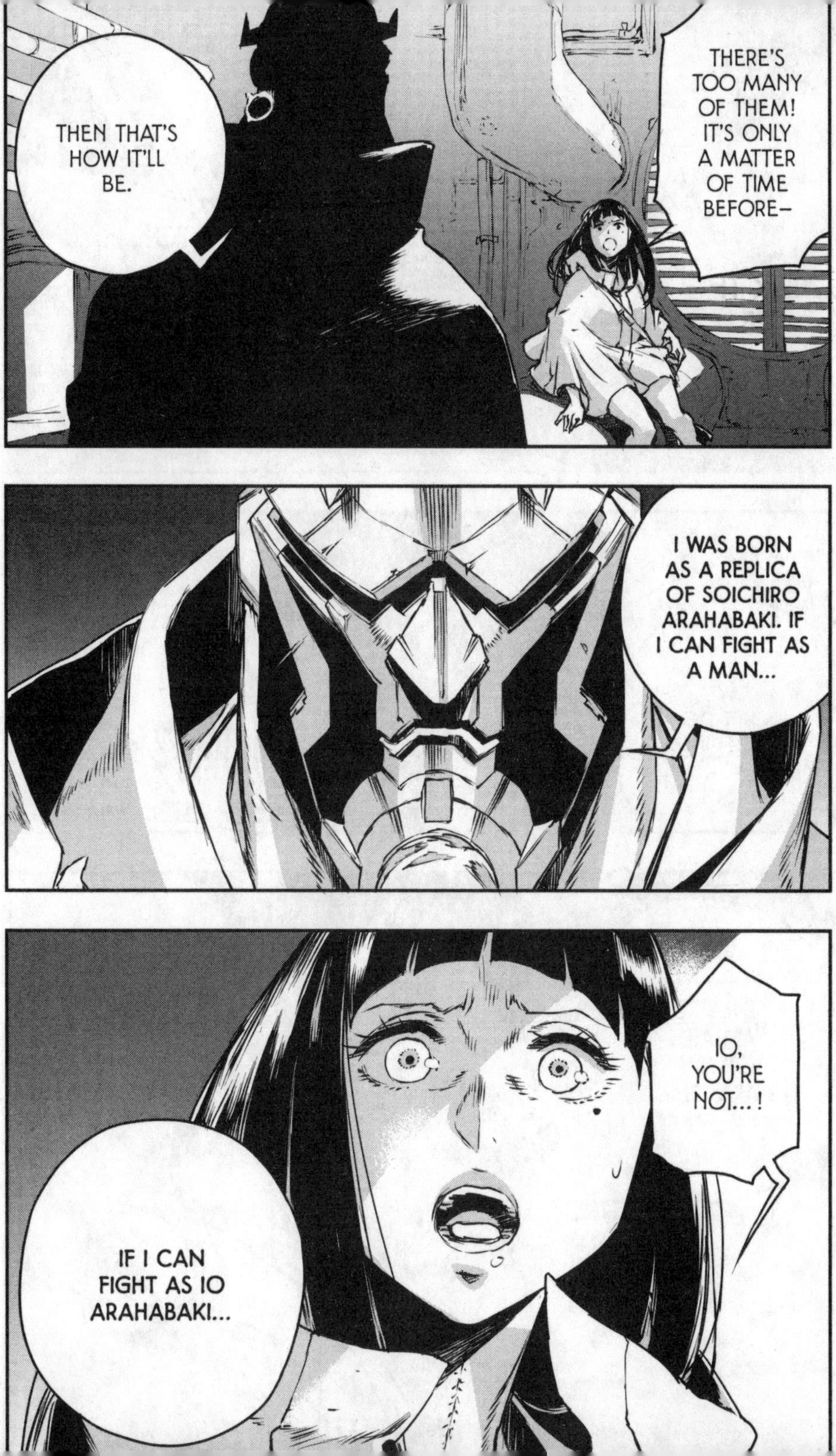
THERE'S TOO MANY OF THEM! IT'S ONLY A MATTER OF TIME BEFORE–
THEN THAT'S HOW IT'LL BE.
I WAS BORN AS A REPLICA OF SOICHIRO ARAHABAKI. IF I CAN FIGHT AS A MAN...
IO, YOU'RE NOT...!
IF I CAN FIGHT AS IO ARAHABAKI...

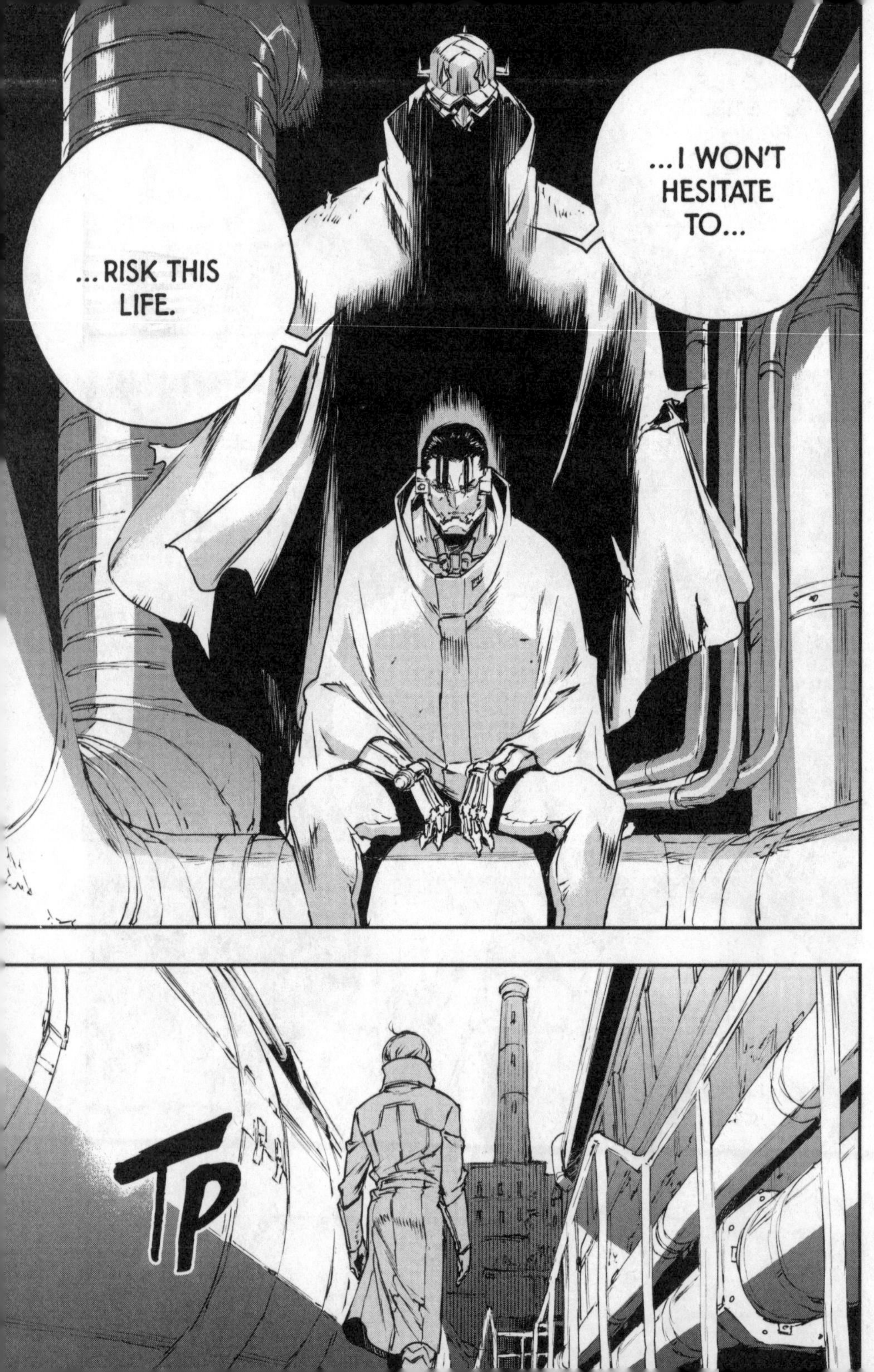
...I WON'T HESITATE TO...
...RISK THIS LIFE.
TP

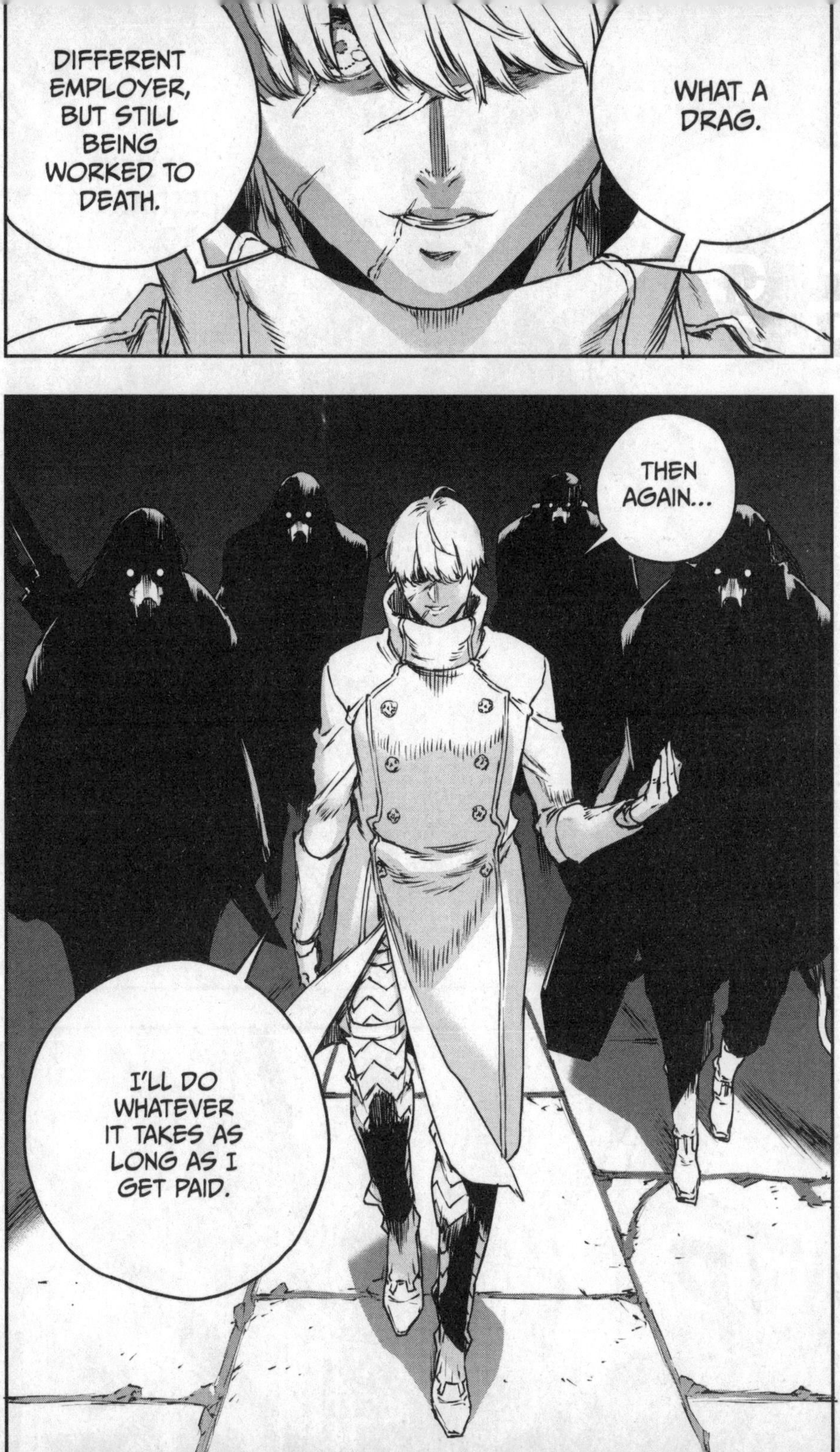
WHAT A DRAG.
DIFFERENT EMPLOYER, BUT STILL BEING WORKED TO DEATH.
THEN AGAIN...
I'LL DO WHATEVER IT TAKES AS LONG AS I GET PAID.

NO GUNS LIFE

The gunsmoke drifts, the muzzle talks

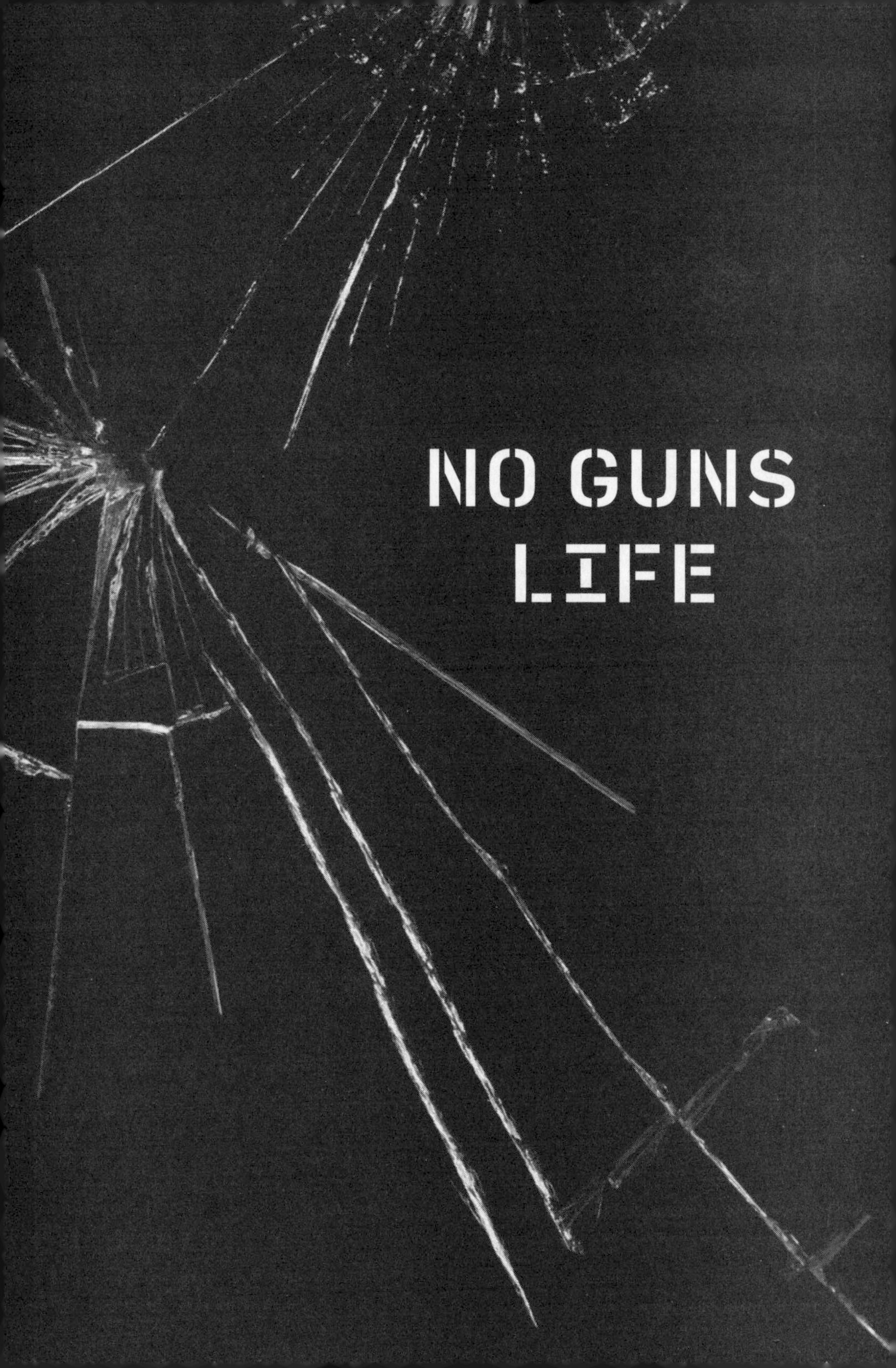
NO GUNS
LIFE

Chapter 69
Antipathy

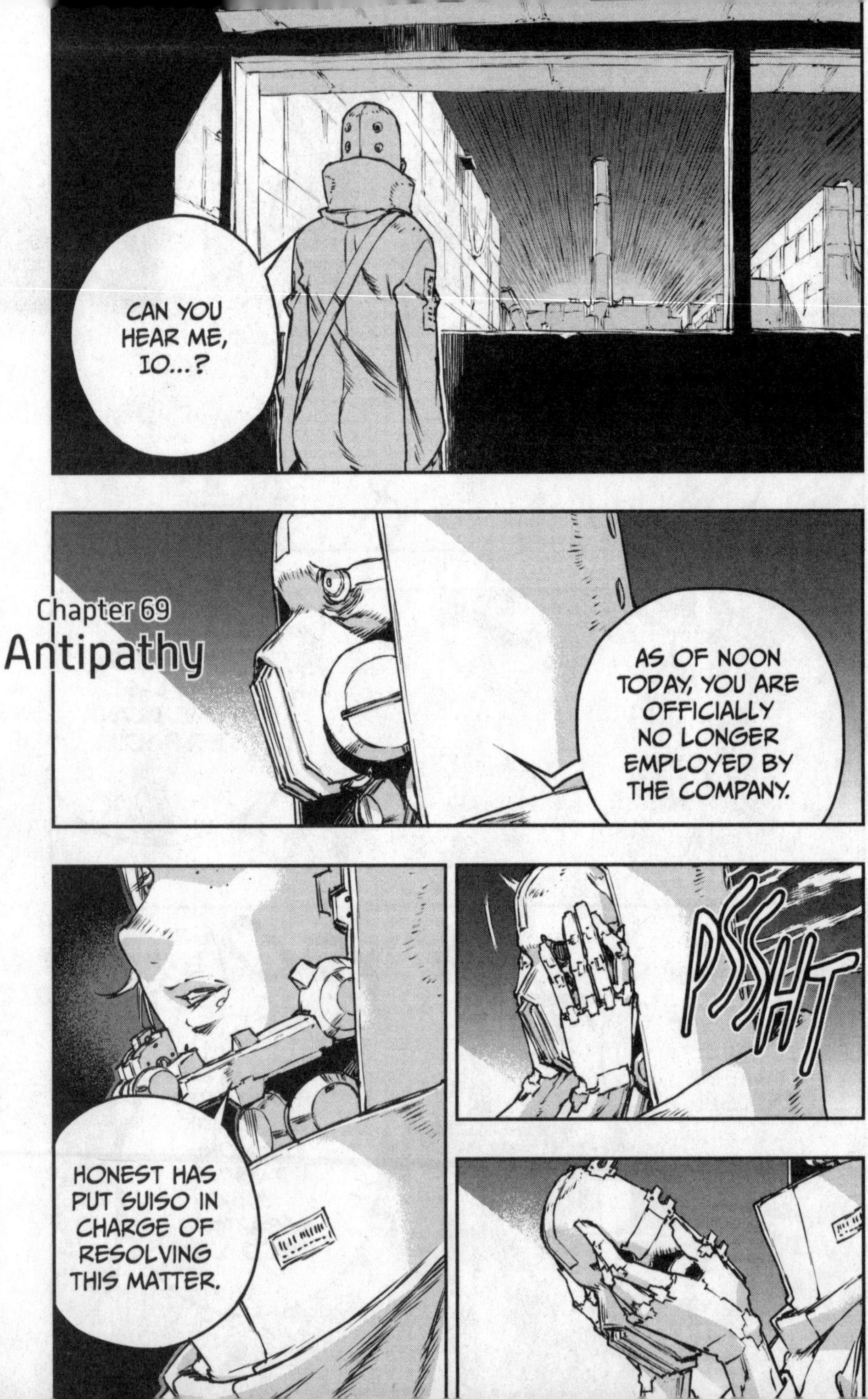
CAN YOU HEAR ME, IO...?
AS OF NOON TODAY, YOU ARE OFFICIALLY NO LONGER EMPLOYED BY THE COMPANY.
PSSHT
HONEST HAS PUT SUISO IN CHARGE OF RESOLVING THIS MATTER.

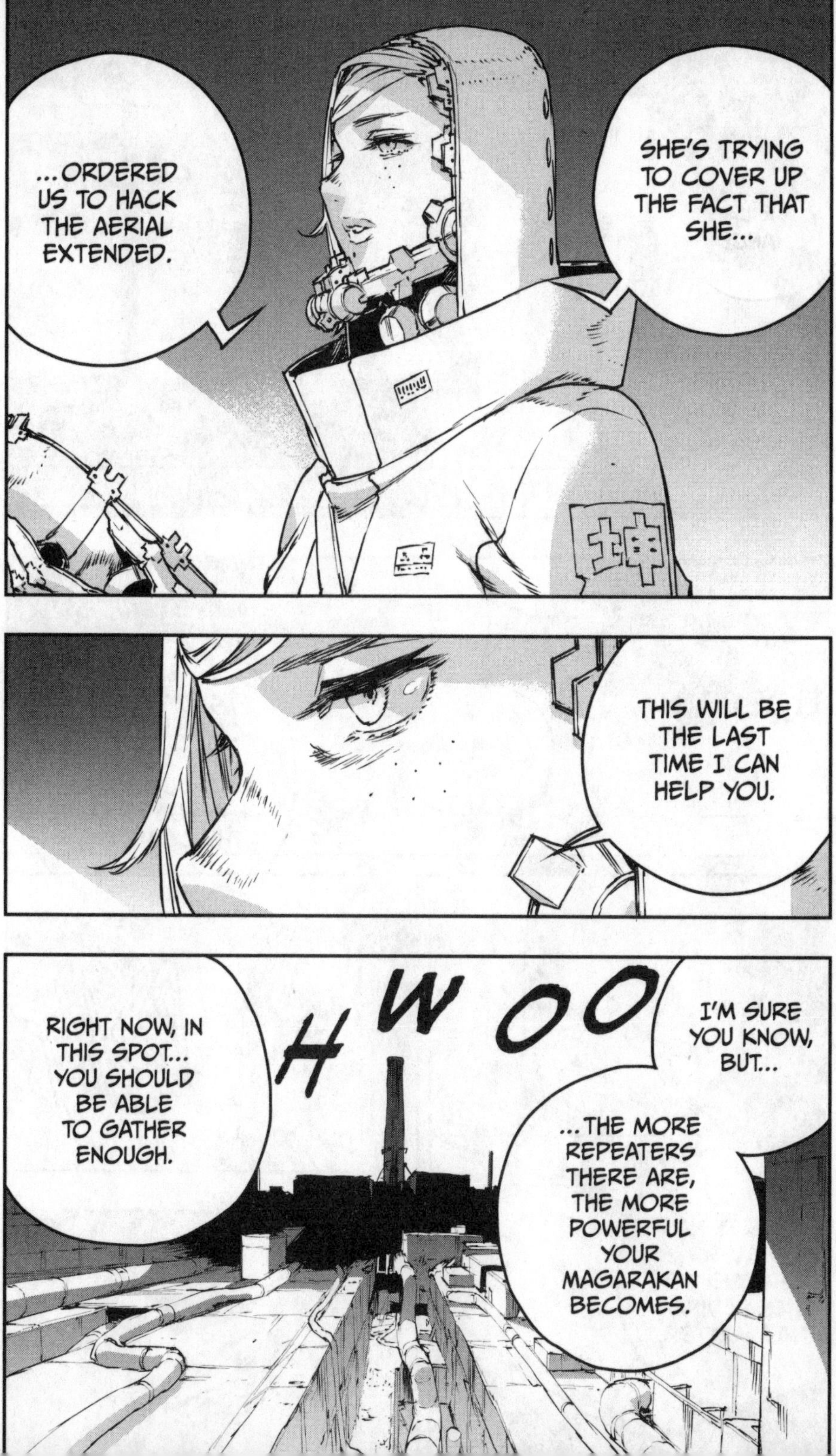
SHE'S TRYING TO COVER UP THE FACT THAT SHE...
...ORDERED US TO HACK THE AERIAL EXTENDED.
THIS WILL BE THE LAST TIME I CAN HELP YOU.
I'M SURE YOU KNOW, BUT...
...THE MORE REPEATERS THERE ARE, THE MORE POWERFUL YOUR MAGARAKAN BECOMES.
HWOO
RIGHT NOW, IN THIS SPOT... YOU SHOULD BE ABLE TO GATHER ENOUGH.

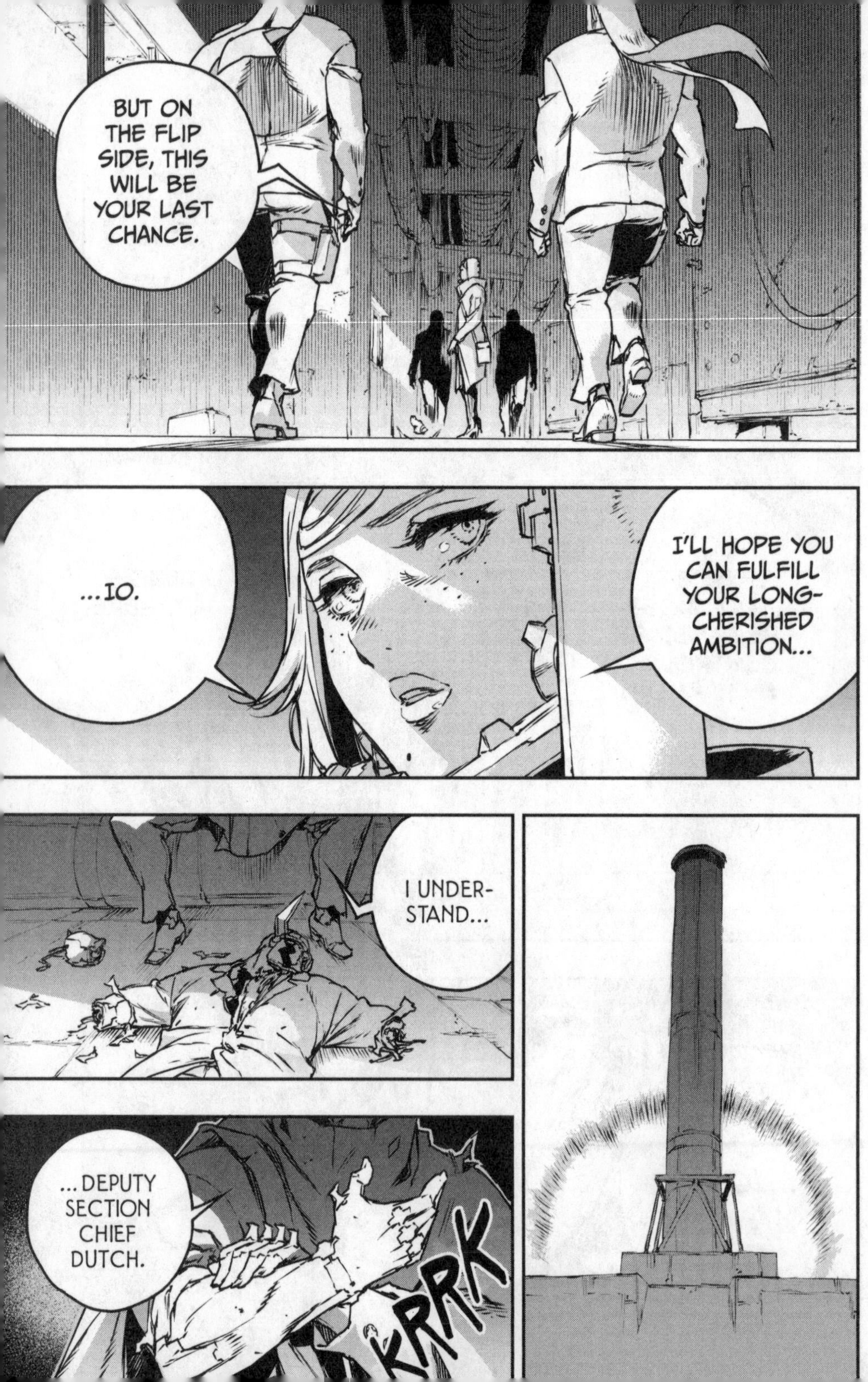
BUT ON THE FLIP SIDE, THIS WILL BE YOUR LAST CHANCE.
I'LL HOPE YOU CAN FULFILL YOUR LONG-CHERISHED AMBITION...
...IO.
I UNDER-STAND...
...DEPUTY SECTION CHIEF DUTCH.
KRRK

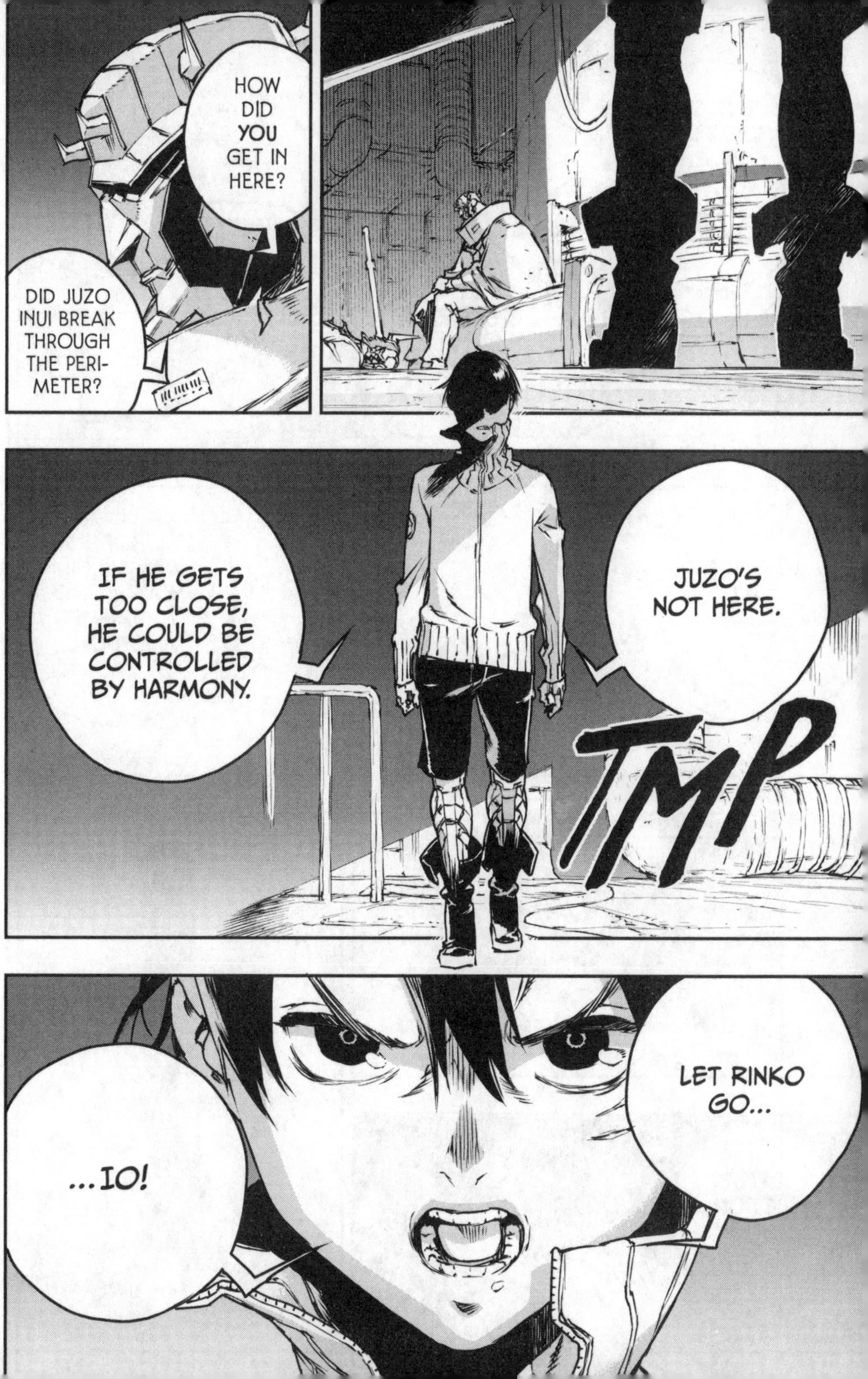
HOW DID YOU GET IN HERE?
DID JUZO INUI BREAK THROUGH THE PERI-METER?
JUZO'S NOT HERE.
TMP
IF HE GETS TOO CLOSE, HE COULD BE CONTROLLED BY HARMONY.
LET RINKO GO...
...IO!

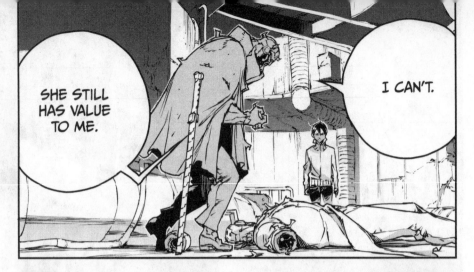

SHE STILL HAS VALUE TO ME.

I CAN'T.

BESIDES, WHY DO YOU CARE ABOUT HER?

YOU'RE THE REASON RINKO AND THE REST OF US BROTHERS HAVE SUFFERED.

?!

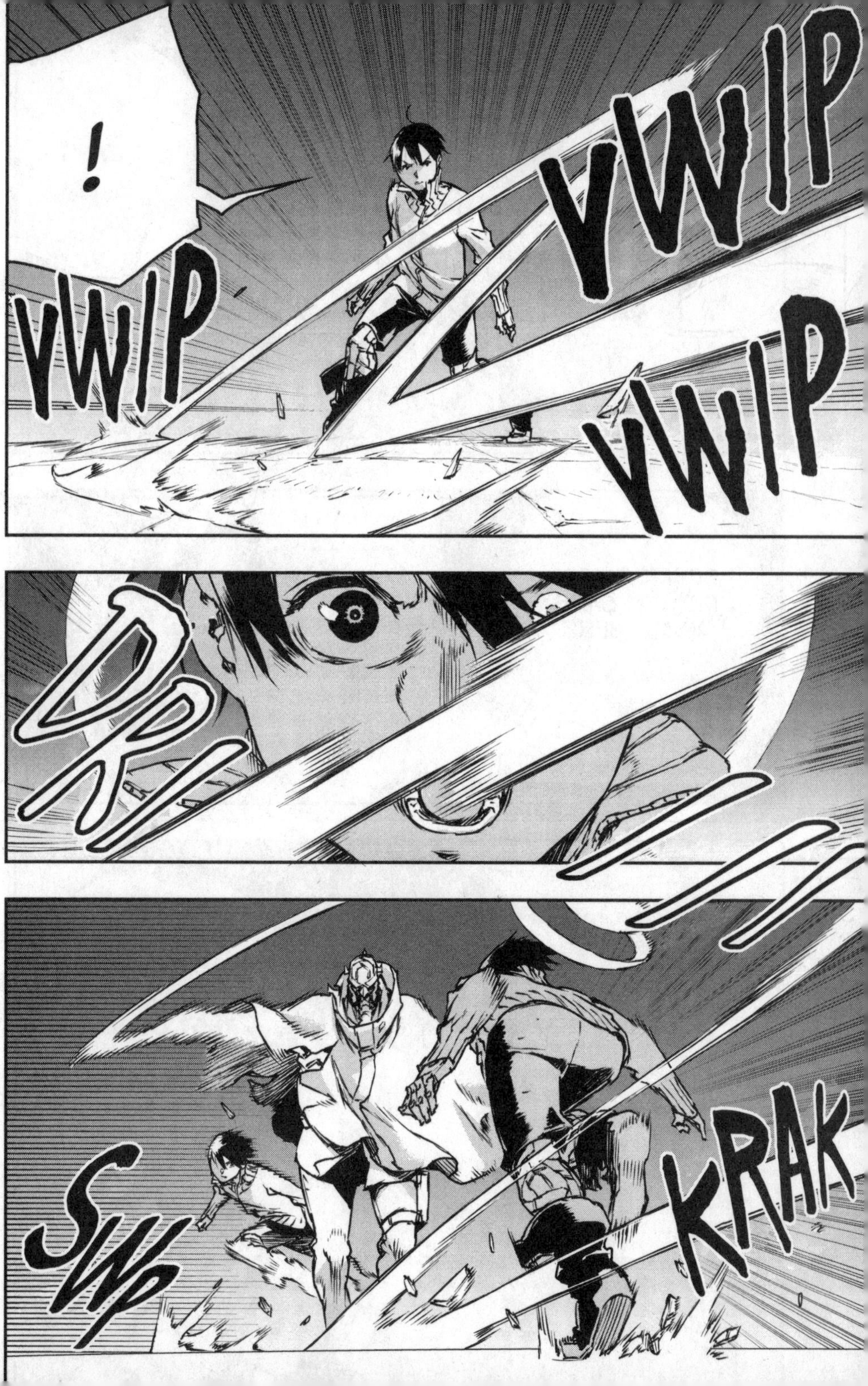
VWIP
VWIP
!
VWIP
DRI
KRAK
SWP

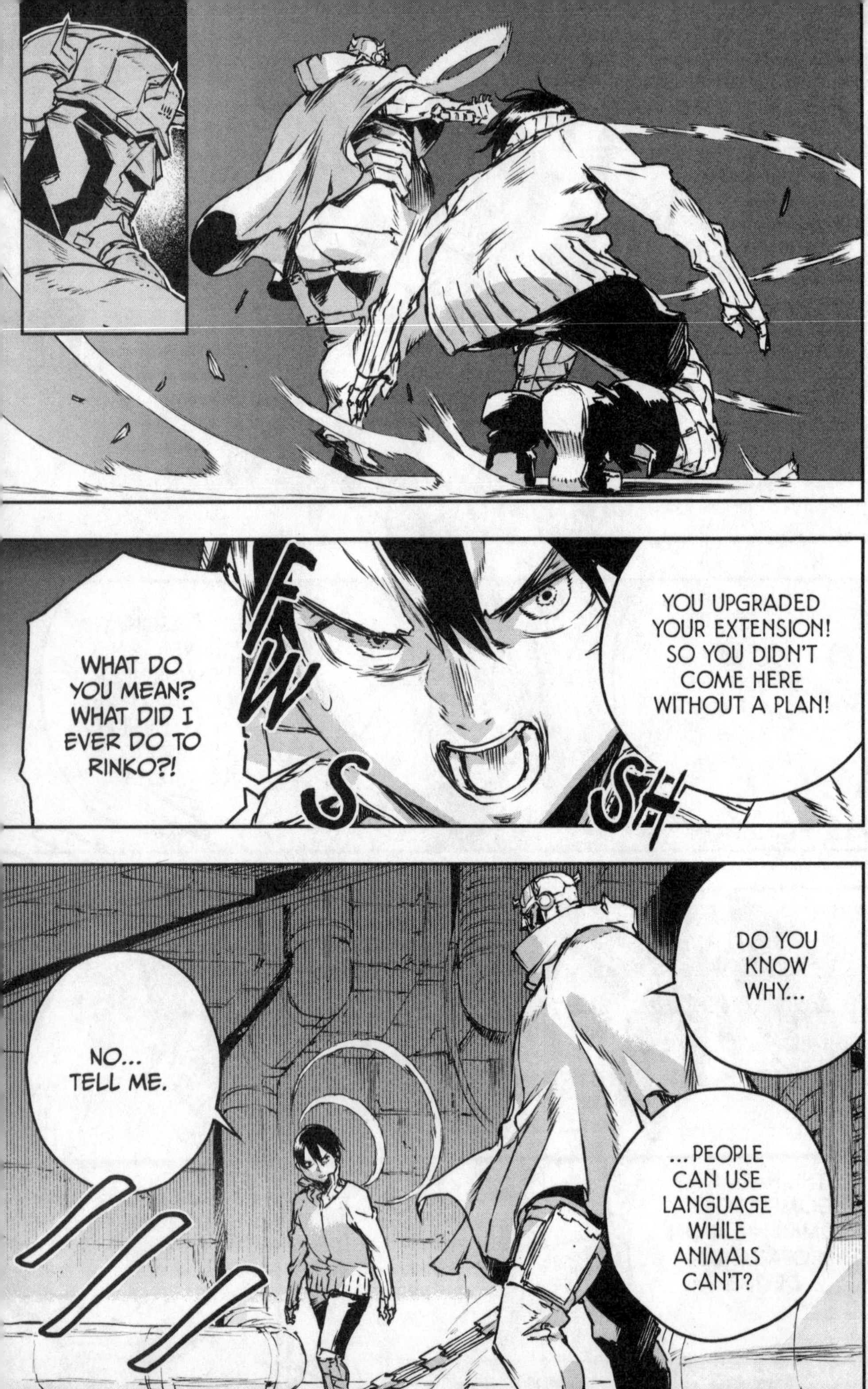
YOU UPGRADED YOUR EXTENSION! SO YOU DIDN'T COME HERE WITHOUT A PLAN!
FWSSH
WHAT DO YOU MEAN? WHAT DID I EVER DO TO RINKO?!
DO YOU KNOW WHY...
NO... TELL ME.
...PEOPLE CAN USE LANGUAGE WHILE ANIMALS CAN'T?

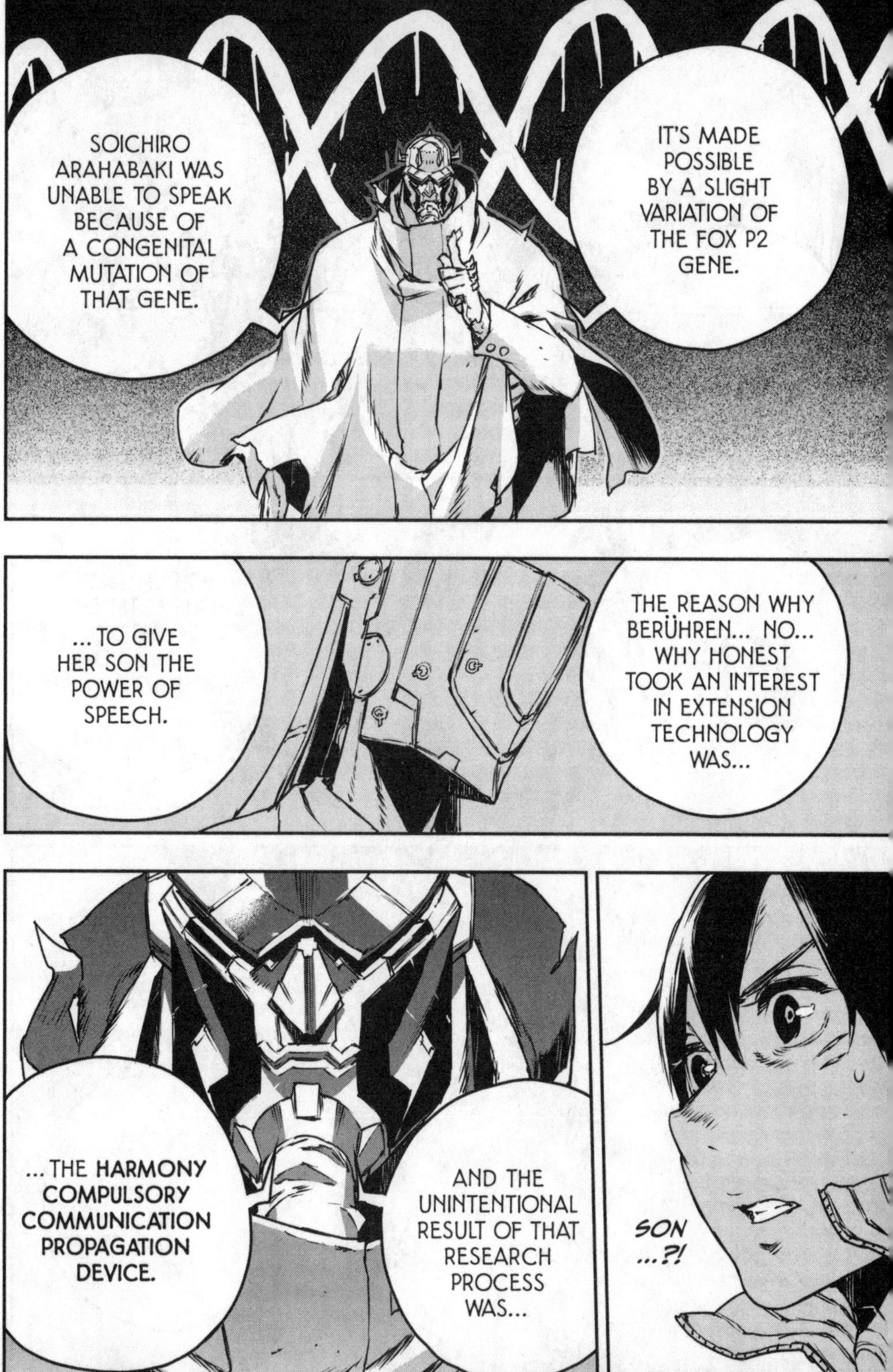
IT'S MADE POSSIBLE BY A SLIGHT VARIATION OF THE FOX P2 GENE.
SOICHIRO ARAHABAKI WAS UNABLE TO SPEAK BECAUSE OF A CONGENITAL MUTATION OF THAT GENE.
THE REASON WHY BERÜHREN... NO... WHY HONEST TOOK AN INTEREST IN EXTENSION TECHNOLOGY WAS...
...TO GIVE HER SON THE POWER OF SPEECH.
SON ...?!
AND THE UNINTENTIONAL RESULT OF THAT RESEARCH PROCESS WAS...
...THE **HARMONY COMPULSORY COMMUNICATION PROPAGATION DEVICE.**

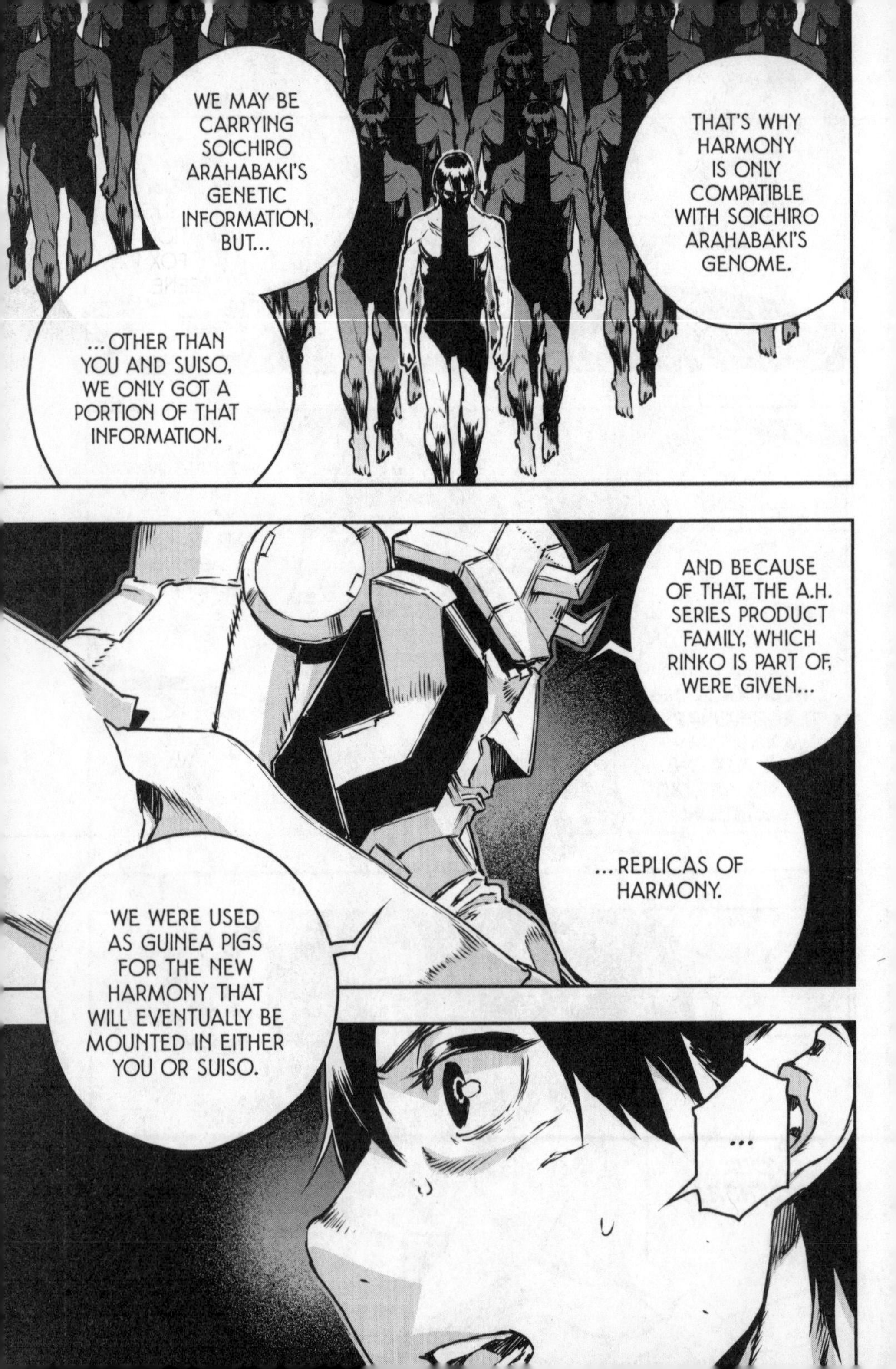
THAT'S WHY HARMONY IS ONLY COMPATIBLE WITH SOICHIRO ARAHABAKI'S GENOME.
WE MAY BE CARRYING SOICHIRO ARAHABAKI'S GENETIC INFORMATION, BUT...
...OTHER THAN YOU AND SUISO, WE ONLY GOT A PORTION OF THAT INFORMATION.
AND BECAUSE OF THAT, THE A.H. SERIES PRODUCT FAMILY, WHICH RINKO IS PART OF, WERE GIVEN...
...REPLICAS OF HARMONY.
WE WERE USED AS GUINEA PIGS FOR THE NEW HARMONY THAT WILL EVENTUALLY BE MOUNTED IN EITHER YOU OR SUISO.
...

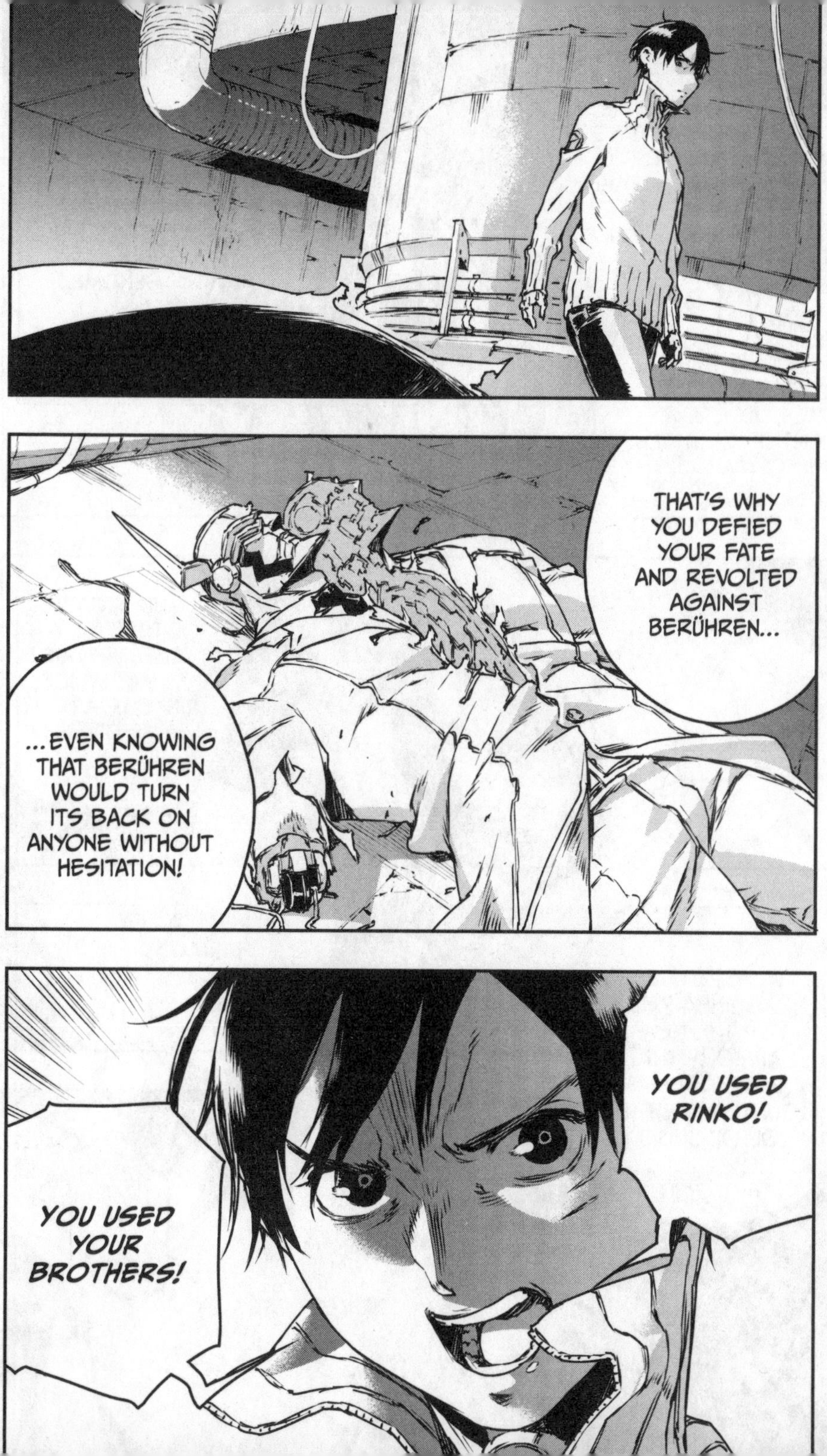
THAT'S WHY YOU DEFIED YOUR FATE AND REVOLTED AGAINST BERÜHREN...
...EVEN KNOWING THAT BERÜHREN WOULD TURN ITS BACK ON ANYONE WITHOUT HESITATION!
YOU USED RINKO!
YOU USED YOUR BROTHERS!

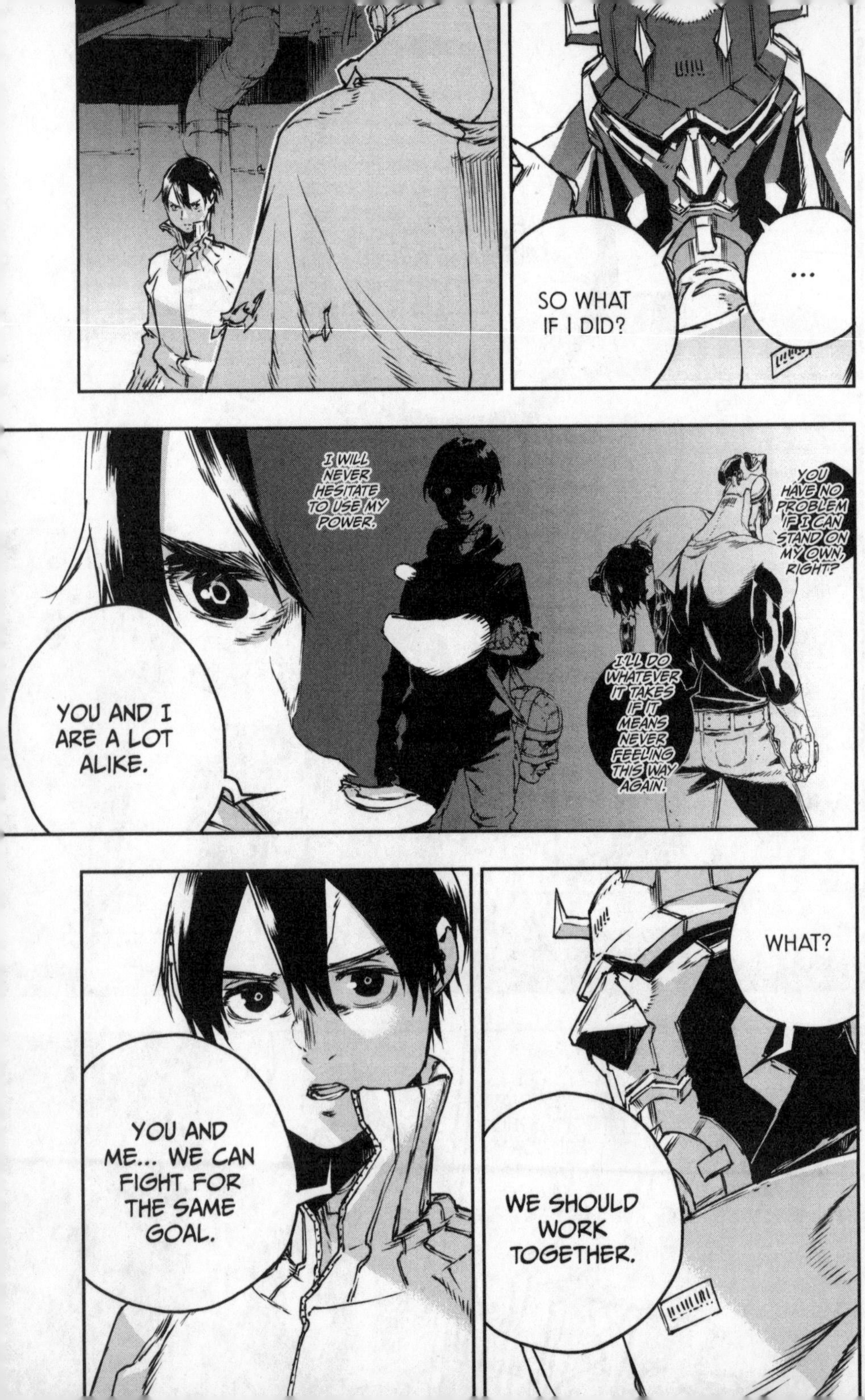
...
SO WHAT IF I DID?
YOU HAVE NO PROBLEM IF I CAN STAND ON MY OWN, RIGHT?
I WILL NEVER HESITATE TO USE MY POWER.
I'LL DO WHATEVER IT TAKES IF IT MEANS NEVER FEELING THIS WAY AGAIN.
YOU AND I ARE A LOT ALIKE.
WHAT?
WE SHOULD WORK TOGETHER.
YOU AND ME... WE CAN FIGHT FOR THE SAME GOAL.

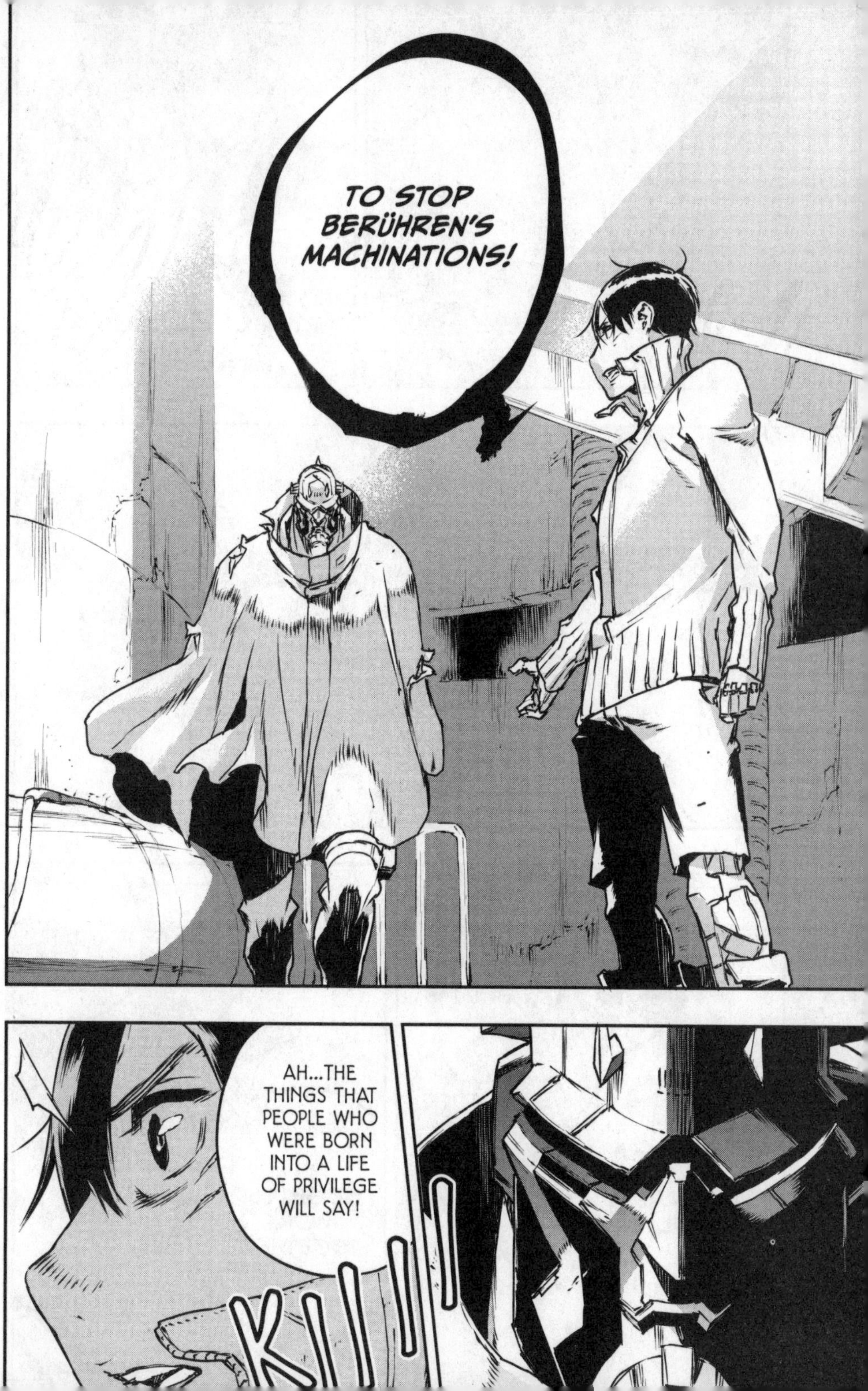
TO STOP BERÜHREN'S MACHINATIONS!
!!
AH...THE THINGS THAT PEOPLE WHO WERE BORN INTO A LIFE OF PRIVILEGE WILL SAY!

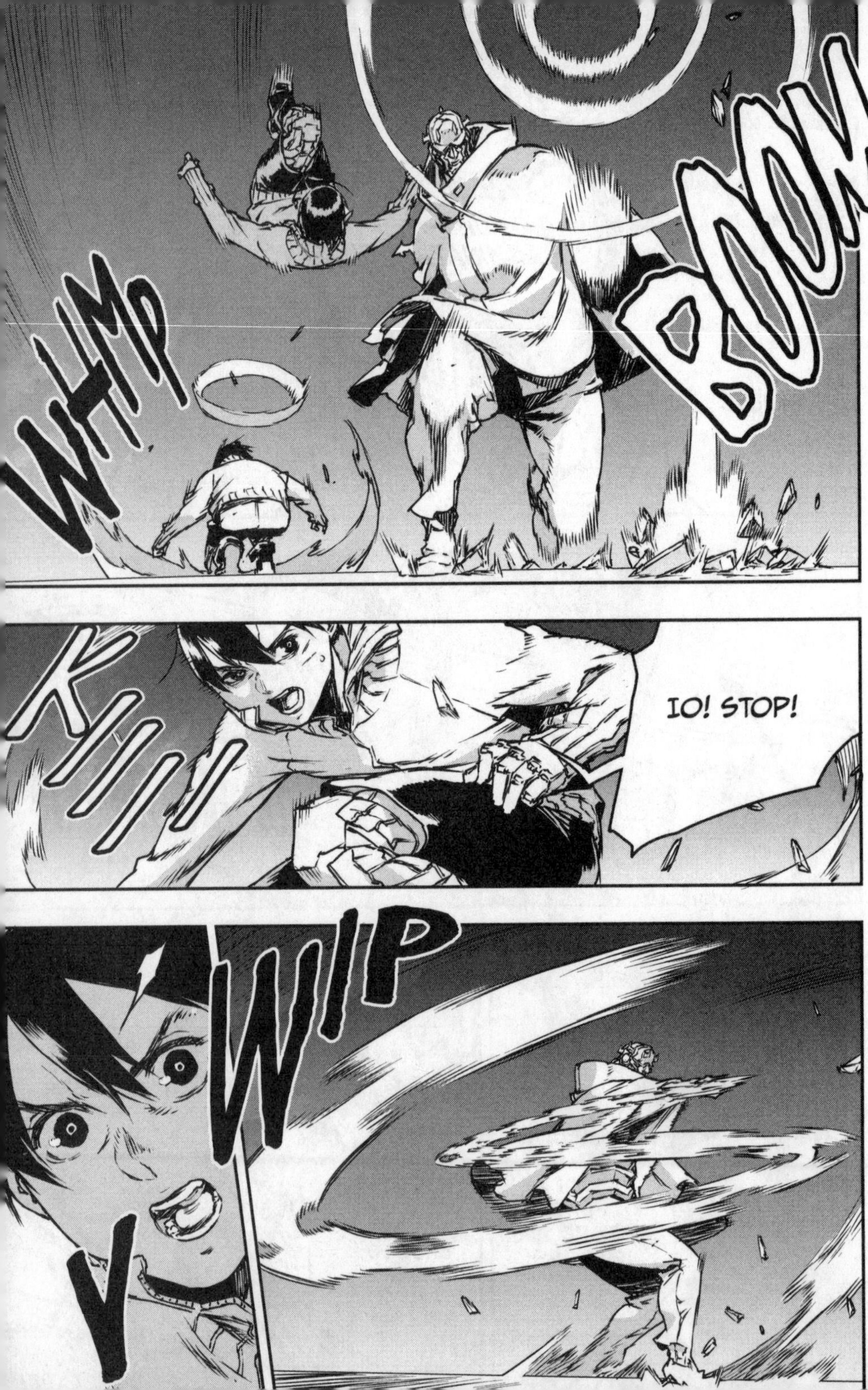
BOOM
WHMP
IO! STOP!
KHII
WHIP

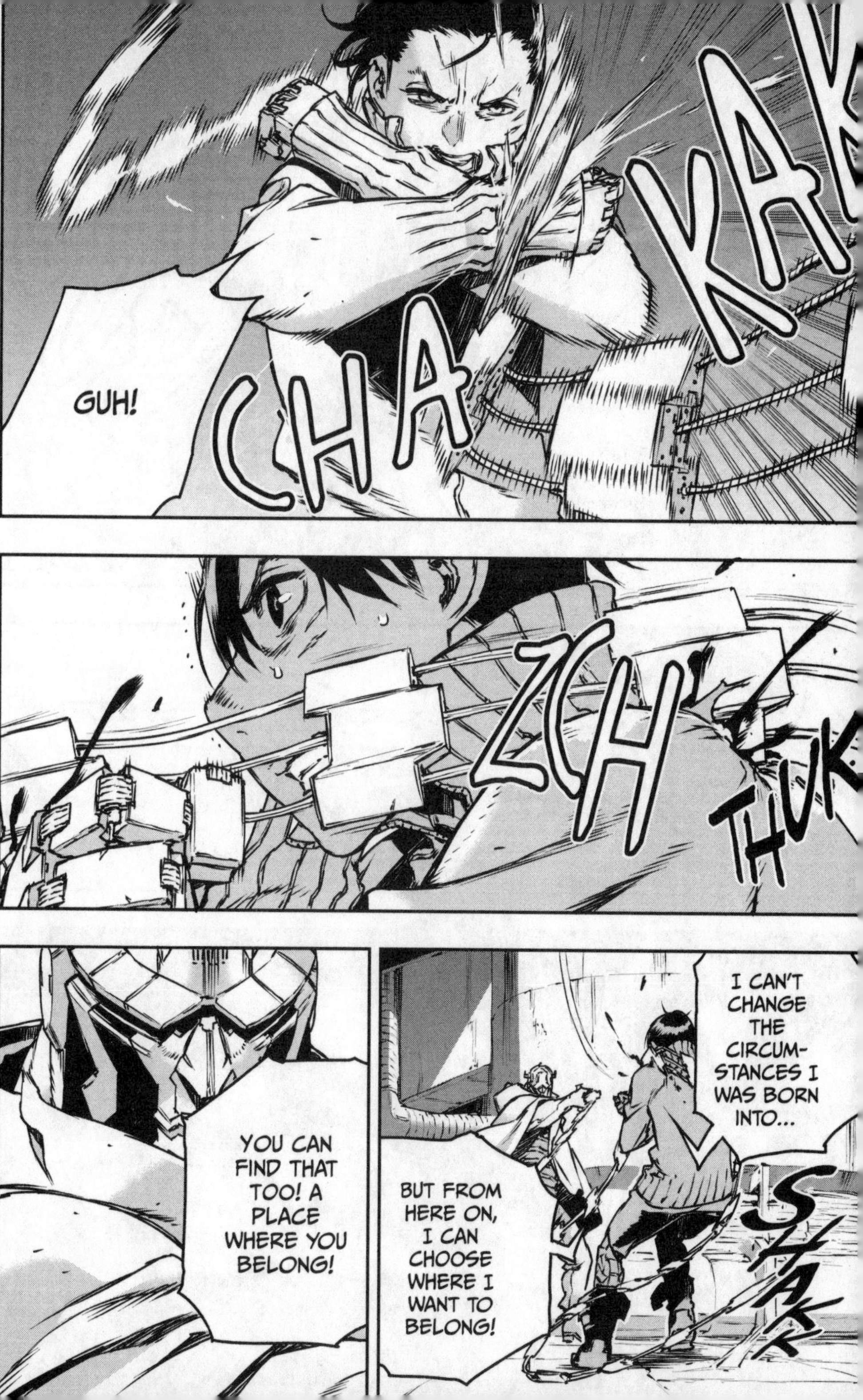
KAK
CHA
GUH!
ZCH
THUK
I CAN'T CHANGE THE CIRCUM-STANCES I WAS BORN INTO...
BUT FROM HERE ON, I CAN CHOOSE WHERE I WANT TO BELONG!
SHAK
YOU CAN FIND THAT TOO! A PLACE WHERE YOU BELONG!

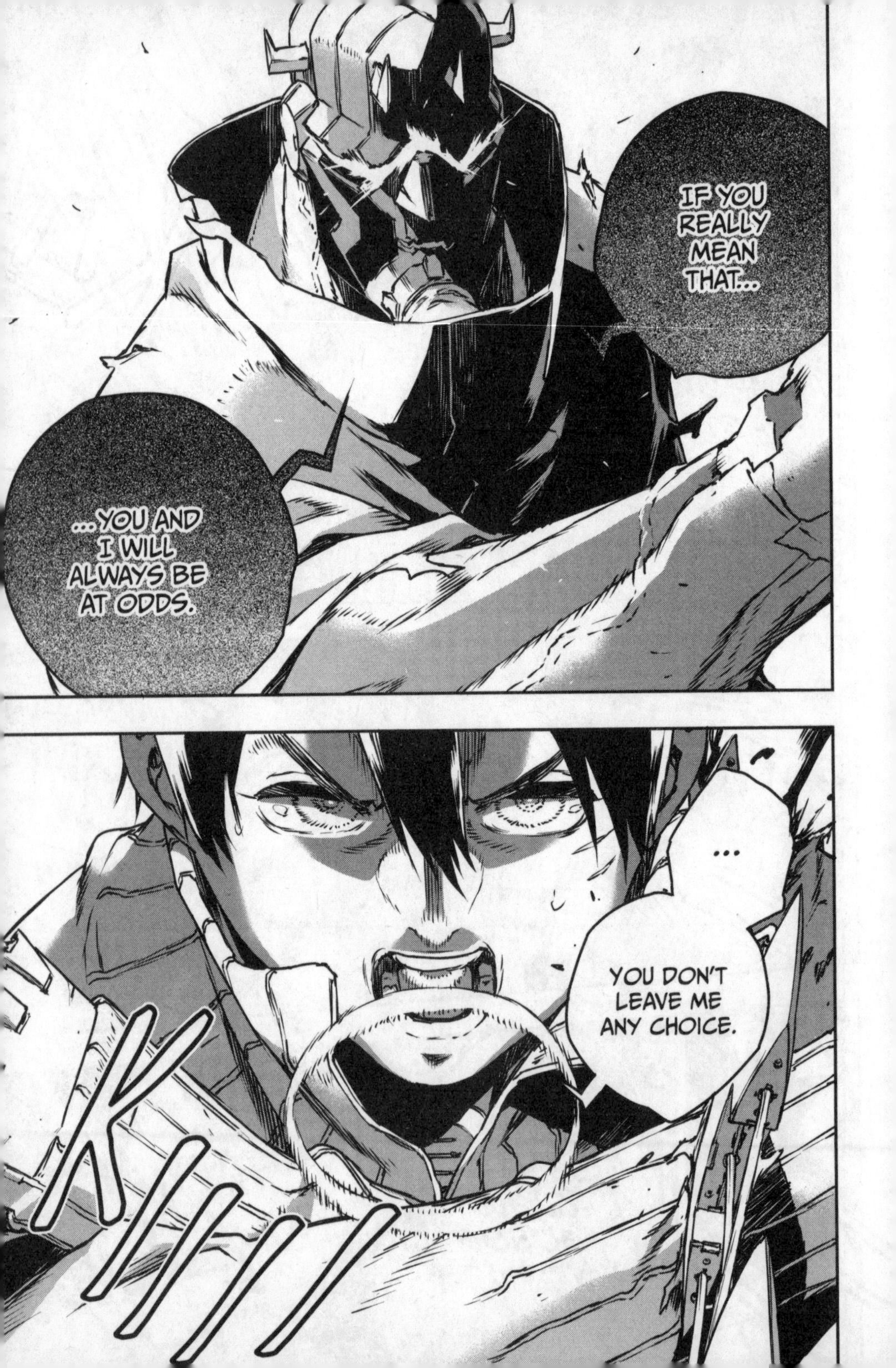
IF YOU REALLY MEAN THAT...
...YOU AND I WILL ALWAYS BE AT ODDS.
...
YOU DON'T LEAVE ME ANY CHOICE.
KIIIII

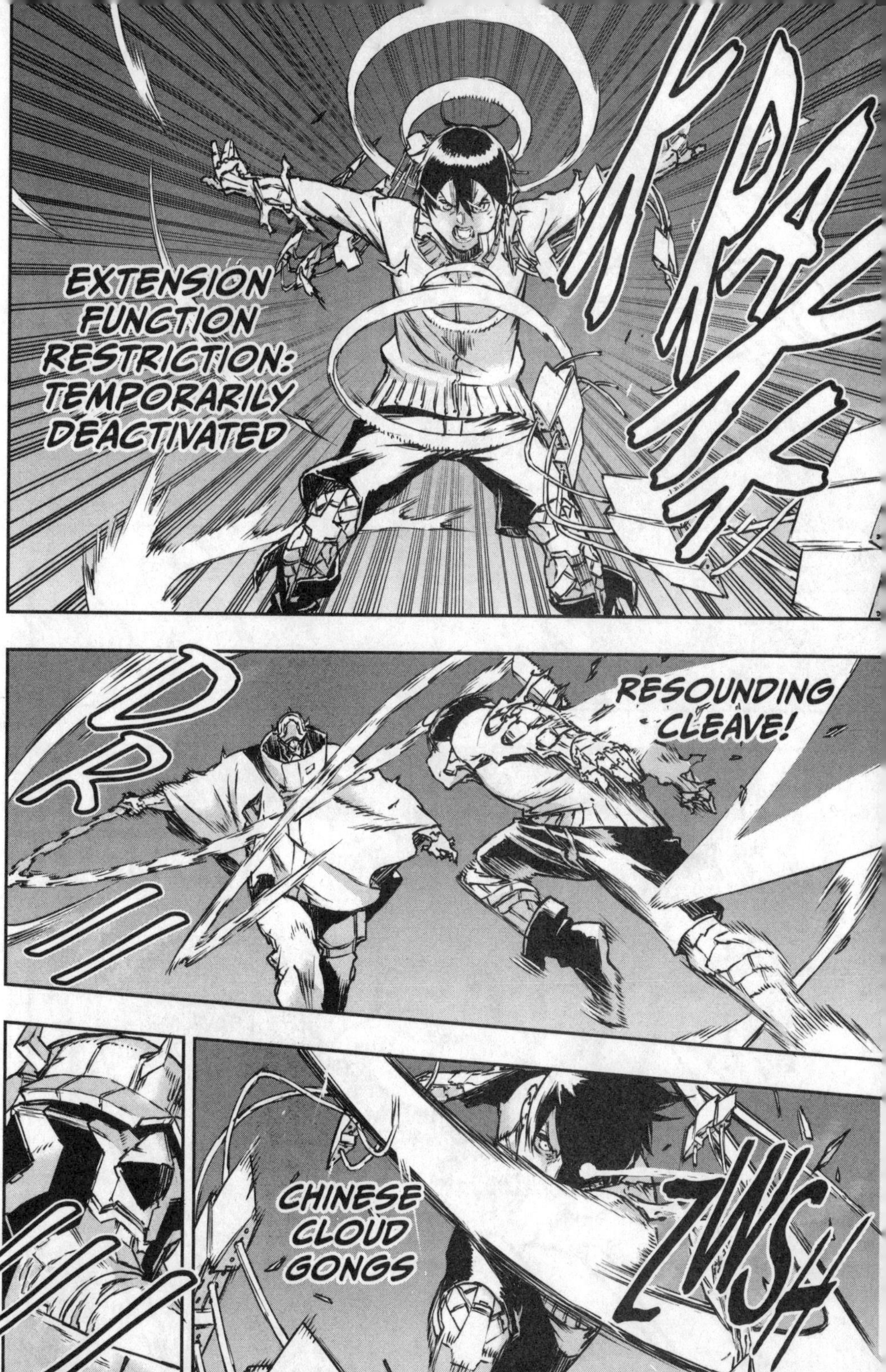
EXTENSION FUNCTION RESTRICTION: TEMPORARILY DEACTIVATED
RESOUNDING CLEAVE!
CHINESE CLOUD GONGS

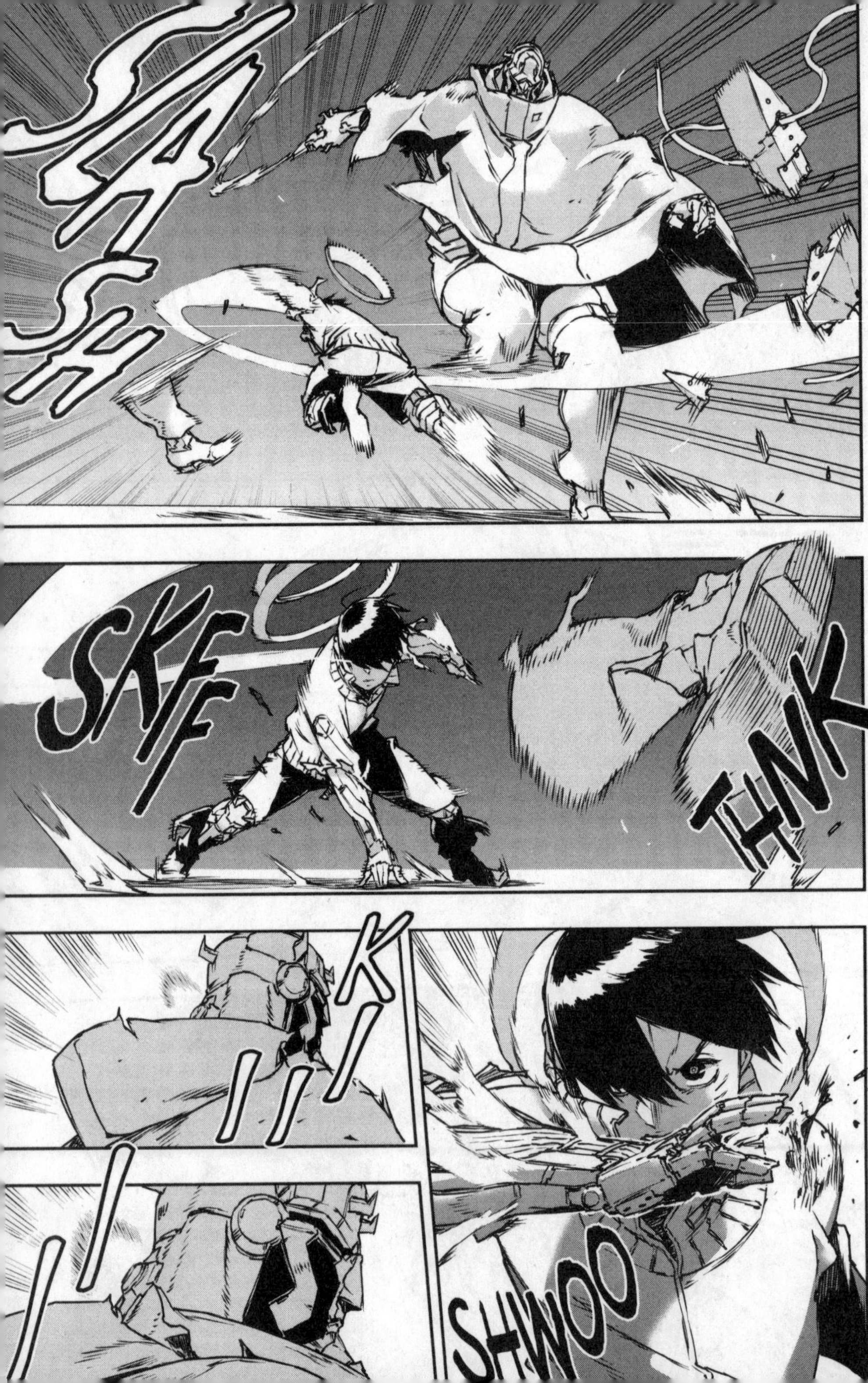
SLASH
SKFF
THNK
SHWOO
KIIIIII

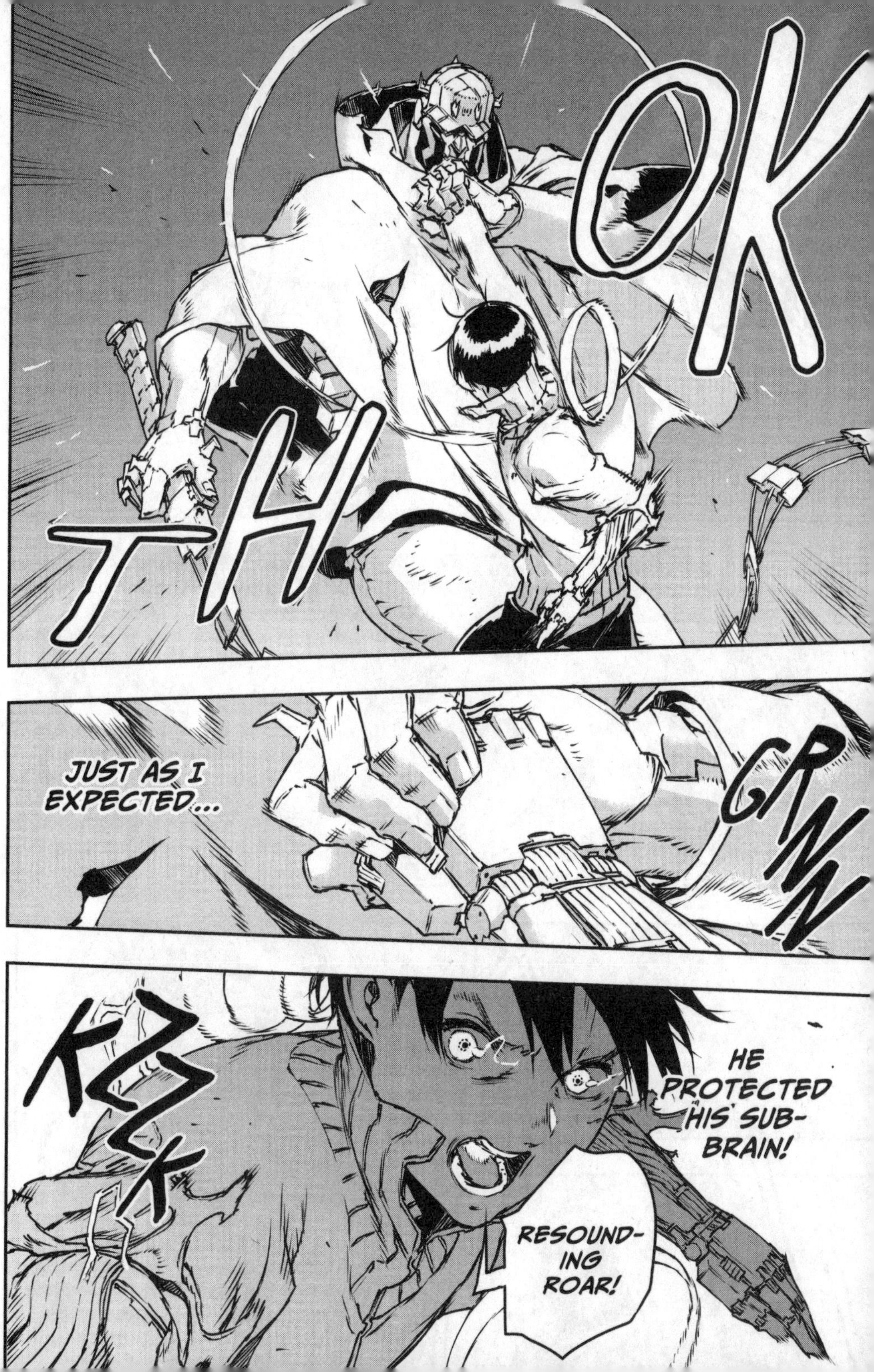
THOK
GRNN
JUST AS I EXPECTED...
HE PROTECTED HIS SUB-BRAIN!
RESOUNDING ROAR!
KZZK

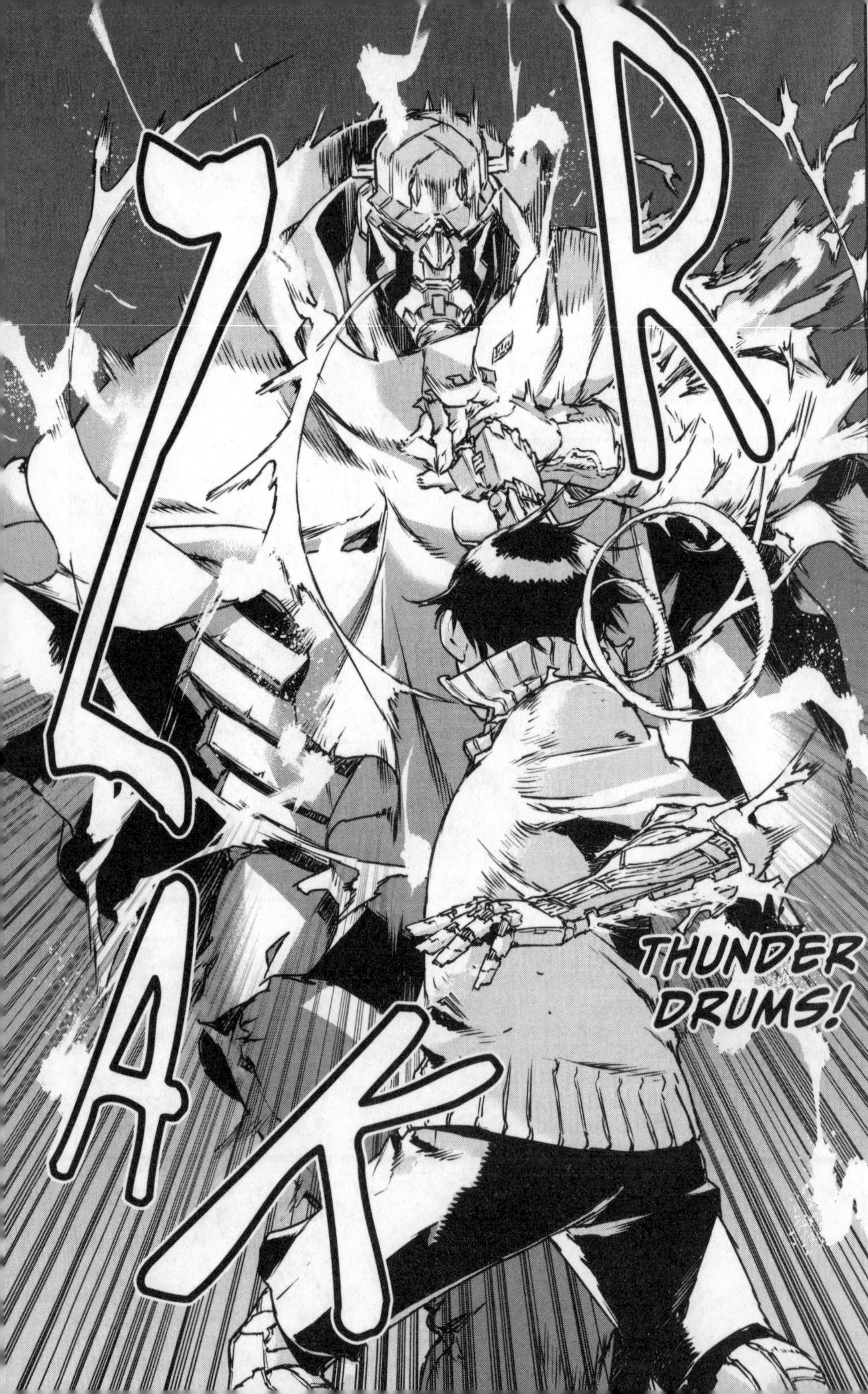
ZRAK
THUNDER DRUMS!

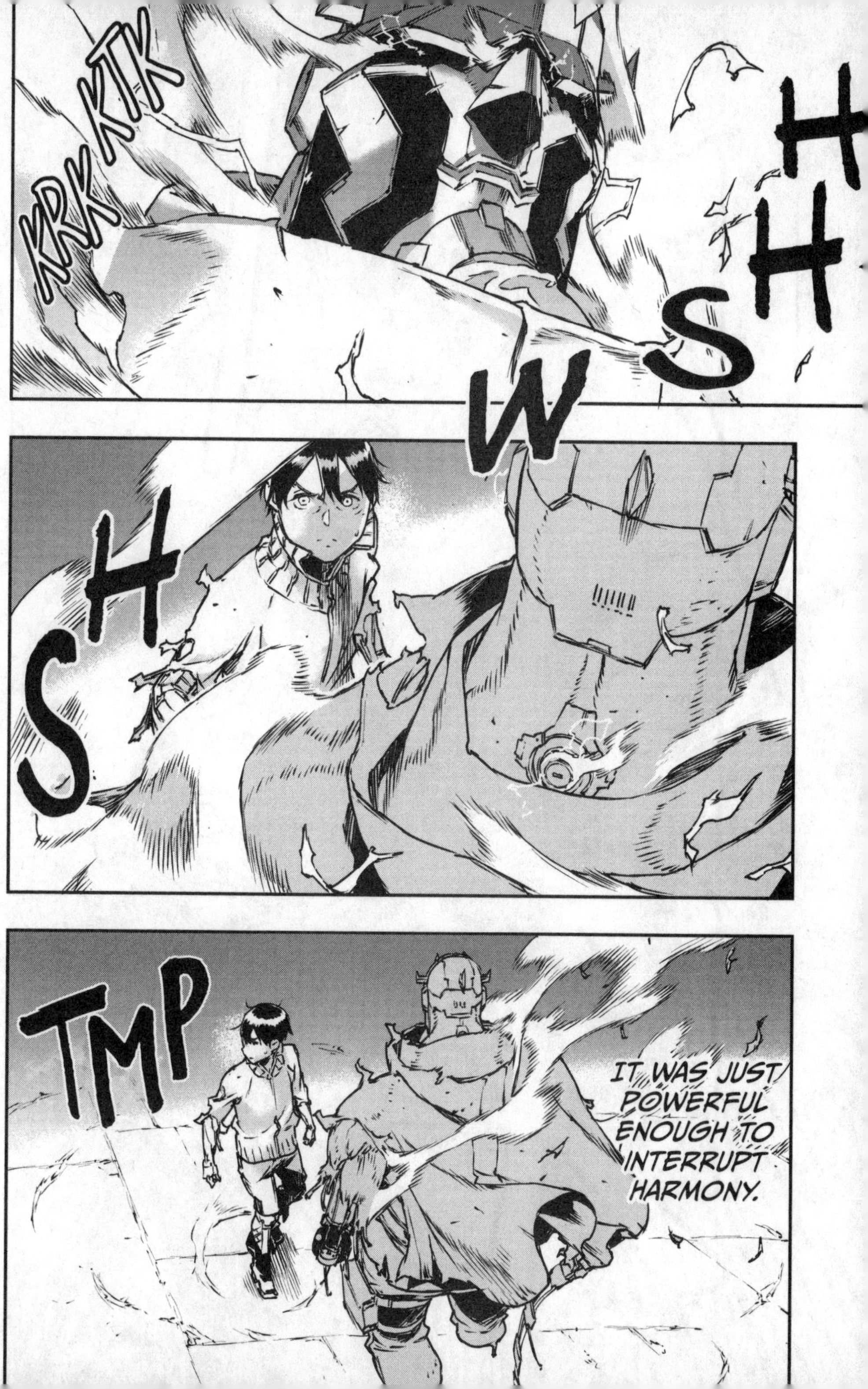
KRK KTK
SHWSH
SH
IT WAS JUST POWERFUL ENOUGH TO INTERRUPT HARMONY.
TMP

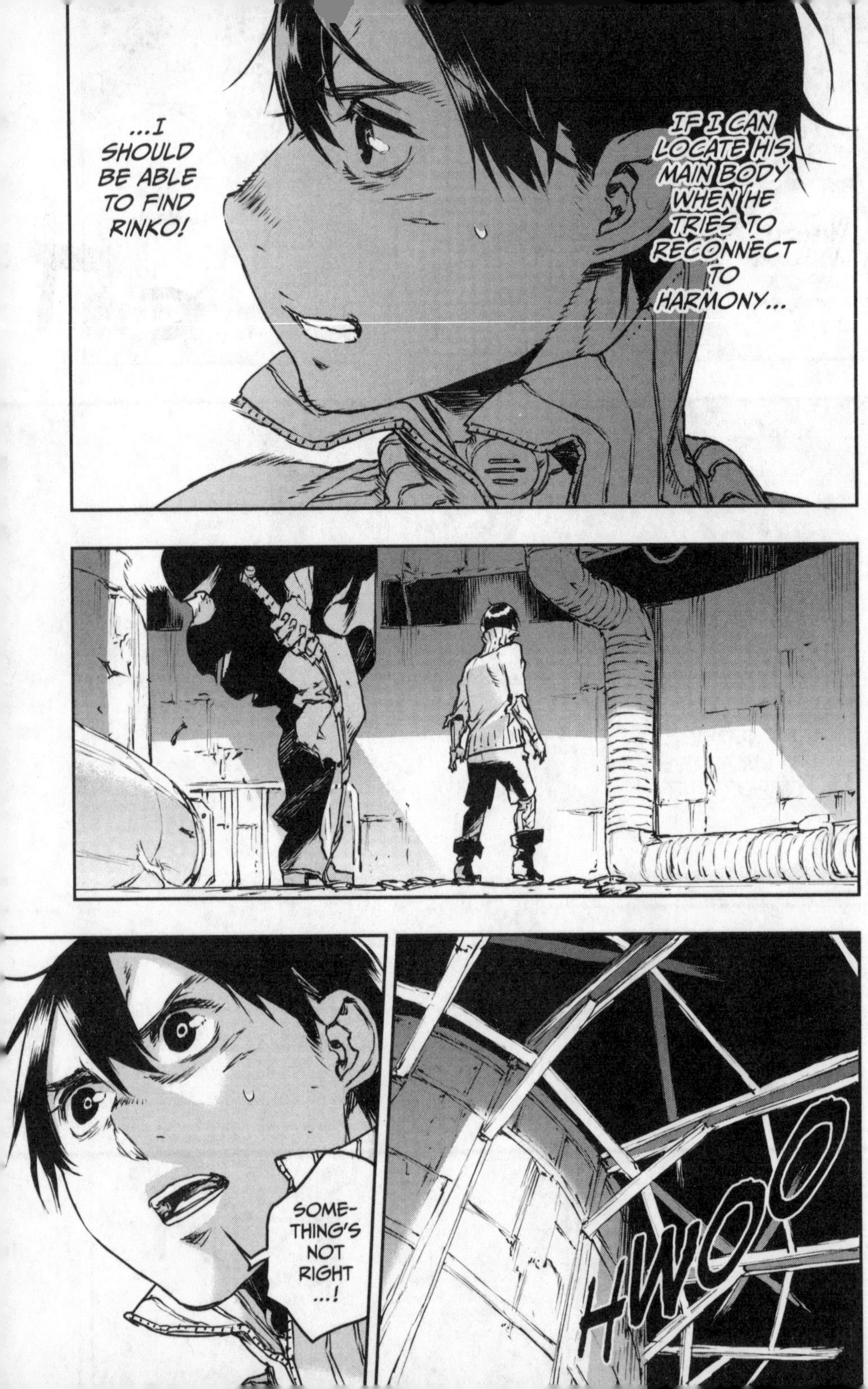
IF I CAN LOCATE HIS MAIN BODY WHEN HE TRIES TO RECONNECT TO HARMONY...
...I SHOULD BE ABLE TO FIND RINKO!
HWOO
SOME-THING'S NOT RIGHT ...!

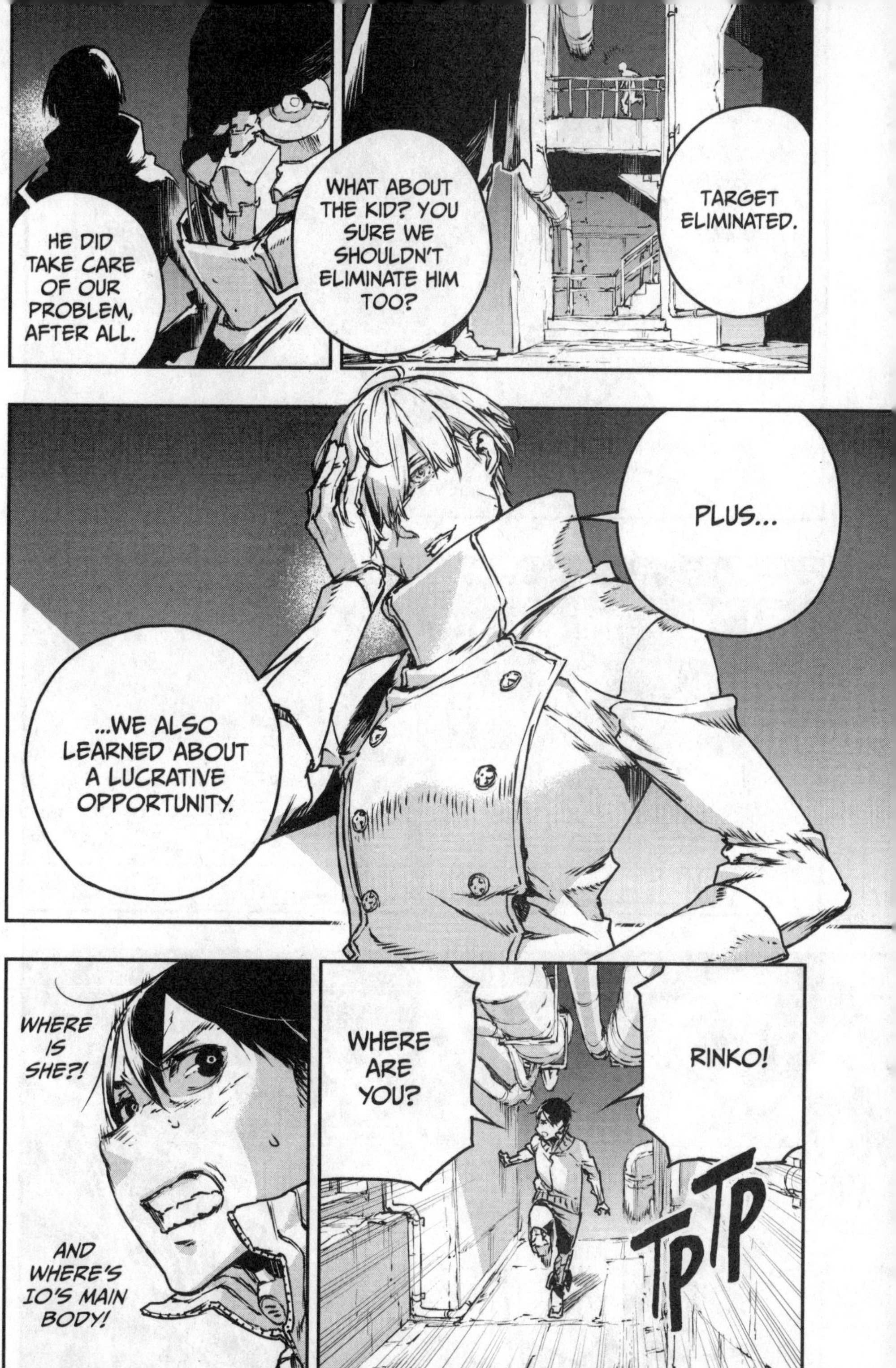
TARGET ELIMINATED.
WHAT ABOUT THE KID? YOU SURE WE SHOULDN'T ELIMINATE HIM TOO?
HE DID TAKE CARE OF OUR PROBLEM, AFTER ALL.
PLUS...
...WE ALSO LEARNED ABOUT A LUCRATIVE OPPORTUNITY.
RINKO!
WHERE ARE YOU?
TPTP
WHERE IS SHE?!
AND WHERE'S IO'S MAIN BODY!

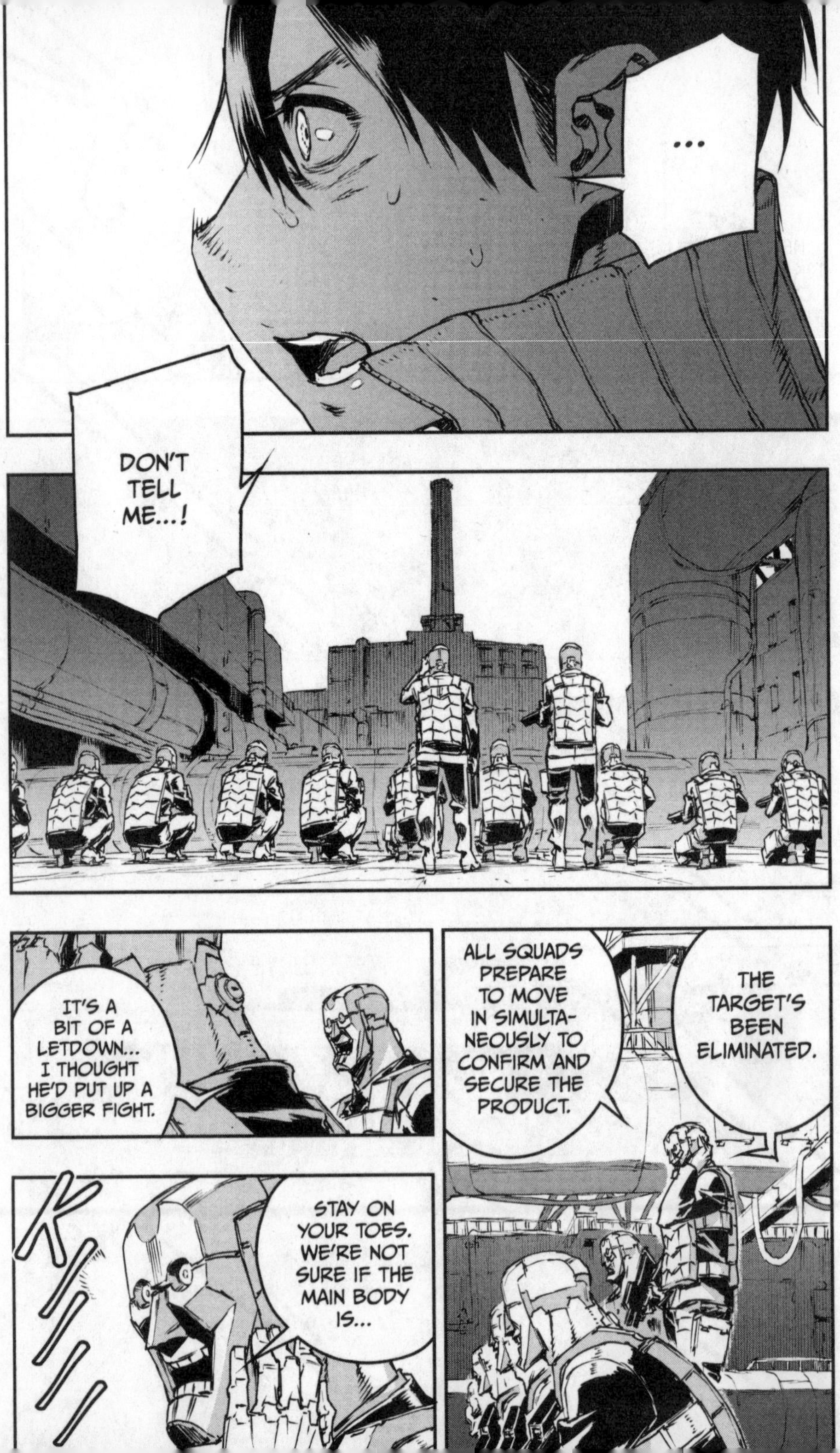
...
DON'T TELL ME...!
THE TARGET'S BEEN ELIMINATED.
ALL SQUADS PREPARE TO MOVE IN SIMULTANEOUSLY TO CONFIRM AND SECURE THE PRODUCT.
IT'S A BIT OF A LETDOWN... I THOUGHT HE'D PUT UP A BIGGER FIGHT.
STAY ON YOUR TOES. WE'RE NOT SURE IF THE MAIN BODY IS...
K

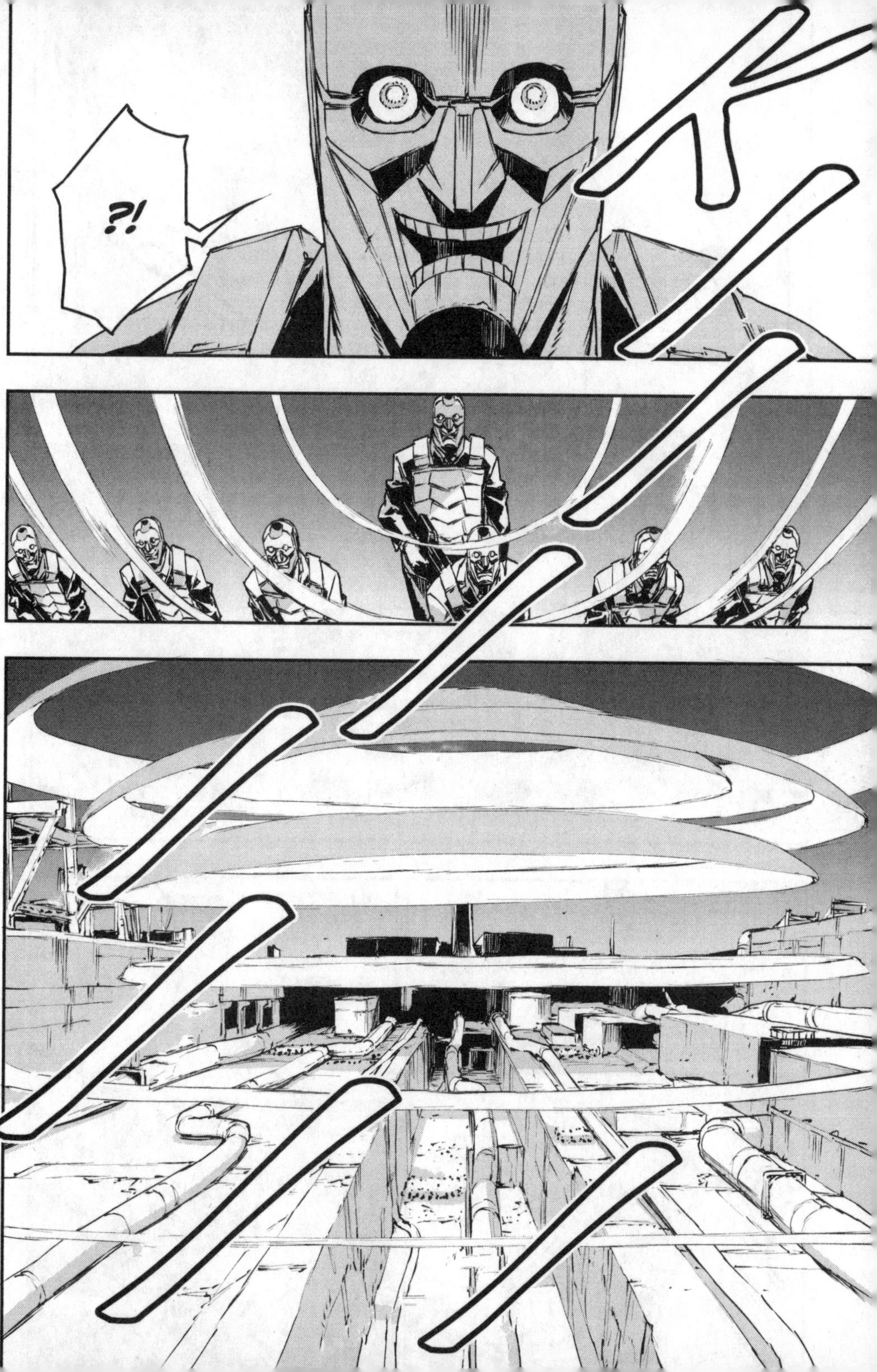
?!

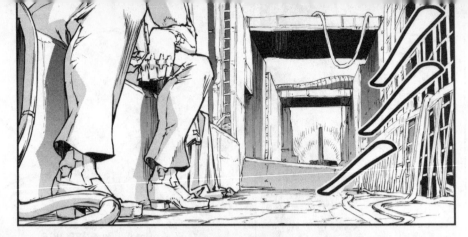

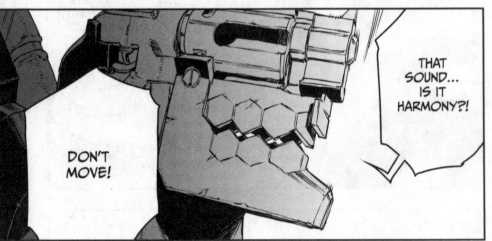

THAT SOUND... IS IT HARMONY?!
DON'T MOVE!
I'M MAKING THE FINAL ADJUST-MENTS.
BESIDES, IT CAN'T REACH THIS FAR.
TINK
CHK
HURRY IT UP, MARY. I GOT A FEELING SOMETHING'S ABOUT TO GO DOWN.
I KNOW!
SHF

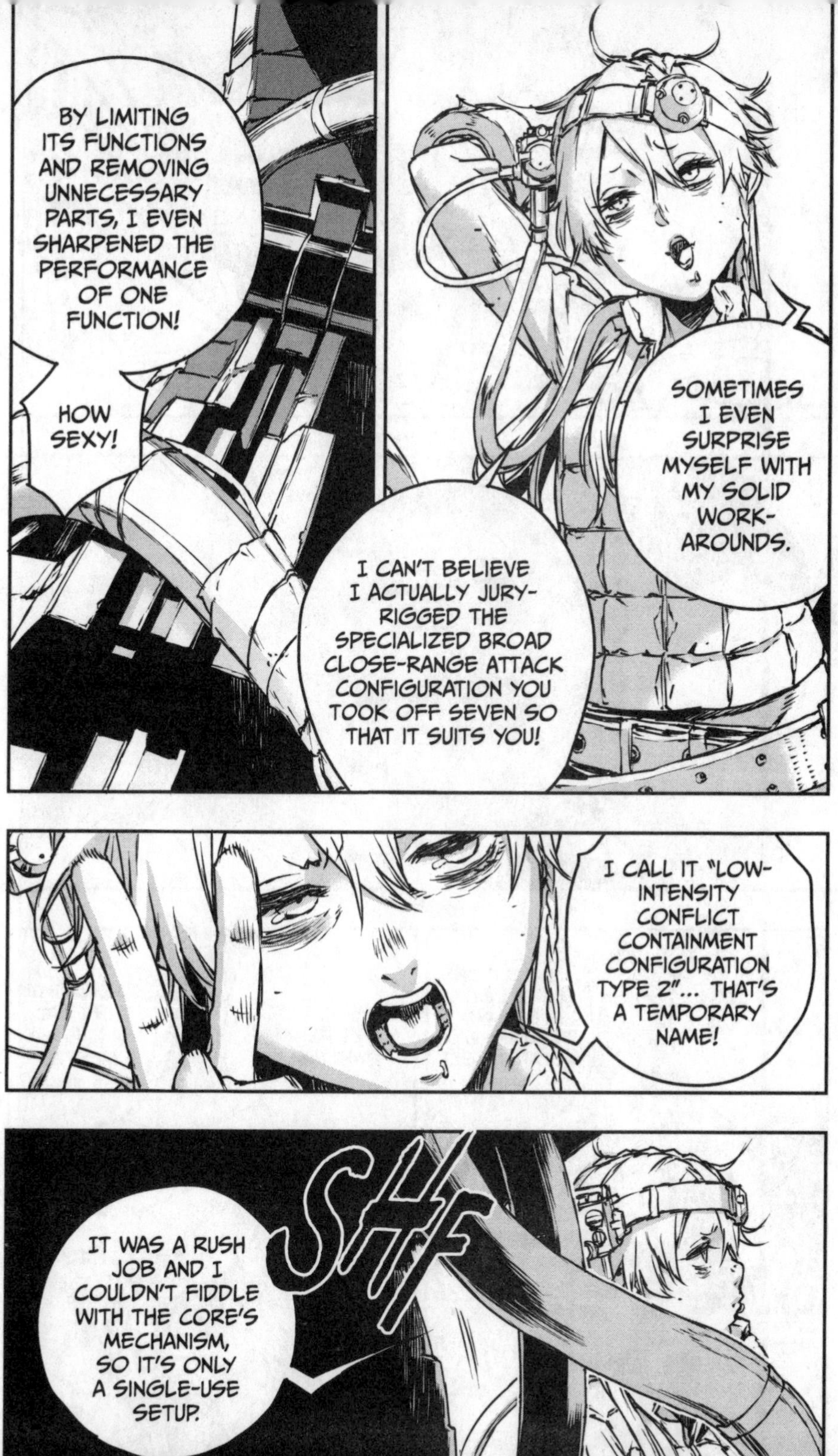
SOMETIMES I EVEN SURPRISE MYSELF WITH MY SOLID WORK-AROUNDS.
I CAN'T BELIEVE I ACTUALLY JURY-RIGGED THE SPECIALIZED BROAD CLOSE-RANGE ATTACK CONFIGURATION YOU TOOK OFF SEVEN SO THAT IT SUITS YOU!
BY LIMITING ITS FUNCTIONS AND REMOVING UNNECESSARY PARTS, I EVEN SHARPENED THE PERFORMANCE OF ONE FUNCTION!
HOW SEXY!
I CALL IT "LOW-INTENSITY CONFLICT CONTAINMENT CONFIGURATION TYPE 2"... THAT'S A TEMPORARY NAME!
SHF
IT WAS A RUSH JOB AND I COULDN'T FIDDLE WITH THE CORE'S MECHANISM, SO IT'S ONLY A SINGLE-USE SETUP.

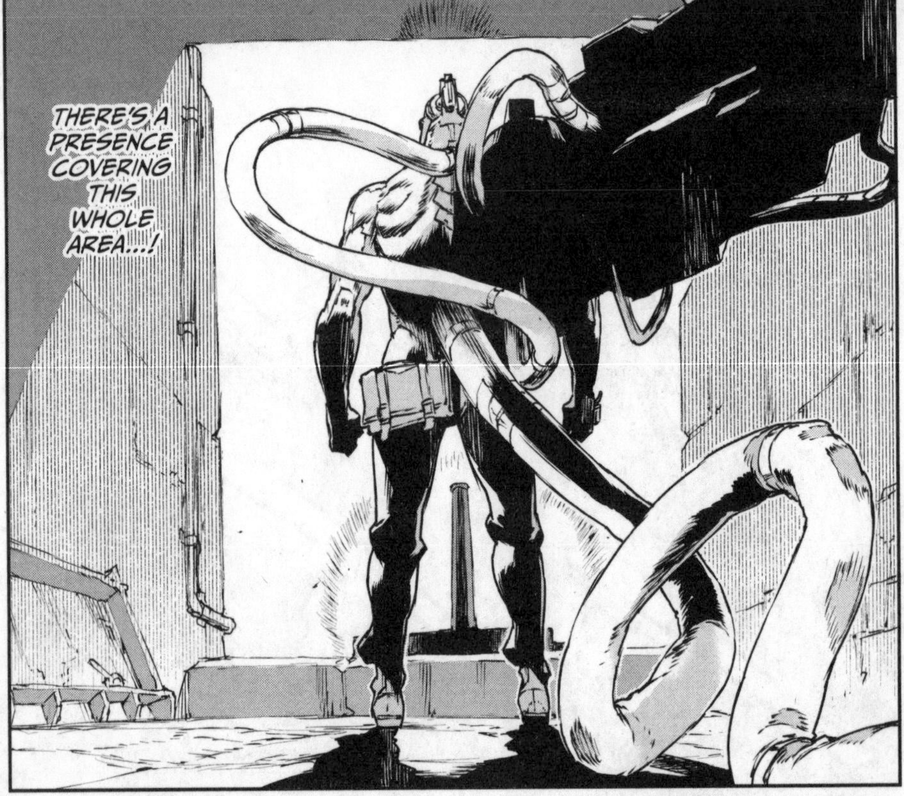
THERE'S A PRESENCE COVERING THIS WHOLE AREA...!

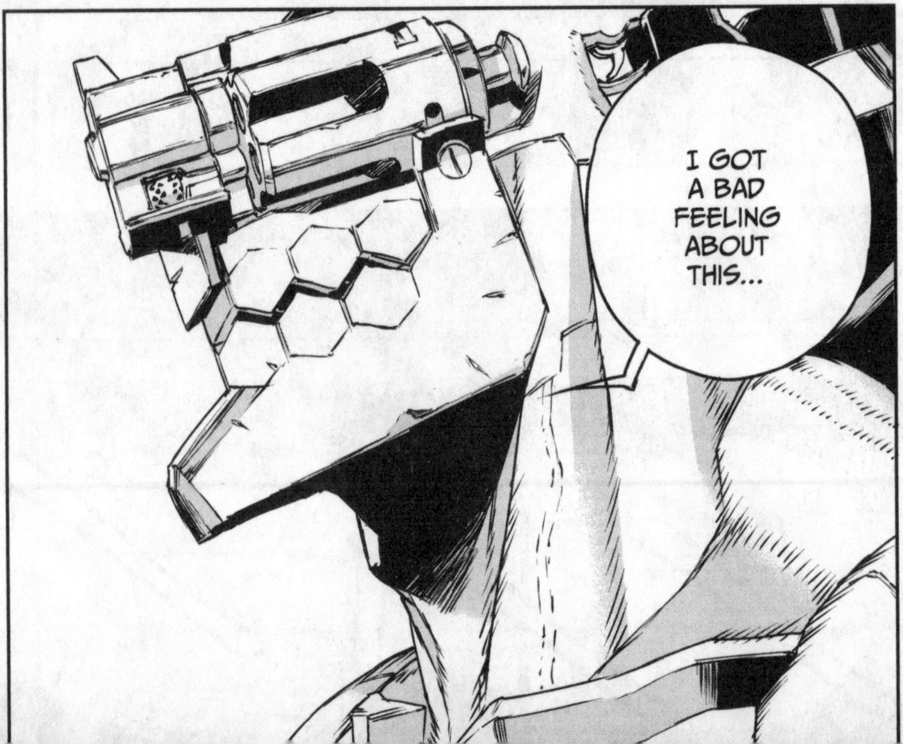
I GOT A BAD FEELING ABOUT THIS...

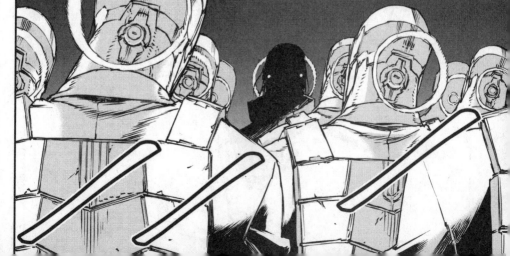

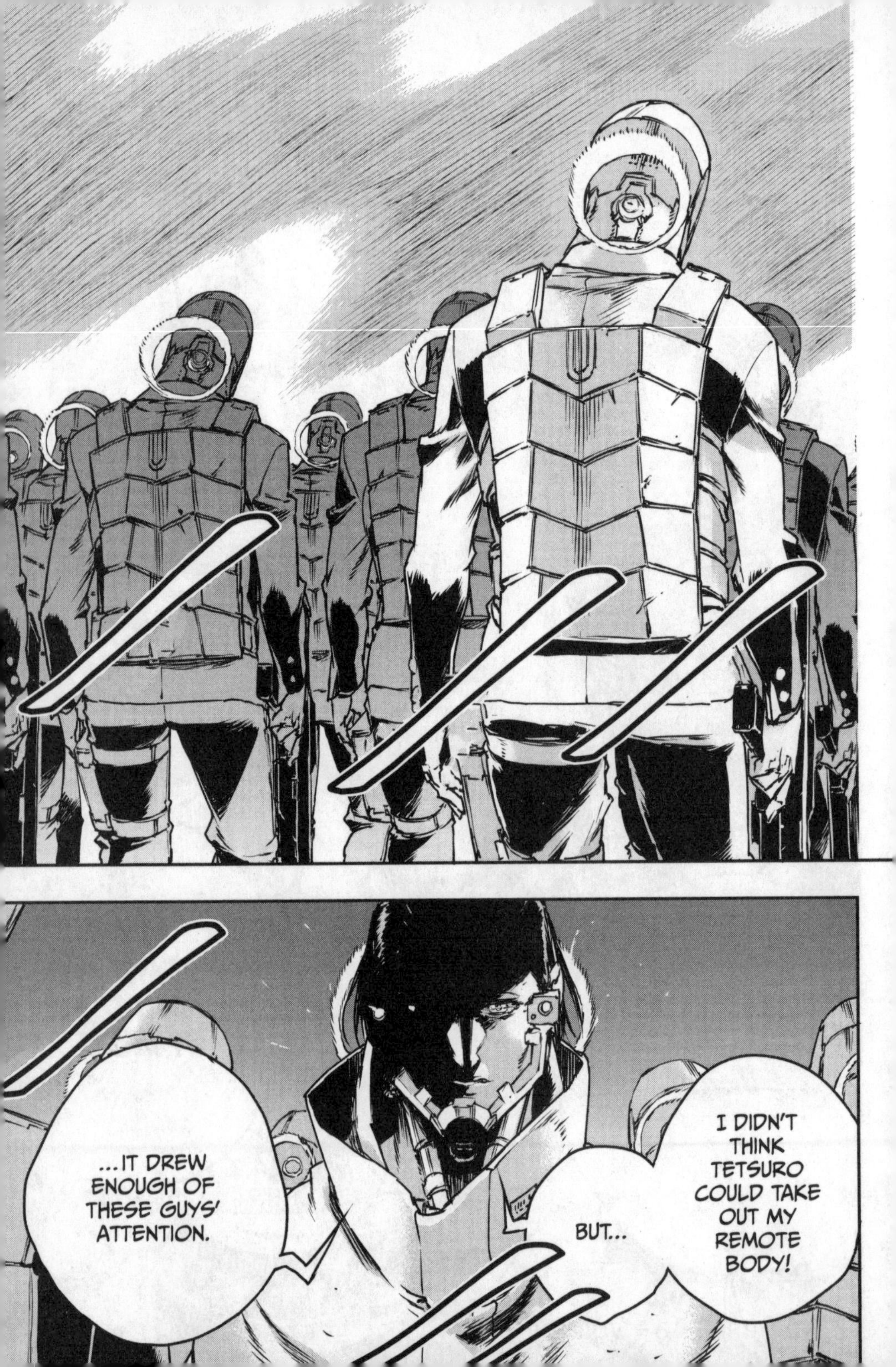
I DIDN'T THINK TETSURO COULD TAKE OUT MY REMOTE BODY!
BUT...
...IT DREW ENOUGH OF THESE GUYS' ATTENTION.

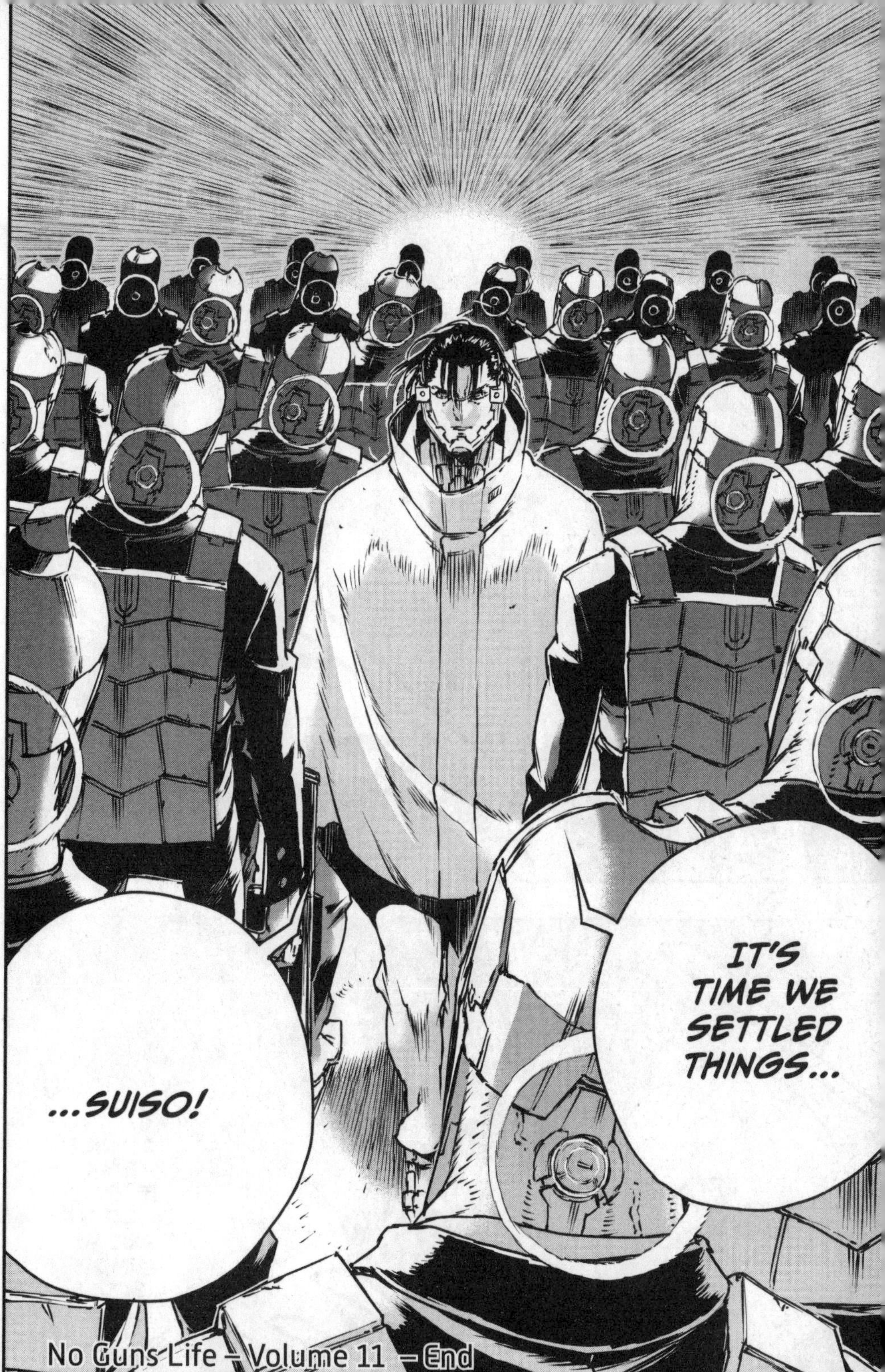
IT'S TIME WE SETTLED THINGS...
...SUISO!
No Guns Life – Volume 11 – End

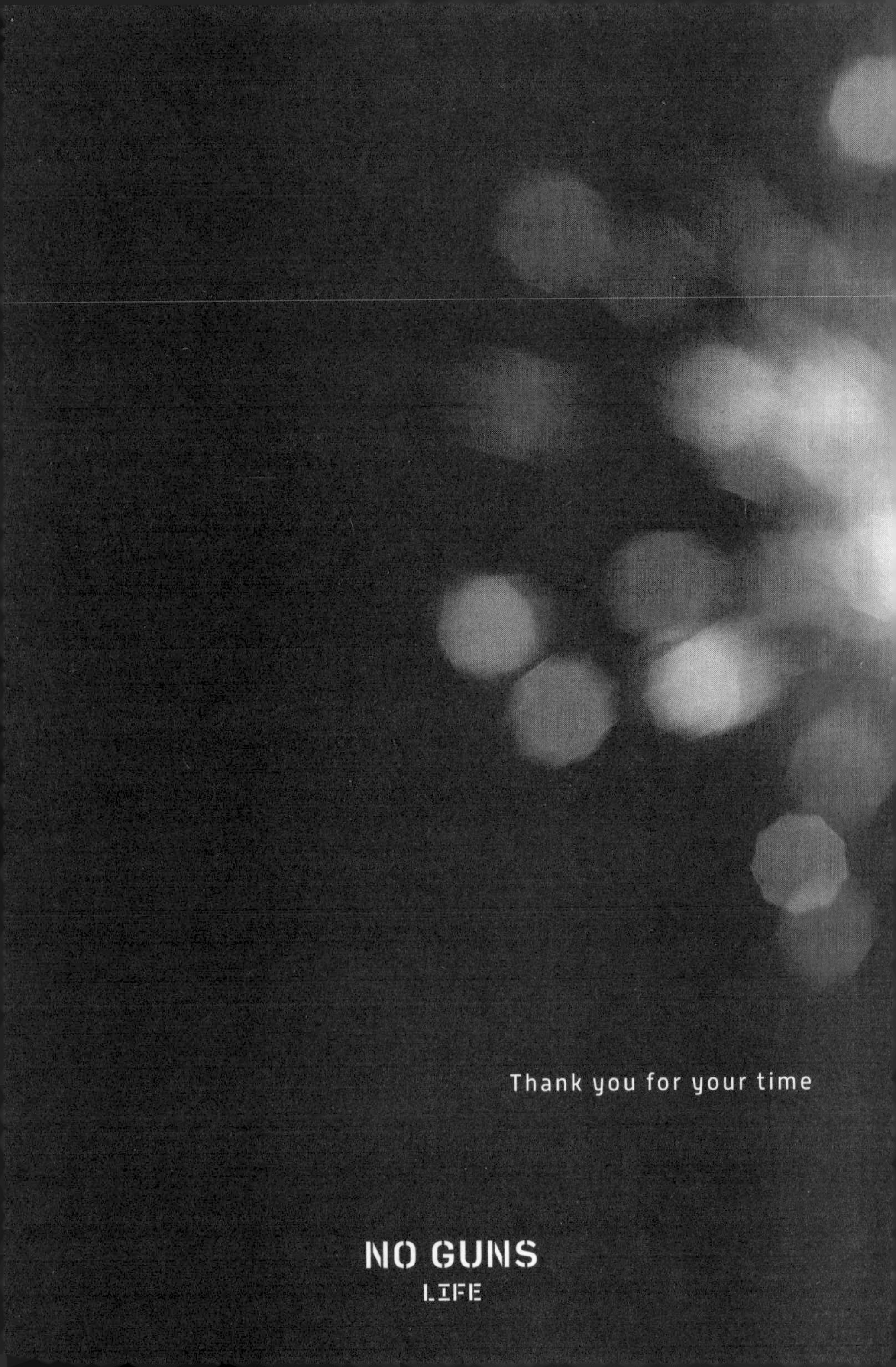
Thank you for your time
NO GUNS
LIFE

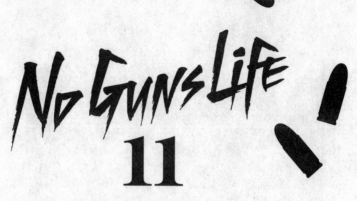

NO GUNS LIFE

11

STORY AND ART BY
TASUKU KARASUMA

VIZ SIGNATURE EDITION

TRANSLATION Joe Yamazaki
ENGLISH ADAPTATION Stan!
TOUCH-UP ART & LETTERING Evan Waldinger
DESIGN Shawn Carrico
EDITOR Mike Montesa

First published in Japan in 2014 by SHUEISHA Inc., Tokyo.
English translation rights arranged by SHUEISHA Inc.

Printed in Canada

Published by VIZ Media, LLC
P.O. Box 77010
San Francisco, CA 94107

10 9 8 7 6 5 4 3 2 1
First printing, October 2021

ratings.viz.com RATED T+ OLDER TEEN

PARENTAL ADVISORY
NO GUNS LIFE is rated T+ for Older Teen and is recommended for ages 16 and up. This volume contains violence, strong language, and adult themes.

VIZ MEDIA VIZ SIGNATURE

viz.com vizsignature.com

CONTENTS

NO GUNS LIFE

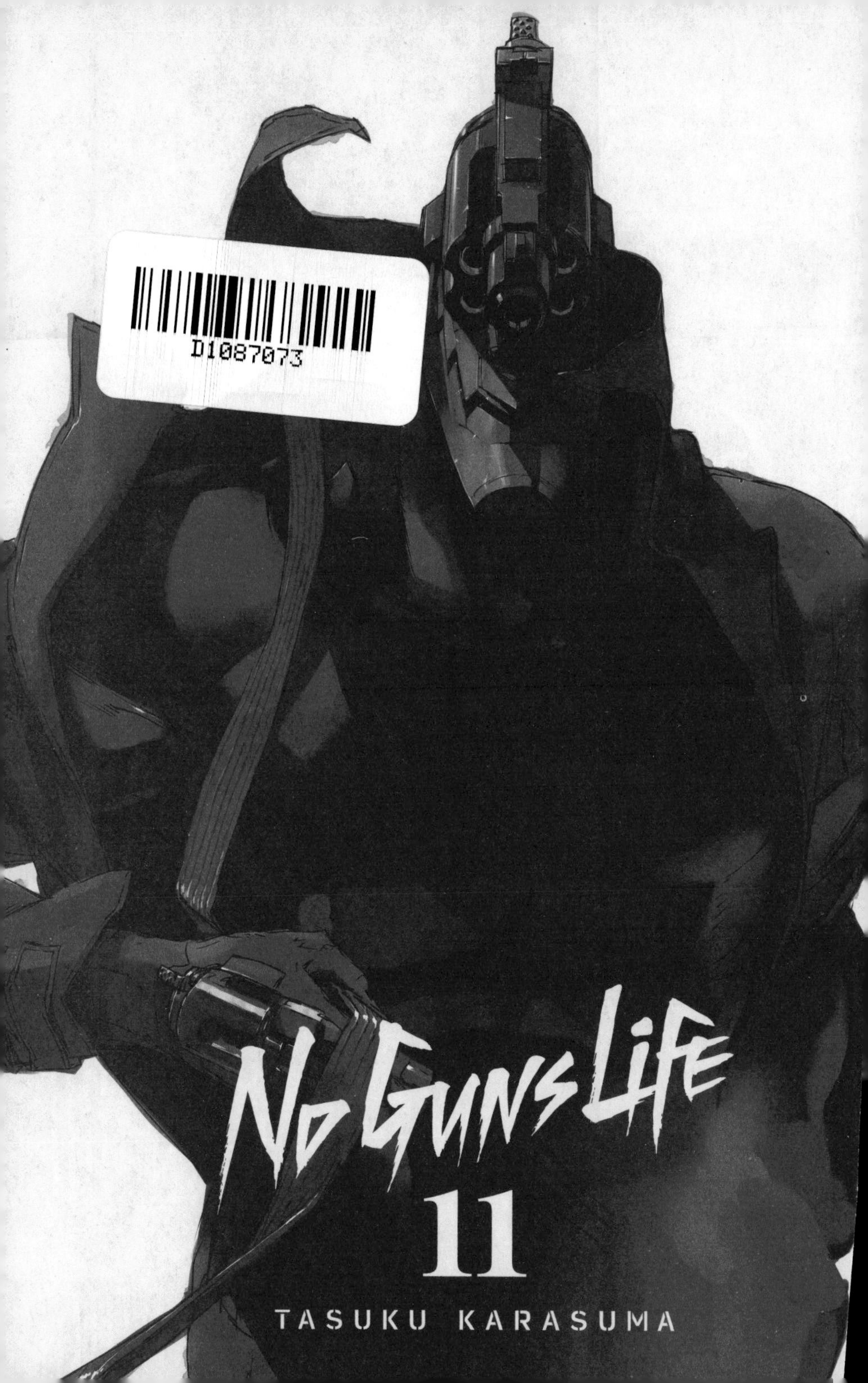
No Guns Life
11
TASUKU KARASUMA